ANTHROPOLOGICAL PERSPECTIVES
on
ORGANIZATIONAL CULTURE

Edited by

Tomoko Hamada

and

Willis E. Sibley

UNIVERSITY
PRESS OF
AMERICA

Lanham • New York • London

Copyright © 1994 by
University Press of America®, Inc.
4720 Boston Way
Lanham, Maryland 20706

3 Henrietta Street
London WC2E 8LU England

Library of Congress Cataloging-in-Publication Data

Anthropological perspectives on organizational culture / edited by
Tomoko Hamada and Willis E. Sibley.
p.   cm.
1. Corporate culture—Congresses.   2. Business ethics—Congresses.
3. Business anthropology—Congresses.   I. Hamada, Tomoko.
II. Sibley, Willis E.
HD58.7.A49   1994   302.3'5—dc20   94–5787 CIP

ISBN 0–8191–9486–7 (cloth : alk. paper)
ISBN 0–8191–9487–5 (pbk. : alk. paper)

 The paper used in this publication meets the minimum requirements of
American National Standard for Information Sciences—Permanence
of Paper for Printed Library Materials, ANSI Z39.48–1984.

CONTENTS

VOICES FROM THE FIELD:
WORKING ORGANIZATIONAL CULTURE
PART THREE

ETHICS AND ORGANIZATIONAL CULTURE
PART FOUR

PREFACE

Willis E. Sibley

This volume of papers grew out of an all-day symposium titled "Studying Corporate Cultures," during the Annual Meeting of the American Association for the Advancement of Science (AAAS). Sibley organized the symposium on behalf of the Society for Applied Anthropology (SfAA) during his tenure as Liaison Person from SfAA to AAAS Section H, Anthropology. The symposium brought together anthropologists interested in what has come to be called organizational culture.

Since the symposium, those papers which have been retained for this volume have been thoroughly revised, rewritten and brought up to date. Additional contributions were sought which augment and broaden the original symposium corpus greatly, resulting in the present volume.

This volume highlights research products which constitute evidence of changes taking place in anthropology in the United States -- changes which have results in a substantial redirection of interests on the part of a growing number of anthropologists from an historical interest in smaller, alien and allegedly simpler cultures toward the analysis of our own complex forms of organization in mass society. The reasons for this redirection speak eloquently to the strong and pervasive influence of economic, political and social forces on the interests of professionals generally, and in this case anthropologists in particular.

Beginning in the 1970s, the effects of much earlier anti-natal procreative decisions on the part of American mating pairs began to show up in rapidly declining growth rates in college and university student populations. This declining growth rate had serious negative affects on the numbers of academic positions available to newly minted anthropologists. Many of them were forced to seek employment outside the academy which had been the traditional home for the overwhelming majority of anthropologists. New employment in both the private and public sectors outside academia brought new perspectives to anthropology and to anthropologists and engendered new research interests in corporate and organizational cultures of large scale organizations in a mass society. Today, approximately one-half of those anthropologists awarded the Ph.D. degree find employment outside the academy. Increasingly, the earlier seeking of non-academic employment as a last resort has changed to a positive interest in the excitement and rewards to be found in a wide variety of positions in both the public and private sectors of the American economy.

No doubt other changes also were consequences of the same powerful forces which led anthropologists initially to seek new employment niches. National problems concerning such areas as the family, schooling, poverty, crime, drug use and economic decline increasingly attracted the attention of anthropologists. No doubt some thought (and think) that anthropology might have useful contributions to make to resolving some of our national problems, complementing the work of our fellow social scientists in such fields as sociology, economics, political science and psychology.

Yet another factor which encouraged anthropological attention to domestic issues was a significant decline in opportunities for research abroad. Federal funding for foreign research became scarcer, and many newly independent nations restricted severely long-term visits by anthropologists. For better or worse, anthropological access characteristic of earlier colonial times ended.

When work on the volume lagged, a pair of Sibley's impatient but helpful colleagues-contributors brought forward an eminently suitable co-editor to help bring the project to conclusion in the form of the present volume of papers titled *Anthropological Perspectives on Organizational Culture*.

Co-Editor Tomoko Hamada, Associate Professor and Chairperson of Anthropology in the College of William and Mary, joined the project in the middle of 1991, and has been a vigorous participant since that time. Sibley continued to manage administrative arrangements, negotiations with publishers and communication with authors, along with undertaking copy editing chores and generating an Index and information concerning authors; Hamada occupied herself with editing papers, along with utilizing her special expertise in the writing of introductory and analytical materials to transform a set of papers into a coherent volume. Co-editor Sibley wishes to state openly in this preface his gratitude to his helpful colleagues, and to express his esteem and admiration for the energetic contributions of Tomoko Hamada. We also wish to express our deep appreciation to Ms. Jean Belvin of the Department of Anthropology in The College of William and Mary, who provided invaluable skills and energies in producing the manuscript for publication.

Jointly, the editors hope that this volume will be found useful not only for college instruction in business and organizational studies as well as anthropology, but also for practitioners (both anthropological and not) in both public and private sector organizations -- persons who deal with and contribute through their participation to the evolution of organizational culture in their everyday work. Through recent time, the field of organizational culture has grown into a major subfield in anthropology, paralleling similar developments in sociology, psychology and management sciences, among others. For anthropologists the study of organizational culture has become an inter-disciplinary endeavor combining perspectives from such fields as linguistics, interpretive anthropology, folklore and economic anthropology.

It is also our hope that this volume will assist in bringing to the attention of its readers the contributions which anthropological perspectives and analyses make to understanding how our modern complex society operates.

PART ONE

ANTHROPOLOGY AND ORGANIZATIONAL CULTURE

INTRODUCTION

Tomoko Hamada

The purpose of this book is to clarify some anthropological perspectives on organizational culture, and to demonstrate how the issue is being researched by industrial ethnographers in actual organizational settings. Our discussion is divided into four parts. The first part reviews the history of anthropological research on organizational culture and discusses key anthropological perspectives on the subject. Part two presents concrete examples of industrial and institutional ethnography drawn from empirical and primary fieldwork. These cases collectively illustrate how researchers observe and discover cultural patterns in organizations in complex industrial societies. The third part of the book investigates the caveat of studying organizational culture. Management consultants and practicing anthropologists together explore theoretical challenges and practical problems involved in empirical analyses of organizational cultures. The fourth and final part of the book is devoted to ethical and moral challenges of industrial and institutional anthropology. The essays examine the roles of the anthropologist-consultant; the concept of organizational culture for social change; the normative orientation of the organization as a reflection of the wider culture; and the organization's conflicting values and ethics.

This book is our collective attempt to define the research agenda of industrial and institutional anthropology and "to clarify the discipline's theories in relations to those of other social sciences and humanities that examine organizational culture." They include management sciences, policy sciences, linguistics, psychology, theology, social philosophy, literary criticism, and sociology.

Being a professionally trained anthropologist, I came to the field of organizational culture study through my ethnographic research on American enterprise in Japan (1991). I have observed first-hand that the topic of culture has flourished in popular literature and language for managers and consultants, and that books on "how-to manage corporate cultures" have increased at an alarming speed, without solid empirical foundation. Despite renewed interest in corporate and organizational anthropology in the 1980s and 1990s, there is still a need for empirical data, more models for analysis, and, most of all, some theoretical agreement on the topic. The relative dearth of ethnographic studies in this area may stem from the fact that the re-emergence of interest in organizational culture and corporate culture studies in the 1980s came not from industrial ethnographers who are comfortable with naturalistic, historical and qualitative research methodologies, but from management scientists and behavioral scientists who were more familiar with hypothesis-testing quantitative methodologies, in spite of the fact that they were dissatisfied with the conventional, positivistic, functional, and bureaucratic models of organization. Matters were further complicated by different interests in the topic because of different professional training and adherence to different professional cultures and their paradigms. While some organizational researchers have an interest in learning more of social relations and symbolic behaviors from interpretive perspectives, others have been attracted to the apparent functional utility of the culture concept in creating organizational changes. For some, culture is to serve as a control mechanism in order to create strong organizational commitment and concerted efforts for attaining specific goals of management.

Theoretical discussion, endless fights over definitions and concepts, anecdotes and other forms of narratives still largely dominated the field (see Alvesson and Berg 1992:199). If the culture concept is to turn into a meaningful paradigm for organizational research, we need to spend more effort on empirical research to build the foundation, rather than on debating opinions. I have concluded that it is vital for anthropologists to present a volume on organizational culture, that simplistic notions of culture must be corrected; that the development of solid empirical data must be encouraged; and that the field must be separated from speculative narratives, anecdotal stories and opinions.

Ethnography with its naturalistic and qualitative methodology appeals to those in organization sciences who have been discontented with the traditional research methodology which emphasized the measurement and quantification of organizational variables, and to those who would like to pursue "folk-representation" (ethno-graphy) of organizational phenomena. By presenting anthropology's tools and examples, I hope to invite those who are seriously contemplating on initiating historically-oriented (and yes, time-consuming), qualitative research on organizations.

Another important objective of mine is to establish the legitimacy of industrial and institutional anthropology within the growing field of organizational culture and within the field of applied anthropology. Unfortunately there still exists a common misconception outside (and sometimes inside) our discipline that anthropologists have not studied organizational culture. For example, a management scientist Sonja A. Sackmann declares:

> Most anthropological concepts of culture have emerged in studies of rather isolated societies. It is, therefore, questionable whether these concepts and their associated assumptions can be directly applied to organizations (1991:2)

Claiming that anthropologists have not studied complex organizations or that anthropological concepts of culture are not directly applicable to organizational studies would appear to me a gross misunderstanding. While the late 1970s and early 1980s saw a vigorous revitalization of interest in the cultural approach to work organization, the origin of industrial anthropology can be traced back to the 1930s North America, not to the study of "isolated societies". While it is true that relatively few anthropologists actively participated in the "growth industry" of corporate culture in the 1970s and 1980s, the important anthropological origin of this field should not be ignored. I would like to clarify these points in this volume.

I also believe that anthropological studies of organizational phenomena provide a different perspective from those of conventional organization sciences partly because anthropology as a discipline is most cross-cultural, eclectic, and interdisciplinary. It may be beneficial to re-affirm that anthropology is the study of the human condition, or the nature of humanity, in all times and places. With a data base built upon information from 3,000 societies, anthropology's time line extends 65 million years into prehistory. Anthropology searches for the essential biological and social characteristics shared by all primates, including homosapiens, and attempts to identify unique characteristics of our species. So far the discipline has articulated an important issue of human variation and similarity. Anthropology has accumulated a distinctive data base on human ideas, customs, traits and principles involving human work life.

I would argue that organizational culture studies undertaken by anthropologists in contemporary western societies should be placed within a much larger framework of ethnology and socio-cultural anthropology of work and human relations across time and space, and that readers on work organizations should include both pre-industrial and industrial societies (cf. Applebaum 1984 a & b) to give some depth in our perspectives. The present study of contemporary organizational culture directly relates to current theoretical debates concerning how a people understand a social phenomenon, how they express themselves, and how language, ideology, artifacts, and socio-political structure are interrelated at a particular historical and temporal point within human civilization. Cultural anthropology's comparative perspectives are supported by the fact that not everyone classifies or enacts the same world in the same way, and that not everyone feels social reality in the same way. Cultural anthropology's knowledge of other human groups and their world views forces us to recognize our own cultural bias and ethnocentrism in our fieldwork and theory-making. To liberate oneself from one's own cultural logic, the anthropologist usually attempts to apply the three principles of holism, relativism and pluralism. The anthropologist does not characteristically set problems (hypotheses) and seek solutions as in the case of many other behavioral scientists. The anthropologist is not necessarily preadapted for the role of discovering the problem, testing the hypothesis, and finding the answer, through statistical analyses. Instead, the first and most important task of the cultural anthropologist is to understand a particular human group and its culture as deeply and holistically as possible. Based upon this viewpoint, the methodology of anthropology is extremely empirical, participatory, longitudinal, and field research-oriented. The discipline's insights gained into the problematic and enigmatic nature of representing the others' cultures make impossible the comfortable and over-simplified assertion that other peoples' cultures can be easily grasped, categorized, analyzed, -- manipulated, or **managed**. Instead, anthropologists tend to pay particular attention to historical context and to attempt to reveal dynamic, and sometimes contradictory, relationships between subjective experiences, languages, symbols, artifacts, collective expressions, behavioral patterns, physical settings, social structures, political alliances, inter-organizational relations, and environments. According to this viewpoint, organization is a social entity embedded in the wider culture of society.

The authors of this volume share the belief that the culture concept as developed in anthropology can be applied to formal organizations in complex societies. They all believe that the culture paradigm can provide significant ideas with which to examine age-old problems of organizational behavior. There are, of course, some caveat in the declaration of its usefulness. Part three explores challenges, possible problems, and difficulties in applying the culture paradigm to organization research and to specific problem-solving. Practicing anthropologists and management consultants attempt to clarify the pros and cons of the organizational culture concept according to their field experiences.

The final goal of the book is to examine ethical issues in studying organizational cultures. Today, professional ethics is a vital concern of the discipline. Applied anthropologists are particularly anxious about how their research can be used for social change, and how the research itself fits into the global formation of power and its symbolic representation. Since the discipline's birth, anthropology has struggled with comparative colonialism, survival of indigenous populations, the third world development, environmental destruction, economic exploitation, wars, and political domination. The last and possibly most important part of this volume discusses the role of the anthropologist-consultant, corporate ethics, the norms of business firms and those of the larger society, anthropology of organization, and international development aid.

In doing research on other cultures, anthropologists implicitly compare, legitimize, or criticize their own culture. The ultimate value of anthropological inquiry may lie in its constructive critique of our own institutions, of our institutional members, and of our own life and values. Comparative organizational culture study encourages a supple and reflective mind for self-doubt. It is invites contemplation on how and why people act across time and space. I hope that this book helps clarify the significance of anthropological research on organization culture and its future challenges.

REFERENCES

Alvesson, M. and Per Olof Berg
  1992   *Corporate Culture and Organizational Symbolism.*   New
                York: Walter de Gruyter.
Applebaum, Herbert, ed.
  1984a   *Work in Market and Industrial Societies.*   Albany: State
                University of New York Press.
Applebaum, Herbert, ed.
  1984b   *Work in Non-Market and Traditional Societies.* Albany: State
                University of New York Press.
Hamada, Tomoko
  1991   *American Enterprise in Japan.*   Albany, New York: State
                University Press.

ANTHROPOLOGY AND
ORGANIZATIONAL CULTURE

Tomoko Hamada

The history of anthropological research on work organization can be discussed in terms of some important anthropological perspectives on the subject. In recent decades, anthropologists have gone through a sort of rite of passage. As a result an increasing number of anthropologists today question the validity of the traditional, all-encompassing, functional-structural-configurational paradigms. To pursue systematic observation and analyses of cultural phenomena, socio-cultural anthropology has diverged into various sub-fields: some anthropologists have constructed theories of contradictions and contested identities (c.f. Rosendahl 1985; E. Wolf 1966); cultural materialism (Harris 1979); structural analysis (Levi-Straus 1963, 1966, 1969, 1978), cultural ecology (Steward, 1955); eco-system (Moran 1983) and adaptive process (Rappaport 1968, 1984). Others have moved into cognitive anthropology (c.f. Goodenough 1971); interpretive anthropology (Clifford and Mercus 1986, Geertz 1973, Rabinow 1977); economic anthropology (Dalton 1961, Polanyi 1947, 1957, 1959, Sahlins 1958, 1961, 1972,1976); anthropology of work (Applebaum 1984 a & b, Buraway 1979) and other related fields.

Gregory (1983) critiqued past organizational studies done by industrial researchers, and pointed out that many were still based on past anthropological paradigms such as structural-functional, and configurationist views, and failed to explore "multiple native views". She argued for a "native-view" paradigm to explore a multi-cultural model of organization. Indeed in any modern organization, multiple identities, double talk, (Brunsson 1989) and separation of formal and informal organizations (Homans 1956) are often important and even necessary phenomena. To an anthropologist interested in post-canonical and post-doctrinal view of reality, an organization is a world locked in a war of meanings.

The present discussion on the historical path leading to anthropology's widely divergent perspectives on organizations today must begin with the problematic paradigm of functional-structural perspectives that gave birth to industrial anthropology some seventy years ago.

THE BEGINNING:
FUNCTIONALISM AND INDUSTRIAL ANTHROPOLOGY

Many anthropologists would agree that the concept of culture was first developed by the British anthropologist Edward Burnett Tylor, who defined it as "that complex whole which includes knowledge, beliefs, art, law, morals, custom and any other capabilities and habits acquired by man as a member of society" (1871). In England, and later in the United States, the functionalist and holistic stances regarded culture as an integrated system, posited that one aspect of a culture was invariably related to others, and that there was a tendency for all aspects of a culture to function as an inter-related whole. Thus the task of functionalists was to seek patterns of such integration. The interest of anthropology in the integrated totality has been well documented in literature by pioneers in the field. For example, Radcliffe-Brown was interested in "a complex network of social relations" (1952:19), while Malinowski focused on "an integral composed of partly autonomous, partly co-ordinated institutions." (1944:40). Evans-Pritchard studied "social institutions as interdependent parts of social systems" (1951:9) and Nadel discussed "the integrated totality of standardized behavior patterns" (1951:29). These pioneers and their students pursued the impossible goal of completely describing a complex inter-related totality.

Industrial anthropology's functional origin in the United States has been well documented (Baba 1986, Chapple 1953, Gamst 1990, Morey and Luthans 1987, Trice 1985). We can trace its birth to W. Lloyd Warner. Warner conducted field work on the Aborigines of Arnhem Land, Australia, where he utilized the functionalist models of his mentors, Malinowski and Radcliffe-Brown (Warner 1933). He was the first anthropologically-trained scholar who applied the functionalist-culture paradigm to industrial organizations in North America. During the 1930s, Elton Mayo of Harvard recruited a number of anthropologists including Warner in long-term organization research such as the Hawthorne Study. In the now well-known participant observations of the bank wiring room at the Hawthorne plant, where, for the first time, "a systematic description of the social organization of an industrial working group was obtained" (Chapple, 1953:820), the researchers investigated the human relationships among workers and ideologies that underlay their work-related behavior. The Hawthorne Studies generated considerable interest in applying anthropological tools to industrial research during the next two decades.

In addition to the Hawthorne studies, Warner applied functionalist theories and participant-observation methodologies in his community studies of "Yankee City", or Newburyport, Massachusetts (Warner and Lunt 1941; Warner and Low 1947), where he and his co-researchers linked characteristics of the regional community and the organizational ideologies and behaviors of the employees. Studies of small communities including their work life were conducted by many anthropologists during this period.

In 1942 Warner moved to the University of Chicago as head of the Committee on Human Relations in Industry to continue his influential work. Among many of Warner's students at Harvard were Conrad Arensberg and Eliot D. Chapple. Arensburg, Chapple, Frederick Richardson and others at Harvard who were interested in "applied anthropology" founded the Society for Applied Anthropology (SfAA) in 1941 along with its journal, *Applied Anthropology* (Now *Human Organization.*) The primary objective of the SfAA was "the promotion of scientific investigation of the principles controlling the relations of human beings to one another, and the encouragement of the wide application of these principles to practical problems." *Applied Anthropology* published a number of articles on business, industry and other formal organizations.

William F. Whyte was a student of Chapple and Arensberg at Harvard during his research on street corner society. Whyte's *Street Corner Society* (1943) is sometimes considered as an exemplary model for ethnographic research (Frost et al 1991). Whyte left Harvard in 1940, and went to the University of Chicago to study for his doctorate under Warner and the sociologist Everett C. Hughes, with a major in sociology and a minor in anthropology.   In 1944 he joined the Committee on Human Relations, and researched human relations in the restaurant industry (1948a and 1949).

Whyte was also a formative editor of *Human Organization* between 1955 and 1961. Under his guidance, the journal published many articles that attempted to capture complex social phenomena by using historical research, naturalistic inquiries, and descriptive narratives. Whyte's own research extended to the human relations of the restaurant, hotel, steel, automobile, glass, and petroleum industries (1961).   Among others, Burleigh Gardner worked as an applied anthropologist from 1937-1942 at the Hawthorne study (Gardner 1977), after the end of the Harvard phase of the project, and he wrote *Human Relations in Industry* (1945).

Burleigh Gardner's work on human relations was one of the pioneering efforts to study the business organization as a socio-cultural system within larger systems of the community and society (1977). Gardner and Whyte worked together on the double bind problems of the supervisor as the man caught in the middle (1945). Other important research included Richardson and Charles Walker's investigation on supervision and assembly line workers of an IBM plant (1948 and 1949). Walker and Robert Guest investigated an automotive manufacture's assembly line and the related informal relations (1952), while Melville Dalton examined the relationship between extra-job patterns of behavior, informal group norms, and work performance of the work groups (1948). Others such as Walter Goldschmidt studied agricultural farm operations in California (1946, 1947).

The human relations school of the study of organization started to decline during the 1950s and especially after 1960.   *Human Organization Research* edited by Richard N. Adams and Jack J. Preiss for the SfAA (1960) was one of the last major collections of anthropological research on organizations using the human relations perspective. After the departure of William Whyte from the editorship of *Human Organization* in 1961, the focus of the journal also shifted away from research on American organizations. Gamst summarizes the problems related to the human relations perspective as follows:

> The functionalist, human relations school has been criticized for:
> being management social science; either ignoring trade unions or
> being biased against them; in a vein of functionalist equilibrium, de-

emphasizing the natural significance in business organizations of the uses of power and the conflicts of factions; and neglecting the influences exerted by extra-organizational political and economic pressures. Especially, the school saw conflict and pressures from workers, union organized or otherwise, as dysfunctional to the organization and in need of a restabilizing correction. Established norms were valued by the school above factional interests. Social control and conformity were emphasized over social change. The school's frequent use of a posited static state as a basis of analyses also posed problems for the validation of studies. (Gamst 1990:20)

In general anthropology, traditional functionalism-structuralism was being contested. Main criticisms of functional analyses were similar to those addressed to the human relations school: (1) functional statements are frequently untestable because they often affirm their consequences; (2) it lacks perspective for radical cultural change; (3) there is often a failure to make explicit the functional hypotheses of self-regulation; (4) the entities to which functional analyses are applied are not always specifically defined or definable; (5) functionalism must be re-defined in the social and historical contexts; (6) it neglects the power dimension inherent in social systems.

With the decline of functionalism and the human relations school by the 1960s, the term organizational culture was rarely mentioned in management science literature. Similar but not identical concepts such as organizational climate were used by organization scientists (Frederiksen 1966, Tagiuri and Litwin 1968, James-Jones 1974), where the concept of organizational climate centered on norms and values of institutions or of individual employees. There was also a shift from ethnological research methods to the clinical psychological or other social science approaches. Major paradigms on organizational phenomena were proposed by social scientists during the era of decline of ethnographical research on organization. Some major paradigms are listed in the following table.

While non-anthropologists were exploring theoretical models for analyzing organizational phenomena during the 1960s and 1970s, industrial anthropologists' focus shifted to the negative consequences of industrialization home and abroad, to cultural analysis framed in terms of dependency and Marxism, to the issue of development of third-world societies, and to race, ethnicity and gender in urban America and elsewhere.

ANTHROPOLOGICAL RESEARCH ON WORK ORGANIZATION

Many anthropologists who were analyzing small-scale societies and who were interested in kinship, local communities and cognitive taxonomies, began to face a new level of integration of the world economy caused by supranational activities of organizations. Many anthropologists experienced firsthand that traditional small-scale economic systems are rapidly changing and are deeply involved in larger regional, national, and international systems (Nash 1966; Ribeiro 1968; Wolf 1959; Geertz 1966; Worsley 1970). As Ted Downing states (1981) in his paper entitled, "The Internationalization of Capital: Mrs. Olsen and Juan Valdez," the internationalization of capital penetrates every corner of the world and every work life of people: Mexican coffee producers become more inter-related to coffee producers in Africa and Brazil, and to consumers in America and Europe, than to non-coffee producing peasants in their own culture areas (Downing 1981:18). Theories of integrated culture in a bounded system are deemed inadequate to meet such new conditions of economic interpenetration.

TABLE 1
MAJOR PARADIGMS ON ORGANIZATIONAL PHENOMENA (1)

PARADIGMS	FOUNDERS	ADVOCATES
Scientific Management	Taylor	Mooney, Reiley, Gulick, Urwick, Brown, Koontz, O'Donnel
Action	Weber	Silverman, Bowey
System Theory	Parsons Bertalanffy	Merton, Ezioni, Gouldner, Blau, Selznick, Miller, Rice, Burns, Stalker, Croizer, Thompson, Lawrence, Lorsch, Dunca
Expectation	Lewin, Tolman	Vroom, Porter, Lawler, Evans, House
Needs	Maslow, Murray	McGregor, Argyris, Herzberg, McClelland, Cumin, Litwin, Stringer
Influence Leadership	Lewin	Cartwright, Sander, Bales, French, Raven, Ohio State Group, Tannenbaum
Exchange	Homans, Blau	Whyte, Jacobs
Resource Dependence	Blau, Emerson, Merton	Pfeffer, Salancik, Hickson, et al.
Conflict	Max, Simmel	Dalton, Walton, Mouton, Coser, Dahrendorf
Decision Making	Simon, March	Cyert, March, Lawrence, Lorsch, Galbraith, Duncan
Bureaucracy	Weber	Udy, Hall, Aston Group
Technology	Marx, Veblen	Woodward, Thompson, Perros, Harvey
Contingency	Fiedler	Thompson, Duncan, Nonaka, Kagano, Tannenbaum, Lawrence, Lorsch

Source: The table was created based upon the tentative categorization presented by Nonaka, I, et al. Soshikigenshou no Riron to Solutei (Theories and Measurement of Organizational Phenomena, Tokyo: Chikuma-shobo 1978).

The theoretical "movements" of the 1960-1970s, curriculum re-organization, and career prospects in the 1980s pushed many anthropologists to domestic and international fields of organized and non-organized work research. Beginning in the 1960s a number of forces exerted pressures on anthropologists to study "us" as well as "them," to genuinely understand the range of behavior. At the same time many anthropologists turned their attention to solving social problems at home (see Cole, J. 1982). As anthropologists explored the totality of human attitudes, values, behavior and social institutions, a number of issues came into sharper focus. For example, those "urban" anthropologists who claimed their theoretical roots in W. Lloyd Warner's "Yankee City", Robert Redfield's Yucatan communities, William Foote Whyte's Boston, Ellen Hellman's Johannesburg, and Oscar Lewis's Culture of Poverty, turned to studies of rural-urban migrant workers, urban class formation, political economy of ethnicity, class and gender, blue-collar work life, and work folklore (see Sanjek 1990 for a review). The result has been an impressive collection of work-related literature that include studies on multinationals and inter-locking capital formation (see J. Nash 1981 for review; Downing 1981; A. Wolf 1977, 1980, 1984); female factory workers (Bookman, et al. 1988; Lamphere, L. 1987; Ong 1987; Sacks and Remy 1984; Zavella 1987), working-class culture and global political economy (Lubeck 1986; Nash and Fernandez-Kelly 1983; Ramaswamy 1983; Rosendahl 1985); work-place crime (Mars 1982); domestic work (Chaney, E. and Castro M. 1989; Cock 1980; Lamphere 1987, Sacks and Ramey 1984); and downward mobility of the middle class (Newman 1988). Ethnographic studies were conducted on American construction workers (Applebaum 1981); police force in Japan and America (Ames 1981, Manning 1977); Chinese factory workers in Malaysia (Ong 1987); a medical center in North Carolina (Sacks 1988); Islam and urban labor in Nigeria (Lubeck 1986); wood-carvers in Hong Kong (Cooper 1980); domestic workers in South Africa (Cock 1980); industrial workers in South India (Ramasway 1983); American railroad workers (Gamst 1980); and American waitresses in a New Jersey restaurant (Paules 1991). Contemporary immigrants' working-class life has been examined in the context of factory labor in Rhodes Island (Lamphere 1987); the social construction of the "old" and "retired" has been analyzed in California and Florida (Francis 1984,

Vesperi 1985); and the meaning of work and lifecourse has been discussed (Plath 1983).

Economic anthropologists who carry on the tradition established by Raymond Firth's description of the Tikopia (1939) and Malay Fishermen (1966); A. I. Richard's work on land, labor, and diet among the Bemba of Northern Rhodesia (1939); and Karl Polanyi's work on trade and market systems (1957) revealed organizational rules of non-industrial societies where work is embedded in the total fabric of social practices. Only in industrial cultures does work become a separate sphere from those of family, religion, politics and kinship (Sahlin 1972). Work, in a vast majority of human societies, is part of a continuum of social roles and status, magic and rituals, political alliance, family and kinship networks, and gender division.

Development anthropologists who participated in overseas aid programs learned that ideological and value changes frequently paralleled political ones that provided the over-all social context for technological and economic development. These observations gave support to those who believe that the groundwork for social change must start with the minds of people, and that their values, meanings and expectations are significant part of the social process. At the same time, as Nolan discusses in this volume, development anthropologists painfully recognize the fact that some development projects fail because of the inability of institutions such as the World Bank, USAID and UN organizations to change their organizational culture: Their institutional orientation is for short-term goals in numerical terms rather than for incorporating long-term needs of local communities into planned change. Detailed ethnographic studies in different work communities have contributed to the discipline's collective knowledge and perspectives that regard organization as a socio-cultural system deeply embedded in the larger societal cultures.

INTERNATIONAL DIMENSION

Outside the discipline of anthropology, the term "culture" was often used in the sense of specific cultures of specific societies--such as German and Japanese, especially during the

1960-1970s. Among social scientists engaged in cross-cultural/international studies of organizations, the convergence-divergence debate dominated the field for two decades. Adherents of the convergence (or universalist) perspective argued that organizational characteristics are mostly free of the influence of specific cultures (Form 1979; Hickson, Hinnings, McMillan & Schwitter 1974; Negandhi 1979, 1985), while the divergence scholars argued that organizations are culture-bound. (Hofsteed 1980; Laurent 1983; Lincoln, et al. 1978, 1981; Meyer and Rowan 1977). For example, Hofstede (1980) in a landmark study of 160,000 employees working in 40 countries for a multinational corporation, identified four dimensions on which styles of work differ: power distance, uncertainty avoidance, individualism/collectivism, and masculinity/femininity. There were, however, few ethnographic researchers who participated in the convergence-divergence debate.

The battle of convergence-divergence was particularly severe in the Japan field as this country continued to grow economically to become the first non-western economic giant in recent history. Maccoby analyzes in this volume how a major challenge to the Tayloristic industrial bureaucracy was posed by the American image of Japanese manufacturers, particularly in the context of total quality management.

Research on Japanese work organization began with an anthropological perspective, notably by James Abegglen who had worked with the founder of American industrial anthropology, W. Lloyd Warner. Abegglen worked with W. Lloyd Warner on occupational mobility in American business and industry, and big business leaders in America (Warner and Abbeglen 1955a and b), and he later moved to Japan to study industrial organizations. His descriptive study, *The Japanese Factory: Aspects of Its Social Organization*, was a pioneer work on Japanese organization. Since then, the structural characteristics of the Japanese company have been discussed extensively by many scholars (Cole 1979, Levin, Okochi and Karsh, 1973; Marsh and Mannari 1971 1972 and 1976; Noda 1975b, Taira 1962, 1970), and the theoretical battle of convergence-divergence began. The convergence-universalist argued that individual economies can be placed at different levels of industrial development and that many characteristics of industrial organizations can be explained by universally applicable structural variables such as size, technology, centralization-decentralization, market, and labor mobility. Two sociologists who utilized ethnographic methodologies to study Japanese organizations are worth mentioning in this respect: Industrial sociologist Cole wrote an ethnographic work on a Japanese factory and Japanese blue collar workers. He maintained a universalist/convergence stand, arguing that there are many "functionally equivalent" features in the Japanese employment system that can be explained by structural variables. On the other hand, a British sociologist Ronald Dore worked closely with Hiroshi Hazama on ethnographic research on Hitachi Electric and British Electric. Dore argued against Japan's eventual convergence toward the Western-style model. His "later development" model predicted, some twenty years ago, that the British style market-oriented labor management system would eventually converge to an alternative participatory management model presented by Japanese management. Dore cast doubt on the validity of all universal models either of economic growth or of rational labor behavior.

In the organizational research field, the influence of Japanese culture on organizational structure became a controversial issue (see Hamada 1980 for a review on this issue.) For example, Marsh and Mannari (1976) stressed that most distinctively Japanese variables such as seniority increments, the life-long employment system, etc. have less causal impact on performance that do more universal variables such as employees' status and job satisfaction.

From the viewpoint of organizational culture, the question in cross-cultural management research became: Do universally applicable structural variables determine people's behavior in organizations, or do national, racial, or ethnic cultural conditioning influence organizational activities (Adler & Jelinek 1986, Chimezie A. B. Osigweh, Yg 1989)? Questioning the universal applicability of theories developed and tested in the West, Azumi (1974) suggested that "if the perspective of social science as developed in the West is inadequate, that must be demonstrated by the creation of a new and better social science instead of developing separate social sciences for different societies" (1974: 527). Maruyama (1980, 1982) relates cognitive dimensions of mapping called mindscapes to comparative management and noted that in any larger culture there are all types of individual mind patterns, but that cultural differences exist in the distribution of various individual types as well as in the social dynamics of the interaction among different types; some types are officially accepted or encouraged while others are relegated to the social periphery, ignored, institutionally suppressed, individually repressed, latent or nonverbalized.

An increasing number of organizational scientists attacked the universality myth in transnational organizational research (see Chimezie A.B. Osigweh 1989 for a review of organizational science abroad) as the interfaces between the western and non-western cultures on organizations became an important area of inquiry (Adler 1983, 1986).

ORGANIZATIONAL ANTHROPOLOGY TODAY

Within the discipline of anthropology, research on North American work organizations flourished in the 1980s, and many scholarly societies experienced a renewed infusion of organizational energy. The Society for the Anthropology of Work was founded in 1980 by Thomas Greaves, June Nash, Frederick Gamst, Herbert Applebaum and others with its periodical, now called *The Anthropology of Work Review*. Reflecting the fact that more than half of new Ph.D.s in anthropology began to work outside academia in the 1980s, the National Association for the Practice of Anthropology (NAPA) was founded as a unit of the American Anthropological Association in 1983. The Society for Economic Anthropology was also formed in 1981. The debate on culture and industrial organization, sometimes quite furious, among scholars began to help define the distinct specialization of organizational anthropology within the discipline: Michael Buraway critiqued the anthropology of industrial work (1979); June Nash explored issues of international capital formation and the division of labor (1981, 1985); Holzberg and Giovannini reviewed anthropological research on industries (1981); Julia Pennbridge produced, for the SfAA, an annotated bibliography on industrial anthropology

(1985). Marietta Baba (1986) provided an historical overview of business anthropology for NAPA. Sachs edited two special issues on anthropological approaches to organizational culture in the *Anthropology of Work Review* (1989). Hamada and Jordan (1991) presented anthropological perspectives on cross-cultural management and organizational culture. *The Anthropology of Work* series, edited by June Nash for the State of New York University Press; the *Anthropology of Contemporary Issues*, edited by Roger Sanjek for Cornell University Press; *City and Society* by the Society for Urban Anthropology; *Anthropology of Work Review* by the Society for Anthropology of Work, and *Human Organization* by the Society for Applied Anthropology, and other scholarly journals have provided much needed venues for anthropological publications in this area.

The recent flood of works on organizational culture both inside and outside anthropology can be seen as a renaissance of the field first begun in the 1930s, although many are not necessarily functionalist. Serrie states that there is still a great need for anthropologists to help work on a range of multicultural topics, including comparative management and international marketing, and that there is great receptivity to anthropologists in both American schools of management and in American corporations (Serrie 1990). Gamst (1989) and Hamada and Jordan (1989) note the difficulty in separating "organizational culture" applied by management specialists from the concept of "culture" used by anthropologists. They oppose the notion of corporate culture as an additive or as a factor to be manipulated for organizational competitiveness. Instead they advocate the organizational culture study as a way to understand organization not as an economic or political entity but as a socio-cultural entity placed in a particular society within a particular historical context. This socio-cultural entity continues to emerge as on-going relationships among subjective experiences of its members, symbolic communication and representation, manifested socio-political alliances, behavioral patterns, collectively expressed artifacts, and physical, socio-political and economic environments. Thus it is safe to say that many anthropologists are interested in "organizing," as well as "organization". Cross-cultural organizational ethnographies are on the rise, especially from the "native's" perspective (Connors 1989, 1990; Briody and Baba 1991; Hamada 1991). Baba (1986) notes that an urgent need still exists for cross-cultural studies of organizations in order to test hypotheses related to the evolution of bureaucratic structures, the convergence of economic and social forms, and the international transfer of work technologies. These needs, she states, can be met empirically by organizational ethnography and conceptually by anthropological theories and research designs.

THE ORGANIZATIONAL CULTURE MOVEMENT
OUTSIDE ANTHROPOLOGY

During the 1980s, the concept of culture was "displaced" from its anthropological origin by non-anthropologists, who introduced the construct to a the general management science readership (Reichers and Schneider 1990). The now well-known development of the "organizational culture" movement outside anthropology began at the historical moment when American society increasingly was faced with evolving ethnic, racial and religious sub-identities, continuing immigration of non-European people, differential fertility rates, growing female labor participation, and increasing international competition. The corporate culture movement in the 1980s and 1990s can be characterized by its curious mixture of extremely divergent viewpoints: In organization culture studies, some conceive culture as being a management tool for developing organization-wide values (Allen and Kraft 1982; Bryman 1984, Peters and Waterman 1982); others see culture as a symbol system (Martin et al 1983; Frost et al. 1991, Smircich 1983). Some view organizational culture as being an engendered entity (Kanter 1977, Mills and Tancred 1992). While others see corporate culture-making as a form of social engineering (Kunda 1992). Although there is a wide and eclectic coverage of topics (see for reviews of literature :Alvesson and Berg 1992, Frost et al. 1985, 1991, Ott 1989, Sackman 1991, Schein 1990), there is relative paucity of empirical data (Denison 1990, Murrin 1988; Goodall 1989; Jones, Moore, and Snyder 1988). Few critiques have been made on the ideological and socio-political nature of the movement itself (Martin and Siehl 1983; Schneider 1990). Let us briefly review the movement itself to highlight how and where the culture concept was constructed throughout the movement.

It was slow in the beginning, as initial attempts by organizational researchers in the 1970s to incorporate anthropological concepts into organizational studies met with mixed success. For example, Stanley Davis (1971) introduced the concept of culture as a new tool for management consultants to manipulate organizational change, while Pettigrew (1979), with only a short reference to Leslie White, defined organizational culture as a system of forms, categories, and images imbedded in the beliefs, rituals and myths of daily organizational life (1979:574). Although Pettigrew advocated anthropological models for studying symbolism, ritual and power, he failed to convince other organizational researchers to follow his suit.

In 1982, interest in corporate culture was suddenly exploded with the publication of popular works such as Deal and Kennedy's *Corporate Cultures* and Peters and Waterman's(1982) *In Search of Excellence*. The impact of their messages spawned research exploring the relationship between culture and productivity. In 1983, two major journals, *Administrative Science Quarterly* and *Organizational Dynamics*, published special editions devoted entirely to the concept of corporate culture. The former contained a variety of articles discussing the definition of corporate culture (Smircich 1983) and studying ethno-semantics (Barley 1983). *Organizational Dynamics* urged their readership to adopt the concept of culture as a practical tool (Sathe 1983; Wilkins 1983; Koprowski 1983). Numerous books (e.g. Frost et al., 1985, 1991; Kilmann, et. al 1985, 1988; and Schein 1985) and articles (e.g., Feldman 1989; Garsombke 1988; and Hebden 1986) followed.

One theory in the emerging organizational culture school suggested that organized action is the product of consensus among organizational participants, who act in a coordinated fashion as a result of sharing a common set of meanings or interpretations of their joint experience. Following this perspective, certain researchers explored a multi-level topology of culture which proceeds from abstract, unconscious assumptions at one end of a continuum to concrete, conscious expressions of culture at the other. For example, Edgar Schein

(1985) developed a definition of organizational culture and described the processes of formation, emergence and change. His structural model of culture operates at three levels: (1) the uppermost level of artifacts and creations, (2) the next level of values that are the conscious, shared group beliefs, and (3) the third and deepest level of basic assumptions that are invisible, often unconscious, and taken for granted (1985:1-22). The dynamics of the model are that culture emerges from small groups within an organization, but that it is leadership which helps shape, embed, transmit and change it. Although Schein is a strong advocate of the ethnographic method for studying corporate culture, he utilizes the "clinical perspective" where a researcher is called in and paid by the client to fix specific problems. Clients, Schein believes, are motivated to reveal things that unpaid observers could not obtain "willingly". This management-centric view on corporate culture, by viewing organization through the short-term client-researcher interaction only, may seriously limit our understanding of organizational culture. There is a serious concern that the clinical perspective methodology, like the traditional functionalist-human relations perspective, may misguide researchers to interpret management subcultures for organizational culture as a whole.

Some scholars who took the narrow definition of organizational culture have developed the "culture-as-another-variable" concept, and contrasted "strong" and "weak" corporate cultures according to the number of important shared assumptions, the pervasiveness of the culture and/or its suitability for accomplishing articulated management goals. According to this group, culture is a variable which can be manipulated by management, a value supposition that may be a product of the American management sub-culture itself. For example, Davis believed that culture is something an organization "has" that it is manifest through its myths and rituals. Of greater concern is his theme that corporate culture is merely a pattern of shared values and beliefs, and thus he reduces such workplace behavior to a "homogeneous, monolithic entity created by senior management" (Giovannini and Rosansky 1990:29). A number of management science researchers sought to change or "manage" culture to fit the current strategic plan for more efficient organization (Beer et al. 1990; Fitzgerald 1988;

Denison 1990). Others have attempted to draw causal relationships between culture and a variety of organizational effects-- the impact of culture on socialization and acculturation (Hebden 1986), mythmaking and revitalization (McWhinney and Batista 1988), financial performance (Siehl and Martin 1990), innovation (Feldman 1989), and coping with militarism (Garsombke 1988). Management literature today consists of a variety of models espousing the need to change values and beliefs (Fitzgerald 1988) by understanding key processes (Barczak, Smith and Wilemon 1987; Zeira and Avedisian 1989). Miller (1989) even presents a grand evolutionary schema vis-a-vis Lewis Henry Morgan, that corporations are like new civilizations going through evolutionary stages-prophet, barbarian, builder, explorer and administrator--, ultimately to reach the final stage of synergizing. Adizes (1988), uses a "lifecycle" model in which growth and death are predictable in corporate culture and individuals in leadership positions play an important role in the corporate life cycle.

On the other hand, it is important to note that a few non-anthropologists who have been disenchanted with these models of planned or managed cultural change have turned to more behavioralist approach, focusing on innovators and change agents. For instance, Kanter (1983) argues that the successful corporate transformations depends on cultures that support innovation and entrepreneurial activities. Thompson and Luthan (1990) believe that culture can be changed only through changes in behaviors and that individuals change behaviors if they see a desired consequence. Thus the individual has the choice of accepting, accommodating, or rejecting any change. Beer, Eisenstat and Spector (1990) present a model for change that suggests that "corporate renewal should start at the bottom through informal efforts to solve business problems" (1990:158). They argue, however, that attitudinal change will not lead necessarily to behavioral change.

The movement for organization culture has so far produced four different ideas about the usefulness of the culture concept: as an analytical tool, a managerial tool, a tool of change, and a cognitive sense-making tool. At present, there is no consensus on the definition of organizational culture among management scientists, and as far as research methodology is concerned, the majority is still directed towards assessment questionnaires and surveys (Rousseau 1990) within the narrow focus of a variety of management problems.   The general scarcity of long-term, organization-wide, participant observational studies may be due partly to the organizational scientists' "cultural" orientation, "objective" data gathering, and hypothesis-testing, and to the time and monetary factors impossed by their clients-employers. The result is the lack of an holistic, longitudinal, cross-cultural, and "native view" approach that is so often taken for granted by the ethnographer. Without solid empirical data, an infusion of well-grounded anthropological theory, and a balanced combination of theory and practice, organizational culture studies may flounder or fail to reach their potentialities.

THE CULTURE PERSPECTIVE

However, it is important to summarize the following assumptions about the nature of organization, presented in this volume, that may distinguish our work from the traditional organizational studies perspectives that emphasize rationality, certainty and linearity.   From anthropological perspectives, organization can be considered as follows: (1) Organization is a socio-cultural system embedded in larger socio-cultural environments; (2) The management culture of an organization is not necessarily **the** organization culture. Management is only one, albeit powerful, sub-culture; (3) Organizational life is more fluid than linear: Decisions, actors, plans and issues continuously carom through an ever-changing labyrinth of meanings, positions, statuses, barriers, and traps; (4) Values are often sub-consciously perceived, and yet they influence organizational members' behaviors, decision-making patterns, and emotional and affective reactions to organizational phenomena; (5) Therefore, we must look at **not only** what happens, but **what it means**. As Turner states, life as lived, life as experienced, and life as told are three different things; (6) Significant events and processes in organizations are often **ambiguous** (multivocal) and **uncertain** (unpredictable);   (7) Socio-political alliances of organizational members are not necessarily the same as the cultural integration of their ideational worlds; (8) The same events can have very different meanings for different people because of differences in their cognitive schema, the amount and content of information, and the methods and forms they use to interpret and create organizational actions; (9) People create, reinvent, and manipulate symbols in order to increase predictability and control over organizational phenomena; (10) Organization is filled with internal contradictions and conflicts, formal and informal realms, double talk and parodies. Organizational rituals often symbolize underlying forces for disintegration as well as integration; (11) As Goffman observed, in everyday life actors are simultaneously the marks as well as the shills of social order.

I believe that the power of the culture metaphor is in its holistic orientation: It unites various aspects of organizational phenomena such as the individual cognitive processes, languages and symbolic aspects, behavioral manifestations, material products, socio-political structures of power and hegemony, and wider and larger environments of the organization, that all contribute to sharing, creating, contesting, denying, interpreting, and changing human activities. Although contemporary anthropologists do not necessarily follow functionalism or configurationalism, it is safe to say that anthropologists are still and always interested in revealing dynamic, and sometimes contradictory, inter-relationships between different aspects of culture such as inter-subjective experiences, symbolic interpretation, reflection, and representation of such experiences, and site-specific development of political, economic, and social structures and power alliances among people.

I am uncomfortable about the "how-to-manage culture" perspective, partly because my professional culture discourages the use of superficial tools for quick results. My normative orientation is guided by the anthropological perspective that respects the inclusiveness, subtlety, and depth as well as the robustness of culture. This issue of the researcher's cultural orientation raises another very important question concerning the professional culture of academic anthropologists and that of applied anthropologists and management scientists.

An important task of applied scientists, including management scientists, is to create organizational change. This outlook for social change is also shared by practicing anthropologists, as discussed in Part Three and Four of this volume. Unlike academicians and particularly academic anthropologists, applied scientists do not approach organizations or cultures as items of study in their own right. However, this does not mean that applied scientists simply want to find tools to support present management ideologies. Under ideal circumstances, these management scientists and practicing anthropologists should be able to create and make organizations better. The action-oriented scientist would always like to improve social institutions that affect many people's lives in many levels. And this is not a lesser vision or task than that of the academic anthropologist. On the contrary, this task may be of greater value because the action-oriented scientists needs to know everything the academic anthropologist does and more. In putting theory into action, one must be keenly aware of one's own cultural orientation, motives and values, normative orientation and ethics. And one must avoid cheap shots at organizational culture.

I firmly believe that we can link the above-mentioned two perspectives, where theory and praxis re-enforce each other. While the scientific community of academic anthropologists can pose persistent and probing questions about methods, paradigms, and approaches in organizational research, practicing anthropologists and management scientists can utilize such knowledge in their search of social change, and bring empirical data back to the theoretical debate. Together we can improve the soundness, feasibility, and applicability of our knowledge.

REFERENCES

Abegglen, James
1956   *The Japanese Factory: Aspects of Its Social Organization.*
         New York: Free Press.

Adams, Richard N., and Jack J. Preiss, eds.
1960   *Human Organization Research: Field Relations and
         Techniques.* Homewood, Illinois: Dorsey.

Adize, Ichak
1988   *Corporate Lifecycles: How and Why Corporations Grow and
         Die and What to do About it.* New Jersey: Prentice Hall.

Adler, Nancy. J
1983a   Cross-cultural Management Research: The Ostrich and
         the Trend. *Academy of Mangement Review* 8(2):226-232.

1983b   Organizational Development in a Multicultural
         Environment. *Journal of Applied Behavioral Science*
         19(3):350-365.

1983c   A Topology of Management Studies Involving Culture.
         Journal of International Business Studies. Fall:29-47.

1986   *International Dimensions of Organizational Behavior.*
         Boston: Kent Publishing.

Agar, Michael H.
1986   *The Dilemmas of Independent Trucking: Independents
         Declared.* Washington D.C.: Smithsonian Institution
         Press.

Allaire, Y and M. Firsirotu
1985   Theories of Organizational Culture. *Organizational
         Studies* 5(3):193-226.

Alvesson, Mats, and Per Olof Berg
1992   *Corporate Culture and Organizational Symbolism.* Berlin: de
         Gruyter.

Ames, W
    1981   *Police and Community in Japan*. Berkeley: University of
                Califronia Press.

Applebaum, H
    1981   *Royal Blue: The Culture of Construction Workers*. New
                York Holt, Rinehart, Winston.

    1984a   (ed.) *Work in Market and Industrial Societies*. Albany:
                State University of New York Press.

    1984b   (ed.) *Work in Non-Market and Traditional Societies*.
                Albany: State University of New York Press.

Arensberg, Conrad M.
    1942   Industry and Community. *American Journal of Sociology*
                49:1-12.

    1954   Community Study Method. *The American Journal of
                Sociology* 60:109-124.

    1955   American Communities. *American Anthropologist*
                57:1143-62.

    1978   Theoretical Contributions of Industrial and
                Developmental Studies. In Elizabeth M. Eddy and W.L.
                Partridge, eds. *Applied Anthropology in America*. Pp.49-
                78. New York: Columbia University Press.

Arensberg, Conrad M., and Douglas McGregor
    1942   Determination of Morale in an Industrial Company.
                Applied Anthropology 1(2):12-34.

Argyris, C
    1958   Some Problems in Conceptualizing Organizational
                Climate: A Case Study of a Bank. *Administrative Science
                Quarterly* 2:501-520.

Azumi, Koya
    1974   Japanese society: A sociological review. In A. D.
                Tiedemann (ed.) *An Introduction to Japanese Civilization*.
                Pp. 515-535. New York: Columbia University Press.

Baba, Marietta L.
1986   *Business and Industrial Anthropology: An Overview.*
        Washington D.C.: National Association for the Practice
        of Anthropology. Bulletin No. 2. Washington D.C.:
        American Anthropological Association.

Barczak, Gloria, Smith, Charles and David Wilemon
1987   Managing   Large-scale   Organizational   Change.
        Organizational Dynamics Autumn:23-35.

Barley, Stephen R.
1983   Semiotics   and   the   Study   of   Occupational   and
        Organizational Cultures. *Administrative Science Quarterly*
        28:393-413.

Barth, Frederik
1963   *The Role of the Entrepreneur in Social Change in Northern
        Norway.*   Universitetsforlaget,   Oslo: Scandinavian
        University Books.

1966   Models of Social Organization. *Journal of the Royal
        Anthropological Institute.* Occasional Paper 23. Glasgow:
        University Press.

1967   On the Study of Social Change. *American Anthropologist*
        69:661-9.

Barth, Frederik
1969   (ed.) *Ethnic Groups and Boundaries.* Boston: Little Brown
        and Co.

Beer, Michael, Eisenstat, Russel A., and Bert Spector
1990   Why Change Programs Don's Produce Change. *Harvard
        Business Review.* November-December: 158-166.

Beneria, L, Roldan, M
1987   *The Crossroads of Class and Gender:Industrial Homework,
        Subcontracting, and Household Dynamics in Mexico City.*
        Chicago: University of Chicago Press.

Blau, Peter M.
    1955   *Dynamics of Bureaucracy: A Study of Interpresonal Relations in Two Governmental Agencies.*   Chicago: University of Chicago Press.

Bookman, A. Morgen, S.,eds.
    1988   *Women and the Politics of Empowerment.*   Philadelphia: Temple University Press.

Briody, Elizabeth K. and M. Baba
    1991   Explaining Differences in Repatriation Experiences: The Discovery of Coupled and Decoupled System. *American Anthropologist* 93:322-44.

Briody, Elizabeth K.
    1990   Organizational Culture: From Concept to Applications. *Anthropology of Work Review* 10(4):4-10.

Brunsson, Nils
    1989   *The Organization of Hypocrisy: Talk, Decisions and Actions in Organizations.*   Trans. by Nancy Adler.   New York: John Wiley & Sons.

Buraway, Michael
    1979   The Anthropology of Industrial Work. *Annual Review of Anthropology* 8:231-66.

Chaney, E., and Castro M., eds.
    1989   *Muchachas No More: Household Workers in Latin America and the Caribbean.*   Philadelphia: Temple University Press.

Chapple, Eliot D.
    1939   Quantitative Analysis of the Interaction of Individuals. *National Academy of Sciences Proceedings* 25:58-67.

    1941   Organization Problems in Industry.   *Applied Anthropology* 1(1):2-9.

    1943   Anthropological Engineering: Its Use to Administrators. *Applied Anthropology* 2:23-32.

Chapple, Eliot D.
　　1953　Applied Anthropology in Industry. **In** A.L. Kroeber, ed. *Anthropology Today.* Pp. 819-831. Chicago: University of Chicago Press.

Chapple, E.D., and C. M. Arensberg
　　1940　Measuring Human Relations: An Introduction to the Study of the Interaction of Individuals. *Genetic Psychology Monographs* 22:3-147.

Chimezie A.B. Osigweh, Y Ed.
　　1989　*Organizational Science Abroad: Constraints and Perspectives.* New York: Plenum Publishing Corporation.

Clifford, J. and Marcus G. E. (eds.)
　　1986　Writing Culture: The Poetics and Politics of Ethnography. Berkeley: University of California.

Cock, J
　　1980　*Maids and Madams: A Study in the Politics of Exploitation.* Johannesburg: Ravan Press.

Colby, Fernandez and Kronenfeld
　　1981　Toward a Convergence of Cognitive and Symbolic Anthropology. *American Ethnologist* 8:436-442.

Cole, Robert, E.
　　1979　*Work, Mobility and Participation: A Comparative Study of American and Japanese Industry.* Berkeley: University of California Press.

Connors, Jeane L.
　　1989　Quality Control in an American Corporation: An Ethnography from the Inside. *Crosscurrents* 3:33-52.

Dahrendorf, Ralf
　　1956　*Class and Class Conflict in Industrial Society.* New York: Free Press.

Dalton, George
　　1961　Economic Theory and Primitive Society. *American Anthropologist* 63:1-25.

Dalton, Melville
    1948   The Industrial Rate-Buster: A Characterization. *Applied Anthropololgy* 7(1):1-16.

Davis, Keith
    1962   *Human Relations at Work.* New York: McGraw-Hill.

Davis, Stanley M.
    1971   *Comparative Management: Organizational and Cultural Perspectives.* Englewood Cliffs: Prentice-Hall

David, Stanley M.
    1984   *Managing Corporate Culture.*   Cambridge: Ballinger Publishers.

Denison, Daniel R.
    1990   *Corporate Culture and Organizational Effectiveness.* New York: John Wiley & Sons.

Dore, Ronald P.
    1973   *British Factory: Japanese Factory: The Origins of National Diversity in Industrial Relations.* Berkeley: University of California Press.

Downing, T.L.
    1981   The Internationalization of Capital: Mrs Olson and Juan Valdez: Thoughts on Exploitation in Agriculture. paper presented at the Annual Meeting of the American Anthropological Association.   Los Angeles, CA December 5.

Deal, Terrence E., and Allen A. Kennedy
    1982   *Corporate Cultures: The Rites and Rituals of Corporate Life.* Reading, Mass: Addison-Wesley.

Denison, Danial R.
    1990   *Corporate Culture and Organizational Effectiveness.* New York: John Wiley & Sons.

Dickson, WIJ., and Fritz J. Roethlisberger
    1966   *Counseling in an Organization: A Sequel to the Hawthorne Studies.* Boston: Harvard University.

Evans, Peter
    1981   Recent Research on Multinational Companies. *Annual
                Review of Sociology* 7:199-223.

Evans-Pritchard, Edward E.
    1940   *The Nuer: A Description of the Mode of Livelihood and
                Political Institutions of Nilolithic People.* Oxford:
                Clarendon Press.

    1951   *Social Anthroplogy.* London: Cohen and West.

Feldman, Steven P.
    1989   How Organizational Culture Can Affect Innovation.
                Organizational Dynamics Summer:57-68.

Fitzgerald, Thomas H.
    1988   Can Change in Organizational Culture Really Be
                Managed? *Organizational Dynamics.* Autumn:5-15.

Firth, Raymond
    1951   *Elements of Social Organization.* London: Watts.

    1963   (c1957) *We the Tikopia.* London: Allen and Unwin.

    1966   *Malay Fishermen: The Peasant Economy.* Hamden, Conn:
                Archon Books.

Firth, Raymond
    1975   (c1965) *Primitive Polynesian Economy.* New York:
                Norton.

Form, W.
    1979   Comparative Industrial Sociology and the Convergence
                Hypothesis. *Annual Review of Sociology* 5:1-25.

Frederiksen, N.
    1966   Some Effects of Organizational Climate on
                Administrative Performance. *Research Memorandum* RM
                66-21.

Frost, P. J., L. Moore, M. R. Louis, C. C. Lundberg, and J. Martin, eds.
    1985   *Organizational Culture.* Newbury Park: Sage.

Frost, P. J., L. Moore, M. R. Louis, C. C Lundberg, and J. Martin, eds.
    1991   *Reframing Organizational Culture.* Newbury Park: Sage.

Fukuda, Hohn K.
    1988   *Japanese Style Management Transferred: The Experience of East Asia.* New York: Routledge.

Gagliargi, P ,ed.
    1990   *Symbols and Artifacts: Views of theCorporate Landscape.* Berlin, New York: De Gruyter.

Gamst, Frederick C.
    1977   An Integrating View of the Underlying Premises of an Industrial Ethnology in the United States and Canada. *Anthropological Quarterly* 50:1-8.

    1980   *The Hoghead: An Industrial Ethnology of the Locomotive Engineers.* New York: Holt, Rinehart and Winston.

    1989   The Concept of Organizational and Corporate Culture: An Ethnological View. *Anthropology of Work Review* 10(3):12-19.

    1990   Industrial Ethnological Perspectives on the Development and Characteristics of the Study of Organizational Cultures. *Studies in Third World Societies* 43:13-47. Williamsburg: College of William and Mary.

Gardner, Burleigh B.
    1945   *Human Relations in Industry.* Chicago: Irwin.

Gardner, Burleigh, B.
    1946   Factory as a Social System. **In** W.F. Whyte, ed. *Industry and Society.* Pp.4-20. New York: McGraw-Hill.

    1977   The Anthropologist in Business and Industry. *Anthropological Quarterly* 50:171-73.

Gardner, Burleigh B.
    1978   Doing Business with Management. **In** E.M. Eddy and W.L. Partridge, eds. *Applied Anthropology in America.* New York: Columbia University Press.

Gardner, Burleigh B., and William F. Whyte
    1945   The Man in the Middle: Position and Problems of the Foreman. *Applied Anthropology* 4(2):whole issue.

Garsombke, Diane
    1988   Organizational Culture Dons the Mantle of Militarism. *Organizational Dynamics.* Summer:46-56.

Geertz, Clifford
    1963   *Agricultural Innovation: The Processes of Ecological Change in Indonesia.* Berkeley: University of California Press.

    1973   *The Interpretation of Cultures.* New York: Basic Books.

    1983   *Local Knowledge: Further Essays in Interpretive Anthropology.* New York: Basic Books.

Giovannini, Mareen J., and Lynne M.H. Rosansky
    1990   *Anthropology and Management Consulting: Forging a New Alliance.* National Association for the Practice of Anthropology Bulletin No. 9. Washington D.C.: American Anthropological Association.

Goffman, Ervin
    1959   *The Presentation of Self in Everyday Life.* New York: Doubleday.

    1961   *Encounters.* Indianapolis: Bobbs-Merrill.

    1967   *Interaction Ritual.* Garden City, New York: Anchor Books.

    1983   The International Order. *American Sociological Review* 48:1-18.

Goldschmidt, Walter R.
    1946   Small Business and the Community: A Study in Central Valley of California on Effects of Scale in Farm Operations. Washington, D.C.: U. S. Government Printing Office.

    1947   *As You Sow.* New York: Harcourt.

Goldschmidt, Walter R.
    1955   Social Class and Dynamics of Status in America. *American Anthropologist* 57:1209-17.

    1979   *The Uses of Anthropology.* Washington D.C.: American Anthropological Association.

Goodall Jr., H. L.
    1989   *Casing a Promised Land; The Autobiography of an Organizational Detective as Cultural Ethnographer.* Carbondale and Edwardsville: Southern Illinois University Press.

Goodenough, Ward
    1956   Componential Analysis and the Study of Meaning. *Language* 32:195-216.

    1971   *Culture, Language And Society.* Reading, Mass.: Wesley Modular Publications No. 7.

Gouldner, Alvin W.
    1954   *Patterns of Industrial Bureaucracy.* New York: Free Press.

Greenfield, Sidney M., Arnold Strickon and Robert T. Aubey, eds.
    1979   *Enterpreneurs in Cultural Context.* Albuquerque: Univeristy of New Mexico Press.

Gregory, Kathleen L.
    1983   Native-view Paradigms:Multiple Cultures and Culture Conflicts in Organizations. *Administrative Science Quarterly* 28:359-76.

    1984   Signing-Up: The Culture and Careers of Silicon Valley Computer People. PhD. Dissertation, Anthropology, Northwestern University.

Hamada, Tomoko
    1989   Perspective on Organizational Culture. *Anthropology of Work Review* 10(3):5-7.

    1991   *American Enterprise in Japan.* New York: State University of New York Press.

Hamada, Tomoko and Ann Jordan, eds.
1990   *Cross-cultural Management and Organizational Culture.*
Vol. 42 *Studies in Third World Societies.* Williamsburg:
College of William and Mary.

Hamill, James F
1990   *Ethno-logic: The Anthropology of Human Reasoning.*
Urbana: University of Illinois Press.

Harris, Marvin
1979   *Cultural Materialsim.* New York: Random House.

Hebden, J. E.
1986   Adopting an Organization's Culture: The Socialization
of Graduate Trainees. *Organizational Dynamics.*
Summer:54-72.

Hickson, D. J., Hinnings, C. R., McMillan, C. M. M and J. P.Schwitter.
1974   The Culture-Free Context of Organization Structure: A
Tri-national Comparison. *Sociology* 8:59-80.

Hofstede, G
1980   *Culture's Consequences: International Differences in Work-
Related Values.* Beverly Hills: Sage.

Holzberg, Carol S., and Maureen Giovannini
1981   Anthropology and Industry: Reappraisal and New
Directions. *Annual Review of Anthropology* 10:317-360.

James, L. R., and A. P. Jones
1974   Organizational Structure: A Review of Structural
Dimensions and Their Conceptual Relationships with
Individual Attitudes and Behavior. *Organizational
Behavior and Human Performance* 16:74-113

Jones, Michael O., Michael D. Moore and Richard C. Snyder, eds.
1988   *Inside Organizations: Understanding the Human Dimension.*
Newbury Park: Sage.

Kanter, Rosabeth Moss
1977   *Men and Women of the Corporation.* New York: Basic
Books.

Kanter, Rosabeth Moss
      1983   *The Change Masters: Innovation and Enterpreneurship in the American Corporation.* New York: Simon and Schuster.

Kardiner, Abram
      1981   *The Psychological Frontiers of Society.*   Westport: Greenwood Press.

Kerr, C. J., Dunlop T, Harbison, F., and C. A. Myers
      1952   *Industrialism and Industrial Man.*   Cambridge Mass.: Harvard University Press.

Keys, J. B. and T. R. Miller
      1984   The Japanese Management Theory Jungle. Academy of Management Review 9:342-353.

Kilmann, Ralph H., and Marry Saxton, Roy Serpa and Associates, eds.
      1985   *Gaining Control of the Corporate Culture.* San Francisco: Jossey-Bass.

Kilman, Ralph H., and Teresa Joyce Covin and Associates, eds.
      1988   *Corporate Transformation: Revitalizing Organizations for a Competitive World.* San Francisco: Jossey-Bass Publishers.

Kluckhohn, Clyde
      1943   Covert Culture and Administrative Problems. *American Anthropologist* 43:413-19.

Koprowski, Eugene J.
      1983   Cultural Myths: Clues to Effective Management. *Organizational Dynamics.* Autumn:39-51.

Krader, Lawrence
      1972   *The Ethnological Notebooks of Karl Marx.* Assen: Van Gorcum.

Krader, Lawrence
      1975   *The Asiatic Mode of Production.* Assen: Van Gordum.

Kroeber, A. L. and C. Kluckhohn
      1952   *Culture: A Critical Review of Concepts and Definitions.* New York: Vintage Books.

Kunda, Gideon
    1992   *Engineering Culture: Control and Commitment in a High-Tech Corporation.* Philadelphia: Temple University Press.

Lammers, C. J.
    1976   Towards the Internationalization of the Organization Sciences. **In** G. Hofstede and M. S. Kassem, eds., *European Contributions to Organization Theory.* Amsterdam: Van Gorcum.

Lammers, C. J. and D. J. Hickson
    1979   *Organizations Alike and Unlike.* London: Routledge and Kegan Paul.

Laurent, A
    1983   The Cultural Diversity of Western Management Conceptions. *International Studies of Management and Organization* XIII(1-2):75-6.

Lamphere, L
    1987   *From Working Daughters to Working Mothers: Immigrant Women in a New England Industrial Community.* Ithaca: Cornell University Press.

Levi-Strauss, Claude
    1949   *The Elementary Structures of Kinship.* Translated by J. Bell and J. von Sturmer, R. Neeham. Boston: Beacon Press.

    1961   *Tristes Tropiques.* New York: Criterion.

Levi-Strauss, Claude
    1963   *Structural Anthropology.* C. Jacobson and B.C. Shoepf, trans. New York: Basic Books.

    1966   *The Savage Mind.* Chicago: University of Chicago Press.

    1969   *The Raw and the Cooked.* John Weightman, trans. New York: Harper and Row.

    1978   *Myth and Meaning.* New York: Schocken.

Lewis, Oscar
    1961   *The Children of Sanchez: Autobiography of a Mexican Family.* New York: Random House.

Lincoln, J. R. and A. L. Kalleberg
    1990   *Culture, Control and Commitment.* New York: Cambridge University Press.

Lincoln, J. R., Hanada, M. and K. McBride
    1986   Organizational Structures in Japanese and US Manufacturing. *Administrative Science Quarterly* 31:338-64.

Lincoln, J. R. Hanada, M., and J. Olson
    1981   Cultural Orientations and Individual Reactions to Organizations: A Study of Employees of Japanese-owned Firms. *Administrative Science Quarterly* 26:93-115.

Lincoln, J. R., Olson, J., and M. Hanada
    1978   Cultural Effects on Organizational Structure; The Case of Japanese Firms in the United States. *American Sociological Review* 43:829-47.

Lincoln, Y. S. and E. G. Guba
    1985   *Naturalistic Inquiry.* Beverly Hills: Sage.

Litwin, G. H., and R. A. Stringer
    1968   *Motivation and Organizational Climate.* Boston: Harvard Business School, Division of Research.

Lubeck, P
    1986   *Islam and Urban Labor in Northern Nigeria: The Making of a Muslim Working Class.* Cambridge: Cambridge University Press.

Malinowski, Bronislaw
    1922   *Argonauts of the Western Pacific.* New York: Cutton.

    1931   Culture. Encyclopaedia of the Social Sciences 4:621-46.

    1933   *A Scientific Theory of Culture.* Chapel Hill: North Carolina Press.

Malinowski, Bronislaw
    1935   *Coral Gardens and Their Magic: A Study of the Method of Tilling the Soil and of Agricultural Rites in the Trobriand Islands* (two vols.) London: G. Allen.

    1939   The Group and the Individual in Functional Analysis. *American Jouranl of Sociology* 44:938-64.

Manning, Peter K.
    1977   *Police Work.* Cambridge: MIT Press.

Marsh, R. and M. Mannari
    1971   Lifetime Commitment in Japan: Roles, Norms and Values. *American Journal of Sociology* 76:795-812.

Marsh, R. and M. Mannari
    1972   A New Look at Life-time Commitment in Japanese Industry. *Economic Development and Cultural Change* 20:611-31.

Marsh, R. and M. Mannari
    1976   *Modernization and the Japanese Factory* Princeton: Princeton University Press.

Marcus, G. E. and D. Cushman
    1982   Ethnographies as Texts. *Annual Review of Anthropology* 11:25-69.

Marcus, G. E. and M. J. Fischer
    1986   *Anthropology as Cultural Critique.* Chicago: University of Chicago Press.

Mars, G.
    1982   *Cheats at Work: An Anthropology of Workplace Crime.* London: Allen and Unwin.

Martin, Joanne, and Caren Siehl
    1983   Organizational Culture and Counterculture: An Uneasy Symbiosis. *Organizational Dynamics* 12(2):52-64.

Maruyama, Magoro
    1980   Mindscapes and Social Theories. *Current Anthropology* 21(5):389-600

Maruyama, Magoro
    1982   New Mindscapes for Future Business Policy and
              Management. *Technology, Forecasting and Social Change*
              21:53-76.

    1984   Alternative Concepts of Management: Insights from
              Asia and Africa. *Asia Pacific Journal of Management*
              1(1):100-111.

Maslow, A. H.
    1970   *Motivation and Personality.* end ed. New York: Harper
              & Row.

McGregor, Doublas
    1960   *The Human Side of Enterprise.* New York: McGraw Hill.

McWhinney, Will and Jose Batista
    1988   How Remythologizing Can Revitalize Organizations.
              Organizational Dynamics. Autumn:46-58.

Meyer, J. W. and B. Rowan
    1978   The Structure of Educational Organizations. In Meyer,
              M. ed., *Environments and Organizations.* San Francisco:
              Jossey-Bass.

Mills, Albert J., and Peta Tancred, eds.
    1992   *Gendering Organizational Analysis.* Newbury Park: Sage.

Miller, Lawrence M.
    1989   *Barbarians to Bureaucrats: Corporate Life Cycle Strategies.*
              New York: Clarkson N. Potter.

Moran, Emilio,ed.
    1983   *The Ecosystem Concept in Anthropology.* American
              Association for the Advancement of Science.

Morey, Nancy C. and Fred Luthans
    1987   Anthropology: The Forgotten Behavioral Science in
              Management History. *Best Paper Proceedings*, 47th
              Annual Meeting of the Academy of Management, New
              Orleans Pp. 128-132.

Morgan, Gareth
1986   *Images of Organizations.* Beverly Hills: Sage.

Nadel, S. F.
1951   *The Foundations of Social Anthropology.* Glencoe, Illinois: Free Press.

Nash, June
1981   Ethnographic Aspects of the World Capitalist System *Annual Review of Anthropology* 10:393-423

1985   Segmentation of the Work Process in the International Division of Labor. In S. Sanderson, ed. *The Americas in the New International Division of Labor.* Pp. 253-72. New York: Holmes & Meier.

Nash, J. and M. Fernandez-Kelly (eds)
1983   *Women, Men, and the International Division of Labor.* Albany: State University of New York Press.

Nash, Manning
1966   *Primitive and Peasant Economic Systems.* San Francisco: Chandler.

Negandhi, A. R.
1979   Convergence in Organizational Practices: An Empirical Study of Industrial Enterprise in Developing Countries. In C. J. Lammers and D. J. Hickson eds., *Organizations Alike and Unlike.* Pp. 323-45. London: Routledge & Kegan Paul.

1985   Management in the Third World. In P. Joynt and M. Warner eds. *Managing in Different Cultures.* Pp. 69-97. Oslo Norway: Universitetsforlaget.

Newman, K.
1988   *Falling From Grace: The Experience of Downward Mobility in the American Middle Class.* New York: Free Press.

Nolan, R.
1986   *Bassari Migrations: The Quitest Revolution.* Boulder: Westview.

Ong, A.
    1987   *Spirits of Resistance and Capitalist Discipline: Factory Women in Malaysia.* Albany: State University of New York Press.

Ortner, S.
    1973   On Key Symbols. *American Anthropologist* 75:1338-1346.

    1984   Theory in Anthropology since the Sixties. *Comparative Studies in Society and History.* 26:126-166.

Ott, J. Steven
    1989   *The Organizational Culture Perspective.* Chicago: Dorsey Press.

Ouchi, William G.
    1983   *Theory Z: How American Business Can Meet the Japanese Challenge.* Reading, Mass: Addison-Wesley.

Ouchi, W. G. and A. L. Wilkins
    1985   Organizational Culture. *Annual Review of Sociology* 11:457-83.

Parsons, Talcott
    1951   *The Social System.* Glencoe: The Free Press.

Pascale, R. T. and A. G. Athos
    1981   *The Art of Japanese Management.* New York: Warner Books.

Paules, Greta Foff
    1991   *Power and Resistance Among Waitresses in a New Jersey Restaurant.* Philadelphia: Temple University Press.

Peters, T. J. and R. H. Waterman, Jr.
    1982   *In Search of Excellence: Lessons from America's Best-run Companies.* New York: Harper and Row.

Pettigrew, A. M.
    1979   On Studying Organizational Cultures. *Administrative Science Quarterly* 24:579-81.

Pettigrew, A. M.
1985 The Awakening Giant Oxford: Basil Blackwell.

Plath, David, ed.
1983 *Work and Lifecourse in Japan*. Albany: State University of New York Press.

Polanyi, Karl
1947 Our Obsolete Market Mentality. *Commentary* 3:109-17.

1957 The Economy as Instituted Process. In Polanyi, K, Arensberg C., and H. Pearson, eds. *Trade and Market in the Early Empires*. Glencoe: The Free Press.

1959 Anthropology and Economic Theory. **In** Fried, M. ed., *Readings in Anthropology*, Vol 2. New York: Crowell.

Pondy, L. R., Frost, P. J., Morgan, G., and T. Dandridge
1983 *Organizational Symbolism*. Greenwich, Conn.: JAI Press.

Rabinow, Paul
1977 *Reflections on Fieldwork in Morocco*. Berkeley: University of California Press.

Radcliffe-Brown, A. R.
1935 On the Concept of Function in Social Science. *American Anthropologists* 37:394-402.

1940 On Social Structure. *Journal of the Royal Anthropological Institute* 70:1-12.

Ramaswamy, U
1983 *Work, Union and Community: Industrial Man in South India*. Delhi: Oxford University Press.

Rappaport, Roy A.
1968 *Pigs for the Ancestors: Ritual in the Economy of a New Guinea People*. New Haven: Yale University Press.

Richards, A. I.
1939 *Land, Labour and Diet in Northern Rhodesia: An Economic Study of the Bemba Tribe*. London: Oxford University Press.

Richards, A. I.
    1956   *Chisungu.* London: Faber and Faber.

Richardson, Frederick L. W.
    1955   Anthropology and Human Relations in Business and
              Industry   **In** W. L Thomas, Jr., ed.   *Yearbook of
              Anthropology.* Pp. 397-419. New York: Wenner-Gren
              Foundation for Anthropological Research.

    1961   Talk, Work, and Action: Human Reactions to
              Organizational Change.   Society for Applied
              Anthropology Monograph No. 3.

Richardson, Frederick L. W. and Charles R. Walker
    1948   *Human Relations in an Expanding Company.* New Haven:
              Labor Management Center, Yale University.

    1949   Work Flow and Human Relations. *Harvard Business
              Review* 27:107-22.

Roethlisberger, Fritz J.
    1960   *The Human Problems of an Industrial Civilization.* New
              York: Viking.

    1977   *The Elusive Phenomena.* Cambridge, Mass.: Harvard
              University Press.

Roethlisberger, Fritz J., and William J. Dickson
    1939   *Management of the Worker.* Cambridge Mass.: Harvard
              University Press.

Rosendahl, M.
    1985   *Conflict and Compliance: Class Consciousness among
              Swedish Workers.* Stockholm: Dept. of Anthropology,
              University of Stockholm

Sackmann, Sonja A.
    1991   *Cultural Knowledge in Organizations: Exploring the
              Collective Mind.* Newbury Park: Sage.

Sacks, K.
    1988   *Caring By the Hour: Women, Work, and Organizing at Duke
              Medical Center.* Urbana: University of Illinois Press.

Sacks, K and D. Remy, eds.
1984   *My Troubles Are Going to Have Trouble With Me: Everyday Trials and Triumphs of Women Workers*. New Brunswick: Rutgers University Press.

Sahlins, Marshall
1958   *Social Stratificiation in Polynesia*. Seattle: University of Washington Press.

1961   *Moala*. Ann Arbor: University of Michigan Press.

1972   *Stone Age Economics*. New York: Aldine Publishing.

Sahlins, Marshall
1976   *Culture and Practical Reason*. Chicago: University of Chicago Press.

Sandy, Peggy Reeves
1979   The Ethnographic Paradigm(s). *Administrative Science Quarterly* 24:570-81.

Sathe, V.
1988   *Culture and Related Corporate Realities*. Homewood Illinois: Irwin.

Schein, Edgar H.
1985   *Organizational Culture and Leadership: A Dynamic View*. San Francisco: Jossy-Bass.

1987   *The Clinical Perspective in Field Work*. Beverly Hills: Sage.

1990   Organizational Culture. *American Psychologist* 45(2):109-119.

Schneider, Benjamin, ed.
1990   *Organizational Climate and Culture*. San Francisco: Jossey-Bass.

Sergiovanni, T. J. and J. E. Corbally, eds.
1984   *Leadership and Organizational Culture*. Urbana, Illinois: University of Illinois Press.

Serrie, Hendrick, ed.
   1984   *Anthropology and International Business, Studies in Third World Societies*, Volume 28.   Williamsburg, Virginia: College of William and Mary.

Siehl, Caren and Joanne Martin
   1990   Organizational   Culture: A   Key   to   Financial Performance? In Schneider, B.,ed. *Organizational Climate and Culture*. Pp. 241-81. San Francisco: Jossey-Bass.

Smircich, Linda
   1983   Concepts of Culture and Organizational Analysis. *Administrative Science Quarterly* 28:339-58.

Steward, Julian
   1955   *The Theory of Culture Change*.   Urbana: University of Illinois.

Tagiuri, R, and G. H. Litwin, eds.
   1968   *Organizational Climate*.   Boston: Graduate School of Business Administration, Harvard University.

Turner, Victor
   1969   *The Ritual Process*. Chicago: Aldine.

Turner, Victor
   1974   *Dramas, Fields and Metaphors*. Ithaca, New York: Cornell University Press.

   1982   *From Ritual to Theatre: The Human Seriousness of Play*. New York: PAJ Press.

Van Maanen, John, ed.
   1979   *Qualitative Methodology*. Newbury Park: Sage.

   1988   *Tales of the Field*. Chicago: University of Chicago Press.

Van Maane, John, James M. Dabbs, Jr., and Robert R. Faulkner, eds.
   1982   *Varieties of Qualitative Research*. Newbury Park: Sage.

Van Willigen, John, and R. Stoffle
  1984   The Americanization of *Shoyu*: American Workers and
          a Japanese Employment System. In Hendrick Serrie (Ed.)
          *Anthropology and International Business, Studies in Third
          World Societies*, Volume 28. Pp.125-162. Williamsburg:
          College of William and Mary.

Vesperi, M.
  1985   *City of Green Benches: Growing Old in a New Downtown.*
          Ithaca: Cornell University Press.

Walker, Charles R., and Robert H. Guest
  1952   *The Man on the Assembly Line.*   Cambridge
          Mass.:Harvard University Press.

Warner, W. Lloyd
  1933   Kinship Morphology of Forty One Australian Tribes.
          American Anthropologist 35:63-86.

  1936   American Caste and Class. *American Journal of Sociology*
          42:234-237.

  1945   The Committee on Human Relations in Industry.
          Applied Anthropology 4(2):1.

  1953   *American Life: Dream and Reality.* Chicago: University of
          Chicago Press.

Warner W. Lloyd, and James Abbeglen
  1955a   *Occupational Mobility in American Business and Industry,
          1928-1952.* Minneapolis: Minnesota University Press.

  1955b   *Big Business Leaders in America.* New York: Harper.

Warner, W. Lloyd, and J. O. Low
  1943   *The Strike: A Social Analysis.*   New Haven: Yale
          University Press.

Warner, W. Lloyd, and J. O. Low
  1946   The Factory in the Community. **In** W. F. Whyte, ed.
          Industry and Society, Pp. 21-45. New York: McGraw-Hill.

Warner, W. Lloyd, and J. O. Low
    1947   *The Social System of the Modern Factory*. New Haven: Yale University Press.

Warner, W. Lloyd, and Paul S. Lunt
    1941   *The Social Life of a Modern Community*. New Haven: Yale University Press.

Warner W. Lloyd, and D. B. Unwalla, and J. H. Trimm, eds.
    1967   *The Emergent American Society. Vol. I: Large Scale Organizations*. New Haven: Yale University Press.

Weber, Max
    1947   *The Theory of Social and Economic Organization*. New York: Oxford University Press.

Weick, Karl E.
    1979   *The Social Psychology of Organizing*. 2nd edition. Reading, Mass: Addison-Wesley.

Whyte, William F.
    1943   *Street Corner Society*. New York: McGraw-Hill.

    1948a   *Human Relations in the Restaurant Industry*. New York: McGraw-Hill

    1948b   Incentive for Productivity. The Case of the Bundy Tubing Company. *Applied Anthropology* 7(2):1-16.

    1949   The Social Structure of the Restaurant. *American Jouranl of Sociology* 54:302-310.

Whyte, William F.
    1953   Interviewing for Organizational Research. *Human Organization* 12(2):15-22.

    1961   *Men at Work*. Homewood Illinois: Dorsey Press.

    1969   *Organizational Behavior: Theory and Application*. Homewood Illinois: Richard D. Irwin and Dorsey Press.

Whyte, William F.
    1979   Organizational Behavior Research **In** Elizabeth M.
            Eddy and W. L Patridge, eds. *Applied Anthropology in
            America*. New York: Columbia University Press.

    1982   Social Inventions for Solving Human Problems.
            American Sociological Review 47:1-13.

    1983   Worker Participation. *Journal of Applied Behavioral
            Science* 19:395-407.

Whyte, William F., and B. B. Gardner
    1945   The Man in the Middle: Position and Problems of the
            Foreman. *Applied Anthropology* 4(2).

Wolfe, Alvin W.
    1963   The African Mineral Industry: Evolution of a
            Supranational Level of Integration. *Social Problems*.
            Fall:153-164.

    1977   The Supranational Organization of Production: An
            Evolutionary Perspective. *Current Anthropology*
            18(4):615-35.

    1980   Multinational Enterprise and Urbanism. In Thomas W.
            Collins, ed. *Cities in a Larger Context*. Pp. 76-96. Athens:
            University of Georgia Press.

    1984   The Multinational Corporation as a Form of
            Sociocultural Integration Above the Level of the State.
            Studies in Third World Societies 28:163-90. Williamsburg:
            College of William and Mary.

Wolf, Eric
    1959   *Sons of the Shaking Earth*. Chicago: University of
            Chicago Press.

    1966   *Peasants*. Englewoood Cliffs: Prentice Hall.

Worsley, Peter M.
    1970   *The Third World*. Chicago: University of Chicago Press.

Zavella, P.
    1987   *Women, Work, and Family in the Chicano Community.*
                Ithaca: Cornell University Press.

Zeira, Yoram and Joyce Avedisian
    1989   Organizational Planned Change: Assessing the Chances
                for Success. *Organizational Dynamics.* Spring: 31-45.

PART TWO

ETHNOGRAPHY AND
ORGANIZATIONAL CULTURE

INTRODUCTION

Tomoko Hamada

   Alvesson and Berg noted that organizational culture and symbolism research, after more than ten years of intensive studies, continues to experience "endless fights over definitions and concepts, anecdotes and other forms of narratives" (1992:199), rather than a rapid accumulation of empirical research.   This part is a reply to the call for more ethnographic work on organizational culture by anthropologists.   The seven chapters in this part illustrate anthropological studies on organizational culture conducted in such locations as a federal agency, a local government office, a computer firm, a subsidiary of a Japanese multinational, and an American auto-maker. The authors use participant observation methods, content analyses, critical events analyses , and historical re-construction, in order to decipher the meanings of cultural phenomena under observation.
   One of the traditional tasks of anthropologists was to record previously un-represented, or un-recorded ideas, and consequently to give voices to alternative world views and alternative systems of knowledge and logic.   Thus the first significant task of the anthropologists, on which all the rest of their analytical endeavors depend, is to describe specific organizational phenomena adequately. Our mission in organizational studies is to understand and describe, in all its richness, the work of life in organization, as fully as possible, from the inside. Differences between the vista of an "objective" outside observer, and the view of the "natives" situated within ever-changing organizational phenomena can be best described with the following analogy: Imagine that you are a passenger in an helicopter looking down at the rough sea, where a small sailing boat is attempting to make

its way toward a harbor. You can capture the characteristics of the environment under observation that may include the relative position of the boat, its distance to the harbor entrance, the height of the waves, the speed of the tide, the direction of the wind, the location of other boats nearby, the sites of rocks, buoys, and the lighthouse, and so forth. From this perspective, it is reasonable to describe the scene in terms of broad general characteristics such as environmental structures, categories, variations, and distances. On the other hand, suppose you are a person in this small boat heading towards the harbor, being swept along by the rapid tide. The high walls of waves are rushing toward you, the rocks, the cliffs, and the lighthouse are moving, the harbor entrance appears and disappears, the floating debris blocks your path, and the view of the shoreline twists and turns. You are faced with a series of interpretations, choices, decisions, and consequences, that are specifically defined, limited, and dictated by your perception of the most immediate and ever changing features of the environment. Your comprehension of and reaction to this environment may be quite different if you are a seasoned captain, or a novice crew member. The anthropological lens must be situated inside the boat to capture all these meanings. Schwartzman and Berman believe that the reason why the world is much too clear as seen through the eyes of social scientists is that social scientists have managed to avoid getting inside the everyday activities and events that individuals and groups use to constitute and re-constitute their worlds. The world seems too clear from the "above", because we can then see what we want to see--our structures, values, categories, variables. Schwartzman and Berman guide to us to see the ambiguity, confusion, and contrasting interpretations that make up the real world by moving into the world of the small boat, that is much murkier and more confusing. Through the analysis of everyday meetings as provinces of meaning, the authors explore how the meetings as forms are used to create a sense of imagined order in such a disordered world.

Shirley Fiske argues that organization culture is not a monolithic entity. She believes that organization is composed of multiple layers and loci of shared meanings, that have varying degree of strength and cohesion. Layers of intraorganizational culture can develop among horizontal relationships around functions, positions, job series and staff-management roles of individuals who are inter-connected with other individuals of federal agencies. For example, pan-bureaucratic layers of cultural codes of behavior often dictate the way they handle organizational ambiguity, concurrence system, informal ranking system, and delegation of responsibility. Specific lexicon, vocabulary, symbols and rituals may adhere to certain positions within the bureaucracy, job series, and roles. On the other hand, the locus of culture can be found at the agency level or smaller functional work groups of people who share similar professional values, backgrounds, and frequent interaction. These are agency-specific core values, symbols and ideologies, ceremonial cycles and myths and legends. As a federal employee herself, Fiske observes that participation in these layers and loci of culture invokes a web of identities, languages, and rule systems, that are not static. An individual calls on knowledge of appropriate behavior as his or her cultural competence develops through experiences in the networks of panbureaucratic, occupational, agency-wide, and work-group- specific subcultures.

Gregory-Huddleston moves our analysis to cultural change and individual careers in Silicon Valley computer firms. Although Silicon Valley's fast and rapidly changing career paths together with quick rises and fall of firms do not conform to the traditional model of career and lifecourse, Gregory-Huddleston nevertheless finds that individual perceptions of career options, individual ideas of work, and incentives, and the consequences of their decisions are directly interacting with a shift from one phase of organizational development to another, namely from a start-up, fluid, and risk-taking operation, to a more established and stable organization. According to Gregory-Huddleston, almost all currently successful companies experience cultural conflicts between the "pioneers" who have taken a risk to found the firm, and the "settlers" who have joined the firm at the latter phase. Her analysis of cultural conflict between the two groups links her theory of "native perspectives" directly with her analysis of rapid organizational change. In addition, she asserts that the cultural conflict between the two groups within one firm actually helps maintain the vitality and diversity of Silicon Valley industry at large, where size and growth dimensions of firms often dictate natives' choices of employment. She presents the anthropological perspective that organizational culture must be analyzed as an entity embedded within its larger socio-cultural environment.

The linkage between organizational culture, regional sub-culture, and national culture is explored by White and Rackerby in their investigation on the transferability of Japanese management practices to the United States. The authors see a number of parallels, rather than differences, between Japanese culture and that of the agrarian South, including the concepts of honor, family and work ethic. By focusing on value similarities among peoples, they set forth a hypothesis that particular management practices born out of a particular culture can be transferred if preconditions in the recipient culture also possess similar values and norms. Substantial regional sub-cultures exist in the United States and the linkage between organizational culture and regional community culture must be explored further.

The interface between these levels of culture are explored in the next two case studies. First, Kleinburg's ethnographic research applies a cultural domain analysis to a Japanese-American, bi-national firm. Organizational identities within a Japanese subsidiary firm in the United States presents a natural setting for Kleinburg to illustrate how cultural domains and themes are constructed, and how people in organizations utilize various "cognitive sketch maps" in their attempt to make sense of the organizational contingencies and critical issues. She indicates that the process of organization-wide integration, subcultural differentiation, and organizational fragmentation are not three separate processes, but rather three manifestations and interpretations of one organizational process, and that the interpretations of the integration-differentiation-fragmentation process are themselves deeply embedded in social and national cultures, such as those of Japanese and Americans. In addition, while working in such multi-cultural settings increases the level of organizational ambiguity, ambiguity exists not only because of the divergent cognitive sketch maps, but also because of the uneven power distribution, structural constraints and politics, changing environments, unpredictable strategic decision making and reorganization. She observes markedly different interpretations of, and strong concern or lack of concern with, ambiguity expressed by Americans and Japanese. She concludes that the definition of organizational ambiguity itself is culturally constructed. Her research exemplifies a growing field of inquiry in which organizational studies, international and cross-cultural management research, and cognitive anthropology together can bring forth a deeper understanding of organizational phenomena.

Hamada and Yaguchi also examine a Japanese firm in the United States, where their attention is given to the disintegration process of a particular corporate ideology. They call it the "Yin" side of the cultural process. According to the "Yin" perspective, culture is not only a process of developing, generating, and perpetuating consensus, but also something that is being mutilated, shrunk, deformed and hollowed. Applying "critical events" analyses to this setting, they chronologically record how the most overt and dominant organizational ideology is being "displaced", contradicted, and hollowed out. The management's cultural concept of "the company as one big family" comes from the paternalistic principles of the traditional Japanese household. Once having transplanted into America, however, this principle begins to show cracks as a schism grows between its manifested symbols and the management's perceptions of local conditions. In the process, the ideology becomes fragmented in its application, while management in its efforts to reconcile symbol-logic dissonance shifts its taxonomy boundary. Their multi-vocal culture perspective allows us to become sensitive to the fact that the dominant corporate ideology of managers develops in relationship to the managed, and that there are always more possibilities than those that are overtly enacted in organization. They caution that an apparently dominant corporate ideology may turn out to be an amalgam of incomplete value pieces patched together under a surface label of a mission statement presented by top management.

Organization is also embedded in history. Briody and Baba's analysis of the overseas assignment in General Motors traces the causes of two different types of repatriation experiences of GM employees to two different cultural patterns developed within General Motors--one pro-international and the other anti-international. Their work suggests that cultural contact often stimulates and brings to surface latent differences within organization, and that management actions often create an unexpected new set of organizational problems. Once organizational structures, philosophies, and behaviors are established within an organization, they tend to persist over very long periods of time, long after their initial utility seems to have ended and modern substitutes have evolved to replace them. The following chapters provide ethnographic examples, a framework in which ethnographic research is conducted, and an agenda for future research in organizational settings.

MEETINGS:
THE NEGLECTED ROUTINE

Helen B. Schwartzman and Rebecca Hanson Berman

> Imagine that you enter a parlor. You come late. When you arrive, others have long preceded you, and they are engaged in a heated discussion, a discussion too heated for them to pause and tell you exactly what it is about. In fact, the discussion had already begun long before any of them got there, so that no one person is qualified to retrace for you all the steps that had gone before. You listen for a while, until you decide that you have caught the tenor of the argument; then you put in your oar. Someone answers; you answer him, another comes to your defense; another aligns himself against you, to either the embarrassment or gratification of your opponent, depending upon the quality of your ally's assistance. However, the discussion is interminable. The hour grows late, you must depart. And you do depart, with the discussion still vigorously in progress (Kenneth Burke, *The Philosophy of Literary Form*, 1973:110-111).

The world is much too clear as seen through the eyes of social scientists. One reason that it looks so clear is that we have managed to avoid the everyday activities and commonplace events that individuals and groups use to constitute and re-constitute their worlds.[1] In this session we suggest that the world looks much murkier when seen through a meeting---we hear individuals making ambiguous statements (and we wonder if this is deliberate), we follow actors wandering in and out of discussions and listen as they contest each other's interpretations of what "really" was said, we formulate our own tentative interpretations of what happened on a particular occasion and find that our informants are no longer concerned with the issue. It is easy to see why meetings have been ignored, but if we wish to understand and critically examine relationships between agency, action, structure and culture it is to events like meetings (with all their ambiguities, uncertainties and frustrations) that we must begin to turn. Of course, as Mark Hobart (1990) suggests, we do not have a discourse for analyzing these issues and when we do discuss them we are inevitably trapped by cultural premises and assumptions that push us to see some things and neglect others. In fact the treatment of meetings in the social science literature is an excellent example of how our research knowledge is culturally mediated.

MEETINGS AND CULTURAL ASSUMPTIONS: A CAMEL IS A HORSE ASSEMBLED BY A COMMITTEE

In the West we believe that meetings should exemplify our basic values of pragmatism, task orientation, efficiency and rationality. We are frustrated when we find that meetings do not seem to accomplish or display these values. The classic joke about the functioning of committees as meeting groups: "A camel is a horse assembled by a committee," reflects this folk wisdom about meetings but the research literature makes use of it as well.[2] In general three orientations have been taken toward meetings (see Schwartzman 1989 for a more detailed discussion of these orientations): 1) meetings are viewed as *tools* for tasks and researchers have used them to study other things (e.g., leadership in groups, the effect of group size on group performance, testing decision models); 2) meetings are evaluated as ineffective tools and treated as either the symptoms of or cure for a host of organizational problems (e.g., Drucker 1974); and 3) researchers and managers (frequently working together) attempt to "fix" meetings (e.g., "How to" books).[3]

One important assumption that ties these orientations together is the view that there is (or should be) a tight connection between individual (or group) intentions and action (March and Olsen 1976).[4] If something happens that interferes with this relationship---meetings would be a good example according to many people---then it is the event or the form that must be fixed. Clarity and connection between action and intention is an important value and one that has made it very difficult to see meetings as anything other than a nuisance, a bore or a very bad joke (remember "a camel is a horse assembled by a committee").

RE-IMAGINING MEETINGS

In order to make meetings a topic as opposed to a tool of research Schwartzman has suggested elsewhere (1989) that we need to re-imagine meetings and that we can use anthropology (especially research on political language) to do this. An anthropology of meetings conceptualizes meetings as speech events which must be examined as they are embedded within a sociocultural setting (an organization, a community, a society) as a constitutive social form. An appreciation of the idea that the world does not appear as formalized concepts (such as structure or culture, or hierarchy and value), but only in particular routines and gatherings composed of specific actors (or agents) attempting to press their claims on one another and trying to make sense of what is happening to them motivates the approach/orientation described here. In this way it is possible to see how the process of meeting contributes to the production and reproduction of the structures of everyday life. However, while meetings are accomplished these structures are often interpreted and experienced as objective entities which are external and unrelated to these actions and occasions. In this way meetings have been pushed out of the picture although they are in fact partly responsible for creating such structures.

It is necessary to recognize that situations, routines and gatherings are themselves "practical accomplishments" as the ethnomethodologists have demonstrated repeatedly. These events are constructed by actors and researchers out of what is frequently "a blooming, buzzing confusion" and whatever order is achieved is always precarious and tentative. Meetings, as Myers (1986) reminds us for the Pintupi, are "delicate achievements" but they are "achievements" in every society. Meetings are involved in the construction and imposition of order in individuals' lives. We suggest that meetings are responsible for both the construction of order and disorder in social systems, and so they must be conceptualized as occasions with both conservative (as sense-makers and social and cultural validators) and transformative capacities.

When participants engage in the construction of speech events like meetings, they are also involved simultaneously in their interpretation and evaluation as cultural texts. This is how meetings may be seen to generate "provinces of meaning," "rubrics of understanding," "interpretive schemes" (Schutz 1972) or cultural patterns which come to serve as models of and models for (Geertz 1973) activities and beliefs. As texts, meetings are like Geertz's Balinese cockfights where actors act as both the subjects and objects of their jointly created event. In the process (or practice) of producing and reading meetings as texts, before, during and after their occurrence, participants generate, affirm and transform cultural values and beliefs. Successive interpretations of meetings may serve to legitimate or de-legitimate meeting content, social relations or cultural systems. In this paper we discuss the "ordering" and "disordering" features of meetings as we observed and experienced them in an American mental health center and in task force work in a city government.

SEEING WITH MEETINGS

Organizational or environmental constraints are problematic features of agencies and structures: Individuals do not and cannot act outside of forms such as speech events like meetings. They use meetings to generate interaction as well as to interpret what it means (*we are greeting each other, we are bargaining, we are playing, we are meeting*). It is in these forms, and only in these forms, that individuals are able to transact, negotiate, strategize and attempt to realize their specific aims. But cultural systems and social structures are "bred into" these forms as Ranson, Hinings, and Greenwood (1980) suggest. It was my (Schwartzman's) gradual understanding of this point which helped me realize that I could only portray the experience of working, as well as conducting research, at Midwest Mental Health Center **through** the meetings (I called them key meetings) which informants used to make sense of or "see" the organization and their actions in it. In this particular context staff and board members saw their world as a battleground and they became caught up in a battle for control while at the same time viewing each other's activities, as "out of control". Staff and board members saw the organization and their actions quite differently because they were seeing events, and trying to understand

and interpret them, through different meetings (staff meetings vs. board meetings). To explain these differences in terms of the different roles which individuals occupied in the organization does not help us understand how these differences were experienced and generated in the daily actions of individuals.

Individuals also use meetings to read and/or see their place in particular social systems. We say that an individual is or is not a powerful person, but often we only "know" this based on how we read and interpret events in a meeting. This was certainly the case for participants at Midwest where there were very few ways outside of meetings for individuals to negotiate and/or determine their status and social ranking, and where their status was frequently in flux. In some cases it was only be astutely reading meetings (e.g., who knows about, was/was not attending, calling/canceling, arriving or leaving, etc., a meeting) that an individual might learn about his/her place in the status system of the Center.

The linkage of intention with constraint brings out the difficult issue of intended and unintended consequences, that has been discussed by many social scientists (e.g., Giddens 1979). Ortner (1984) comments on the ironic consequence of an intention as follows:

> Major social change does not for the most part come about as an **intended** consequence of action. Change is largely a by-product, an **un**intended consequence of action, however rational action may have been....To say that society and history are products of human action is true, but only in a certain ironic sense. They are rarely the products the actors themselves set out to make (p. 157).

The work of James March and Johan Olsen (1976) on choice-making examines the "loose" connection between action and intention in organizational systems such as organized anarchies (i.e., organizations characterized by: ambiguous or inconsistent goals; unclear or "fuzzy" technologies; fluid participation of members; unpredictable environ-ments; and confusing histories). In this model an organization is construed as "a set of procedures for argumentation and interpretation as well as for solving problems and making decisions" (1976:25). Decision situations in such a context become a "meeting place for issues and feelings looking for decision situations in which they may be aired, solutions looking for issues to which they may be an answer, and participants looking for problems or pleasure" (**ibid.**). Problems, issues, feelings, solutions, participants, and goals are not tightly connected in this model, although after the fact, participants often describe them **as if** they were. It is these descriptions and interpretations which provide some stability in such systems as "consensual anticipations, retrospectations, and understandings" develop as "interpretive schemes" (Weick in Ranson, Hinings and Greenwood 1980:5). But do forms, such as meetings in these contexts, provide individuals with opportunities for making sense of what is happening? (the assumption is that what is happening is not entirely clear to any of the actors involved in the setting, **including the researcher**). Do meetings on forms control our sense-making while we produce, reproduce and sometimes transform the social and cultural system?[5] In the following example I use a series of decisions (related to the hiring/firing of the executive director and assistant director and the selection of a replacement) made at Midwest to examine how the need to make decisions in meetings became the means by which participants constituted the sense of "an organization" for themselves, activated new relationships as well as old hostilities and divisions, solidified groups and provided everyone with a reading of their current status in the frequently shifting and confusing social system of Midwest (summarized from Schwartzman 1989).[6] In this way I try to illustrate how contested and ambiguous social relations and cultural values may emerge out of formal and informal meetings processes and how meeting may serve as a sense-making form for individuals and groups in specific contexts.

DECISIONS MAKE MEETINGS:
TALKING WORK IN AN ORGANIZED ANARCHY[7]

The decision which initiated the series of committee and board meetings which will be examined in this section was a decision that no one at Midwest knew they had to make.[8] However, once the **need** for decision was generated, these meetings became crucial contexts for Center staff and board to use to interpret their relationships and conflicts to each other and, in the process, to transform these relationships and the Center's leadership. Mary Kassen remembers how she discovered, on reading the Center's by-laws, that it was necessary to initiate a contract review not later than six months prior to the termination of the contracts of all administrators earning $15,000 or more per year. She brought this to the Board's attention in the following way:

> As sort of the guardian of the by-laws what I did was a thing I'd often done in the past, I would get excerpts from the by-laws pertaining to the point, print them up for everybody, distribute them at the meeting so that one person can't hold the by-laws and say this is what they say, everybody had an equal chance to look at them. I summarized the by-laws because they were a little bit confusing as regards to the whole procedure. I gave them a step by step summary of exactly how the by-laws said you were supposed to handle the renewal of the Executive Director's contract starting with the first question you had to ask, "Does Freed [Fred Hart, the current Executive Director or ED] want to renew?" This is where you start and then I went from there and mimeographed the thing and give it to everybody at the meeting as part of the Personnel Committee Report. The reason for that was that I went to the PC and said "Hey, this is coming up, do you want to do anything about it?" and they said well no, it's the Executive Committee's job to do the hiring of the ED. They're the ones that have to make the move. So I said, "Okay, as a part of the PC report at the next meeting, can I include some information about this?" and they said "fine" so I handed them [the Executive Committee] this and they were a little startled at first. "Okay, we will have to do it obviously because this is what they by-laws say." So that's how the whole thing got going....So, of course, chaos kind of broke loose at that point. Fred, I think, was completely nonplused when he realized that the Board was actually going to evaluate his performance.

At the May meeting of the board, Mary Kassen distributed the procedures, which she refers to above, to the board members and moved that the Board begin renegotiating the contract of Fred Hart as Executive Director. A five member Contract Negotiating Committee was immediately established and charged with the task of initiating this process and reviewing Fred's performance and reporting back to the Board. This action precipitated a process which brought staff and board together in a series of committee and sub-committee meetings which became key meetings for the Center. The need to make a decision about the contract of the Director reactivated long-standing controversies about the Center's Associate Director (Paula Gray), ambiguity and conflict about the nature of the Center's goals and training philosophy, and confusion about the relation of the Center to the community. After one month of deliberations by this committee (four meetings), confusion and chaos (as Mary Kassen suggested) did indeed seem to have been produced. As reflected in the minutes and memos of the Board and Council, this process produced: 1) a recommendation by the Contract Negotiating Committee not to renew the contract of the Director; 2) the resignation of the Director because of his feelings about the way the Committee was doing its job; 3) a demand and petition by staff that Fred reconsider his "impetuous" resignation; 4) an apology by Fred written in the form of a memo to staff and the Board for his resignation and his agreement to remain for one-year as a "consolidation year"; and 5) the creation of a joint staff and board "Evaluation Committee" to develop "clear, objective and comprehensive criteria for evaluating the performance of executive staff." This committee was expected to implement an evaluation of the five senior administrative staff which included at this time, Fred Hart and Paula Grey, Paul Chase as Education Director, Rodger Barnes as Clinical Director, and John Dante as Business Office Director.

These actions initiated a four month meeting process which lasted from June to November as the Evaluation Committee composed of 15 staff and 15 board members began the arduous process of establishing "objective evaluation criteria" for administrative staff. The need to decide on these criteria provided individuals with an important topic to use to discover as well as assert differences between the groups (staff accused board of being incompetent and not objective, while the board accused staff of being biased and crazy). This process led to an exacerbation of the differences in perspective and orientation which already existed between board and staff, but by having a common topic to discuss, and by engaging each other in a meeting, these occasions also provided individuals with an important opportunity to assert the existence of the organization. This occurred publicly and continually in the meeting process which began to consume everyone's time.

After four months of meetings a series of criteria were established which were sent out in questionnaire form to affiliated organizations (most of these organizations refused to fill out the form saying that it was up to the Center to evaluate their own staff), to community individuals and organizations (minimal response), and to board and staff (most responses here). The results of the evaluation produced no surprises, Paul Chase, Rodger Barnes and John Dante were given good to adequate evaluations and Fred Hart and Paula Gray were given more negative evaluations. Finally, in a special board meeting held in November the decision was made to renew the contracts of Paul, Rodger and John and to extend the contracts of Fred and Paula only until the end of December. A motion was also made at this time to allow them the option to resign.

This decision immediately created the need for another decision---a temporary replacement for the Director. Once again a committee was established of board and staff and this group was charged with the task of deciding on procedures for selecting an Acting Director, and with evaluating the three "in-house" candidates who applied for this position. The result of the final meeting of this committee was the elimination of all but one candidate (Paul Chase) as viable applicants. In this way a decision by default was made which resulted in the selection of one individual whom a number of staff did not want. One staff member (who was a member of this committee) explained the decision to himself and others as follows:

> There's the dynamics of the meeting that leads you to a certain decision and people on the outside wonder, "How in hell did you decide that," and if you weren't at the meeting you really can't appreciate how it was done.

Participants interpreted the process and significance of this meeting to each other by telling stories about "the 4:00 in the morning meeting" which emphasized that this was one of the few committees "ever" to make a decision and take responsibility for it. In the process of making this decision staff and board found it necessary to re-constitute their alignments as these discussions created an uneasy agreement between groups which were frequently in conflict with each other. But this was an agreement, in my view, which could only be supported by continued and continual meetings and the need to select a permanent Executive Director created this opportunity. A "Selection Committee" was established, once again composed of members of staff and board. This committee met over the course of a year, first establishing procedures, then soliciting applications for candidates and, during the late summer and early fall, inviting three candidates to interview for the position, along with Paul Chase. The Selection Committee met during as well as at the end of this process and the final meeting of the Board which selected Paul Chase as permanent Executive Director is described in detail here. When the decision was announced, everyone spoke of it as if the decision had already been made before the meeting began. As a participant in this meeting I initially accepted this interpretation, but as I examine what happened in this event now, it is no longer clear to me that a decision to select Paul Chase had been made before this meeting began. Instead, this meeting now illustrates to me how the need to make a decision created a context for individuals to talk themselves into the organization as they talked themselves into a decision. It turns out that at this moment in time Paul Chase was the best vehicle for this talk.

THE MEETING

The final meeting to decide on the permanent Executive Director was held in the home of Greg Stone, the Board President. I arrived at 9:00 a.m. and was greeted by Greg's wife. She was obviously used to meetings, and had prepared coffee-cake, donuts and coffee which were arranged in the center of a large dining room table which became the meeting table for the day. Individuals began to filter in between 9:00 and 10:00 a.m. as the meeting began approximately at 9:30 a.m. with the announcement that Sheila Jones, a member of the Selection Committee, wanted to personally address the Board. The report of this committee eliminated two candidates immediately and presented only Paul Chase and Walter Ellis as viable candidates. It was reported that two votes had been taken regarding these candidates and in each case a draw had been produced. it was also reported that two staff members had resigned from the committee which confused the results.

Discussion then centered on the two candidates and a summary of their pros and cons was offered. Walter Ellis was said to have organized a community advisory board even though he was not mandated to do this, it was also said that he had good administrative skills. Paul Chase's ability to "deal well" with external administrative agencies was evaluated positively, and he was also said to have skills and good relations with the community, but not with the staff.

Shiela Jones was allowed to speak to the committee at this point as a staff representative of the Selection Committee. She reported that if Paul Chase was hired she felt that several of the staff would leave. She felt that the problem with the Center was not the staff but the administration, especially Paul Chase and his "style", which in her terms meant that input was not used or wanted and it was the case that "whoever gets there latest with the mostest gets what they want." The theme of accountability recurred throughout this meeting, as Sheila Jones stated it, the cabinet did not hold each other accountable, Paul Chase did not hold the cabinet accountable and the Board did not hold the Director accountable. In keeping with this theme, Sheila Jones raised the issue of who was in charge of the Center, and she criticized Paul Chase for "cowtowing" to funding sources, but she also suggested that the current saying at the Center was that Paul "had the Board in his back pocket." She also criticized the fact that there was no staff input directly into the Board. Mildred Rose and James Ratner responded by saying that it was impossible to know what was happening at the Center. And Greg Stone told a story which illustrated how difficult it was for members of the Board to know what was going on on a daily basis at the Center.[9]

Shiela left the meeting shortly after this discussion, and a shift in focus occurred as the question was asked "what's our next move?" Blanche Wright asked if we should get more information on Walter Ellis because there was only one reference report. At this point Charles Parsons suggested that "The strengths of Paul Chase are his people relations which seem to be Walter Ellis' strengths, but are these necessarily strengths?" He pointed out that "a good person always steps on people's toes." (This became a recurring transition theme introduced by Charles Parsons throughout the meeting. "Is Walter Ellis good enough to replace the known quality of Paul Chase?" It was this argument, which was introduced repeatedly by Charles Parsons, that more than any thing else seemed to direct discussion and became the "rhetoric" which individuals used to convince themselves of the appropriateness of selecting Paul Chase in this meeting.)

At this point eleven people were participating in the meeting and it was 11:30 a.m. Sandwiches and more coffee replaced the donuts and coffee-cake. Individuals periodically stood up, walked into the living room, stretched, and engaged in private conversations, while the meeting continued in the dining room. When I returned from such a break, three types of skills had been written on the flip chart.

Administrative Skills
Community Skills
Clinical Skills

The group was now discussing ground-rules for making a choice and rating candidates according to the above three skills. Once again Charles Parsons introduced a series of questions, "Is Paul Chase functioning effectively?; Do we want to replace him, do we want to fire him?" Is Walter Ellis good enough to replace Paul Chase?; Do we want to change from something good to something unknown?" Mildred Rose suggested a variant of this point by saying "We may not like what we have, but is it worth it to replace him?" Ellis Marsh asked what structural changes could be made to improve the ability of the Executive Committee to control and run the Center. She said that she thought that the Board had lost contact with the Center: "we gave up, we threw our hands up in horror and gave up." At this point the idea of selecting Paul Chase "with riders" was suggested by Mary Kassen and this appeared to be seen as a possibility.

Individuals now turned to the "three skills chart" and began to define the various criteria. Administration was defined and divided into: budgeting, relations with funding agencies, affiliate relations and staff management and delegation. (Training was later added to this category.) Discussion proceeded around the table with each participant suggesting a percentage figure for how weight should be attached to each sub-skill in evaluating the candidates. For example, in regards to administrative abilities, Sue Holland said "I don't know, maybe 40%." Charles Parsons said "50%." Ellis Marsh thought "40%," James Ratner said "60%" and so on. This occurred for each skill category.

After enumerating and ordering these criteria, discussion then shifted to consideration of each category and comparison of the two candidates, Walter Ellis and Paul Chase. Budgeting was the first issue to be discussed, and James Ratner spoke about Walter Ellis, "His experience is light here, he does have experience with a department but not a large budget." Greg Stone spoke about Paul Chase, "He is heavy in experience here, he took an impossible situation with the Center and turned it around, although we do still have the problem of salary inequities." By the time discussion reached staff management and delegation the entire discussion focused on Paul Chase, as everyone said, "We have no information on JW here, his personal style seems good but we don't know what he does with authority. We have been told he delegates well but we really don't know." Charles Parsons suggested once again that Paul Chase was "a known quality" and the discussion of his abilities at staff management and delegation led to a lengthy discussion of administrative and decision processes at the Center, personal evaluations of a range of staff, the relation of the Board of Staff and current and past history in all these areas.

At one point, following the discussion, the idea that the board should delay its decision and acquire more information about Walter Ellis as well as staff input was mentioned. In conjunction with this idea of waiting to make a decision until after the union election was held was also discussed (but this is the last time that Walter Ellis' name appears in my notes). In the end, however, everyone felt that they **had** to make a decision today "or we will be thrown out and rightly so" (in Ellis Marsh's terms). And so turning attention to how to present their decision to staff, a motion was passed, "That Paul Chase be appointed as Executive Director with certain conditions to be worked out subject to conditions to be defined." The vote was unanimous. It was also decided to present the decision and the process of rating candidates in writing to staff and that Greg Stone should attend the first staff meeting.

Participants divided themselves into two groups to prepare the wording of their statement. It was now 3:30 p.m. and when everyone reassembled in the dining room it was 4:00 p.m. and individuals began to review and critique statements of the process and the statement of "riders and conditions" which had also been prepared. Side comments at this time were made like "I can't believe it, we really made a decision" but when the list of riders and conditions was presented Blanche Wright said "It sounds like we are saying that we don't have any trust in the man we are selecting."

A phone call was made to Paul Chase at 4:30 p.m. and he came to Greg Stone's house at 5:30 p.m. while everyone was "polishing" the wording of the statement. He was informed, very solemnly, of the decision along with the issues and problems which had been raised in the discussion, and the riders and conditions which were presented. The statement which had been written was read to him. He then made his own statement about how he looked forward to working at the Center as the permanent Director and to resolving the problems and working toward "goals in the future."

At 6:30 p.m. when Paul Chase left, participants also began to leave, although several individuals (including the researcher) went on to a restaurant to continue discussion and to congratulate themselves on "the process." There was, in these post-meeting discussions, a sense of both exhaustion and accomplishment. The "fact" of the decision, more than anything else, was the major focus of comments and it seemed a confirmation of the authority and leadership and the continues existence of the organization.

TALKING ACTION: RESULTS AND ALTERNATIVE RESULTS

Once the decision was announced everyone assumed that it was the **only** decision that could have been made, and, in fact, that it had already been made before the final meeting of the Board. The idea that the Selection Committee had been "set-up" to consider only "weak" candidates, that individuals had intentionally neglected to follow-up thoroughly on candidates, and that everyone had already made up their mind, dominated staff's interpretation of this decision.

In my view this decision was not pre-determined or set-up, not because there was no one who wished and tried to do so, but because, this was not a context which any individual controlled in any clear-cut fashion. This was a context which was produced by and controlled, to the extent that it was, by meetings. If one took an individual perspective it would be possible to interpret all of the events, beginning with the establishment of the first contract negotiating committee, as an inevitable and predictable plan and process designed by those individuals who wished to oust Fred Hart and Paula Gray and install their own replacement. From the meeting centered perspective presented here, however, this does not reflect the course of events at Midwest. Adopting the approach of March and Olsen (1976) which suggests a loose connection between individual or group intention and organizational events, and suggests that different circumstances could have produced different results (see especially, pp. 10-23) it is possible to see how the manufacture of the first decision (the contract negotiation decision) created a process which could have produced various results and multiple scenarios. After the fact, each of these decisions would have been interpreted as predictable and inevitable. For example, Fred could have chosen to stay and Paula could have left (this was, in fact, what many people stated that they wanted to happen). Alternately, another staff member (Rodger Barnes) could have been chosen as Acting Director during "the 4:00 in the morning meeting" and finally, Walter Ellis could have been chosen as permanent Executive Director. Any or all of these alternative results would certainly have changed the ongoing story (and drama) of Midwest but the leadership decisions may not have been to the most important accomplishment of these meetings. As a constitutive form for the organization a major accomplishment of the meetings (and the decisions) was to assemble staff and board together during a difficult, conflictual and transitional time period and to label these assemblies as organizational work or business. In this way while attempting to talk about a particular decision, individuals were able to talk about their relationship with each other and also to talk themselves into, and sometimes out of, the organization. In this case the decision gave participants something to do, while the meeting gave them a place to do this as well as range of other things as well.

The final meeting of the Board was particularly important as this process certified this group as the major decision-making body of the Center, and Board members legitimated this status to themselves by making a decision about the executive director. Participants also legitimated this process to themselves by developing what they believed to be an objective and rational series of evaluation criteria and then proceeding to evaluate candidates on this basis. This was an important legitimating process for the executive committee as they were frequently accused of behaving irrationally, incompetently and subjectively. This was an important process because it allowed board Members to demonstrate to themselves and to others that discussion proceeded in a rational and objective manner.

Dialogue and discussion in the final meeting frequently focused on issues of leadership, accountability and responsibility, as executive committee members used this meeting opportunity as a way to re-assert their position at the Center (which had been considerably challenged by Fred Hart and Paula Gray). This meeting was also an occasion for evaluating other administration and leadership skills of staff and it also provided participants with an opportunity to instruct new, or relatively new, members in the history and on-going construction and re-construction of history at the Center. Along with this individuals were also able to learn current information about what was happening at the Center (always confusing given the nature of the setting).

This meeting also provided individual Board members with an opportunity to assert themselves as they attempted to direct or control discussion. In the case of the final board meeting, Charles Parsons, who had played a relatively insignificant role in discussions and meetings up to this point, was extremely effective in asserting himself with the theme already identified "we know Paul Chase, why do we want to try something new." This idea, more than any other point, seemed to allow individuals to convince themselves to the appropriateness of choosing Paul Chase. This illustrates, again, the importance of meetings and speech for influencing specific decisions/events. Charles Parsons was not a "powerful" person, by anyone's judgment, and yet in this meeting, on this day, his statements significantly influenced the course of the discussion and the leadership decision.

In one sense, Charles Parsons' comments were most significant because they always shifted the focus of the discussion back to Paul Chase, and the discussion of Paul Chase was the perfect vehicle for generating, learning about and "seeing" the organization. There was so much to say about Paul (it really did not seem to matter whether it was good or bad), he had a history at the Center and everyone had experience with him.   When Paul Chase was the topic of discussion, discussion of a range of issues about the Center flowed naturally in the meeting. In talking with Walter Ellis, there was really very little to say, except that he "seemed good" but there was "no personal experience," and so there was no way for Walter Ellis to lead to a discussion of specific issues at the Center, there was no way that Walter Ellis as a topic could allow individuals to create and see the organization in action. Talking about Paul Chase and talking about the organization began to merge in the "evaluation discussions" in the final Board meeting and one-third of their way into the list of evaluation criteria, everyone stopped talking about Walter Ellis and also about the criteria. Talking about Paul Chase invoked the organization for meeting participants, talking about Walter Ellis invoked abstract concepts (leadership skills, ideals about staff delegation of authority), but while these might produce a discussion about an ideal person or and ideal organization they could never produce "the organization" (i.e., Midwest).

From this perspective, Paul Chase was selected in this long, wandering, sometimes exciting and very exhausting discussion because his candidacy gave participants the organization, "their" organization, to talk about. In talking themselves into the organization, participants talked themselves into (or, in this case, back into) Paul Chase. However, I'm told that Paul Chase did not stay too long as other "leaders," other issues, other crises and other solutions wandered onto the "stage" and into the meetings at Midwest (March and Olsen 1976).

And so long after the struggle over Paul Chase has been forgotten it is "the unending meetings"[10] (long discussion, uncertain actions, heated debates and contested interpretations), and the individuals working with and within them, who continue to make, re-make and sometime un-make the organization I call Midwest.

The above case shows that meetings serve as sense-making forms of organization. Meetings can also serve as both sense-making and sometimes nonsense-making forms in organizations. In order to illustrate such a process we now turn to research conducted by Berman on task force meetings in a large metropolitan government, referred to here as Union City.

Union City government task forces were studied by Berman from June of 1984 through October of 1985 (see Berman 1988). The research focused on four of task forces within this government setting. These four meeting groups had fluctuating memberships encompassing a wide variety of meeting participants from city departments and offices, from aldermen's offices, from other municipal agencies, from federal and state agencies, from private sector for-profit and not-for-profit organizations, and from coalitions and other task forces. Representatives were often department heads and executive directors, but actual attendees usually also included middle and lower level managers, technical staff and "support staff" from the department in chairing the task force. Research on these groups was conducted using observations of meetings as well as interviews with participants.

SENSE AND NONSENSE IN
UNION CITY GOVERNMENT TASK FORCES

Complex organizations in Western societies often turn to interagency, interdepartmental or temporary committee meeting mechanisms to deal with broad issues, transitory problems or change. These interdepartmental groups parade under a variety of titles---commissions, targeted action groups, ad hoc committees, project teams, coordinating committees and focus groups. One such meeting group is the "task force," a term originally coined by the United States Navy (*Encyclopedia Americana*, 1983) and adopted in American government to refer to interagency or public/private sector groups operating as a part of presidential advisory systems. The label now enjoys widespread popularity as it is used to describe groups that are mandated the tasks of developing policy, implementing recommendations, or coordinating processes. In such groups it is expected that specific **tasks** will be identified and group effort will **force** solutions and solve problems.[11] The idea that policy making and implementation tasks proceed in an unproblematic and fairly straight-forward fashion underlines the literature that examines the "work" of task forces in organizations.

> A task force is by definition a temporary group that is given a specific problem to solve or project to handle. The expectation is that the group will be dissolved once its work is completed. The task force may involve its participating members full or part time. Participants are drawn from several departments, and frequently from several levels, and are selected not only because of their interest or ability with respect to the work of the task force but also because of their stature in their own departments (Scott 1981:219).

Task force participants defined a "task force" as any interim gathering of individuals focused on a specific issue which often, but not always, had an ideal "horizon" or end and whose "scope" had been identified as beyond the organizational responsibilities of any one of the group participants alone. Over their lifetime of meetings task forces were considered to be "worthwhile" if they accomplished their task, fostered communication and cooperation among represented organizations and departments (including "opening up City Government" and "involving people in the democratic process") and advertised their accomplishments to intended audiences for purposes of political support and making their issues "visible." At the same time complaints about ineffective meetings and the ability of these groups to solve **any** problems or accomplish any tasks were rampant among task force participants and observers. Even so most participants were unwilling to evaluate an entire task force experience as worthless, as long as something in one of the above areas was believed to be accomplished.

Prompted by participants' unwillingness to dismiss task force meetings despite their problems this case study focuses on how individuals in Union City Government made sense of their task force meetings while at the same time discounting, upsetting and reversing these occasions and the work that occurred within them. One study that was particularly helpful in attempting to examine what I call the sense and nonsense of task force meetings was Susan Stewart's (1978) study of nonsense in folklore and literature. Here she identifies a number of language operations by which sense is transformed into nonsense in written and oral discourse. These include reversing and inverting common sense categories, playing with category boundaries through misdirection, over signification, under signification and the use of formal procedures, playing with infinity through reflexivity, repetition, nesting, and circularity, and using simultaniety to arrange and rearrange common sense within a close field. This paper argues that similar processes occur in task force meetings.

MEETINGS AS REVERSIBLE EVENTS:
SIDE-TALK. FOOTNOTING AND POST-MORTEMS

In the process of trying to make sense of meetings, both during and after their occurrence, it was not atypical for individuals to discount portions of meetings, entire meetings or even entire task forces and committees. Participants in Union City Task Forces frequently used side-talk or footnoting (i.e., side conversations going on during regular meeting talk) as a means to interpret and/or discount events occurring in a meeting. For example, during a particularly confusing funding committee meeting of one task force, a participant commented to me on the side "This is ridiculous!" Later in the same meeting other participants gradually disintegrate into a number of side conversations bemoaning the particularly confusing discussion that was occurring.

> Eric: Why can't we nail them out?...

> Eric is upset and confused over what they are trying to decide while people attempt to explain it to him.

> Pam: Ai, ai, ai [groaning]..

> One woman got up and left as the meeting disintegrated into animated conversations yet one more time.

Jokes about the tendency of meetings to complicate (and stall) rather than simplify (and solve) problems were not uncommon.

> After a somewhat involved discussion of one problem the chair person turned to the woman taking minutes...

George: OK, you got that all?

The room broke into laughter.

Patrick: Why don't you put it in a committee and stall it for a while!
More Laughter.

In the above example it is the group itself that negates its own behavior but on an individual level each participant does his or her own share of discounting meeting talk. As one participant put it, "80 percent of a meeting doesn't pertain to you." Another person describes how a certain task force's subcommittee does not pertain to him.

> I'm totally disinterested in those portions of it and some of it I find just not to my liking at all. I think they are tilting at windmills. Some of these things that they're doing aren't that much use. Maybe I'm biased in that respect because I just don't care about that section at all.

Much of this kind of negation occurs during the meeting itself. In fact, participants may engage in side conversations in part because they do not feel that portion of the meeting properly pertains to them.

Post-mortem accounts, e.g., post-meeting and other after-the-fact talk, play a special role in offering participants an opportunity to dismiss a meeting as irrelevant. After a meeting has taken place, participants can deny that the entire meeting had any validity or sometimes can ignore that some portions of it happened at all. In a post-mortem of one meeting a participant told me, "I don't know what they think they were doing. We got nothing done!" The tendency of individuals in many American organizations to ridicule and disparage the meeting format (see previous discussion) may be one reason why many organizations operate on a "weak information base" (see Cohen and March 1974) and find themselves constantly replicating ideas (this is commonly referred to as the "reinventing-the-wheel phenomenon"). It is also important to note that when meetings are easy to discount they are also easy to reconstruct and re-interpret in a variety of ways.[12]

"FIGURING OUT" MEETINGS

Along with activities that might negate or reframe specific meetings or entire task forces, individuals also spent a good deal of time trying to "figure out" their meetings and the "workings" of Union City Government. While processes like footnoting might upset and disrupt task force meetings, their content also provided individuals with another way of "figuring out" meetings. These simultaneous mini-meetings contained a wealth of explanatory information on the meeting at hand as well as on other meetings. Figuring out other participants' "agendas" was a very common activity in meeting footnote. In fact participants were quite eager to use footnotes to "explain" to me what was happening during a meeting, e.g., what certain individuals were "really" saying, what was happening with a specific agenda item or why participants were behaving in a certain way.

Pre- and post-meeting talk also contained a great deal of information about people, issues, and processes which was helpful for understanding what went on in the city government and for discovering how a participant might fit in (this was not necessarily obvious). In pre-meeting talk, participants might discuss upcoming business, banter and joke with one another, negotiate other meeting schedules, and gather information about the role of other participants, departments and organizations. The following description of pre-meeting talk illustrates some of these activities.

> As people drift in, conversation in groups of two's and three's can be heard concerning the details of issues to be covered during the meeting. A new member who has just entered is introduced as "taking Janice's place...She's going back to school." There is a brief interlude of social chatting about her plans and what she is doing among those who know her. Conversations then return to a variety of issues relevant to the upcoming meeting and exchanging information about time lines and schedules. As the wait for others to arrive lengthens, one participant begins to play with the light switch and jokes about modern technology. Another begins to offer people coffee, water, etc. This instigates a round of fun about "taking orders for food." People go about stocking up on beverages as another participants begins eating her lunch. Another couple of participants begin talking about a news story they saw on TV of interest to the task force's problem focus. Someone else asks a question concerning what departments occupy the building they are

meeting in and it is explained to her. Two other people begin a cynical but humorous verbal; exchange concerning social problems in a foreign country from which one of the women has just returned. Laughingly, the other woman says to her, "It's on the Task Force agenda for tomorrow" implying that she must prepare something to talk about. Meanwhile other participants continue to discuss issues relevant to the business at hand, exchange information. One woman arranges an informal meeting with another participant immediately following this one, saying "you want to come down and look at it?" The chairperson mentions some problems they are having on one of the task force's projects and several people ask questions and make suggestions. The woman in charge of the project explains some of the misconceptions they deal with from the people they are trying to serve. Finally someone asks why they are still waiting to start the meeting and others answer that they are waiting for the arrival of a particular committee member [who is viewed as necessary for making decisions]. Nevertheless, the committee chairperson says, "Let's start...because I have to leave..."

Post-meeting activities and commentary were also important for "figuring out" what had just happened as well as for continuing to talk (out of meeting frame) about work that must be accomplished.

Tony: I'll call you...on that map.

Carol [the chairperson]: That would be helpful.

Some people are leaving rather quickly. Carol is talking to a lot of people, catching them before they go out the door, thanking them and asking for them to contact her concerning various items of business. She then moves into a longer conversation with Kris concerning the conservation issues which had brought out some disagreement during the meeting. At the same time an intern and Elizabeth are going over some charts from one of the reports. Elizabeth is explaining to the intern what they mean. Carol and Kris are disagreeing and Carol expresses her concern for tailoring things to the community they are referring to.

Carol: Lets first talk to Joe [Kris' boss] about this. I'll give you a call and we can get together with Wendy.

Carol then came over to talk with me. I questioned her about the schedule of the task force and she gave me a history on their activities and then began talking about today's meeting.

Carol: This meeting was fair, discussion wise. We made several decisions at this meeting. [When I asked what they were she told me.] We decided what charts and tables are to be used in the report. That's important!!! And secondly, we decided to try and get a handle on the cost of doing business in this area versus others. At the previous meeting we decided what businesses to include. It's been very difficult to get Economic Development to come up with things. I ask Dan only for very specific things I know they have. This meeting I asked him for lists of businesses they're working on. The general, more esoteric things we do in [this] Department. As a result of this meeting we will conduct some sort of review of the literature, but more than that we will contact these firms to get information on costs. We talked about that last time. We're also contacting the Fire Department for their records. That conservation stuff...Kris' boss, Joe Roberts didn't like the conservation idea. I was trying to force a decision. Kris came up to me after the meeting and talked about it...saying "maybe we should talk to Joe again" and so on.

As individuals reconstruct meetings for themselves and for researchers they may either discount or affirm the actions that occur during the event. In the above example, the meeting was evaluated positively because "decisions" (e.g., the charts and tables to be used in the report, the need "to get a handle" on costs) and action were taken following from the discussion.

The use of minutes for re-construction and re-writing task force meetings was also quite common in this context. Minutes were most often a support staff version of what a meeting accomplished, written by one person and sometimes reviewed by others but rarely corrected in subsequent meetings. Minutes were usually interpreted as the "official" version of a task force meeting, but it was widely understood that these were documents that were easy to re-write and manipulate. On one occasion I acted as the "minute taker" and was later given instruction by a staff person about how to record the minutes. For example, I was told to leave out many of the details of what had happened in reference to a rather heated portion of the meeting. I was also told not to put anything in the minutes about the memos regarding the incidents that had been circulated after the meeting. Of course, the memos were another form in which individuals interpreted and contested what happened in this particular meeting. In order to avoid many of these "interpretive" problems I was instructed to only include what was moved and passed and to change "pending" decisions to "suggestions."

In this section we have tried to illustrate some of the ordering (sense-making) and disordering (nonsense-making) processes of task force meetings. It was in the process of generating, attending (and not-attending), interpreting and contesting these meetings that participants constructed, and in effect, created "Union City Government."

CONCLUSION

When we look **behind** social forms (like meetings) everything seems so clear, because we see what we want to see -- our structures, values, categories, variables, etc.[13] This is how the researchers' culture effects his/her study in ways that make it difficult to see the processes and forms, such as meetings, that reveal the informant's culture "as something that is contested, emergent and ambiguous" (Van Mannen 1988:127). When we look **at** meetings we begin to see with our informants and what we see is the ambiguity, confusion and contrast interpretations that make up the "stuff" of everyday life. We see how meetings create pockets of order in an often disordered world, but we also see how meetings may be responsible for reversing, inverting, upsetting and disassembling organizational worlds. In this paper we have tried to illustrate how we came to **see** Midwest Mental Health Center and Union City Government through the meetings that were an important link between individual action and organizational structure and culture in these settings. We argue that researchers must turn to events like meetings in organizations in order to understand how individuals in their everyday actions and routines constitute and reproduce the worlds which they inhabit.

NOTES

1. The most recent call for a turn to the everyday is from researchers with a practice orientation (see Ortner 1984 and especially Giddens 1984; Bourieu 1977). As Giddens suggests in presenting his theory of structuration, "All social systems, no matter how grand or far flung, both express and are expressed in the routines of daily social life .. (1984:36). Of course, enthnomethodologists have been calling for the study of the commonplace world over 20 years:

    > The distinctive features of [this] alternative perspective...reside in the proposal that the objective struc-tures of social activities are to be regarded as the situated, practical accomplishments of the work through and by which the appearance of objective structures is displayed and detected. *The apparent strangeness of this perspective is due to the fact that it introduces a strange and hitherto largely unexplored domain of inquiry---the commonplace world* (Zimmerman & Pollner 1970:103, italics added).

    The work of symbolic interaction researchers in sociology as well as ethnoscientists and ethnography of speaking researchers in anthropology has also been significant for laying groundwork for a language (communi-cation) centered approach to the study of social occasions and social structure.

2. Committees are the most obvious of institutionalized group meeting forms in the West, and a form that by definition is "given" a specific task (it is "referred" or "committed" to the committee (see Wheare 1955). It is probably for this reason that committees are the most ridiculed and frustrating of meeting groups for Westerners and especially Americans. The range and number of jokes, parodies and cartoons about meeting is enormous and is most evident in books like *I Hate Meetings* (Baker 1983). Jokes about committees invariably focus on the irrationality and inefficiency of this form of activity as in the well-known definition "a committee is an aggregation of the unwilling, appointed by the incompe-tent, to do a task that is unnecessary" (Carnes 1980: 61).

3. One of the dominant themes in this literature is the need to improve meetings in order to more effectively use them as a management tool. This specific interest has inspired its own genre of management literature, the "how-to-make-meetings-better" books with titles like *Making Meeting Work* (Bradford 1976), *Effective Meetings for Busy People* (Carnes 1980),

and *You and I Have Simply Got to Stop Meeting Like This* (1978). This literature illustrates and reinforces the dominant image of meetings as tools for tasks. It is built on the premise that meetings are currently ineffective tools and therefore must be fixed immediately in order to improve task performance and productivity. Unfortunately, even though this approach focuses on the meeting form directly, it also takes this form for granted by assuming either that meetings transparently reveal the problems in organizations or that meetings are naturally ineffective and unproductive and therefore in dire need of improvement. This tells us something about what managers/consultants think about meeting, but it does not constitute a study of the meeting form itself.

4. James March and Johan Olsen's work on organizational decision-making (e.g., 2976) is interesting for anthropologists to consider because it challenges the folk-model embedded in our theories about organizations, models that privilege decisions (as tasks) and individual intention in attempting to explain how choices are made in these systems.

5. In Karl Weick's terms it is often the case that we need to "talk in order to discover what [we] are saying, [to] act in order to discover what [we] are doing"(1977:195).

6. Here I am reversing the assumption that **decisions** (or other meeting tasks) are what meetings are **about**. Instead I am suggesting the possibility the **meetings are what decisions, crises, and other problems are about.** For this vantage point, tasks such as decisions and problems such as specific conflicts and crises occur because they produce meetings and in many social systems, such as Midwest, it is meetings that produce "organization", although it is much more common to assume the opposite.

7. One of the key transformations that a meeting frame makes is to turn the behavior of individuals into organizational action (March and Olsen suggest that it is the decision process se 1976:11) The meeting form performs this transformation because as a social form it frames the behavior that occurs within it as concerned with the "business" of a group or organization. In this case, meetings and meeting talk as objectified in minutes, reports, etc. become the major evidence of organizational action, results, decisions and control. From this perspective, talk is not expressive or reflective of action, power, control, it **is** action, power, and control. Gronn (1983) suggests this in his study of how talk is used among Australian school administrators:

What all the structured observation studies [of school admin-
istrators] do reveal is that **talk** is the work, i.e., it consumes
most of an administrator's time and energy. The next step is
to make clear the circumstances under which talk **does** the
work, that is, to show how talk is the resource that school
personnel use to get others to act (Austin 1978). To see talk
in such terms is to view it as an instrumental tool...for
performing actions like influencing, persuading, manipulating,
and so on. (p.2).

8. The information in this section was taken from interviews and documenta-
    tion of committee and board activities available in minutes, memos, and
    other records of meetings held before the research project began, and it
    is also based on my participation in the final selection committee process
    and the final meeting of the board to decide on a permanent executive
    director. This example is taken from Schwartzman (1989:222-239).

9. This story was first recorded on tape in an interview with Greg Stone, but
    according to my note it is essentially the same story that he told at this
    meeting.

Let's just go back, way back. I used to walk into the Center
and I used to hear all kinds of complaints about Paula Gray
and when I mentioned the name don't even tell me. Every
time I walked in the door there was another Paula Gray story.
Finally we had a showdown with Fred and got to do away
with Paula Gray and you know what happened it seems that
all of the staff critizing her dried up. Either staff didn't want
to stand up, we don't know what the final outcome will be,
maybe they should just keep it inside. Nevertheless, we as
Council or Board members were left out on a limb and we
thought that we were really trying to do something to help the
Center, and we really didn't know whether we really had the
staff behind us or not. All we could go by were all the things
we had hear in the past. [After this] Toni Michaels was
hired. I come walking in here one and oh, Paula Gray is
back again. If I heard it from one person I heard it from five
people. That was somewhat resolved but now Toni Michaels
has submitted her resignation. There are letters from people
in support of her not leaving, some of those letters are from
the same people who said oh, we have another Paula Gray
here. You know, let's face it, the Council or Board people,

are not here everyday, the wind blows one way one day and one way another day.

10.   I am re-phasing Kenneth Burke here as he asks, "Where does the drama get its materials? From the "'Unending conversation that is going on at the point in history when we are born" (1973:100).

11.   A striking example of problems with this assumption is Robert Alford's (1975) analysis of the efforts of 20 different task force/commissions of investigation created to examine problems of New York health system. After investigating the task force's activities over a 20 year time period, he discovered that the last commission was asking the same question as the first.

12.   As Hogart suggests, "Events are what agents make of them and often make of them subsequently" (p.15). This is why the relationship between meetings and stories about them is crucial to examine (see Schwartzman 1989:243-269 for an extended discussion of this issue).

13.   Rento Rosaldo (1980) makes this point about Ilongot stories. "Ilongot stories not only contained but also organized perceptions of the past and projects for the future. In other words, the only way I could apprehend Ilongot lifeways was by looking through (not somehow around or directly behind) the cultural forms that they used to represent their lives to themselves" (p. 17).

REFERENCES

Alford, R. R.
      1975   *Health Care Politics*. Chicago: University of Chicago Press.

Austin, J. L.
      1975   *How to Do Things with Words*. Cambridge, MA: Harvard University Press.

Berman, R. H.
      1988   "Task Force" Meetings and Life in a City Government: Making Nonsense and Sense. PhD. Thesis, Department of Anthropology, Northwestern University. Evanston, Illinois.

Bourdieu, P.
1977   *Outline of a Theory of Practice*. London: Cambridge University Press.

Bradford, L. P.
1976   *Making Meetings Work*. San Diego, CA: University Associates.

Burke, K.
1973   *The Philosophy of Literary Form*. Berkeley, CA: University of California Press, Third Edition.

Carnes, W. T.
1980   *Effective Management for Busy People*. New York: McGraw-Hill Book Company.

Drucker, P.
1974   *Management*. New York: Harper & Row.

Dunsing, R. J.
1976   *You and I Have Simply Got to Stop Meeting This Way*. New York: AMACOM.

Geertz, C.
1973   *The Interpretation of Culture*. New York: Basic Books.

Giddens, A.
1984   *The Constitution of Society*. Berkley, Ca: University of California Press.

Gronn, P. C.
1983   "Talk as the Work: The Accomplishment of School Administration." *Administrative Science Quarterly*, 28, 1-21.

Hobart, M.
1990   "Complex Agents: On Meetings in Bali." Paper presented at the Annual Meeting of the American Anthropological Association, November 28-December 2, 1990, New Orleans, Louisiana.

March, J. G. and J. P. Olsen (Eds.)
1976   *Ambiguity and Choice in Organizations.*   Bergen, Norway: Universitetsforlaget.

Myer, F. R.
1986   "Reflections on a Meeting Structure, Language and the Polity in a Small-Scale Society. *American Ethnologist, 13*, 430-447.

Ortner, S.
1984   "Theory in Anthropology Since the Sixties." *Comparative Studies in Society and History,* 1984, pp. 126-166.

Ranson, S. B. Hinings and R. Greenwood
1980   "The Structuring of Organizational Structures." *Administrative Science Quarterly, 25,* 1-17.

Rosaldo, R.
1980   *Ilongot Headhunting 1883-1974.*   Stanford, CA: Stanford University Press.

Schutz, A.
1972   *The Phenomenology of the Social World.* London: Heinemann.

Schwatzman, H. B.
1989   *The Meeting: Gathering in Organizations and Communities.* New York: Plenum Press.

Scott, W. R.
1981   *Organizations*: Rational, Natural and Open Systems. Englewood Cliffs, NJ: Prentice-Hall.

Stewart, S.
1978   *Nonsense: Aspects of Intertextuality in Folklore and Literature.* Baltimore: Johns Hopkins Press.

Van Maanen, J.
1988   *Tales of the Field.* Chicago: University of Chicago Press.

Weick, K. E.
1977   "Re-Punctuating the Problem." *In* P.S. Goodman and J.M. Penning, *New Perspectives on Organizational Effectiveness.* San Francisco: Jossey-Bass.

1979   *The Social Psychology of Organizing.* Reading, MA: Addison-Wesley, Second Edition.

Wheare, K. C.
1955   *Government by Committee: An Essay on the British Constitution.* london: Oxford University Press.

Zimmerman D. H., and M. Pollner
1970   "The Everyday World as a Phenomenon." *In* J. Douglas (Ed.), *Understanding Everyday Life.* London: Routledge and Kegan Paul.

FEDERAL ORGANIZATIONAL CULTURES: LAYERS AND LOCI

Shirley J. Fiske[1]

I had been in government less than a week, starting as a policy analyst in a staff office to the Administrator, when my office mate, a seasoned bureaucrat, took me aside in a mentor-like fashion and told me that there was something that I should know about successful government service. He said, "Stay high enough to make the job interesting, but not high enough to be vulnerable." He followed with the explanation, "Don't get too close to political appointees." I was starting work on a special project for the Undersecretary. And I appreciated this advice from a veteran of over 20 years of federal service, although at the time I did not fully understand the warning and assumptions it contained.

This revelation turned out to be the tip of an iceberg of cultural knowledge among upper level civil servants. My colleague was drawing on a systematic set of beliefs about relationships between civil servants and political appointees that I later found to be elaborated broadly among the civil service upper levels. This advice about proper survival behavior is one example of pan-bureaucratic belief system among upper level bureaucrats that provides a framework for behavior.

The assumptions about interrelationships betweeen political appointees and civil servants are part of the conceptual and emotional landscape of upper level program managers and professional staffers who are distrustful of political appointees. "Schedule C" appointments come and go very quickly (average tenure, 18 months), cause a flurry of activity, and are often troublesome because they have particular political agendas they want to advance. These agendas, such as the President's initiative to eliminate fraud, waste and abuse, or the push to contract out government services to the private sector are usually seen as troublesome or as nuisances because they divert attention away from the 'real' mission of an agency, whether it is customs and immigration, environmental monitoring, or providing human services.

Furthermore, a close association with a political appointee (running a task force, an evaluation, a new program) can result in being "labeled" by associates as an enemy of the organization, especially if one does something that shakes up the organization. It can result in decapitation of a program, loss of funding, loss of status, or even RIF'ing -- that dreaded acronym for the abolishment of civil service positions in downsizing or re-organizing efforts of the federal government.

The units at the top of the organization, that is those which answer directly to the Secretary, Undersecretary or the like and act as his or her staff, are the most vulnerable to the quixotic whims of political fate: when a new Secretary or new Deputy Director is sworn in, they are likely to change the structure of the organization to suit their style and management needs and bring in people who share their vision for the agency; the units at the top are most likely to topple or be re-organized. Being close to political appointees is considered dangerous territory and must be negotiated very carefully by civil servants. On the other hand, to the ambitious or creative young civil servant, new political agendas can provide fertile ground for establishing one's leadership and can offer avenues of career advancement. I have seen several meteoric rises in the civil service riding on the coattails of political agendas, but the staying power of these individuals remains to be seen. In the eyes of longer-term civil servants there is much to be overcome in their behavior and actions before there is true cooperation and acceptance.

This kind of knowledge comes under the general rubric of pan-bureaucratic survival skills for senior staffers and senior program managers. It is exemplary of one piece of cultural knowledge that a program analyst or other staff need to know to survive upper level interactions with political appointees. This is just one example. This paper will describe examples of pan-bureaucratic cultural norms that civil servants need to conduct everyday business (implicit knowledge that is held across agencies and allows for the conduct of everyday business in an orderly fashion) but which you will never find written in an Office of Personnal Management (OPM) manual nor agency operating procedures. I will also describe two other loci for culture -- agency cultures and workplace cultures.

The interpretations presented here stem from four years of observation and participation in a variety of federal settings. I arrived in the federal government fresh from academia, albeit familiar with the practices and stereotypes in civil service from my years of teaching in public administration. Still, I was not prepared for the wealth of cultural behavior, norms, covert knowledge and assumptions that underlie people's behavior. Such assumptions about behavior, purpose of employment, ways of thinking, and patterns of affect can only come from socialization into a system of cultural knowledge. I was astounded at the pervasive cultural phenomena in civil servant worklife. I became aware that federal organizational cultures are complex nets of identities, languages, interpersonal exchanges, ceremonies and ceremonial behavior; that they overlap on different levels; that they are often situational, such that the individual can pick and choose between roles and identities; and that some slices within organizations are more complete organizational cultures than others.

I start from the conceptualization of organizational culture as used by Louis (1985) in which organizations are seen as "culture-bearing milieus," because they "provide opportunities for affiliation out of which may come sets of shared understandings that are relevant and distinctive to some group" (1985:75). Additionally it is fairly well established that there are many sites or loci within an organization where organizatinal culture can develop. Intraorganizational culture can develop with a workgroup, an office or division. Or, aspects of culture can develop among 'horizontal' slices of an organization, as Louis points out, such as among individuals who share a similar role or function within an organization (budget officers in federal agencies, for example). Cultures can develop along 'vertical' lines, such as a major operating component within a federal agency -- the National Weather Service, a part of the National Oceanic and Atmospheric Administration (NOAA) comes to mind.

This paper describes layers and loci of cultural phenomena in the executive branch, each of which is found with varying intensity in multiple locales througout the executive branch. Layers of culture such as pan-bureaucratic norms in the opening illustration are horizontal slices of cultural phenomena that adhere to positions, job series (for

instance program analyst) and roles (staff, managment) in the government. These layers contrast and overlap with cultural loci which are
'locales' where cultural systems can be found, such as in office culture.
The cultural phenomena at locales depend more on social interaction,
a shared workcycle, and agreement on organizational mission -- they are
more complete systems, as I'll show shortly. I'll describe in turn (a)
pan-bureaucratic norms, (b) agency cultures, and (c) workgroup or
office cultures as I came to see them.

LAYERS AND LOCI OF
FEDERAL ORGANIZATIONAL CULTURES

Pan-bureaucratic Norms

Pan-bureaucratic norms, knowledge and behavior are understandings
and beliefs that allow negotiations to occur, interagency work to
proceed, and underlie the assumptions and values among upper GS-level
staffer personnel and operating managers. The earlier illustration of
beliefs and appropriate behavior vis a vis political appointees is one
example. These belief systems are a locus of culture... threads of
understandings about what can and cannot be said, modes of operating,
and about one's positions in the organizations that are **pan-bureaucratic**. This specialized knowledge is shared by people who work in the
executive branch and informs their behavior in everyday work life.

I will give examples here from beliefs about effective behavior,
norms for insuring managerial flexibility, interpreting status and ranking
systems, common language systems, and the symbolism of delegating
authority and responsibility. All are elements of cultural systems that
exist in the culture-bearing milieux of organizations.

Unravelling Ambiguity

One of the everyday challenges as agency staff is to figure out what
to do in ambiguous situations, where your only clues are paper memos,
directives, and where you can't always have first-hand knowledge about
everything nor speak to the head boss directly. I remember when I first
joined government service, my solution to ambiguity was simple: why
not just go and ask the Undersecretary what he meant by the 'one-stop

service center,' or what he really wants to do with a certain program. I assumed staff had open and direct access to the Undersecretary any hour night and day. It took a while to sink in that staff's job, as ironic as it may seem -- is not to bother the Undersecretary with every little detail, but to interpret, advise and help the Undersecretary think or make decisions. And to do all this without continual clarification or access. Instead, you have to make appointments, write background and decision memos, and personal access is formalized. Consequently a staff person has to interpret ambiguous directives, memos, or verbal comments to figure out what's wanted.

> One morning I watched as two top-level analysts from different agencies were trying to determine how much authority a document had to change the work patterns of the operating units of their organizations. Almost in unison they flipped through the document to the cover memo to see if it had been signed yet by the Secretary, knowing that the unsigned draft document carried little weight but a signed version was enormously powerful and influential. When signed, it would mean gearing up all the operating agencies for a major management effort; and whether or not that set of activities was inevitable, the two staffers knew that when unsigned, it bought them several weeks to a month before they had to generate the effort while last-minute details were still being worked out and the 'concurrences' were being sought. Amazingly, it took them only 10 seconds for the whole transaction, and not a word was spoken, yet there was complete communication on what they were doing. (Incidentally, the document was not signed, and they decided to do nothing.)

This kind of knowledge -- assessing the level of authority inherent in various forms of a document, and being able to take appropriate action on the knowledge is an example of pan-bureau cultural knowledge shared among federal civil servants.

In fact, this general category of knowledge is a valued commodity. People who "know the right level of action" are admired as skilled civil servants. This phrase means that they know how to respond to requests from higher status office directors or political appointees without causing an over-reaction or appearing to do nothing. They know how to judge the political winds and estimate how serious the topic or request is, make a moderate investment of time, and develop a responsive product without wasting anyone's time spinning wheels -- the appropriate level of activity.

The Importance of Concurrences

The concurrence system means getting higher-level bosses to sign off on an action. The cumbersome and slow-moving nature of bureaucracies is a national joke. It can take weeks or months of writing briefing papers, decision memos based on the briefing papers, re-drafting and recirculating, and redrafting the final revision just to get people to "sign off" on the memo. There are offices of people who do nothing but read the paper trail, distribute and track the memos, looking for appropriate concurrences ('Exec Sec,' or Executive Secretariat offices). By getting concurrences, information of an action is spread around and de jure agreement is achieved. 'Concurrences' can involve literally dozens of levels and offices from various agencies. Some have called it "CYA" (Cover Your Ass) syndrome. The general effect, often satirized by political humorists, is that if everyone participates in concurring an action, no one can be blamed individually for any particular action. Nonetheless, concurrences have a functional value as well as the symbolic CYA attribute. For organizations such as large bureaucracies, the sharing of information is important for coordination, and concurrences contribute to coordination.

An Oxymoron: How to Get Something Done in a Bureaucracy (!)

The converse of continual concurrence is the frustration with not being able to get something done in a timely manner. This leads to a corollary principle of behavior that I have heard invoked more than once. Here is a typical scenario:

> The scene is an intraagency meeting of the heads of the public affairs units of the operating divisions of the agency. A new member bemoaned that she could not understand the process for getting promotional brochures approved through official channels. She had labored for months trying to get a pamphlet approved for printing. She could see no consistency or reason to the thinking of higher authorities, and finally announced that she was going to confront the head of the department and demand that they describe the rules by which one could get brochures approved.

> She was advised by her colleagues: "Don't ask. You might get an answer. Just do it. It's easier to ask for forgiveness than it is to ask for permission." The unspoken interpretation is that where rules and

regulations are not codified, there are opportunities for action; and that higher officials might (and likely would) create rules when they realize the void. The wise manager consciously avoids formalizing anything that could potentially restrict action, thus preserving ambiguous circumstances and the ability to act.

How to Judge Someone's Status

There are formal, overt status systems in federal agencies which rank individuals in seniority, authority, and prestige. The formal ranking system is the General Schedule (GS) personnel system, managed by the U. S. Office of Personnel Management, which ranks people according to grades, and within the grade according to steps, by seniority. Grade and step together are powerful determinants of status in Federal organizations, and are used informally as a shorthand calculus for categorizing individuals and ranking them, for composing task forces and working groups, and assessing the credibility of a product. It's bad form to ask someone directly "What's your GS level?" (tantamount to how much income a person makes). Instead, one inquires circumspectly to see who outranks whom.

> Rank is important: A group of high ranking managers were negotiating the membership on a task force that would be mandated to conduct an evaluation of a sensitive political program. The selection of individuals was guided by two important principles: (a) to have people at a "similar level" to avoid "imbalance" in the group but (b) to keep the appointments at a low enough level to avoid escalation of concern and exposure to high level officials. (The higher rank you pull into a task force, the more closely it is watched by Assistant Secretaries and their staffs and the more politicized it becomes.)

In addition to the formal ranking system, there are many other indicators of status. Office furniture subtly signals status and power. A large office, with windows, a new desk and multiple pieces of office furniture signal a high status individuals or one with longevity. A small couch demonstrates power and prestige; a credenza or bookshelf, on the other hand, are nice complements to one's furniture, but do not have much status by themselves. An entire room to oneself with a door that closes and walls that go all the way to the ceiling is clear status. Window drapes are beyond the pale of most bureaucrats, and if one has them, it is obvious that one has great pull. Framed agency awards for meritorious performance hung on the walls, detail the status of individuals.

Symbolic Aspects of Delegation of Responsibility

Delegation of authority is one of the pillars of bureaucratic organization, as Weber noted long ago. Not all managers can personally participate in every activity, so they can choose to delegate the responsibility depending on how important the mission is. Positions rather than individuals are named to work groups or task forces, but the degree of participation is a matter of their available time and discretion. "Principals" may attend all meetings personally or they may choose to send a delegate who is lower in status. An delicate gage of success of a group is the grade level of the delegate and the frequency with which the delegate is sent rather than the named official. A high turnover rate among delegates is a bad sign - a symbolic assessment about the lack of value of the group. After just the second meeting of a group, as a staffer, one can judge its importance, likelihood of success and target one's own investment of time and energy according to the number of delegates and their rank. These are subtle and critical indicators for a task force chair and for the staff persons attending the meeting if they are concerned about the outcome and process of the group activity.

Alphabet Soup and Inherent Meanings - Lexicon

Shop talk is not a language system in itself, since it relies on the host language (English), but the terminology is specific to bureaucratic life. Every executive branch worker becomes proficient in the 'alphabet soup' of federal conversation: How are things at OMB? Did NASA sign the MOU with NOAA?, and so on. While the specifics of the MOU or the meaning of the acronym may not be known, its generic referent is familiar to bureaucrats, and one can carry on extended conversations at this level.   There is meaning, intent, affect and information ascribed to each of the acronyms. They are symbols for greater culture.

The above are examples of broadly understood pan-bureaucratic norms from the cultural repertoire of upper level federal workers. A fully socialized civil servant understands the covert rule systems in each of these situations. It would not matter whether one was an employee of the U.S. Department of State, or Department of Labor -- these situations and the behaviors they generate are be familiar to managers and staff across them all.

Pan-bureaucratic behaviors and rules are layered cultural norms -- layered beacause they belong to roles, to positions or identities across the government, but are not necessarily adherant to particular work-places or corporate enterprises such as agencies. Organizations are culture-bearing milieux, and the pan-bureau culture associated with role and strata are cultural threads that weave in and out of agencies at different levels.

In comparison, there is a difference in intensity and elaboration betweeen pan-bureau norms, where there is little corporate interaction or agreement on mission, and **agency and workplace cultures** which have a more fully-elaborated cultural systems, including a dedicated language, shared purpose, continuous face-to-face interaction, and ceremonial events. At this locus, the cultural system is fairly complete and intense, although cultural constructions vary enormously at varous places within a federal agency.

Any civil servant is called upon to use pan-bureaucratic norms for interagency and federal bureau behavior. At other times one partici-pates in the culture of a specific federal agency and uses values and behaviors for that specific organization. And at the most specialized level, individuals are part of office or workgroup cultures. Calling upon each of these cultural affiliations is situational, depending on the setting, status and identity of individuals present.

Agency Culture

Organizational culture at the federal level has been relatively neglected. Most anthropological work on public sector organizations has looked at public service delivery systems at the local level or private non-profit groups. At the national level, Gold's study of successful organizations in the public sector is one of the few works describing culture in federal agencies. Gold examines successful and unsuccessful organizations in the public and private sectors and concludes that strong federal agency culture derives from a clear mission or charter, a shared sense of history, pride in the unique service an agency provides, similar professional background among the operational personnel, a shared value system about the mission of the agency and the types of actions appropriate to meet those goals, a socialization process which enhances the broadly shared values, and a set of symbols for the organization. The cognitive rules for appropriate behavior and affect are distinctive to that particular organization. There are both expressive and material aspects to an organization's culture. Some agencies embody the sense of agency culture more fully than others. In fact, I have observed very few bureaus which have this unique sense of culture.

Gold identified a small number of federal level organizations which "embody an identifiable organizational culture that serves to integrate a tradition and philosophy with a well-defined mission" (Gold 1982:569). The federal agencies he identifies are the U.S. Forest Service (corroborating Kauffman's early work of 1967), the U.S. Customs Service and the U.S. Passport Service. In each of these he finds well-articulated and well supported objectives, a sense of uniqueness and pride in the organization, and a cluster of management principles which are people-centered. Organizational culture at the level of the total institution may not occur in every federal agency, or may not be elaborated to the same degree, but there is evidence that culture can exist at this level of description under certain ideal conditions.

The cultural system has interrelated and interdependent parts. There are core value systems, organizational symbols and ideologies, ceremonial cycles, and organizational myths and legends which support and legitimate the organization's activities.

Core Value System: The centerpiece of organizational culture is the core value system which informs behavior, illustrates evil and good, and validates worthwhile goals in the organization. This aspect is frequently described in the popular literature by Deal and Kennedy (1982) and Peters and Waterman (1982) and Schein (1985) who use culture to mean shared values about the organization's mission. Gold sees culture as a perception of 'specialness' that distinguishes an organization from others in its products and operation and contributes to a feeling of organizational pride.

In federal organizations the core value system usually derives from unique and special expertise in a particular area. In some cases where there is an unusually dynamic or long-standing director, core values can be enhanced by the top administrator through his or her management of the institution. The FBI under the leadership of J. Edgar Hoover is a case in point. Core values shift at the margins over time, responsive to changes in politics and public opinion but generally are long-standing and revered.

In the following passages Gold describes agency-specific core values:

> For example, the primary mission of the U.S. Forest Service, management of the forest land, may be somewhat unusual for a government agency in terms of clarity and visibility. This awareness of mission by Forest Service managers appeared to be quite significant, and represented a deep sense of understanding and personal commitment that had developed over time. Moreover, this mission is one that has been extremely stable over an extended period of time.
>
> A fundamental component of this shared sense of mission is the personal commitment found among individuals. The vast majority of Forest Service officials have spent their entire government careers in the agency, and almost all of them entered as foresters in the field (1982:569).
>
> In addition to the high level of awareness of mission, the nature of the mission itself clearly plays a significant role. Management of the forest lands is a wholesome, relatively noncontroversial mission that is a source of substantial pride, and something which they believe the whole country feels good about (1982:572).

While a shared sense of mission is crucial for organizational culture, shared, specific goals across all individuals is not necessary. Core values are beliefs about the framework values of the organization -- the general values and objectives, or "paradigm congruence," as Wilkins and Ouchi refer to it. They make the point that members may share general orientations, assumptions, and values regarding the interest of the collective, but not necessarily the specific knowledge or shared goals (Wilkins and Ouchi 1983:471-2).

Organizational ideology: Organizational ideology is closely related to core values. An organization needs an explanation for its role and special contributions to the productive sector of the U.S. The ideology legitimates the unique political and economic interests of the organization and its work. For U.S. Federal agencies, the ideology typically **legitimates the government role in providing services or regulating an industry or resource.** Most bureaus' ideology emphasizes that their services are essential to fill a gap in the market, to regulate a market that is inequitable, or to provide essential services that no one else will or can do. The ideology for a national program in oceanic data collection, for example, runs thusly:

> "We (the Feds) run the national repository for oceanographic data because the States can't do it, and there are not enough incentives for private industry to take on this responsibility. It is very important to have this data for reasons of public information -- to maintain a public archive."

Gold finds the sense of specialness in product and operation to be an important feature of federal organizational culture (1982). The agency for which I work, the National Oceanic and Atmospheric Administration (NOAA), was created relatively recently in 1970 by joining several distinct, previously independent agencies, two of which had historical roots in the 19th century and each of which had its own sense of mission and strong organizational culture. It is not surprising that much of the effort of successive heads of the agency have been spent trying to figure out how to develop a more unified, coherent, NOAA agency culture, and how to get the recalcitrant operating agencies to give up their individual symbolism and identify with the new agency. In one particularly dramatic move, the agency head mandated that National Weather Service to change its name to the **NOAA** Weather Service, to promote identification with the composite umbrella organization.

Subsistence activities: All organizations attempt to establish control over their financial and human resources. Of course this is not the same as subsistence activities in the traditional ethnographic sense, but it is a symbolic form of subsistence activity. An agency captures resources, both fiscal and human, which insure the continuity of the organization. Many civil servants have described the annual budget process as competition with other agencies for resources and see themselves pitted against other agencies during the appropriations process.

Once established by statute, federal organizations are dependent for their subsistence base on Congress and the American public. Their subsistence activities revolve around the annual appropriations and authorization cycle of the Federal government. Agencies must justify their budget to Congress and OMB, justifying enhancements for new expenditures, and nurturing relationships with constituencies who can help in the appropriations and authorization process. The strategies for promoting programs and for securing authorization and apppropriations from Congress have been well described in Wildavsky's book *The Politics of the Budgetary Process* (1979).

Ceremony and ritual: Ceremony and ritual in organizations bring life under control and crystallize key values for the members of the organization. Ritual is traditionally linked with religious occasions, but Moore and Meyerhoff (1977) have shown that public life is filled with secular ritual. Secular ritual endows occasions with evocative particular interpretations of social reality and endows those occasions with legitimacy. A ceremony arranges information in an expressive manner and calls attention to the status of certain people.

> The Annual Awards Luncheon, a yearly rite of intensification in most large federal organizations, is a public ceremonial which crystallizes for the participants of my organization the core values for employee behavior. As a case in point, the National Oceanic and Atmospheric Administration (NOAA) chose to honor several employees: one person who had achieved international scientific recognition; another who had cracked an international ring of fishery poachers in American territorial waters; and another who had written a manual for a piece of technical equipment and thereby raised the level of productivity of that unit. Each of these individuals embodied core values of NOAA - scientific excellence, the sanctity of American fishing rights, and the importance of conquering technical equipment to enhance productivity.

The awards luncheon not only honors individuals but also unifies the organization by identifying and honoring employees from many units throughout the organization, and from different levels of the organizational hierarchy. It enhances both horizontal and vertical integration. It demonstrates, essentially, that "this is excellence in employee behavior and this is behavior for which you will be honored, **no matter how far from the top you may be**."

Organizational myths and legends: Employees in most organizations have been told confidentially, "You remember Marty F.? He used to be the head of X Division...... Well, he set off every red flag of the Administrator, and now he's in the field office in Topeka!"

Organizational stories have been shown by Martin, *et. al.* (1983) to follow common themes such as "Is the Big Boss human?" "Can the little guy rise to the top?" and " Will I get fired?" These themes occur over and over because they capture inherent tensions between individuals and organizations. Organizational stories help an individual make sense out of life and struggles in the organization. Organizational stories also take the form of legends about particularly influential individuals or myths about organizational creation.

Organizational legends illustrate a point, or describe heroic individuals in the past. They are narratives which refer to real world activities after creation, and are more common in organizations than true organizational myths. A top career official in NOAA's Weather Service is reverently described by his employees as an empire-builder who "protects his people" against the predations of the higher ranking officials and the Office of Management and Budget "coyotes" who want to cut his budget. This administrator was the only head of the operating units who refused to propose any cuts in his subsistence base, and this renegade behavior earned him legendary respect because he managed to resist budget and employee cuts and hold his job as well.

Myths, as compared to organizational legends, are sacred narratives explaining how the organization came to be in its present form. They are set in the remote past, prior to the actual creation of the organization. Culture heroes are sometimes associated with myths, and bring to the organization some sorely needed items - a charismatic ideology or leadership for program development, a large budget, or some other resource needed by the agency. Examples can often be found in young, enthusiastic organizations such as the U.S. Peace Corps in its early years, or an older organization under a long-tenured, strong, and controversial director, such as the Federal Bureau of Investigation under Hoover.

Obviously these illustrations of the agency organizational culture have not been exhaustive. Noticeably missing is a discussion of enculturation into organizations, the excellent ethnographic work by Kauffman on the U.S. Forest Service (1960), and other more recent work in that area (Charles 1982; Starr 1982). The previous examples illustrate the tip of the iceberg of cultural systems at the agency level.

Localized Cultural Systems - Workplace or Office Culture

The locus of organizational culture can be at the agency level or it can be smaller units within large institutions. Within each federal agency, regardless of whether or not there is coherent organizational culture as a whole, there are subunits which develop cultural systems. These may be the locus of strongest culture, because culture often forms around functional work groups which have similar professional backgrounds, share the same office space, and have the potential for frequent interaction between members.

The following example of workplace culture takes place in a federal budget office. Imagine the following if you will. The Budget Office has forty-four employees, with four Divisions and three Branches. It is a staff office to the top officials in the organization and produces budget documents for the five operating units and seven staff offices of the agency. The Budget Office is ultimately one of the most important in the agency because it plans and tracks spending for a budget of over $3 billion and 24,000 employees.

The material culture of the budget shop belies its importance. The power of the office is not reflected in luxurious furniture, symbols of accomplishment, or symbols of integration with the organization (e.g. pictures depicting agency activities). The carpets are worn, metal desks are standard, walls need painting, and venetian blinds (not drapes!) need repair. Most employees do not have offices, but have modular spaces surrounded by five foot high room dividers which partition the area. The space is divided along organizational units, with individuals in the same Division or Branch grouped together. There are no shared spaces or amenities such as a lounge area or conference room. The material culture suggests that it is a serious, work oriented office [not a brainstorming or socializing office where conference space is for sharing group interaction].

Core values in the budget shop are expressed through individual behavior, by concerns voiced at staff meetings, and particularly by everyday choices made by managers in the office. The core value propositions are the following:

(1)   "The cornerstone of a good reputation is timeliness in getting out the documents."

The Budget Office is responsible for producing three major documents in a yearly cycle: the Secretarial Submission, the OMB Submission, and the Congressional Submission. The schedule for getting these budget documents is set years in advance and is largely outside the Office's control, depending on OMB and Congressional schedules. As the deadlines near, crucial pieces of information are always missing: justification for line items, different figures, changes ordered from a higher department official, and so on. The budget shop always works overtime and on weekends on a predictable cycle to get the documents completed by the deadline.

> (2)   "The Budget Office collects information from the line and summarizes it. Never second guess the line."

This proposition describes the proper relationship vis à vis the line units. Their mission is to collect and coordinate the spending plans and spending allowances of the operating units. The opearating units have a monopoly on the technical information underlying costs; budget analysts are not technically trained and believe it's difficult to second-guess the line when your background is not technical.

Therefore they must rely on the cooperation of the line to provide that information in a timely fashion. Independent analysis of the spending levels or questions about programmatic priorities would jeopardize that delicate relationship. The proposition supports and legitimates lack of "second guessing" the line and a production orientation rather than an analytical one.

> (3)   "Beware of 'Washington Monuments' offered by the line."

When forced to make cuts, program managers will offer to cut those programs which are politically popular, expecting that Congress will put them back in the budget. The phrase comes from a lengendary story about the National Park Service which traditionally offered to cut funding of the most popular public attraction in Washington, the Washington Monument. Of course Congress never agreed to cut the budget of the Monument, so the National Park Service always received their funds. "Washington Monuments" are danger signs for a budgeteer because Congress may put the item back in the budget but not appropriate any money, so the agency has to pay for the program by taking money from other efforts.

(4)   "Maintain as much flexibility as possible in your budget."

One of the continual chores of a budget office is to find money to pay for unexpected expenditures or sometimes expected ones. A well-defined budget structure that is clear to Congress or OMB hinders movement of funds from one activity to another. Therefore the goal is to use categories of reporting or line items that do not fully reflect the complexity of the budget, so that things can be hidden. A corollary value is to refrain from revealing too much to OMB or Congress about the organization's activities through the agency's budget documents. "Reprogramming," moving money from one account to another, is an important tool in the budget tool kit.

The constellation of these core values reflects a production orientation, rather than analytical or managerial orientation. The most important activity of the office is timely production of the budget documents. Ironically, despite the emphasis on production, virtually no thought seems to be given to the process or the people who put the budget documents together. Because of the heavy emphasis on production, new ideas, innovative approaches, and professional development are neglected. They simply get in the way of production. There is no time for them. Consequently the system perpetuates itself and its values.

The ceremonial elements of the cultural system of this particular Budget Office are few and far between. There is only one formal event in the annual cycle, and that is the Christmas Party. The other formal events occur only when people leave the office through retirement (most commonly) or lateral transfer to other parts of the agency. Retirement luncheons honor the individual for their years of work in the budget office and they also affectionately parody the distinctive work of budgeteers (occupational norms). Conspicuously absent, given the product orientation of the organization, is any ritual or ceremony at the completion of any one of the cycles of budget documents.

The Budget Office has an elaborate lexicon. They use the words in English sentences, but to uninitiated, the meaning of the sentences is a mystery:

"Floyd is working on the juniors, and the spreadsheets and narratives are almost ready for the Secretarial submission. But we'll need a cross-walk for the-ATBs and reimbursables. The Weather Service is offering up some Washington Monuments, and you know Congress'll

never close those WSOs, so we'll have to eat them. Do you think we
can reprogram from some of the Fish Funds, or sort out the carryover
in the ADF to see how much goes back to the line?"

Much of the language and acronyms are shorthand communication
which help budgeteers talk about things in an efficient way. They all
share the semantic referents behind the code. Some functions of the
highly specialized language, however, are dysfunctional in an organization - especially when dealing with other units in the agency or
outsiders trying to understand the budget process. Specialized language
is often a way of screening information from other people, and can
result in isolation, miscommunication, and de facto power over other
units.

To summarize, the culture of the Budget Office centers around
production of documents to meet short term deadlines, and at the same
time it discourages innovation and professional development. Hierarchical relationships with individuals are the normal operating mode. A
memo generated by a budget analyst at the lowest level is re-written by
the Branch Chief, who passes it up next door to the Division Chief, who
then passes it up to the Director who re-drafts it and asks his Deputy to
check it. Individual jobs are specialized by function, and the functions
are traditional ones passed on from generation to generation. There is
a long enculturation period in the Budget Shop. Budget employees are
hardworking, long-term employees, staying seven to eleven years and
viewing budget work as a career. The ceremonial cycle is thin and does
not regularly validate (legitimate the value of) the work being done or
individuals in the office.

An awareness of office culture can be useful to managers facing
certain problems. The new Director of the Budget Office faced poor
morale, lack of commitment and enthusiasm for work, and a pervasive
sense of futility about their jobs and the work of the government in
general. Budget documents were routinely produced late -- after the
deadlines. People felt isolated, neglected, and undervalued.

Culture can be a sensitive key to and indicator of morale and also
gives some insight into factors contributing to the problem. Ideally, the
culture of an office should reflect its core values -- production of budget
documents and at the same time should legitimate the value of the
individuals and the work they perform. In this case there was a
disjunction - a core value that prescribed production but there was no

emotional valuing of the factors of production -the people who produced the budget and the process by which it was produced.

Events such as Christmas parties, pot luck dinners, birthday celebrations, Friday afternoon beer sessions are all part of the expressive and ritual system of the agency or workgroup, and play an important role in legitimating values.

In this budget office there was little value placed on the accomplishments of groups or employees during the yearly budget cycle. "Formulation" is an emic category for the coordination and preparation of the next fiscal year's budget; it is a time when people usually have to work overtime and on weekends, and there is a natural end point with the printed, hardcover product. This is a natural time for ceremonial affirmation of the core values of the office. Opportunities such as these to confirm organizational values exist in most organizations. The Budget Office had no ritual events for celebrating the end of a seasonal cycle, a well-done job, or status reversal and informal communication in the face of a very hierarchical system. In fact there were few ceremonies except for retirement parties; and retirement parties honor individuals retrospectively rather than applauding their contributions to the on-going production and execution of budgets.

CONCLUSION

I have sought to illustrate the layers and loci of federal organizational cultural phenomena which interdigitate organizational life in the federal executive branch.

Culture in federal organizations is both an external and an internal variable. Organizations absorb from and reflect the values and behaviors of the culture around them, but they are not simply undifferentiated extensions of American national culture. Participation in a Federal bureaucracy requires specialized cognitive knowledge, behavior and values not required by the general cultural system. Operating successfully in the bureaucratic world requires specialized knowledge and behavior about appropriate activities for survival and proper forms of interaction that are distinct from behaviors on the "outside." Bureaucratic culture develops specifically for use in the organization, and although it is derived from generalized Western culture, it is distinctive from it.

Federal organization culture is dotted with multiple cultures and multiple loci of culture. Agency culture and localized cultures exist side by side in federal bureaus. Agency culture, in which members of an organization agree on the framework of values and interests of the organization, can co-exist with more localized cultures oriented around workgroups and professional norms. They do not always support each other in the organization, and the potential for conflict exists. In addition, the intensity and content of culture at each level is a matter of empirical determination, as Gregory points out (1983).

I have often felt that we are stretching the term 'culture' by applying it wholesale to organizations and claiming that they have cultures. However, I am certain that organizations are culture-bearing milieu as Louis (1985) describes them and that some locales within the organization have more complete cultural systems than others. I have tried to demonstrate this by describing agency and workgroup cultures. From my perspective, agency or workplace culture involves more than shared values or norms -- it means common understanding about the best interests of the organization, opportunities for group interaction, shared ceremony and enculturation, organizational ideology and key organizational stories, shared symbols within the organization, and a sense of uniqueness about the work of the organization.

From my observations of culture at the federal level, it appears that culture is linked with organizational performance, but we have only begun to explore the relationship and have only rudimentary theory at this point. This is the critical empirical question for business and public management -- to understand **if** and **how** culture relates to productivity, job satisfaction and "the bottom line." I would argue that organizational culture is a critical variable, that it affects productivity, job satisfaction, and the constellation of factors that go along with it, when management is strongly people oriented. This is not to say that culture does not exist in badly managed organizations, because it can; but it is more likely to affect organizational performance in an organization which has a base of good management. I suspect culture is an intervening variable between management practices and organizational performance. Its relative importance compared to other variables such as budget reductions, political salience, Congressional and interest group pressure, etc., has not been determined but is a fruitful area for research.

Another social science and managerial dilemma is whether organizational culture can be managed and manipulated. I suspect the answer is both yes and no. The implicit part of the question is an ethical one: **should** organizational culture be changed for management purposes? Managers should understand the cultures of their organizations and how it serves needs of individuals or leads to conflict, loss of morale and productivity. But at the same time culture is not a totally deterministic system; and culture constantly changes and can be changed. Change will certainly be more informed if based on cultural knowledge. The observations of federal organization culture described here fall somewhere between the purely deterministic view of organizations in which individual or group behavior is a result of being part of a functional system, as typified by the structural functionalist theories, and the purely voluntaristic view of organizations in which CEOs or managers construct a cultural system to meet the needs of top executives or managers. The latter view is found most frequently among business consultants or public managers who look to culture as a panacea, a quick-fix for organizational woes in the tool box of consultants. Culture as described in this paper is both functional and voluntaristic in approach.

Lastly, I have tried to portray the layers and loci of federal cultures not as stratigraphic features deposited in impervious layers. Participation in executive branch culture invokes a web of identities, languages, and rule systems that are not static. Individuals are suspended in networks of pan-bureaucratic, sometimes occupational norms such as - budgeters, program analysts, and personnel specialists; at any one time an individual is also a member of an agency and office culture. An individual calls on knowledge of appropriate behavior much as in the sociolinguistic sense of communicative competence.

NOTE

1. The views in this paper are those of the author's, and do not represent the view of my employer, the National Sea Grant College Program, nor National Oceanic and Atmospheric Administration.

REFERENCES CITED

Administrative Science Quarterly
    1983   Organizational Culture. 28(3), September. Ithaca, NY: Graduate School of Business and Public Administration, Cornell University

Astley, W. Graham and Andrew H. Van de Ven
    1983   Central Perspectives and Debates in Organization Theory. *Administrative Science Quarterly* 28:245-273.

Bee, Robert
    1982   *The Politics of American Indian Policy.* Cambridge, MA: Schenkman Publishing Company

Boje, David M., Donald Fedor, and Kendrith Rowland
    1982   Myth Making: A Qualitative Step in OD Interventions. *Journal of Applied Behavioral Science*, 18(1):17-28.

Britan, Gerald
    1981   *Bureaucracy and Innovation, an Ethnography of Policy Change.* Beverly Hills: Sage.

Burrell, Gibson and Gareth Morgan
    1979   *Sociological Paradigms and Organizational Analysis.* London: Heinemann.

Chapple, Eliot and Conrad Arensberg
    1940   Measuring Human Relations: An Introduction to the Study of the Interaction of Individuals. *Genetic Psychology Monographs*, 22:3-147.

Charles, Michael T.
    1982   The Yellowstone Ranger: The Social Control and Socialization of Federal Law Enforcement Officers. *Human Organization*, 41(3):216-222.

Deal, Terrence E., and Allan Kennedy
    1982   *Corporate Cultures. The Rites and Rituals of Corporate Life.* Reading, MA: Addison-Wesley.

Gold, Kenneth A.
1982   Managing for Success: A Comparison of the Private and Public Sectors. *Public Administration Review* 568-575.

Goffman, Erving
1961   *Asylums.* Garden City, NY: Doubleday.

Gregory, Kathleen L.
1983   Native-View Paradigms: Multiple Cultures and Culture Conflicts in Organizations. *Administrative Science Quarterly* 28(3):359-376.

Harrison, Roger
1972   Understanding Your Organization's Character.   *Harvard Business Review*, May-June.

1970   Choosing the Depth of Organizational Intervention. *Journal of Applied Behavioral Science* 6(2):181-202.

Joyce, William F. and John W. Slocum, Jr.
1979   Climates in Organizations. In, Steven Kerr (ed.), *Organizational Behavior.* Columbus, OH: Grid Publishing Company, pp. 317-333.

Kauffman, Herbert
1960   *The Forest Ranger.* Baltimore: Johns Hopkins.

Louis, Meryl Reis
1985   An Investigator's Guide to Workplace Culture. **In** *Organizational Culture.* Frost, Peter J., Moore, L., Louis, M., Lundberg, C., and Martin, J. Beverly Hills, CA: Sage.

Martin, Joanne, Martha S. Feldman, Mary Jo Hatch, and
Sim B. Sitkin
1983   The Uniqueness Paradox in Organizational Stories. *Administrative Science Quarterly* 28(3):438-453.

Moore, Sally F. and Barbara Myerhoff (eds.)
1977   *Secular Ritual.* Atlantic Highlands, NJ: Humanities Press.

Moris, Jon R.
1981   The Transferability of Western Management Concepts - A Fourth World Perspective. *Development Digest*, 9(1):56-65.

Peters, Thomas J. and Robert H. Waterman, Jr.
    1982   *In Search of Excellence. Lessons from America's Best-Run Companies.* NY: Harper and Row.

Richardson, Frederick W.
    1948   *Human Relations in an Expanding Company.* New Haven: Yale Labor and Management Center.

Roberts, John   M.
    1951   Three Navaho Households: A Comparative Study of Small Group Culture. Cambridge, MA: *Papers of the Peabody Museum of American Archaeology and Ethnology,* 40:3.

Rosengren, William R.
    1984   Environmental Condition and Organizational Change: Rational vs. Natural Systems. *Human Organization* 43(1):54-60.

Schein, Edgar H.
    1985   *Organizational Culture and Leadership.* San Francisco, CA: Jossey - Bass.

Schwartz, Howard and Stanley Downs
    1980   *Matching Corporate Culture and Business Strategy.* Cambridge, MA: Management Analysis Center.

Smircich, Linda
    1983   Concepts of Culture and Organizational Analysis. *Administrative Science Quarterly* 28(3):339-358.

Starr, Paul D.
    1982   Military Socialization in the University: The Role of Subcultures in Navy-Marine ROTC. *Marine Organization,* 41(1):64-69.

Tagiuri, R. and G. Litwin
    1968   *Organizational Climate: Explorations of a Concept.* Boston: Harvard Graduate School of Business.

Taylor, Carol
    1970   *In Horizontal Orbit: Hospitals and the Cult of Efficiency.* NY: Holt, Rinehart, and Winston.

Turner, Barry
1971   *Exploring the Industrial Subculture.* London: Macmillan.

Weatherford, J. McIver
1981   *Tribes on the Hill.* NY: Rawson, Wade Publishers, Inc.

White, Orion F.
1983   Improving the Prospects for Heterodoxy in Organization Theory. A Review of Sociological Paradigms and Organizational Analysis, by Gibson Burrell and Gareth Morgan. *Administration and Society* 15(2):257-272.

Whyte, William Foote
1948   *Human Relations in the Restaurant Industry.* NY: McGraw-Hill.

1955   *Money and Motivation.* NY: Harper and Row.

Wildavsky, Aaron
1979   *The Politics of the Budgetary Process* (3rd ed.). Boston: Little, Brown.

Wilkins and Ouchie
1983   Efficient Cultures: Exploring the Relationship Between Cultures and Organizational Performance. *Administrative Science Quarterly* 28:468-81.

Wolcott, H.
1973   *The Man in the Principal's Office: An Ethnography.* NY: Holt, Rinehart, and Winston.

Woodward, Warner and Reed Nelson
1976   Witch Doctors, Messianics, Sorcerers, and OD Consultants: Parallels and Paradigms. *Organizational Dynamics.* Autumn.

CULTURE CONFLICT WITH GROWTH: CASES FROM SILICON VALLEY

Kathleen Gregory-Huddleston

INTRODUCTION

Most social scientific, and human resources analyses of work are based on a limited, rational model of work which assumes that jobs equal formal titles, work can be summarized by job descriptions, and careers consist of a series of formal job transitions, salary increases, and changes of employer. This formal model of work is powerful. It lets us compare diverse occupations and industries in terms such as labor statistics, turnover rates, and salary scales. It persists because most real jobs and careers can be at least partially described in these terms, and because such comparisons are important in our society. It can also prevent us from considering the complexities and subtleties of real work, or even from recognizing when the formal model fits poorly. We can usefully supplement external, formal perspectives by looking at insiders' perspectives on their own work and careers.

In the 1980's I conducted research on work and careers in Silicon Valley computer companies. As an anthropologist, I wondered how technical professionals themselves conceptualized the high-opportunity Silicon Valley environments and incentives portrayed in the literature. What type of shared cultural knowledge did they possess and use to navigate their careers? Although technical professionals were visible and valued participants in the Silicon Valley work world, no studies had been undertaken to systematically discover their own viewpoints about careers in the valley.

Technical professionals in Silicon Valley do not view their work and careers in traditional terms. Professionals frequently hear about jobs through the grapevine and get hired through professional connections with a rubber stamp from personnel. Real work often does not fit the job description or there hasn't been enough time or stability to develop job descriptions. Individual careers rarely correspond to the idealized career ladders described in the personnel handbook. Ladders of positions change long before anyone can scale them, and even if they exist, they do not adequately represent technical professionals' career goals.

Although Silicon Valley career conceptions do not conform to the official model, I found that a clearly patterned conceptual landscape of options and considerations is culturally shared among technical professionals. In this paper I focus on one important aspect of this cultural system--how organizational life-cycles interact with individuals work and careers and the resulting conflicts.

Many Silicon Valley high-technology companies face a dilemma. Entrepreneurial teams found start-up companies because they are attracted to the excitement, opportunity, and intimacy of a small aggressive firm, a place where "we can things can get done." But success leads to growth and a change in the company's culture and status. It's no longer a lean, mean start-up. It has become a large mature company with customers to support, products to maintain, shareholders to pacify. The larger company doesn't support or reward entrepreneurism as well as the start-up did, and thus it doesn't attract the same breed of risk-takers. New employees arrive who value security. The original team members, who made the company successful, feel as if they are being colonized by the bureaucratic large-company culture they once escaped.

I call this the cultural conflict between the pioneers (entrepreneurial individuals who explore uncharted territory) and the settlers (who come later from other "settled" places once the territory is more civilized). This conflict has confronted nearly all the currently large, successful Silicon Valley companies at some point. In this paper I will elaborate the conflict by describing Silicon Valley insiders' perspectives, or culture, about large and small-companies and examine one company as it changes through time.

CULTURAL ANALYSIS

I discovered this dilemma while conducting a broader anthropological study of work and careers in Silicon Valley during 1982-83. My goal was to understand native perspectives, or culture, about work and careers. This is a particular approach to cultural analysis (see Gregory 1983, 1984). I interviewed more than 100 technical professionals and managers, and observed in several settings over time. I especially looked at software engineers' culture, but also talked with hardware engineers, marketing professionals, and technical writers. Most of what I found is common to all these professions.

Using an in-depth, open ended approach, I asked insiders to teach me about their work-world, from their own points of view. I systematically collected descriptions of familiar situations, goals, and problems to discover the values and meanings behind their way of life. Much culture is tacit, taken for granted by those who use it as simply "the way things are." I presented my native consultants with opportunities to make their culture explicit, by teaching it to me, an outsider.

The first step in cultural analysis is to develop a concrete description of a native perspective in native terms. Native language is critical. Even though we assume we all speak the same language, special terms and specialized meanings for common terms develop within any social group and are the key to unlocking the way a people see their world. Culture develops socially, so much of it is shared among those who interact, but individuals have unique collections of culture that reflect the history of their social experiences across numerous settings. The second step in cultural analysis is to compare individual accounts and look for patterns of similarity and variation that may indicate important subcultures. We try to understand the bases of variation and the local implications of culture and its variance. Finally, we can compare a particular culture with other cultural systems, at a more abstract level. Of course the process is not linear, but recursive, and is somewhat more complex than I've indicated here.

THE SILICON VALLEY CAREER SYSTEM

Silicon Valley is the well-known, high-technology industrial concentration located just north of San Jose, CA. Over 70% of local employees are associated with high technology industry that is composed of electronics companies, research institutes, universities, industry-related services, and other organizations. The valley is characterized by rapid growth. It is also a tightly knit professional community. Organizations and individuals are interconnected in complex networks of cooperation. It is perhaps best known for the rapid emergence of new technologies and start-up companies.

To make sense of this turbulent environment, especially when considering where to work, Silicon Valley technical professionals have developed cultural typologies of kinds of companies. They particularly distinguish between large and small companies and between stable and rapidly growing companies. Newcomers to the valley pick up the typologies quickly and learn to see the valley in these terms.

The cultural concept of "company size" packages a number of criteria for technical professionals including the number of employees and dollars of revenue, but it is also associated with organizational styles and characteristic problems. At any given time, the valley offers an array of all types of options. [Over 95% of the companies in Silicon Valley employ fewer than 500 people, but the largest companies provide the bulk of the total jobs.]

According to my interviewees, large companies provide: a variety of interesting projects, opportunities to advance technically and as a manager, formal training programs, opportunities to specialize in a narrow technical area, and greater job security. They also provide important opportunities to meet many others socially and professionally, and greater fringe benefits and perquisites. Some, like Hewlett Packard have the atmosphere of college campuses. Large companies are usually well-known and their individual reputations go far beyond the large-small dimension. On the other hand, large companies are seen as bureaucratic which means they have more rules, more internal politics, require many levels of management to make decisions, and may be slower and less likely to get particular products "out the door." Reorganizations and project cancellations occur frequently.

In contrast, small companies are said to be "non-bureaucratic" which means products may get out the door with a minimum of red tape, policies are flexible and can be individualized, and individual input can make more of a difference. Smaller companies also offer employees fewer, but possibly more interesting projects; a chance to be more of a generalist; and the ability to know everyone at the company, including top managers.

Over time, technical professionals select job options that put them into the type of work environment they prefer. Some choose large companies; others choose small companies. Technical professionals commonly describe a normal career path related to company size. One usually goes to a large company immediately after school to gain technical experience and meet people, then moves to a smaller company if desired, later on. One of my interviewees, a student just about to graduate from Stanford with a Bachelor of Computer Science degree, described the advice he was given by co-workers at his part-time job:

> "The consensus was I should go to work for Hewlett Packard for a
> few years. They told me, get out of school, get your master's at
> HP, then you can go to work wherever you want to."

Company growth complicates this picture. Small companies, if successful, may become large companies, sometimes very quickly. The transition process is exciting, but can also be painful and treacherous. This is evidenced in part by company survival rates. Ninety-five percent of Silicon Valley start-up companies survive their first four years, a rate significantly above the national rate, but twenty-five percent collapse during the second four years when they fail to make the transition from start-up to mature company.

Insiders cross-cut their small-large company distinction with a growth dimension. Growth companies are said to provide internal career opportunities to be "pushed up the ladder" rapidly into newly created positions, or to "grow an organization beneath yourself." They also offer excitement and feeling of potential associated with structural change, and may offer increasing financial rewards tied to profit sharing or stock options if the company maintains its success. Growing companies are often less formally structured or described as constantly in flux. Individuals have a lot of latitude and opportunity, but if the company is too unstructured, the work environment can be unstable, even crazy. Individuals who stay near the bottom of a growing company can see levels of management grow over their heads, moving them symbolically down even though their official position is unchanged.

The ultimate growth opportunity may be found in the newly founded, start-up company. Among many of those I interviewed, working for a start-up has taken on the status of the Silicon Valley dream, and invitations to join start-ups are coveted. In a start-up, a new product must be developed and released quickly. Start-ups are perceived to be intense, high-risk, single-purpose efforts, that demand a lot of overtime from employees. They usually offer a small company's lack of bureaucracy, and in addition, an intense sense of team effort that appeals to ambitious high-talent individuals. Initial pay and benefits may be low, but potential profits through stock options are much greater than in a mature company. Mere engineers have a chance, however slim, of striking it rich when the company eventually goes public.

Silicon Valley natives use size and growth dimensions to match their interests to existing work opportunities, but those who choose start-ups or fast-growth companies, may soon find themselves working in a substantially different kind of company than the one they joined.

RAPID GROWTH AND CHANGE AT INSTEP CORPORATION

I will now describe the process of growth and cultural change in one company, looking at it from the perspectives of insiders. To maintain confidentiality, I call the company Instep. Instep Corporation grew from a small start-up with ten employees to a Fortune 500 corporation with 4000 employees and nearly a billion dollars in sales within seven years.

Instep, like many Silicon Valley companies, was founded by a few entrepreneurial engineers and marketers. Each of the founders had previously worked for a large company and become dissatisfied with red-tape, project cancellations, and limited opportunities for advancement. One of the founding engineers had tried to persuade his large-company employer to develop a product he designed, but was told it didn't fit into the current strategic direction. So the founders, who had worked together previously, quit their jobs and founded Instep to develop the product on their own.

By the end of their first year, Instep had ten employees drawn from the founders' circle of professional friends, people they could trust and had worked with successfully in the past. One early employee I interviewed described coming to Instep in those days as "taking a flyer." Start-up companies like Instep were going belly-up every week. At Instep, the start-up team worked intensively in total commitment to get their product out the door. Eighty-hour work weeks were not uncommon, but they were bolstered by the anticipation of seeing their product get into the hands of customers, and the team spirit that developed. Everyone was "on critical path." No one wanted to slip. There was no personnel department. Each new employee was hand-picked and given the idea that it was a privilege to become part of the Instep team. The pay was low, but everyone hoped the stock options would be worth a fortune if they succeeded. Impromptu parties celebrated each step toward the goal and provided occasional relief from the pressure.

During its first four years, Instep grew very rapidly but was still considered a small, innovative company within the valley. The work environment continued to be intense and devoted to developing new products. Instep's hot-shot engineers had little desire to maintain existing products beyond adding new features that had not made it into the first release, and since their products were so new, support was not the priority at Instep during the early years.

Instep did succeed, and in its third year it started gearing up to go public, which refers to offering stock on the open market to raise capital. Going public is a major rite of passage for many Silicon Valley start-ups. In preparation, the founders hired a few seasoned managers from large companies and instigated a formal human resources effort. The founders explained it was necessary to look serious and grown-up to impress the financial community and potential investors. Business suits started to appear, just one of many changes that indicated that the start-up days were ending.

At the end of its fourth year, when Instep went public, many of the early employees became overnight millionaires from the sale of their stock options. The public offering and success attracted more new employees. They "flocked in" as one described it. Early employees described the newcomers as being of a different type -- more security-seeking, less experienced -- and of Instep as having changed its character as a result of growth.

Those who came to Instep after it went public essentially joined a different company, a "large company" rather than a "start-up." The organizational structure was more clearly defined, complex, and stable. There were numerous, sometimes internally competing products rather than it being a single-purpose effort. With the growing customer base, initial products had to be supported, so maintenance programming became necessary. There was little immediate risk of failure, because as one put it, "With a company this large, it would take some time for it to fail." Stock options had been devalued by the offering -- they were now at market value.

However, to a large extent the original company lay embedded within the new one. One could, and still can, recognize "oldtimers," as they're called, by their badge numbers. All Instep employees have clip-on picture ID badges with sequentially assigned employee numbers. At Instep, numbers under 100 mean millionaires. Numbers under 1000 mean you joined when Instep was still small. New employees today are receiving badge numbers in the 8000's.

The "oldtimers," who are in their early thirties, are a recognized subgroup in the company. They share a separate culture based on knowing each other well during the intense, small start-up period and through relatively long association in an industry where two years is the average tenure at a company. Oldtimers who are wealthy, also share an interest in investing, not shared by newcomers living on salaries. Also, oldtimers share a more fully dimensioned knowledge of the founders that helps them interpret executives' behavior. To newcomers, the founders are like legends, a view the oldtimers find amusing. Finally, oldtimers share an enthusiasm for the individualistic, intense work-style that characterized Instep as a "start-up." Their values are cultural rather than individual because they were formed socially in the start-up where this workstyle was validated by their success.

CULTURAL CONFLICTS AT INSTEP

Two forms of cultural conflict are associated with the change. First, there has been a change in the dominant culture. The oldtimers have essentially been colonized by a population of "large-company" types, and suffer from having their own values and cultural knowledge now in conflict with the predominant style of work. Second, there are many one-to-one conflicts between individuals of the two different viewpoints where majority is not the main concern.

An example of the first type of conflict is oldtimers' negative reactions to the increasing number of formal policies, the growing red-tape concerning salary levels, hiring, and project scheduling, and the conservative emphasis on product maintenance. Although the founders still exercise considerable power at high levels, seasoned managers recruited from successful large companies have had a civilizing influence. Newly hired human resources professionals have instigated formal policies for hiring, and as a result, fewer individuals with "odd credentials" get in. One oldtimer complained, "It keeps getting duller and duller around here." Recently hired employees take the changes for granted, and even welcome them. In fact, they are consistent with their expectations about working for a large company.

An example of culturally based individual conflict is the conflict between systematic engineers and what are called "weekend project teams." Weekend project teams are often oldtimers who program intuitively rather than by the rules, but who, from the perspective of the systematic engineers, overestimate their abilities to successfully complete high quality projects on schedule. The following quote from one systematic engineer who joined Instep after it went public illustrates the newcomer view of weekend project types:

> In the early days there were a lot of weekend projects here. They all were problems, and some were pure junk. Of course, that's not how many people saw them. There was a certain bravado about it, especially among the executives of this company who believed the company was built on people like that, people who just cranked out magical software that did everything, and cranked it out over the weekend. The executives of this company believed where the industry really went wrong was in hiring all those professionals who actually design, who plod along like Clydesdale engineers.

Arguments about project scheduling are frequent instances of conflict between the two groups. Oldtimer managers who believe that Instep should practice entrepreneurial intensity get accused of demanding too much overtime and setting impossibly short targets for release. "There is never time to do it right, but always time to do it over," their subordinates say. "Settler" managers get flack when they ask oldtimer engineers to schedule their magic.

So, why don't oldtimers just move on to the open spaces of the next start-up? In Silicon Valley, stock options must be exercised over time, a practice that makes them golden handcuffs. Early employees would often be leaving hundreds of thousands of dollars on the table if they were to leave before their options were up. Therefore, they stay, but sometimes unhappily. There is also considerable reluctance to leave the social organization one founded. There is prestige in being an oldtimer, and some real satisfaction in interacting within the embedded oldtimer organization. There are even a few oldtimers recognized as "lifers."   "A lifer is someone who will just sit there and ride every swell," in the words on one interviewee. It's important to keep the relativity of this world in mind. These "lifers" are in their early thirties and the lifetime of the company is barely eight years, so far.

The distinction between oldtimers and newcomers is widely recognized in most successful Silicon Valley companies that have grown rapidly. In time, many oldtimers do leave. Usually, the exodus takes place when the golden handcuffs are off. Often, those who leave are the very engineers who made the company successful initially, and those who stay behind are concerned about how to harness their continued efforts.

IMPLICATIONS AND CONCLUSIONS

My purpose in presenting this case is to identify the basis of this particular form of conflict as cultural. Most studies of organizational culture have focused on static, structurally-based subcultures rather than looking at subcultures based on organizational changes through time which are particularly important in rapidly changing companies like Instep, but may occur any time an organization changes in such a way that newcomers have different values and assumptions from existing employees.

In Silicon Valley, recognizing the existence of this cultural conflict can help, but probably cannot eliminate it. In some large organizations, management has encouraged entrepreneurism and offered profit-sharing incentives and has buffered innovative engineers from red-tape trying to maintain the positive elements of the start-up days. They have had some success.   Settler-style managers and human resources professionals can become more aware of oldtimer perspectives on their rational policies, and can try to preserve informal atmospheres. To some extent, oldtimers can change their values to appreciate the new requirements of operating in a large company, and some do so. Recognition of the different work-styles and values, and appreciation for their bases in shared experience can help. Finally, new shared experienced can create new culture that can tie individuals together.

However, this conflict is more often worked out at an industry-wide level over time. Oldtimers who cannot find comfortable niches in the large company eventually leave to join small or start-up efforts elsewhere - places where their experience with a successful start-up makes them particularly valuable. The successful large company adjusts to its new role in the valley, as a secure work environment and a training ground for future entrepreneurs. It is most realistic for companies to consider their image in the valley's cultural system as a whole. Cooperative efforts between large and small companies probably have a better chance of providing large companies with the benefits of start-up style entrepreneurism than do attempts to preserve this style internally.

REFERENCES

Gregory, Kathleen L.
   1983   Native-view paradigms: multiple cultures and culture conflicts in organizations. *Administrative Science Quarterly* 28:359-376.

   1984   Signing-up: The Culture and Careers of Silicon Valley Computer People.   Ph.D. dissertation. Northwestern University Department of Anthropology, (Available through University Microfilms, Ann Arbor, Michigan #8423239).

A REGIONAL PERSPECTIVE ON THE TRANSFER OF JAPANESE MANAGEMENT PRACTICES TO THE UNITED STATES[1]

Donald D. White and Frank Rackerby

It seems like only yesterday that scholars and managers, alike, were heralding the promise of incorporating Japanese management practices in organizations throughout the United States. Today, however, a backlash of writers and researchers are claiming that cultural differences between American workers and those in Japan are likely to impede the effective transfer of these methods from one society to the other.

These views recently have been exacerbated on both sides of the Pacific by political rhetoric and the popular press. (Shapiro, 1992) This "cross-cultural bashing" continues to support beliefs that differences between our two countries, and therefore, "between our two cultures", are significant and are likely to impede the effective exchange of management practices and their underlying philosophies.[2]

This paper explores the thesis that regional subcultures exist in the United States. Furthermore, it suggests that certain regions (and therefore, subcultures) share values and attitudes that closely resemble those of Japanese workers and Japanese society in general. We will examine values that have been viewed as fundamental to Japan's industrial success and compare them to analogous modes in the United States. Specifically, we will examine concepts related to honor, family, work ethic, and military orientation to determine whether or not cultural predispositions to these factors may be similar in Japan and certain regions in the United States.

WESTERN INTEREST IN JAPANESE MANAGEMENT

Although American observers have shown an interest in Japanese management practices for nearly three decades, (Abegglen, 1956; Adams and Kobayashi, 1969; Steward, 1972) serious attention was first given to the postwar success of the Japanese during the late 1970's. A number of writers (Vogel, 1979; Ouchi, 1981; Pascale and Athos, 1981) have focused attention on Japanese management concepts, methods and techniques. Among the first to gain widespread attention, was the work of UCLA management professor, William Ouchi. Ouchi's "Theory Z" and similar models were received enthusiastically in business as well as academic circles. Writers lauded the "Japanese management style" and called for its adoption by American managers. Although some were cautious, most authors enthusiastically supported the call for change.

Recently, however, questions have been raised concerning the transferability of many of the concepts and techniques that had gained popularity. Challenges to transference typically are based on the cultural differences which purportedly exist between the two countries. Anthropologist Kenneth Ehrensal (1982), for example, concluded, "...the authority of the structures under examination resides in the traditional cultural values of the Japanese, values that typical Americans do not share." Similarly, Management professor Nan Weiner (1983) concluded that many Japanese management practices that managers in the United States find appealing are "inconsistent with the U.S. industrial culture," and that some characteristics of the approach would be totally unacceptable given the "U.S. culture". Even Ezra Vogel, whose book, *Japan as Number One*, was among the first to popularize the movement toward Japanese management practices, himself concluded, "I fear that one of the greatest dangers is the premature incorporation of Japanese patterns without adequate preparation." (Vogel, 1979)

Some comparative studies of Japanese and American management practices have drawn distinctions between the respective systems and stressed their differences (Tsurumi, 1991). Not surprisingly, these differences sometimes have been viewed as insurmountable problems that likely would inhibit the effective transfer of desirable organizational patterns from one culture to another. Such dissimilarities often are arrayed in trait lists (Flynn, 1982; Keegan, 1980) (e.g., see Figure 1).

Such models tend to reflect the extremes of behavioral continua. They are useful for highlighting gross cultural differences but may impede dialogue concerned with operationalizing cultural change.

FIGURE 1

CONTRASTS IN CULTURE, TRADITION, AND BEHAVIOR

United States	Japan
1. Individualistic	1. Collective
2. Independent	2. Dependent
3. Authoritative decision making	3. Participative decision making
4. Competitive	4. Cooperative
5. Style: Confrontation	5. Style: Compromise
6. Quick decision making	6. Slow (due to consensus) decision making but quick implementation
7. Direct	7. Indirect
8. Short-term view	8. Long-term view
9. Communications are one way and secretive	9. Communications are interactive and open
10. Efficiency oriented	10. Effectiveness oriented
11. Management is control oriented	11. Management is customer oriented
12. High job mobility and low loyalty	12. Life employment and high loyalty
13. Incompetence is fatal	13. Shame is fatal
14. Heterogeneous society: dynamic melting pot	14. Homogeneous society: graduate screening process
15. Relaxed and casual in attitude	15. Tense and formal in attitude
16. Enjoyable	16. Serious
17. Specialist is valued	17. Generalist is valued
18. Freedom and quality	18. Reliance upon order and hierarchy

Adapted from a list prepared by Chikara Higashi, World Bank

Source: Keegan, J. W., *Multinational Marketing Management*, 1980, p. 127.

Concern over the wholesale transfer of management techniques from Japan to the United States is not restricted to observers in the U.S. The Japanese generally do not claim communicability or universality for their own culture (Nagai, 1983; Howard, Shudo, and Umeshima, 1983). For example, Ishida (1981) identified problems such as group-oriented behavior, egalitarianism in performance appraisal and compensation, and informal and flexible organization, that foreign cultures may encounter when attempting to copy the Japanese employment system. In fact, American managers have been surprised to find that quality circles, perhaps the most imitated Japanese management technique have not been widely promoted by Japanese companies operating in the United States. Thus, the debate continues between those who advocate adoption of the "Japanese style" and those who reject it in part or in whole based on differences between the two host cultures.

THE QUESTION OF TRANSFERABILITY

The concept of "culture" has been loosely employed by writers in the business literature, although many fail to grasp its complexity. This complexity is perhaps best illustrated by Kroeber and Kluckhohn (1963) who catalogued 164 different definitions of the term. Each of these definitions reflect a particular theoretical orientation. However, it generally is accepted that two distinct **levels** of culture exist. (For example, see Kardiner, 1939, primary and secondary institutions; Steward, 1955, core culture; Levi-Strauss, 1963, structuralist theory; and Chomsky, 1965, linguistic models.) For our purposes, we will use the terms, "surface culture" and "deep culture" to refer to these two levels.

Surface culture is characterized by observable behavior; deep culture, on the other hand, represents a culture's deeply embedded values. The elements of surface culture, (e.g., food, clothing, work hours, seniority systems) are particularly noticeable to the casual observer, yet they are generally adaptable to change. Deep culture (e.g., attitudes toward family and authority, concepts of the soul and after life), however, is more rigid, less immutable and more resistant to change.

Cultural differences, at any level do not necessarily prevent adaptation, although, certain types of change (e.g., core values in the deep culture) may take generations to occur. We are concerned with **cultural similarities** which promote or at least are conducive to directed, purposive behavioral change. This avenue of inquiry offers greater potential for cross-cultural sharing of knowledge and practice than does the position of those who argue that the "uniqueness" of each culture prohibits effective, directed culture change.

As we have pointed out, the idea that cultural patterns can be transferred from one socio-political system to another is not new to the management literature, although questions have persisted as to whether such transfers can be accomplished successfully. Murayama (1981) suggested that "transfer characteristics" can be classified as **culture free** (those which can be transferred intact with no concern about local adaptation), **culture specific** (those which meet considerable local resistance when transferred), and **culture adaptable** (those which can be adapted when transferred). Furthermore, he concludes that certain "preconditional business settings" (business-specific environmental conditions), in particular, the business value system, must exist if an effective transfer of managerial patterns is to take place.

The concept of culture-specific characteristics, along with that of preconditional business settings, raises fundamental questions concerning the transferability of Japanese management methods and constructs. To the extent that such characteristics exist and environmental conditions are incongruous, transferability can present a significant obstacle. However, narrowing the scope of culture-specific characteristics and/or locating areas in which preconditional settings are similar should result in a less obstructed, more successful transfer of management practices. This paper focuses on the second area, preconditional settings, i.e., the environmental suprasystem within which management practices must be employed and upon which they depend.

REGIONAL SUB-CULTURES: AN ALTERNATIVE PROPOSITION

Comparative researchers have given attention to two broad generalizations that are particularly relevant to the thesis of this paper. (1) Japan is an insular nation that historically has had little interaction with other countries. Consequently, it has developed as homogeneous society. (2) The United States, in contrast is a "melting pot" and is a heterogeneous society.

The assumption that the United States, as a whole, is heterogeneous does not preclude the possibility that there are regional subcultures which themselves have homogeneous core values. (See Table 1) Moreover, the modal patterns of one or more of these subcultures may be analogous to the homogeneous nature of Japanese society and be likely to possess preconditional settings that would be conducive to the transfer of Japanese management practices.

In fact, for a number of years, American researchers have been interested in subcultural differences that exist within socio-political systems. More recently, attention has been focused on regional patterns as a basis for those differences. Rubenstein (1982) identified nine "regional states of mind". Each region consisted of a number of States with the State boundaries, themselves, defining the respective regional boundaries. Data were assembled from studies conducted by the Institute for Social Research at the University of Michigan and a survey conducted by the National Opinion Research Center to examine how people think about themselves and their lives. Six measurement scales including (1) outlook on life, (2) stress, (3) positive feelings, (4) negative feelings, (5) personal competence, and (6) overall satisfaction, were used to compare the data by region.

Garreau (1981), on the other hand, also identified nine regions but allowed conceptual, rather than geographic boundaries to define each. He concluded that the regions, "...look different, feel different, and sound different from each other, and few of their boundaries match the political lines drawn on current maps." Furthermore, he suggested that each region had a "...distinct prism through which it views the world." Figure 2 provides one example of a regionally-, rather than nationally-based, trait list.

The present paper does not confine itself to, nor align itself with, regional delineations set forth by either of these studies. Instead, it focuses on the ethos of the rural South and its parallels to Japanese society, in general.[3]

FIGURE 2

"Most Typical Traits" Most Frequently Ascribed to
"White Southerners," "White Northerners," and
"Americans," by 47 White Southern College Students

White Southerners		White Northerners		Americans	
Percentage Ascribing Trait	Trait	Percentage Ascribing Trait	Trait	Percentage Ascribing Trait	Trait
51	conservative	49	industrious	70	*materialistic
40	tradition-loving	38	*materialistic intelligent	45	intelligent industrious
30	conventional	30	progressive	32	pleasure-loving
26	courteous	23	sophisticated	30	progressive
23	generous	21	aggressive	26	ambitious
21	*intelligent	17	arrogant, loud	23	scientifically-minded
19	pleasure-loving lazy	15	rude ambitious conceited	19	imaginative aggresswive extremely nationalistic
17	kind, honest *materialitic	13	ostentatious (showy)		
15	faithful, loyal to family ties	11	alert mercenary	15	ostentatious (showy)
13	stubborn, ignornat, extremely nationalistic	9	boastful deceitful evasive efficient imaginative individualistic rdical	13	sportsman-like
				11	individualistic
9	very religious stupid, nativ straight-forward sportsmanlike shrewd			9	sophisticated gluttonous

*Attributed to both Northerners and Southerners

Source: Reed, J. S. *The Enduring South: Subcultural Persistence in Mass Society*, 1972.

THE AMERICAN RURAL SOUTH: A SEARCH FOR ANALOGIES

Notable similarities exist between Japanese society and the American rural South. First, many observers have attributed the homogeneity and enduring nature of Japanese culture to the nation's geographic location as well as the socio-political isolation brought about by xenophobic attitudes of ruling warlords during the Tokugawa period. The Southern region of the United States experienced similar isolation. Nineteenth century Southern leaders tried to prevent outside influences and controlled the spread of "foreign" ideas. Eaton (1940) referred to these efforts as an "intellectual blockade".

Second, Japan's current industrial society has its origin in a feudal, agrarian culture. Again, one region of the United States that closely parallels these conditions is the rural South. The rural South has its economic and social roots in the rigid social hierarchy of the plantation system. In an anthropological sense, cultural, similarities such as these suggest that structural parallels may exist between Japan and the rural South.[4] The balance of this paper is devoted to examining parallels in selected values, practices and institutions from both cultures. In particular, we will look at cultural similarities relative to honor, family, work ethic, and military influence.

Gimu and Giri / Southern Honor. Gimu and Giri are values of honor and obligation to nation, family, and work, which strongly influence behavior in Japanese society (Benedict, 1946). According to the Japanese scholar, Minamoto (1969), "giri" (obligation) "originates in the natural human feelings of wishing to respond to, and in some manner return, acts of kindness received from persons..." Furthermore, he distinguishes "cold" giri (acts performed out of obligation in response to social pressure) from "warm" giri which develops from emotional relationships. Sanctions against a violation of these ethics, a state of dishonor, are generally perceived as a "loss of face" (Norbeck, 1976).

Scholars have been aware of the similar characteristics in the South since the mid-nineteenth century. Olmstead (1953), referring to characteristics of the Southerner, observed that he, "...never values life or aught else more than he does his honor. This 'honor'...is often really far nobler and makes a nobler man that what **often** passes for religion in the North."

Honor, as a cultural norm, is of great value to both Southerners and the Japanese. It is ingrained in their deep cultures and also manifest in the surface cultures of both groups. Eaton (1967) observed that a:

...keen sense of personal pride and honor was, of course, not peculiar to the Southern people of the antebellum period. The Japanese, for example, have had until recently a code of conduct which exalts honor to fantastic extremes and seems to be the vestigial remains of a feudal society. The Southern sense of honor, too, had a feudal background... honor and personal pride were part of the code of a gentleman in the Old South.

And Henry Stanley (the noted African explorer), observing mid-nineteenth century business transactions in Arkansas, was amazed to see his "...fellow clerks and the plain farmers who visited the store bowing to a stern code of honor that was aristocratic in origin -- the obligation to uphold personal honor" (Eaton, 1961).

Finally, Wyatt-Brown (1982) argues that while "honor" is not exclusively a Southern phenomenon, "...in that part of the continent its tenets were more sacrosanct, more integral to the whole culture, than they were elsewhere." Furthermore, he contends that devotion to family and the subordination of all to community values are still values of honor that are paramount in the contemporary South.

Dozuku-Iemoto / Family-Clan. The term, "dozuku", generally translated into English as "clan", can be used to describe the social corporation in Japan. These ties are the traditional form of village organization in agrarian Japan. Beardsley (1959), in his classic study of village Japan, stated that Japanese sociologists have used the term "dozuku" (common kin) to define the village group, consisting of a hierarchy of households linked by kinship or fictive kinship ties. "Kinship", therefore, is not limited to blood or marriage ties. Proximity alone, sometimes is sufficient to establish a person as "kin". In fact, according to Murayama ("Over Sake!"), it is the spirit of these village kin ties and their attendant reciprocal obligations (giri) that has been transmuted into what we see today as "the corporation as family." The village community in Japan (in the past as a phenomenon and today as a value), provides an insulating cocoon that facilitates communication flow and engenders an egalitarian spirit in industry.

Hsu (1975), discussing some inadequacies of the term, dozuku, offered instead, the concept of "iemoto" as being more descriptive of the kin or fictive-kin based system of obligatory and reciprocal behavior patterns that characterize Japanese family life and Japanese business. In a test of theories underlying the Japanese "lifetime employment" system, Sullivan and Peterson (1991) concluded that "the stronger the 'ie' concept, the stronger is organizational 'benevolence' in the form of lifetime employment." In fact, both terms, dozuku and iemoto, suggest that Japanese society has values deeply rooted in family and kinship.

FIGURE 3

Japan and the Rural South: Historical Analogues

	Japan	Rural South
Socio-Political Isolation	Xenophobic attitudes of ruling war lords	Intellectual blockade by Southern leaders
Economic and Social Roots	Feudal agrarian society	Plantation system

Reischauer (1981) found that the modern family in Japan was "not very different" from that in the United States, although there generally was a stronger survival of the stem family (ie) system in Japan. He observed that the nuclear family in Japan was not as eroded as its American counterpart. "Parental authority is stronger, and family ties on a whole are closer...basically the Japanese nuclear family is reminiscent of the American nuclear family as it existed a half century or so ago." On the surface, Reischauer's conclusions would appear to be well founded. As we suggested earlier, however, comparisons between values and institutions in Japan and the United States, as a whole, may be misleading.

The plantation society of the Old South emphasized the family to a much greater degree than did the industrial society of the North. Family graveyards were a familiar sight in the South. The family altar was part of religious mores and devotion to kin was expressed in the term "kissing cousins". (Eaton, 1967) Moreover, Wyatt-Brown (1982), referring to the early settlement of Alabama, concluded that the entire state was dominated "...politically, economically, and socially by the 'cousinry'". Southerners tended to evaluate people not so much as individuals but as belonging in some manner to a family or clan. Traditionally, the family has been the predominant social unit and force in Southern culture. "In the decades after the Civil War the family was the core of southern society; within its bounds everything worthwhile took place" (Simkins 1947).

Like Japan, this emphasis on family solidarity, which characterizes the South, has its origins in the traditional values of an agrarian social system. Vance (1982) argues that this aspect of the South's social organization is most resistant to change. "The changing structure of Southern society has not undermined the importance of a family, but the institution has become more limited in function, less authoritarian in character, and less romantic in sentiments". Similarly, a lessening of importance of the extended family also has been observed in Japan.

The Southern "clan", although not strictly a clan in the anthropological sense, it nonetheless shares certain similarities with both dozuku and iemoto. In both cultures, it is important to **believe** that there is some kin tie with another individual or family, however tenuous. Once such a tie is established, feelings of affiliation and loyalty are developed toward those who are identified accordingly. Finally, both nuclear and extended families are important sources of values, particularly obligation, in Japan and the rural South.

SAMURAI SPIRIT/PROTESTANT WORK ETHIC

Writers have noted parallels between the Japanese code of honor and the Protestant work ethic. Reischauer (1981) writes:

> Many observers have noted that the emphasis on hard work, individual drive, and economic achievement, pridefully described as the "Protestant ethic" in the West, is even more characteristic of the Japanese, who have no Christianity, let alone Protestantism, in their background.

And he concludes that the roots of feudalism may have been responsible for making economic achievement a goal in itself in both cultures. Similarly, Frigstad (1980) states, "as in the U.S., Japan also has a strong work ethic, called the "Samurai Spirit", which is; similar to our Protestant Ethic. In Japan, diligence and hard work are the keys to success and social acceptance. Norbeck (1976) makes a similar observation concluding that "achievement" is one of the most highly cherished Japanese values, and Howard, et. al. (1983) concludes that achievement motivation is an important factor in Japanese productivity.

George Copeman (1974), in his commentary on Furstensberg's study of Japanese business, agrees that the feudal Samurai tradition has influenced modern industry and given a special code of behavior to managers and supervisors. He identifies several parallels between the Samurai tradition and certain Western traditions including the "North English and Scottish non-conformist small business tradition; this was later labeled in America as the Protestant Ethic.

The **Bushido** or Japan's "Warrior Code" (Musashi; 1982) is deeply imbedded in Japanese culture. Originally based on the philosophies and practices of Zen Buddhism (Reischauer; 1981), much of the contemporary ethical mores of Japanese culture are rooted in this code of honor. (Also, see F. G. Rivera, 1990.) The ethics and traditions of Protestantism are similarly uniform in the southern region of the United States. In fact, the most striking feature of religion in the rural South probably is that the region is (and has been since before the Civil War) almost monolithically Protestant. Between 1954 and 1966, 28 attitude surveys were conducted, and reported by Reed (1972); ninety percent of the Southerners interviewed during this period identified themselves as Protestant, as opposed to 60% for non-Southerners. The ethics of Protestantism, therefore, are more homogeneously embraced in the South than anywhere else in the United States.

Samurai Managers / Colonel Sanders. Sayle (1982) concludes that Japanese business journalism has perpetuated the military theme of the Samurai using such phrases as "markets are invaded and major offenses launched." Further, he observes that titles such as **bucho**, **kacho**, etc., actually were ranks used in Samurai armies of Japanese clans. Many of these clans have, today, become companies. Follath (1983), in an article entitled, "Business is War", reported that some business executives in Japan were being tested in the ancient Japanese warrior tradition. "Young Japanese businessmen are imbued with the virtues that made the Samurai famous: discipline, concentration and the will to sacrifice even to the point of suicide." Sayle concludes, "the Samurai legacy has given Japan the most dependable, diligent middle management in the world" (Sayle 1982).

Military titles are sometimes used in everyday commerce in the South as well. According to Eaton (1961), this is a reflection of earlier usage and bygone glory in Southern society. It was not uncommon by the mid-19th century for a stage driver to be addressed as "captain", an innkeeper as "colonel", and a lawyer or large plantation owner as "general".[5] Vestiges of these labels still remain in some sectors of Southern industrial settings. In a manner similar to the Japanese respect for Samurai traditions, the South also has long held military tradition and allegiance in high esteem.

FROM OBSERVATION TO EMPIRICISM

This paper sets forth a unique hypothesis concerning the transferability of Japanese management practices to the United States. We suggest that such practices, even those that may appear to be culture specific, may be transferred if preconditional settings in the recipient culture parallel or otherwise are similar to such settings in the culture of origin.

We propose that regional subcultures in the United States should be examined to determine the extent to which their homogeneous core values are similar to core values in Japanese culture. In particular, we focused on similarities between selected values and institutions of the Japanese and those existing in the rural South and found evidence to suggest similarities in certain elements of each society's deep culture.

Agrarian origins and xenophobic isolation in both societies along with notable parallels in important values like honor, family, and work ethic, suggest that regional analyses of American subcultures might contribute to the successful transfer of apparently effective Japanese management practices to certain areas in the United States.

Writers in the past have touched indirectly upon this thesis referring, for example, to Southerners as the "American Japanese" (Reed, 1972). Other evidence from historical writings and some empirical studies lend further support to the possibility of such a "Southern Connection."

Logically, the next investigatory step must include gathering and analyzing data sets which reflect regional and subcultural influences that are relevant to the effective management of human resources. One such study using Hofstede's Work-Related Values Model (White and Jensen, 1987) already has been completed and other studies are being designed. The results of this and comparable research must then be evaluated. Such inquiry should provide further insight into questions

pertaining to the transfer of management practices from Japan to the
United States and/or its regional subcultures.

FIGURE 4

Important Cultural Values: Japan and the Rural South

	Japan	Rural South
• Honor	Gimu/Giri Extreme sense of responsibility and boligation to others	Honor as a cultural norm enforced to the extreme
• Family	Dozoku/Iemoto - Reciprocal obligaitons between kin and fictive - kin Village Spirit	Family/Clan More important in South and North Core of Southern social system Southern clan may extend beyond family
• Work Ethic	Samurai Spirit Roots in feudaliam; Bushido (Warrior Code)	Protestant Work Ethnic Roots in feudaliam Southern Protestantism
• Military Influence	Samurai influence Development of early armies into companies Present day managerial titles	Presistence of military titles beyond military service

NOTES

1. The authors would like to acknowledge the suggestions and
contributions of Willard Gatewood, Chancellor and Distinguished
Professor of History, University of Arkansas, Motofusa Murayama,
Professor of Management, Chiba University, and B. B. Hendrick,
Professor of Anthropology, University of Alaska.

2. Results of a January 30, 1992 TIME/CNN Poll conducted by
Infoplan/Yankelovich International provide insight into perceptions
of Japanese and United States citizens about one-another. The
Poll suggests the need to clarify beliefs and misunderstandings that
impede intercultural cooperation.

3. The South also was the focus of another value comparison with an Asian country, Java (Peacock, 1981). We do not mean to imply in this paper that similar value matching cannot be fruitfully conducted between other regions of the United States and other parts of the world, nor that of all the world's cultures and societies only Japan and the rural South share cultural similarities. Our basic thesis remains that Japanese management concepts and techniques might best be accepted where they do not violate existing cultural mores and where the preconditional setting for such transfers is appropriate.

4. The South, itself, may be divided into "subcultures" that can be identified by unique historic and geographic factors. Presumably, Japan also can be subdivided in a similar manner. For our purposes, however, Japan is treated as a relatively homogeneous unit; our concept of the American rural South is viewed as developing out of the White dominated plantation system and is similar in scope to the concept of the "Old South" as discussed by Wyatt-Brown (1982).

5. Under the militia system of the South, officers generally were elected by their men. According to Wyatt-Brown (1982), many men, once having gained an elective title, cared little about them and promptly resigned. "But once a major or colonel, always one...making these titles especially coveted by those whose property holding might otherwise not have provided them with status."

REFERENCES

Annonymous
1991   A Gran Alliance. *Pacific Basin Quarterly*, No. 18, Summer/-Fall; 13-14.

Adams, T. E. M. and N. Kobayashi
1969   *The World of Japanese Business*. Tokyo: Kodansha International.

Abegglen, J.
1956   *Japanese Factory*. Glencoe: The Free Press.

Azumi, K., Hull, F., and R. Wharton
1989   Organization Design in Japan and America: A Preliminary Comparison (working paper), Rutgers University.

Beardsley, R., J. Hall and R. Ward
1959   *Village Japan*. Chicago: The University of Chicago Press.

Benedict, R.
1946   *The Chrysanthemum and the Sword*. New York: New American Library.

Black, M. and J. S. Reed., eds.
1981   *Perspectives on the American South*. New York: Gordon and Breach.

Chomsky, N.
1965   *Aspects of a theory of syntax*. Cambridge, Mass.: The MIT Press.

Copeman, G.
1974   *Appendix*. In F. Furstenberg, *Why the Japanese Have Been So Successful In Business*. London: Leviathian House.

Eaton, C.
1940   *Freedom of Thought in the Old South*. Durham, N.C.: Duke University Press.

Eaton, C.
1961   *The Growth of Southern Civilization -- 1790-1860.* New York: Harper and Row.

1967   *The Mind of the Old South.* Baton Rouge: Louisiana State University Press.

Ehrensal, K. N.
1983   Culture and Employee Behavior: The Japanese System. *MBA Papers of Distinction*, Vol. IV, No. 1. New York: Lubin Graduate School of Business, Pace University.

Firgstad, D. B.
1980   *A Comparative Analysis of U.S. and Japanese Management Science.* Indianapolis: Central Research Systems.

Flynn, D.
        Japanese Values and Management Processes. In S. M. Lee and G. Schwendiman (eds), *Japanese Management.* New York: Praeger Publishers, pp. 182.

Follath, E.
1984   Business is War. Hamburg: *Stern*, 1983. (reprinted in *World Press Review*, February, p. 8.).

Furstenberg, F.
1974   *Why the Japanese Have Been So Successful in Business.* London: Leviathan House.

Garreau, J.
1981   *The Nine Nations.* New York: Houghton-Mifflin.

Howard, A., Keitaro, S., and M. Umeshima
1983   Motivation and Values Among Japanese and American Managers, *Personnel Psychology*, 36(4):883-894.

Hsu, F.
1975   *Ieomoto: The Heart of Japan.* New York: John Wiley & Sons.

Ishida, H.
     1981   Japanese Employment System in Cross-Cultural Settings.
                   Paper presented at Japan-United States Business Conference,
                   Lincoln, Nebraska, October.

Jensen, T. White, D. and R. Singh
     1990   Impace of Gender. Hierarchial Position, and Leadership
                   Stypes on Work-related Values. *Journal of Business Re-
                   search* 10(2)March:145-152.

Kardiner, A.
     1939   *The Individual in His Society.* New York: Columbia
                   University Press.

Keegan, W.
     1980   *Multinational Marketing Management.* New Jersey: Prentice
                   Hall.

Keene, D.
     1976   *World Within Walls.* New York: Grove Press, Inc.

Levi-Strauss, J. C.
     1963   *Structural Anthropology.* New York: Basic Books.

Morrow, L.
     1992   "Japan in the Mind of America/America in the Mind of Japan,
                   Time, Vol. 139, No. 6, February 10, pp. 16-23.

Murayama, M.
     1973   "Kazokushugi" & "Shudanshugi" Management Approach
                   Sophia Economic Review, Vol. XIX, No. 2, 3: March, pp.
                   69-96.

Murayama, M.
     1981   Essential Characteristics for the Establishment of Japanese
                   Type Multinational Enterprises. *Soka University Review of
                   Business Administration*, Vol. 5, No. 2, Tokyo.

Musashi, M.
     1982   *The Book of Five Rings.* New York: Bantam Books.

Nagai, Y.
    1983   "In Spite Of" or "Because Of"? Japan's Success and Japanese
                Culture. *Speaking of Japan*, Vol. 4, No. 36, Tokyo, pp. 7-11.

Ouchi, W.
    1981   *Theory Z: How American Business Can Meet the Japanese
                Challenge*. Reading, Mass: Addison-Wesley.

Pascale, R. and A. Athos
    1981   *The Art of Japanese Management*. New York: Simon and
                Schuster.

Reed, J. S.
    1972   *The Enduring South: Subcultural Persistence in Mass
                Society*. Lexinton, Mass.: D.C. Heath and Co.

Reed, J. S. and D. J. Singal, eds.
    1982   *Regionalism in the South: Selected Papers of Rupert Vance*.
                Chapel Hill: The University of North Carolina Press.

Reischauer, E. O.
    1981   *The Japanese*. Cambridge: The Harvard University Press.

Rivera, F. G.
    1990   "The Way of Bushido in Community Organization Teaching,"
                Administration in Social Work, Vol. 2, No. 2, pp. 43-59.

Rubenstein, C.
    1982   Regional States of Mind. *Psychology Today*, February, pp.
                22-30.

Sayle, M.
    1982   The Yellow Peril and the Red Haired Devils.   *Harpers
                Magazine*, November.

Shapiro, Walter
    1992   "Japan Bashing on the Campaign Trail", *Time* Vol. 139, No.6,
                February 10, pp.23-24.

Simkins, F. B.
    1947   *The South: Old and New*. New York: Knopf.

Steward, J.
1972   *The Japanese.* New York: William Morrow and Company.

Sullivan, J. J. and R. B. Peterson
1991   "A Test of Theories Underlying the Japanese Lifetime Employment System", *Journal of International Business Studies*, Vol. 22, No. 1, First Quarter, pp. 82, 79-97.

Tsurumi, Yoshi
1991   "Adaptive Corporations for the Global Age, *Pacific Basin Quarterly*, No. 18, Summer/Fall, pp. 5-10, 20.

Vance, R.
1982   *Family and Work in the South.* In Reed and Singal, eds., ibid:317-335.

Vance, R.
1982   *Southern Labor Comes of Age.* In Reed and Singal, eds., ibid:301-307.

Vogel, E. F.
1979   *Japan as Number 1.* Cambridge, Mass.: Harvard University Press.

Weiner, N.
1981   Transportability of Japanese Human Resources Management Practices to the United States. *Working Paper Series 81-92.* Ohio State University College of Administrative Science.

White, D. D. and T. Jensen
1990   Redefining Cross National Comparison: The Case for Subcultural Analysis, Academy of Management National Meeting, August, 1987.

WORKING HERE IS LIKE WALKING BLINDLY INTO A DENSE FOREST

Jill Kleinberg

Quoted above are words uttered by an American who has worked for several years in a Japanese subsidiary in Los Angeles. They illustrate the pervasive feeling among the company's employees, American and Japanese, that you can never quite see your way, that circumstances are never clear or predictable.

The company is LASCO (Los Angeles Subsidiary Company, a pseudonym), and its organization-wide culture is the central focus of this study. The paper describes and explains an organization-wide culture which can be characterized as a culture of ambiguity. Ambiguity is an overarching theme which threads through several sets of commonly shared assumptions. The organization-wide culture not only recognizes various sources of ambiguity, it encompasses, to some extent, ambiguous or fragmented response to these sources.

Results of the LASCO case study are especially relevant to current concerns in organizational culture research and in comparative and cross-cultural management research. Scholars in both areas show mounting interest in the organizational implications of the meeting of cultures in the workplace, noting the virtual lack of systematic, empirical studies (Adler, Doktor & Redding, 1986; Baba, 1989; Boyacigiller & Adler, 1991). Moreover, some organizational culture scholars are rethinking prevailing conceptual frameworks which promote either the notion of a single, integrated (and integrating) organization-wide culture or the notion of clearly bounded, cohesive, and usually oppositional subcultures. An emerging conceptual framework proposes instead a broader perspective that simultaneously incorporates notions of organization-wide integration, subcultural differentiation, and organization-wide and subcultural fragmentation

(Frost, Moore, Louis, Lundberg & Martin, 1991; Martin, 1992; Martin & Meyerson, 1988; Meyerson & Martin, 1987).

The following section develops a framework for understanding the processes by which cultural integration, differentiation and fragmentation arise in this particular binational (Japanese - American) work setting. It first defines culture, then considers the relationship between societal culture and organizational culture and, finally, introduces the cultural construct of nation-specific work sketch maps. The value of the paper lies as much in its contribution toward a framework for conceptualizing and analyzing culture in this kind of binational setting as in its contribution to "local knowledge," i.e., what it is like for Americans and Japanese to work together at LASCO.

THE ANALYTICAL FRAMEWORK

A Theory of Culture

Cultural researchers, whatever their unit of analysis, variously conceptualize culture and, consequently, variously shape the research design and results. This study employs a theory of culture that draws from the tradition of cognitive anthropology (Frake, 1988; Goodenough 1961, 1981). It is concerned with discovering the acquired cultural knowledge people use to give order to their world, to interpret experience and to generate social behavior (Spradley, 1979, 1980). According to this theory, cultural knowledge is widely shared by a group of people; its configuration is distinctive to the group; and it is constructed, passed on, and reinforced among group members through social interaction. Cultural knowledge may be explicit, as in the norms and values that people consciously espouse, or it may be the tacit assumptions that many consider to be the innermost core of culture.

Culture is viewed as a dynamic process. Agar (1982:83), for instance, emphasizes that cultural knowledge "is not a framework that is mechanically applied to the world to make sense of it. Instead, it is a resource in terms of which things get done, given the historical contingencies and human purposes of the moment." Frake introduces the metaphor of "cognitive sketch map." Like Agar, he cautions that culture does not simply provide a blueprint which people acquire and learn to read; rather, it provides a set of principles to use for map making and navigation.

People are cast out into imperfectly charted, continually shifting seas of everyday life. Mapping them out is a constant process resulting not in an individual cognitive map, but in a whole chart case of rough, improvised, continually revised sketch maps (quoted in Spradley, 1979:7).

In this study of LASCO, the reconstruction of organizational culture is pieced together using conventional ethnographic techniques associated with cognitive anthropology. Data were gathered through long-term participant observation and intensive ethnographic interviews. Cultural knowledge is inferred from the verbal utterances of organizational members, from their observed behaviors, and from the material artifacts they use. A kind of content analysis known as domain analysis (Spradley, 1979, 1980) is utilized to surface cultural knowledge. Domain analysis seeks to discover (1) cultural domains -- categories of knowledge or symbolic meaning, and (2) cultural themes -- broad cognitive principles which recur in a number of domains.

Societal and Organizational Culture

In order to understand the culture of a binational organization like LASCO, it is necessary to conceptualize the relationship between societal culture and organizational culture. A set of interrelated assumptions found, with varying degrees of explicitness, in the comparative and cross-cultural management literature provides basic building blocks for an appropriate framework.

First, researchers assume that societal culture helps shape behavior in and of organizations (see, for example, Adler, 1991; Rohlen 1974; Silin, 1976). To elaborate, organizations in any country tend to evolve management ideologies and practices compatible with the values and normative patterns of social interaction characteristic of the larger society. People from different countries therefore acquire different expectations about formal and informal organzational arrangements. These expectations can be thought of as part of a generalized, nation-specific business or organizational culture (Morgan, 1986:114-120; Terpstra & David, 1985:9-10). In any specific organization, a unique culture evolves within the constraints of the generalized business or organizational culture. Enz (1986), for example, hypothesizes that in culturally homogeneous societies such as Japan there will be less cultural diversity across organizations, while diversity will be greater in culturally heterogeneous societies such as the United States.

Researchers further assume that the societal background of an organization's members influences the way they respond to organizational arrangements. In intercultural situations, when confronted with unfamiliar or unexpected circumstances, individuals' responses to the cultural gap are likely to be negative. At the least, some kind of cultural compromise or accommodation is required (Adler, 1991).

The promise of the above theoretical assumptions is yet to be realized, as many critiques of comparative and cross-cultural management research point out (see, for instance, Adler, 1983; Bhagat & McQuaid, 1982; Child, 1981; Roberts & Boyacigillar, 1984; Smircich, 1983). Our understanding of the process by which societal culture affects organizations and their members is severely handicapped by the fact that most empirical research fails adequately to define culture as a social construct. "Culture" and "nation" tend to be used synonymously; thus we find, for example, numerous cross-national comparisons of the values and attitudes of managers. (It is important to note that most research directs attention exclusively to managers.) Furthermore, the positivistic research paradigm which dominates management studies cannot capture the complexity of organizational process, relying as it does on survey research and measurement of readily quantifiable attributes or behaviors. (See Lincoln & Guba, 1985, for comparison of the positivistic and naturalistic research paradigms.)

Several studies of Japanese firms is the United States illustrate this point (Lincoln, Hanada & Olson, 1981; Lincoln, Olson & Hanada, 1978; Pascale, 1978). They rest on the premise of "cultural effect" or "Japanese effect" which holds that the Japanese managers are carriers of a unique culture and that the more Japanese employees there are in an organization, the more "Japanese" it is likely to be in its structures and practices. A standard for "Japaneseness" with regard to such conventional organizational attributes as levels of hierarchy and centralization of decision making is extrapolated from sociological and anthropological studies of Japanese companies. The statistical correlations tend to obscure relationships that ethnographic research reveals.

My own research shows, for instance, that the proportion of Japanese employees in a binational firm is less critical a factor in determining behavior in and of the organization than the relative distribution of home office Japanese and American employees among key positions in the firm. "Cultural effect," moreover, is better understood in terms of the way Japanese and American employees make sense of the binational setting -- the meaning they attach to the daily experience -- than by static measures of attitudes and organizational structures.

Consideration of organizational culture, more than anything else, helps us understand the meaning that the meeting of nations has for persons working together within the boundaries of a firm. A decidedly multi-level or multi-cultural perspective on organizational culture emerges from the study of LASCO. Although this paper mainly addresses LASCO's organization-wide culture which, to some degree, integrates Americans and Japanese, other distinct and significant cultural groupings develop around American and Japanese employees, respectively (Kleinberg, 1991), as well as around specific work groups (Kleinberg, 1992). These various cultural groupings not only intersect, but the understandings of any one are influenced by and simultaneously influence the others. In all instances, nation-specific cultural expectations that people bring to LASCO help shape the emergent organizational cultures.

Nation-Specific Work Sketch Maps

That a link exists between societal culture and the behavior of people in organizations becomes intuitively clear during prolonged fieldwork. To cite a simple example, Japanese very often are observed to communicate thoughts indirectly, or not communicate them at all, at least verbally. Americans, on the other hand, frequently verbalize their feelings of 'I think this,' or 'I want this,' sometimes so emphatically that the Japanese consider them uncomfortably ego-centered and direct. These behaviors reflect the commonly recognized contrast between Japanese implicit and American explicit communication styles (Pascale & Athos, 1981). In order to analyze the impact of societal culture on an organization, however, that culture must be represented systematically as a social construct.

In this study, the construct of nation-specific work sketch maps, akin to the generalized business or organizational culture mentioned earlier, substitutes for a necessarily unwieldly construct representing societal culture. Work sketch maps grow out of individuals' experience as members of society and members of work organizations. Compared to representations of societal culture, work sketch maps have immediacy for persons trying to get a job done. Because the construct attempts systematically to represent social categories and patterns of thinking from the natives' own perspective, they enable us to visualize concretely what happens when an employee's assumptions about work collide with those of the cultural other, or are transgressed by formal and informal organizational arrangements.

Particular Japanese and American work sketch maps have been surfaced through a pilot study broadly aimed at seeing what it is like for Americans and Japanese to work together. The pilot study centered on six Japanese owned and managed firms in the Los Angeles area, including LASCO. During a one-year study, loosely structured, open-ended interviews were conducted with at least three American and three Japanese employees in each firm. Domain analysis of the taped interviews showed significant commonality among Americans and Japanese, respectively, in how they conceptualize their job with regard to such things as title, authority, responsibility and pay and how they conceptualize the process of getting a job done (Kleinberg, 1989). The major findings are briefly summarized below.

Figure 1 partially represents the way each group organizes cultural knowledge around a broad theme that I have labelled "concept of the job." The mostly tacit assumptions or categories of cultural knowledge largely reflect parts of Japanese and American work-related sketch maps which are somehow challenged in the binational setting. These particular principles for navigating the world of work find voice because of the often intense cultural clash surrounding them. A brief comparative summary of the sketch maps follows.

Although both Japanese and Americans dwell on a theme "concept of the job," each maps it differently. Each conceives a domain of cultural knowledge "concept of position." But, within this domain, Americans stress knowing the parameters of their job and achieving what they consider to be the proper correspondence among their title, their responsibilities, their level of authority and their pay. Japanese, on the other hand, stress their relative status or positioning vis-a-vis co-workers in the parent organization.

FIGURE 1

Organization-Wide Culture

WE ARE UNIQUE*	CHANGE IS A CONSTANT	WE ARE A COMPANY DIVIDED
Attempting Something Extraordinatry	New People	"Japanese"
Japanese and Americans working together Unusual strategy	Chuzaiin Japanese visitors Local hires	Status (position, assignmetn, information, influence Relationship to the firm (pay, benefits, and independence Way of thinking
Special Challenges	Reorganization	"American"
Communication gap Cultural gap	Restructuring subdivisions Reassignment to work groups New reporting relationships	Status (position, assignment, information, influence Relationship to the firm (pay, benefits, and independence Way of thinking

*Categories of Cultureal Knowledge
- All letters capitalized = theme
- First letter of wrod capitalized = domain
- Underlined = subdomain

The Americans' concept of the job also includes the notion of a relationship between responsibility, authority and risk. Specifically, they believe that if you have responsibility for a task, you should have adequate authority to ensure that the task is done right; otherwise the risk is too great. The Japanese, in contrast, view responsibility flexibly. They expect flexibility in the formal (and informal) allocation of tasks and in the range of action taken to do a job. Moreover, they expect to take considerable responsibility for developing co-workers. The Japanese concept of the job, in addition, includes the idea of a proper adjustment between concern for one's own interests and the interests of the group, with the group welfare predominating.

The description of the binational setting which follows gives some insight into why LASCO's Japanese and American members find these particular aspects of their respective work sketch maps challenged.

THE BINATIONAL SETTING

The Organization

My particular understanding of LASCO comes from long association with the company. After completing the pilot study mentioned above, I did ethnographic research exclusively in LASCO for more than one year. Research activity included naturalistic observation, participation in every day and ceremonial activities, and informal conversations and taped interviews with organizational participants. I spent an additional year in Tokyo doing the same kind of research at the headquarters and TOSCO (Tokyo Subsidiary Company). Follow-up research was done in both Los Angeles and Tokyo.

At LASCO, I interviewed all of the managerial and professional employees, most of the secretaries, and many of the clerical and technical workers. People were asked to talk about the kinds of tasks their job entails, their interactions with co-workers, problems that arise in the course of work, how LASCO compares to other companies they have worked in, and so forth. More than 60 interviews were conducted, mainly with people who had been with the company a year or longer. With just a few exceptions, this analysis includes only respondents with at least 6 months experience at LASCO.

LASCO forms the hub of a complex web of organizational subunits which comprise the "computer peripherals group" of one of Japan's largest trading companies. The company's primary business centers on the development and distribution of its own brand-name computer peripherals. Because the trading company has no manufacturing capability, the products actually are produced by various manufacturers in Japan. Although LASCO is the wholly owned subsidiary of the trading company's American arm (TC AMERICA in Figure 2), most communication regarding the peripherals business flows between LASCO and Japan, particularly a sister subsidiary in Tokyo (TOSCO).

Overall strategy for the computer peripherals group evolves through discussion among its top subunit managers and high level executives at the Tokyo headquarters. The question of where the locus of influence will lie, nevertheless, has become an emotion-laden issue within the trading company. The tension is expressed by reference to "differences of philosophy" between "LASCO" and "Tokyo" regarding the future direction of the business group. The relationship with key manufacturers provides another source of tension, interlinked with the intra-organizational power struggle. Outgrowing their dependency on the trading company, manufacturers are beginning to give priority to other aspects of their business.

During fieldwork, in the mid 1980s, LASCO's profits were growing rapidly, as were the total number of employees -- from roughly 90 to 120. LASCO's president, who adopted the "American" name of "Matt," was a key founder of the company, and with it the trading company's peripherals business. He has been with LASCO since its establishment in the mid 1970s. Other Japanese expatriates or *chuzaiin*, persons sent from the headquarters for an assignment of normally 5 years, grew in number from 10 to 15 during fieldwork. *Chuzaiin*, all men, range in age from their early 30s to their early 50s. All have worked for the trading company since graduating from university; many have known each other through prior assignments in electronics related departments. Locally hired employees represent a wide variety of ethnic groups; some in fact are Japanese nationals. These men and women have widely divergent educational and work backgrounds. *Chuzaiin* occupy almost all of the upper and many of the middle and lower managerial positions. Some 20 local hires hold managerial or supervisory positions during the time of fieldwork. Among the highest are a vice president and several group (i.e., middle level) managers. With rare exception locally hired managers are mainstream Caucasian or Japanese-American.

FIGURE 2

The Lasco Computer Peripherals Business

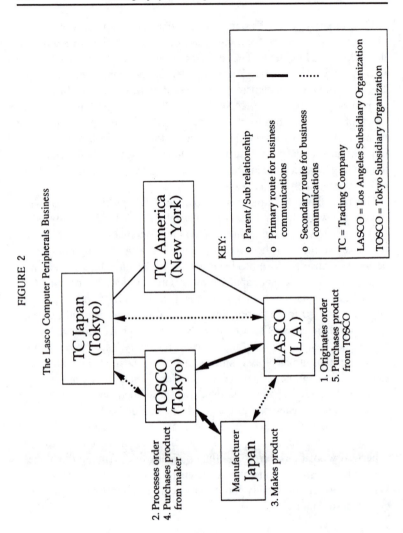

KEY:

o   Parent/Sub relationship

o   Primary route for business
    communications

o   Secondary route for business
    communications

TC = Trading Company

LASCO = Los Angeles Subsidiary Organization

TOSCO = Tokyo Subsidiary Organization

TC Japan
(Tokyo)

TC America
(New York)

TOSCO
(Tokyo)

LASCO
(L.A.)

Manufacturer
Japan

1. Originates order
5. Purchases product
   from TOSCO

2. Processes order
4. Purchases product
   from maker

3. Makes product

Japanese and Americans: Cultural Differentiation

Long before completing domain analysis of the doings and sayings of organizational members, it was obvious that the ethos of LASCO revolves around awareness of the company's Japanese - American binational and bicultural character. Even the organization-wide culture, largely shared by all of LASCO's members, predominately rests on this awareness. Before assessing the content and implications of the organization-wide culture, however, it is important to describe briefly the specifically American and Japanese cultural groupings which have emerged (Figure 3). (See Kleinberg, 1991, for more detailed discussion).

Despite diversity in their backgrounds, locally hired employees at LASCO, labeled "Americans" in a language convention of the organization-wide culture, broadly share the expectations characterized earlier as American work-related sketch maps. The assumptions about life in LASCO that also are generally shared emerge directly in response to frustrated expectations. Americans make sense of the organization mainly by mapping LASCO's differentness from U.S. organizations with which they are familiar and by mapping the limitations on their opportunities within the company. The tenor of these common assumptions is negative, containing a sense of being treated unfairly.

The theme of differentness is reflected in the domain of cultural knowledge that jobs lack anticipated clarity. This understanding proceeds from the fact that people often enter LASCO with a title but no formal job description to provide guidelines. If a formal description exists, it frequently shows little resemblance to job descriptions Americans are familiar with from past experience; moreover, it may not in fact reflect the expectations that their (Japanese) superiors have regarding the activities they should be engaging in.

The absence of clear parameters feeds into a second domain of cultural knowledge -- the understanding that the anticipated correspondence among one's title, responsibilities, authority and pay that develops through experience in a given U.S. industry also is missing. Not only do responsibilities often not match titles, but many of the local hires feel that they are given a lot of responsibility without the necessary, or proper, authority. Frequently too, they are given a higher title and/or increased responsibility without a commensurate raise in salary. Lack of clarity about responsibility and authority can cause considerable anxiety for Americans, especially managers, given their notion of the relationship between responsibility, authority and risk (Figure 1).

FIGURE 3

Major Subgroup Cultures

"American"	

LASCO IS DIFFERENT*
   Jobs Lack Clarity
   No Correspondence
      Title, Duties,
      Authority and Pay
	LIMITED OPPORTUNITY
	   No Career Path
	   Ceiling on Advancement
	   Shut Out of Information Flow
	      and Decision Making

"Japanese"	

LASCO INSEPARABLE FROM
TRADING COMPANY
   LASCO Strategy Part of
      Peripherals Group
      Strategy
	MANAGING LASCO
	   Americans Are A Problem
	   <u>Inflexibility</u>
	   <u>Narrow interpretation of</u>
	      <u>responsibility</u>
	   <u>Concern for power and</u>
	      <u>money</u>
	   <u>Self-interest above group</u>
	      <u>welfare</u>

Competition for Control of Business Group	Structure Reflects Strategic Goals and Individual Capability <u>Reorganize whenever</u> <u>appropriate</u> <u>Japanese most capable of</u> <u>strategic management</u> <u>Separate Japanese and</u> <u>Americans</u>

Career and Personal Identity
   Tied to LASCO
   How to Succeed at LASCO
      Please both Matt and Tokyo
      Get job done
      Avoid mistakes	

*Categories of Cultural Knowledge
- All letters capitalized = theme
- First letter of word capitalized = domain
- Underlined = subdomain
- Italics = subsubdomain

The theme of limited opportunity threads through several domains of cultural knowledge. The perceived absence of an internal career path is one. Indeed, the formal structure of the company does not provide a predictable job sequence. Frequent reorganization, a phenomenon which receives more attention later, further obscures a sense of path. Americans secondly perceive a consciously placed ceiling on their advancement opportunities. Top level jobs, in their opinion, are reserved for *chuzaiin*. A final domain of cultural knowledge revolves around Americans' lack influence: they perceive themselves to be shut out of the flow of information and the process of decision making.

Chuzaiin, or "Japanese" cultural assumptions cover a much broader range than those of the Americans. More than the organization-wide culture and certainly more than the American subgroup culture, they encompass articulated organizational goals and specific notions about how to achieve them.

The notion that LASCO is inextricably linked to the trading company constitutes a major theme. *Chuzaiin* are aware that LASCO's strategy is part of the computer peripherals group strategy. They also are cognizant that LASCO is enmeshed in a struggle for control of this business group. Thirdly, *chuzaiin* live with the knowledge that succeeding or failing at LASCO has ramifications for their place in the trading company organization in which they anticipate a long-term career and from which, in large part, they derive their sense of personal identity. How to succeed at LASCO, therefore, represents an important subdomain in the sketch map regarding career and personal identity. It necessitates somehow pleasing both Matt and Tokyo, making profits and getting new business, and avoiding any big mistakes.

One kind of mistake to avoid is trouble with American employees. A second theme, which centers on how to manage LASCO, encompasses the domain of cultural knowledge that Americans are a problem. Problem areas include their perceived inflexibility with regard to responsibility and their inordinate concern with their own self interest, often focused on authority and money.

The sketch map for managing LASCO, in addition to marking the above pitfalls, includes the notion that organizational structure should reflect the strategic goals of the company and the individual capability of organizational members. Periodic reorganizations are seen as one sub-set of this domain of cultural knowledge. So too is the idea that the Japanese are most capable of strategic management, because only they have the requisite (Japanese) language skills and knowledge of both the trading company and the generalized Japanese business cultures. Another sub-set of the assumption regarding structure and individual capability is that, ideally, Japanese and Americans should be separated as much as possible. Many *chuzaiin* agree with Matt's personal philosophy that "in order to control Americans, you have to be American." All understand that one future goal is to make LASCO a holding company, with most *chuzaiin* located there, and for U.S.-oriented line functions to be centered in subsidiaries mainly managed by Americans.

Cultural Perspectives on Ambiguity

The overview of the binational setting demonstrates that LASCO's members confront many ambiguities in their work. Feldman's (1991:146) definition of ambiguity guides this analysis of the subject:

> Ambiguity occurs when there is no clear interpretation of a phenomenon or set of events. It is different from uncertainty in that it cannot be clarified by gathering more facts.

There are several broad sources of ambiguity. One lies in the very fact that Japanese and Americans work together. Because of divergence in their work sketch maps, a clear and common interpretation of many situations and events cannot be achieved; the basis for respective perception and judgement is too different. Uneven power relations between the two demographic groups exacerbate resulting ambiguity. Additional sources include uneasy relations among players in the trading company's computer peripherals business as well as the structure of the computer peripherals industry. Trading company politics, in the context of ever-changing market forces, drive the pattern of complex and unpredictable strategic decision making and the disruptive phenomenon of reorganization characteristic of LASCO.

Americans and Japanese do not necessarily see ambiguity in the same way however. As Feldman (1991:146) notes, "the meaning of ambiguity is not the same as the ambiguity itself." This has important implications for organizational culture.

> The meaning may vary from person to person and from setting to setting...The meaning of ambiguity for any individual is complex and

influenced by historical, biographical and sociological factors. To the extent that reactions to ambiguity are common among members of the organization, the interpretation may indicate a collective understanding about ambiguity and its effects. This collective understanding is a part of the culture of that organization (Feldman, 1991:146).

Differing collective interpretations of organizational ambiguity help differentiate American and Japanese subcultural groupings. Americans' common concern with ambiguity about the parameters of their job, for example, notably contrasts with Japanese absence of concern. The Japanese recognize some ambiguity regarding who is responsible for what, but have a high degree of tolerance. In fact, they often consider such ambiguity an organizational strength. Furthermore, among themselves, the Japanese are far more certain of what is expected of them than are the Americans.

Where Feldman, above, speaks of culture in terms of collective understandings of ambiguity, she and other researchers simultaneously recognize a variant relationship between culture and consensus. A "fragmentation" perspective, according to Martin (1992:362),

> reconceptualizes consensus in a manner which acknowledges that cultural members sometimes change their views from moment to moment, as new issues come into focus, different people and tasks become salient, and new information becomes available. Group identities (such as gender, race or job classification) do not form stable subcultures in a Fragmentation study. Instead multiple interpretations and reactions are always possible.

In the same vein, Meyerson(1991:131-132), argues that:

> for at least some cultures, to dismiss the ambiguities in favor of strictly what is clear and shared is to exclude some of the most central aspects of members' cultural experience and to ignore the essence of their cultural community.

The following section examines the impact of ambiguity on LASCO's organization-wide culture. Despite the existence of clear subgroup differentiation, at the organization-wide level LASCO's members are bound by what Feldman (1991:154) describes as a "common frame of reference or a shared recognition of relevant issues."

A number of questions inform the analysis.   In what areas do Americans and Japanese conceptualize similar points of ambiguity? Do they map the meaning of such ambiguities in the same way? Are there, perhaps, ambiguous responses to ambiguity -- does consensus fail to coalesce on an organization-wide, or even subgroup basis, except in transient, issue-specific ways (Frost, et al., 1991: 115)? Are there shared principles or understandings that have nothing to do with organizational ambiguity? To what extent do any shared understandings integrate the two groups, in terms of fostering unity or achieving other organizational goals? The concluding section returns to these questions.

The Common Frame of Reference

Three broad themes organize a frame of reference which most LASCO employees, regardless of national origin, share (Figure 4). The following paragraphs examine the shape and texture of each theme, paying particular attention to how these meanings are socially constructed.

We Are Unique

Time and again one hears LASCO's members assert that it is a "unique" company. Its uniqueness revolves around two interrelated domains of cultural knowledge: that the company is attempting something extra-ordinary and the special challenges presented by this fact.

Attempting something extra-ordinary is mapped first of all by cognizance that Japanese and Americans are working together; this fact engenders the expectation of an unusual situation because of differences between the two.   LASCO's members begin to formulate this understanding from earliest contact with the firm. Potential local hires first encounter the Personnel Manager or her assistant. Either way, discussion with the personnel specialists reveals that LASCO is a "Japanese" company and that working here will not be like working in an American firm. Seeing the mix of Oriental and non-Oriental faces, and hearing Japanese and English spoken as they make their way through the halls, visually impresses new hires with the company's binationality.

New *chuzaiin* have an even keener awareness. Almost any trading company employee sent on an extended assignment to the U.S. is likely to "study" on his own about the host country and its business practices. While doing fieldwork in LASCO's sister subsidiary in Tokyo, several times I observed the preparations of a young men for upcoming assignment to LASCO -- for each, his first *chuzaiin* experience. Friends gathered around their outward bound colleague's desk, poring over a book of English-language names in an effort to find just the right name for him. Having an American name was considered the first step toward success in working together with Americans.

Longer association with LASCO allows people to elaborate on the meaning of the company's uniqueness. The extra-ordinary that LASCO is attempting comes to be defined in part by the company's unique strategy. Almost every employee of several months duration has some sense that the company is unusual in the way it pursues its business. This is something the president, Matt, talks about on ceremonial occasions. He enjoys chronicling the history of LASCO and the computer peripherals business, stressing how innovative it is for a trading company to market its own brand-name product. But speeches on such occasions illustrate that business strategy for Matt encompasses a whole philosophy of management.

FIGURE 4

Sketch Maps Regarding CONCEPT OF THE JOB*

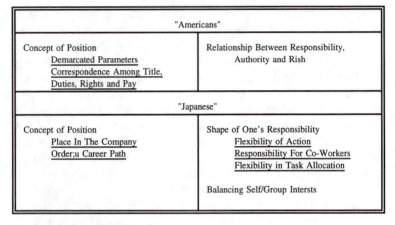

*Categories of Cultural Knowledge
- All letters capitalized = theme
- First letter of word capitalized = domain
- Underlined = subdomain

At the opening ceremony for a newly established subsidiary to handle LASCO's video terminal business, after an historical overview, Matt expands on LASCO'S uniqueness. I quote at length in order to convey the flavor of the official interpretation Matt presents.

> Our operation is very unique way of the operation. There are other Japanese trading companies or electronics companies that have branch or have subsidiaries in the U.S. in order to expand their business. Our philosophy or our way of business quite different from those other people's.
>
> In order to succeed the business in the U.S., we have to combine American way of operation or management with Japanese way of management and operation. That was a key challenge for me from the beginning -- how to hybrid those two good points. First 10 years I tried very hard and established this very unique operation called LASCO. Unfortunately, still, within the LASCO, I could not accomplish this hybrid for 100 percent. In order to, for more expansion, we established one subsidiary and your sister company,

LASCO SYSTEMS (a company which develops and markets computer systems). That is our first venture for getting all American way of operation applied within the Japanese corporation.

Another trial [i.e., experiment] is this new video terminals subsidiary...My basic philosophy for operation of this corporation is the teamwork. Sales department should not be individual. Marketing group should not be individual group. Administration should not be individual group...We would like to apply good point of Japanese way, not only in the management (e.g., teamwork philosophy), but also the product quality, high production capacity, low price. And we like to apply the way of the sales know-how from the American side.

Then, my goal is, not for the short term. This is the way of the Japanese management -- as I said, TC JAPAN business is over 140 years. This [video terminals] company also should be aiming for 100 years reign. In order to do so, everyone's cooperation and loyalty to the corporation very very important.

Members widely vary in their understanding of LASCO's business strategy and official management philosophy. *Chuzaiin* are very knowledgeable about the structure of the daily business as well as the philosophy regarding longevity, teamwork and, something only implicitly acknowledged in the speech quoted above, Matt's goal eventually to separate Americans and Japanese by making LASCO a Japanese run holding company with most of the line action occuring in (mainly) American run subsidiaries. Americans who are most knowledgeable about business strategy are those (male) managers in key business groups whose work brings them into frequent contact with Japan. As distance from the line action grows, the understanding becomes vaguer. I found no evidence that have formulated a clear idea of LASCO's official management philosophy beyond the fact that it emphasizes a (to them) vague notion of combining Japanese and American approaches.

One American manager in the middle of the action provides a partial explanation of the business strategy which gives some intimation of its complexities.

What the company is doing is unique -- putting out a product with no manufacturing capacity. The process you go through to get that

product is unique -- the way we have to do business, the guidelines
we work under.

Another American gives more insight into how difficult the
business is to master as well as the inherent ambiguities. The context
is a group sales meeting at which the possibility of bringing in a
National Sales Manager from outside is debated.

> I think if you bring in someone as National Sales Manager, one of
> the major problems is that we are a unique operating set up. We
> have TC JAPAN, PEC (the manufacturer), and LASCO, and we
> have a philosophy in all of these places. It takes an average person
> 2 to 3 years to understand the real philosophy. So, we bring a man
> on board and all of a sudden he's thrown into this arena, shall we
> say, and he, he's trying to do a good job. But the problem is he
> doesn't understand all of the factors that are involved.

Understanding the (ever changing) philosophy of the business is
complicated for this American by his need to communicate directly with
Japan. His words lead into discussion of what are frequently referred
to as the "special challenges" of the unque work setting. People map
this domain of cultural knowledge in terms of two different yet
overlapping categories of challenges, represented by the terms
"communication gap" and "cultural gap."

A communication problem might refer to situations where there is
difficulty achieving a mutually satisfactory exchange of messages in
English. Such situations occur countless times a day. One illustration
is when Japanese technicians from the manufacturer of a new product
visited to train LASCO's American technicians how to repair a defect.
I observed a long session in which communication proceeded through
demonstration, hand gestures and chalkboard diagrams. Watching it, I
thought the session had been successful, but when the Japanese
technicians left, the Americans rolled their eyes in mock despair.
   Some *chuzaiin* (and Americans) have better English or better
language skills than others. All the *chuzaiin*, nonetheless, make
mistakes in words and syntax and in interpreting the Americans'
meaning. An American, in describing the problems a new co-worker
is having communicating with their Japanese boss, shows that the
difficulties can be overcome.

When he [the new American co-worker] first started, he didn't understand the communication -- I don't want to call it problem, but the little bit of a gap that you can run into in communicating with someone that is even as good as [the Japanese boss] is in language...

And he [the Japanese boss] has now gone to the extreme where he will admit to me that he doesn't understand what I've said. To me, that's a major accomplishment. Originally he wouldn't do that. He would just say, "No way. We won't discuss. That's it. End of discussion." Because he was at the point where he was lost; he didn't understand what I was saying.

[The new co-worker] hasn't developed his approach yet...on how to insure that his idea gets to [the boss] and how to interpret what [the boss] is saying back to him.

Usually, but not always, both Americans and *chuzaiin* treat such communication problems with equanimity. People can even have fun with the language gap. Many times, for instance, I observed the animated repartee as Americans initiate a novice into the mysteries of American slang, scatalogical and otherwise. The difficulty *chuzaiin* have using English, however, is one cause of the American's understanding that they are outside the flow of information. Many *chuzaiin* consciously or unconsciously choose not to make the effort to communicate.

Communication problems often result as much from fundamental differences in ways of thinking as from language problems. Thus, as a category of cultural knowledge, communication gap flows into that of cultural gap. Cultural gap especially encompasses the countless times the cultural other says or does something that is perceived as strange, incompetent or offensive because it transgresses one's own notion of "common sense" or propriety. The challenge of the cultural gap rarely is accepted with equanimity. Pressures generated by the need to get the job done are too strong. A common response when basic cultural assumptions are violated is moral indignation. The specific meaning that the notion of culture gap has for any individual nevertheless depends on his or her particular intercultural experiences.

A case where a Japanese group manager feels that basic principles of work are violated by an American subordinate's relentless drive to clearly define, and expand, his duties and authority illustrates the phenomenon of cultural gap. The American feels he was merely trying to properly align his responsibilities, authority and title of Product Marketing Manager (see Kleinberg, 1989, 1991 for more detail). The Japanese manager interprets the situation differently.

> Judging from experience, I see his character better. He is into a political issue, to sell his name rather than doing the dirty job...He has a unique personality. It is hard to adjust himself to the organization, yet he has a strong inside ambition to be regarded as a big shot...He submitted me a proposal to expand **his** group, the marketing group. He always spends more time on expanding his own responsibilities than on doing the job.

This particular Japanese manager is considered more direct in his communication than most *chuzaiin*, and he says he discussed the situation with the American subordinate several times before he felt compelled to fire him. According to the president's executive assistant, an American who is a LASCO oldtimer, a major point of cultural gap is the Japanese reluctance to communicate certain things, particularly negative feelings, that Americans believe should be communicated. This reticence goes beyond the inconvenience of speaking English. It stems from a conception of the kinds of things one does or does not directly discuss with work subordinates, and is guided by normative patterns of social interaction at the societal level. The executive assistant says:

> That's one of the biggest problems. They don't talk to you beforehand about things, like the salary. It's the same thing when they're unhappy with you. They don't tell you. I've tried to tell them that if they don't say they're not happy, people will go on doing what they are, thinking they are doing a good job. Just make your feelings known...At least Matt will tell me if he's unhappy with Kelly (a secretary), but he never would tell me if he's unhappy with **me**. They never sit down and discuss things, not even salary.

Advice from his executive assistant, and other experiences, have made some impression on Matt, although the insights are not translated systematically into management practice. Matt expounds on the "problems" of managing across cultures when addressing a gathering of academicians and business practitioners. One problem is the Japanese failure to say or do the expected:

In the case of the American staff working with Japanese management, Japanese executives normally do not say "Your job is great,
your job is perfect, you did quite a good job." These words are
very difficult for Japanese to voice, even if they are true. First of
all, Japanese should make every effort to speak out on these
occasions. On the other hand, Americans should take into
consideration this inherent Japanese nature.

The sketch map for working in the binational, therefore, includes
unpredictable obstacles and pitfalls caused by the very things that make
LASCO unique. Those challenges that grow out of the cultural gap, in
particular, articulate with components of the American and Japanese
subgroup cultures.

Change is a Constant

LASCO's members see their world as one in constant flux. The
theme that change is a constant crystallizes in two domains: "new
people" and "reorganization."

Not only do LASCO's members deal with the arrival and
departure of *chuzaiin*, they also host numerous Japanese visitors -- from
the headquarters, from other subunits of the peripherals group, and from
manufacturers. In addition, they must incorporate the many new local
hires that replace leave-takers and accompany the expansion of
LASCO's business. As a social construct, "new people" implies the
frequent renegotiation of work relationships. Beyond this, however,
there is little consensus binding both Americans and Japanese in the
meaning they attach to these three categories of new people.

For *chuzaiin* already at LASCO, an addition to their numbers is
viewed as a compatriot, an ascribed member of an in-group. The new
arrival is welcomed with an all-*chuzaiin* get-acquainted lunch and/or
dinner. He is included in after hours socializing, the weekly evening of
mahjong, and weekend golf and tennis. His family are included in the
various family-oriented get togethers of LASCO's *chuzaiin*.

As a group, *chuzaiin* are seen as impermanent, in the Japanese and
American mind alike. Americans, however, think of a new *chuzaiin*
arrival as "another one of them," the elusive Japanese who dominate the
company. Or, if the new person is to be one's boss, he is viewed as
cause for immediate concern and perhaps resentment over the
adjustments his presence requires.

Japanese visitors, for most American employees, represent another symbol of the fact that LASCO is a Japanese company, and that there exists a complex set of Japan connections that few Americans comprehend. Nevertheless, for some Americans, these visitors signify important contact with business associates in Japan. The American eagerly awaits the arrival of a man who, until first meeting, has been merely a name at the bottom of myriad telexes from TOSCO. Such visits forge friendly relations that can be personally satisfying to both Americans and Japanese. On such occasions, the work group provides the focus for a good deal of socializing among Japanese and Americans.

Chuzaiin view Japanese visitors in terms of the web of reciprocal obligation that governs relations within and between organizations in Japan. They talk about "taking care" of visitors, and carefully plan who will pick the person up at the airport and who among the *chuzaiin* will attend lunches, dinners, and golf or tennis outings. The combination of events and persons in attendance varies according to the relative place of the visitor in the Japanese organizational context. Japanese visitors represent several kinds of opportunities for *chuzaiin*: to conduct business; to maintain one's visibility in the larger trading company organization; and to socialize, sometimes with very close friends. Many Americans view new local hires as potential friends on and off the job. These are people they may eat lunch with or go with to a bar on a Friday night. Both Japanese and Americans perceive the heavy local hiring observed during fieldwork as a sign of restructuring to come. Americans in personnel functions and in the work groups receiving the bulk of new people, furthermore, tend to see them as a symbol of organizational chaos. The Personnel Manager at one point commented that "I don't know who these people are. We didn't have anything to do with hiring them." And, indeed, some of the hiring does skirt the formal procedure set up by the personnel specialists. Out in the business groups, Americans often respond to the situation with statements such as, "We don't know what's going on here. If you figure it out, tell me." The rapid influx of new people leaves many ineffectively integrated into LASCO's work life.

"Reorganization" means the possibility of any of the following to LASCO's members: (1) restructuring and renaming of organizational subdivisions, (2) reassigning individuals to work groups, and (3) realigning individual responsibilities and reporting relationships. Roughly every 6 to 12 months from 1983 through 1987 the process of reorganization has repeated itself. If not anticipating an upcoming reorganization, people are still adjusting to the last.

The frequent reorganizations are a primary source of ambiguity for both Americans and Japanese. This is partly because rumor of reorganization, normally, long precedes the actual fact. Moreover, information proves peculiarly elusive. The comments of the Personnel Manager two months before one particular reorganization transpired give a sense of the elusiveness. The exchange takes place in December, in the midst of rumors that part of LASCO will be splitting off to a new location.

Personnel Manager:
> Nothing is announced yet about the reorganization of course. I guess Components, Marketing and Printer [Groups] are being combined. I heard it from Ken Sasaki (*chuzaiin* head of Printer Group). It looks like we're staying here though. We renewed the lease til June, 86. Terry Shimizu (*chuzaiin* head of Administration Group) told me...

Ethnographer:
> When does this become official?

Personnel Manager:
> Supposedly after the first of the year.

Ethnographer:
> Is it general knowledge already?

Personnel Manager:
> I believe that all the people involved in the transfers are aware, but I don't know for sure...A lot of these changes just happened though, I can tell. I think their budgets were supposed to be done last week. A lot of people who are Group Managers involved in the changes are coming to me now, to resubmit budgets. That's why I think a lot of it is new...It's awful when people (American employees) come to me. They assume I know and I don't...I don't feel I should be involved in the business structure of the company, but

when it comes to moving people around from one type of position to another, I feel I have valuable input.

One oldtimer's perspective on the phenomenon is widely shared by the Americans, except that he is more optimistic than most about the reasons for and the positive outcome of the changes. The way reorganization is handled makes it difficult to know where you stand in the eyes of your (Japanese) superiors.

> Since I've been here, about every 6 months they do a, I don't know if you call it reorganization, but it is an "adjustment," because they may not make a total reorganization per se, but they do adjust to problems, or whatever, in the area...The end result of the changes is positive -- they are well thought out. But the method, the way the changes are handled is difficult...It's just that the people themselves are never given explanations for why those changes are being done. That makes it difficult to adjust to them...The problem is, you don't know where you fit in, so, consequently, you don't know if you're looked at positive or negative because of the change.

Some Americans resent the discombobulation more than others. The manager quoted above is relatively uncomplaining, emphasizing the logic of the moves. Of course, the timing of a conversation makes a difference. A woman just informed by someone other than her boss that she will be moved to another group in an impending reorganization has this to say: "We're not animals, to be moved around at someone's whim. They [the Japanese] see nothing wrong with this."

Beyond the shared framework emphasizing readjustments in work relationships, reorganization holds very different meaning for *chuzaiin* than for Americans. It fits with their assumption that organizational structure should reflect the needs of the business and the particular capabilities of individuals. Periodic, and unpredictable, reassignment is common practice within the trading company. The ambiguities which trouble Americans -- the long wait, continual revision of "information" regarding organizational changes, and chronic lack of clarity about one's position do not frustrate them as much. This is illustrated by a conversation with a *chuzaiin* whose role over the past year has been liaison between LASCO and the systems subsidiary. The conversation, in addition, gives insight into the cultural assumptions which guide perceptions of capability or eligibility for particular jobs. He calmly relates that:

> My title [in this systems subsidiary] is pending. It is difficult to determine my role. Originally I was Operations Manager. That title covers broad things...That should be done by an American. It is more efficient. So I gave that title to an American. In one sense, I am assistant to the [American] Executive Vice President, a kind of "staff"...
>
> My new role, if I have more talent, I think I should be President...This is a possibility. Now Matt is President. But he will return to Japan sometime. At that time, there will be a new President of LASCO and [the systems subsidiary]. If we expand sales, it might be impossible for him to manage both -- then we need a new President for [the systems subsidiary]...But maybe from the Japanese culture standpoint, the next one should be an older guy [than me]. That is Japanese. We respect human relations.

Chuzaiin assume that the form reorganization takes ultimately is Matt's decision. Depending on their personality and link to Matt, they nevertheless seek to influence events. Americans assume only that the Japanese make reorganization decisions. Apart from active brokering in rumor, their understanding prompts them to wait for the announcement and then passively, though not necessarily uncomplainingly, accept the changes. The new organization chart, distributed to all employees on the day the new structure is announced, symbolizes this process which occupies so much of people's thoughts.

We Are A Company Divided

The theme "we are a company divided" reflects understandings that emerge, for many, as a result of often frustrating intercultural experiences and/or bitter disappointments. Persons whose work entails little cross-cultural interaction arrive at a similar understanding through their observations of and conversations with co-workers.

The terms "Japanese (*Nihonjin*)" and "American (*Amerikajin*)" represent the domains of cultural knowledge that reflect this theme. In peoples' minds they stand in inexorable opposition. Being "Japanese," furthermore, is not just a matter of national or cultural identity. Official company documents count the several employees of Japanese national origin who were hired directly by LASCO among the "American staff," along with other locally hired personnel. Only the *chuzaiin*" count as "Japanese staff." Being "Japanese" indicates full membership in the trading company of which LASCO is one important subunit.

It is true that Americans sometimes conceptualize the distinction less rigidly. For example, one lower level manager who is ethnic Chinese but who grew up in Japan often is lumped with the *chuzaiin* by secretaries in his work group. They hear him speaking Japanese with the group manager and observe him going to lunch or dinner with the *chuzaiin*. Moreover, the way he relates to the secretaries -- giving them work "without a please or thank you," is considered "Japanese." *Chuzaiin*, in fact, bestow quasi-in-group status on certain locally hired personnel who are linguistically and culturally Japanese. Nevertheless, they experience no ambiguity concerning the official "Japanese"/"American" dichotomy.

Chuzaiin, however, make distinctions among themselves. This first became clear when a *chuzaiin* was listing his compatriots who would comprise a new Corporate Planning Group to be located in an isolated suite which jokingly came to be called "Japanese Village." He said, looking somewhat sheepish afterwards, "They're a little different from us anyway. It's like they work for Tokyo." Although the trading company ideology fosters unity or oneness, identity and standing at LASCO are determined partly by whether one hails from a support area such as Personnel or General Affairs or from a business area. Matt and most of the men in line positions at LASCO come from the Information Systems Group and most have long been involved in the computer peripherals business. The "Tokyo" referred to means the administrative divisions of the trading company.

Being Japanese or American means, first of all, respective differences in status; that is, differences in a person's formal position, work assignment, access to information and influence. Secondly, it means respective differences in a person's relationship to the firm -- in such areas as pay, benefits, and the degree of independence one has (or feels). Finally, it means different ways of thinking. While the shared culture recognizes and, very broadly, characterizes these categories around which Japanese and Americans are differentiated, once again, the details that fill in the sketch maps reflect subgroup membership and individual experience.

Both Americans and Japanese assume that the Japanese control key positions and information, and make the critical decisions. This general understanding regarding differential status reciprocally proceeds from and guides cultural behavior. *Chuzaiin* oversee the most profitable product groups as well as the administation and corportate planning groups. Matt's office is a focal point for the exchange of information and deliberation; exclusively Japanese meetings take place here almost daily, meetings certain American managers under "normal" circumstances would expect to attend. All Japanese discussions, in fact, occur throughout the day. At lunch time *chuzaiin* usually head for a nearby Japanese restaurant and, at the end of the official work day, they remain to work, read the Japanese newspapers, and chat. Americans make remarks like, "They [the Japanese] decide everything after everyone else has gone home."

As the discussion of reorganization indicates, however, the way Japanese and Americans understand decision making diverges in its specificity. Most Americans consider decision making as monolithically "Japanese." Only a few "know" what all the *chuzaiin* know: that Matt, often unilaterally, makes the important internal decisions. In the words of one *chuzaiin*, "He wants to control *anything*. Even the room allocation of LASCO, Matt did by himself. Even the Vice President of Administration didn't make the decision." It is one general criticism they make of their boss. The Executive Vice President of the systems subsidiary, an American who has worked closely with Matt, jokes about "Japanese - American democracy," where "everyone gives his opinion and then Matt comes in and makes the decision."

Both Americans and Japanese conceptualize the relationship between the individual employee and the firm as much more encompassing for *chuzaiin*. Americans generally have the idea that *chuzaiin* are life-long employees of the trading company and that their salary and benefits are different from those of Americ. Generally they perceive *chuzaiin* salary and benefits as better.

A former member of TC JAPAN, now working at LASCO as a local employee, confirms that part, but only part of the American interpretation of pay differences matches the Japanese reality. The following excerpt from an interview, just as importantly, demonstrates that in his mind the two groups are indeed distinct.

> There is a clear-cut line between the two groups. First of all, the pay system is completely different. Ellen (the Personnel Manager,

an American) can't do anything. This is the untouchable part...The amount of [*chuzaiin*] pay is linked directly to [trading company] pay policy...When I quit [the trading company], and was rehired by LASCO, my pay dropped substantially...If I had the American philosophy, I might argue with the company. But I know the Japanese way, so I never said anything...Then [later], my pay was going up almost constantly. The Japanese pay freezed almost.

Another American manager, in addition to believing the company takes better financial care of its Japanese employees, believes that it exerts inordinate control over them. It is a perception shared by his Japanese co-workers, although they know there is some room for negotiating personal preferences. The context is the possible spin-off and relocation of the business group to which he belongs.

I'm not Japanese. I don't move because someone picks up the phone at 4:00 and says, "Next week you'll be living somewhere else." It wouldn't be such a terrible problem if I felt I would be treated like a Japanese. Meaning, at what expense to me? Because there is no expense to them -- the company pays for it.

Only Americans who work closely with *chuzaiin* begin to piece together concrete notions about their relative lack of control over their work life. The Japanese, however, widely share with Americans the assumption that Americans, in contrast, are not strongly bound to any organization and, thus, its dictates. But in interpreting American independence and mobility as a reprehensible lack of loyalty, many Japanese diverge from the American understanding.

Considerable evidence supporting common recognition of distance between American and Japanese ways of thinking has been cited. In this domain of cultural knowledge, in particular, each individual's understanding reflects personal experience and interests. People puzzle over all manner of things. Some Americans, for instance, compare the relative importance of the family in the U.S. and Japan; many believe that the late night hours of the *chuzaiin* indicate they do not care about their family as much as Americans do. Certain of LASCO's members enjoy philosophizing about Japanese and American differences. For example, an American recently back from his first extended business trip to Tokyo begins to formulate his understandings:

The Japanese don't have the same need for their own space. For Americans it [space] is both a psychological and a prestige need...The Japanese are very regimented with regard to status distinctions; they get to work before their superiors and stay til the boss leaves.

The Japanese man who quit TC JAPAN is especially articulate about differences in thinking. His discussion of the pay issue includes the following insights:

When a Caucasian employee demands real hard a pay raise, that's natural. I understand. That's the normal way. On the other hand, some people from Japan regard that behavior as bad, undesirable behavior. According to the Japanese philosophy, speaking up or demanding is not a good thing. Just go low key and let some other people recognize [your worth]. He himself should not be demanding. Let others do it for him.

That the understandings individuals arrive at sometimes inaccurately reflect the cultural other's reality is less important than the implications of these understandings for the organization-wide culture. Employees tend to verbalize the distinction between being "Japanese" and being "American" in a dichotomy of "we" and "they." Separateness or otherness is a fundamental reality for LASCO's members.

SUMMARY AND DISCUSSION

LASCO's organizational culture hardly exhibits the unity of thought or spirit of oneness that many consider characteristic of Japan's large enterprises (Ouchi, 1981) and America's best managed companies (Deal & Kennedy, 1982; Peters & Waterman, 1982). We find instead the coexistence of essentially oppositional American and Japanese cultural subgroupings and a set of company-wide assumptions which predominately reflects this bifurcation. At the same time, multivalent individual interpretations play below the surface of shared understandings at the company-wide level, colored by personality, personal history, subgroup culture and the circumstances of the moment.

Laying aside the issue of whether an organization-wide culture ever is the integrating, "strong" culture anticipated by many researchers and hoped for by practitioners, it is argued that organizational ambiguities inhibit extensive cultural integration or consensus at LASCO. (See Baba, 1989; Martin, 1992; and Smircich & Calas, 1987, for critiques of corporate culture research which equates management-centered values and assumptions with company-wide culture.)

Clear-cut boundaries differentiate Japanese and American subgroups with regard to certain issues. Within each grouping, the assumptions which comprise the system of meaning not only are widely shared but are understood in much the same way by group members. In other words, there is cultural consensus.

The American subgroup culture emerges largely in response to ambiguities caused by clash between American and Japanese work sketch maps. Americans miss anticipated cues and guideposts which give the work situation adequate predictability. The fact of Japanese political dominance causes further ambiguity, especially with regard to American expectations about access to power, influence, and advancement.

Clash in work sketch maps is a source of ambiguity for *chuzaiin* as well. Their response appears mainly in the domain of cultural knowledge that concerns how to manage LASCO. Because the Japanese conceptualize such things as position and how you go about getting a job done differently from Americans, the exact points around which they perceive ambiguity also differ. Thus Japanese and American interpretations of clash in work sketch maps are not the same. Comparative societal homogeneity, relative homogeneity in prior organizational experience, and their inclination toward frequent and exclusive in-group interaction all promote cultural consensus among *chuzaiin*. This, in addition to their dominant position within LASCO, fosters a subgroup culture that is far more elaborated and management-oriented than that of the American subgroup.

While the meaning that LASCO has for its members owes much to subgroup identity, the zone of mutually shared understandings which Americans and Japanese both traverse also provides meaning. This common zone almost exclusively emerges in response to organizational ambiguities. It represents the framework which gives organization-wide meaning to the many instances in which both Americans and Japanese find no clear interpretation of a phenomenon or set of events. The theme "we are unique" especially reflects differences in societal culture, but it also reflects the ambiguities of LASCO's binational, multi-organizational peripherals business. The theme "change is a constant" mainly reflects the structure of the peripherals business and the volatility of the computer electronics industry. The theme "we are a company divided," in addition to clash in nation-specific work sketch maps, reflects ambiguities caused by *chuzaiin* dominated management practices.

On one hand, it can be argued that the zone of mutually shared understandings is narrow, providing little more than "a shared recognition of relevant issues" (Feldman, 1991:154). The deeper meaning that these issues -- uniqueness, change, and division -- have for organizational participants finds expression either in the way Americans and Japanese make sense of LASCO as distinct subgroups, or in the way individuals autonomously make sense of LASCO.

An alternative view argues that the common framework contributes toward the unity is a primary function of corporate culture. This is evident especially regarding the theme "we are unique." The shared feeling of being part of a company which is attempting something extra-ordinary, and the mutually recognized challenges, draw LASCO'S members together. The principles inherent in this part of the sketch map favor working together to overcome problems; they favor putting aside the resentments caused by communication and cultural gaps. Subgroup and multivalent individual interpretations of LASCO'S unusual business strategy and of the specific dimensions of communication and cultural gaps do not negate these principles.

Not surprisingly, these unifying aspects of the organization-wide culture receive the most official attention. Matt, as formal spokesman, consciously promotes pride in the company and a sense of belonging, not just to LASCO, but to the wider trading company "family." Some sense of the philosophy he espouses sticks with company members; sometimes they recall things he actually has said. For example, one American refers to Matt's comments at the most recent Christmas party:

> He said, 'We have finally learned to work with Americans.' I think really what he's saying is we finally have worked together and have come to terms on how to be successful. And I think they [the Japanese] work very hard at trying to understand us and I think we are a very difficult commodity to really understand.

By espousing a philosophy of uniqueness, Matt follows the tradition of large Japanese corporations. It is management's job to cultivate unity and belongingness (Dore, 1973; Rohlen, 1974). Many other *chuzaiin* try to do this in their daily interactions with Americans. LASCO's management, nevertheless, has not systematically conceptualized the special challenges of LASCO's "uniqueness", or devised management systems and practices which accommodate them. Nor has management addressed the challenges inherent in the related themes "change is a constant" and "we are a company divided." Because of this, tensions caused by the ambiguities of the binational, bicultural setting all too often occupy people's minds. Individual interpretations of situations and events influence and are influenced by the cultural assumptions of a person's (American or Japanese) subgroup.

The cultural analysis of LASCO illustrates interdependence between the processes of integration, differentiation and fragmentation in organizations. It supports the view of organizational culture researchers who contend that "an adequate representation of any cultural context should include the insights of all three perspectives, not just one" (Martin, 1992:406). This study's particular contribution to a framework for conceptualizing culture in organizations lies in the insight it gives concerning interaction between two nationally and culturally distinct demographic groups or, stated another way, the impact of societal culture on organizational culture.

Other studies, in a single national context, have found, as at LASCO, evidence of unity and division [i.e., differentiation] existing in tandem around an issue or set of issues (Martin, 1992; Young, 1991). Studies, in a single national context, also have found, as at LASCO, evidence of fragmented or ambiguous response to organizational ambiguities (Feldman, 1991; Martin, 1992; Myerson, 1991). Future research should broaden our understanding of the processes of integration, differentiation and fragmention so that we can begin to theorize about how one type of organizational setting, such as a Japanese - American binational setting, differs from other types. These issues are likely to receive much more attention than they have in the past as organizational researchers expand the theoretical and methodological boundaries of the field and as dialogue is established between those who pursue the, presently, largely separate interests of organizational behavior (including cultural manifestations) and comparative and cross-cultural management.

REFERENCES

Adler, N. J.
1983   Cross-cultural management research: The ostrich and the trend. *Academy of Management Review*, 8(2):226-232.

Adler, N. J.
1991   *International Dimensions of Organizational Behavior.* Boston: Kent Publishing Company.

Adler, N. J., Doktor, R., & Redding, S. G.
1986   From the Atlantic to the Pacific century: Cross-cultural management reviewed. *Journal of Management*, Vol. 12, No. 2:295-318.

Baba, M. L.
1989   Organizational culture: Revisiting the small-society metaphor. *Anthropology of Work Review*, Vol. X, No. 3, Fall:7-10.

Bhagat, R. S. & McQuaid, S. J.
1982   Role of subjective culture in organizations: A review and directions for future research. *Journal of Applied Psychology Monograph*, Vol. 67, No. 5, October.

Boyacigiller, N. & Adler, N. J.
1991   The parochial dinosaur: The organizational sciences in a global context. *Academy of Management Review*, Vol. 16, No. 2:1-32.

Child, J.
1981   Culture, contingency and capitalism in the cross-national study of organizations. In L. L. Cummings and B. M. Staw (Eds.), *Research in Organizational Behavior*, Vol. 3. Greenwich, CT: JAI Press: 303-356.

Deal, T. E., & Kennedy, A. A.
1982   *Corporate Cultures: The Rites and Rituals of Corporate Life.* Reading, MA: Addison-Wesley.

Dore, R.
1973   *British Factory - Japanese Factory: The Origins of National Diversity in Industrial Relations.* Berkeley: University of California Press.

Enz, C. A.
    1986   New   directions   for   cross-cultural   studies: Linking
              organizational and societal cultures. In R. N. Farmer (Ed.),
              Advances in International Comparative Management, Vol. 2.
              Greenwich, CT: JAI Press: 173-189.

Feldman, M. S.
    1991   The meanings of ambiguity: Learning from   stories and
              metaphors. In P. Frost, L. Moore, M. R. Louis, C. Lundberg,
              & J. Martin (Eds.), *Reframing Organizational Culture*.
              Newbury Park, CA: Sage Publications: 145-156.

Frake, C. O.
    1983   Ethnography. In R. E. Emerson (Ed.), *Contemporary Field
              Research*. Prospect Heights, IL: Waveland Press: 60-67.

Frost, P., Moore, L., Louis, M. R., Lundberg, C., & Martin, J. (Eds.).
    1991   *Reframing Organizational Culture*. Newbury Park, CA: Sage
              Publications.

Goodenough, W. H.
    1961   Comment on cultural evolution. *Daedalus*, 99:521-528.

Goodenough, W. H.
    1981   *Culture, Language, and Society*.   Menlo Park, CA:
              Benjamin/Cummings.

Kleinberg, J.
    1989   Cultural clash between managers: America's Japanese firms.
              In S. B. Prasad (Ed.), *Advances in International Comparative
              Management*, Vol. 4.   Greenwich, CT: JAI Press Inc.:
              221-243.

Kleinberg, J.
    1991   Organizational culture in a binational setting. *Proceedings of
              the Annual Meeting of SCOS* (Standing Conference on
              Organizational Symbolism), Copenhagen, Denmark.

Kleinberg, J.
    1992   The crazy group: Social construction of character, text and
              subtext in a binational work group. *Proceedings of the
              Annual Meeting of SCOS* (Standing Conference on
              Organizational Symbolism), Lancaster, England.

Lincoln, J. R., Hanada, M. & Olson, J.
  1981   Cultural orientations and individual reactions to organizations: A study of employees of Japanese-owned firms. *Administrative Science Quarterly*, 26:93-115.

Lincoln, J. R., Olson, J. and Hanada, M.
  1978   Cultural effects on organizational structure: The case of Japanese firms in the United States. *American Sociological Review* 43:829-847.

Lincoln, Y. S. & Guba, E. G.
  1985   *Naturalistic Inquiry*. Beverly Hills: Sage Publications.

Martin, J.
  1992   *Cultures in Organizations: Three Perspectives*. New York: Oxford University Press.

Martin, J. & Meyerson, D.
  1988   Organizational culture and the denial, channeling, and acknowledgement of ambiguity. In L. R. Pondy, R. J. Boland, Jr., & H. Thomas (Eds.), *Managing Ambiguity and Change*. New York: John Wiley.

Meyerson, D.
  1991   "Normal ambiguity?" A glimpse of an occupational culture. In P. Frost, L. Moore, M. R. Louis, C. Lundberg, & J. Martin (Eds.), *Reframing Organizational Culture*. Newbury Park, CA: Sage Publications: 131-144.

Meyerson, D. & Martin, J.
  1987   Cultural change: An integration of three different views. *Journal of Management Studies*, 24:623-6.

Morgan, G.
  1986   *Images of Organizations*. Beverly Hills: Sage Publications.

Ouchi, W. G.
  1981   *Theory Z: How American Business Can Meet the Japanese Challenge*. Reading, MA: Addison-Wesley.

Pascale, R. T.
1978   Employment practices and employee attitudes: A study of
        Japanese and American managed firms in the United States.
        Human Relations 31(7):597-615.

Pascale, R. T. & Athos, A. G.
1981   *The Art of Japanese Management: Applications for American
        Executives.* New York: Simon and Schuster.

Peters, T. J. & Waterman, R. J., Jr.
1982   *In Search of Excellence: Lessons from America's Best-Run
        Companies.* New York: Harper and Row.

Roberts, K. H. & Boyacigiller, N. A.
1984   Cross-national organizational research: The grasp of blind
        men. In B. M. Staw & L. L. Cummings (Eds.), *Research in
        Organizational Behavior*, Vol. 6. Greenwich, CT: JAI Press:
        423-475.

Rohlen, T. P.
1974   *For Harmony and Strength: Japanese White-Collar
        Organization in Anthropological Perspective.*   Berkeley:
        University of California Press.

Silin, R. H.
1976   *Leadership and Values: The Organization of Large-Scale
        Taiwanese Enterprise.* Cambridge, MA: East Asian Research
        Center, Harvard University.

Smircich, L.
1983   Concepts of culture and organizational analysis. *Administra-
        tive Science Quarterly*, 28(3) September:339-358.

Smircich, L., & Calas, M. B.
1987   Organizational culture: A critical assessment. In F. M.
        Jablin, L. L. Putnam, K. H. Roberts, & L. W. Porter (Eds.),
        Handbook of organizational communication. Newbury Park,
        CA: Sage:228-263.

Spradley, J. P.
1980   *Participant Observation.* New York: Holt, Rinehart and
        Winston.

Spradley, J. P.
    1979   *The Ethnographic Interview*. New York: Holt, Rinehart and Winston.

Terpstra, V. & David, K.
    1985   *The Cultural Environment of International Business*. Cincinnati: South-Western Publishing Co.

Young, E.
    1991   On the naming of the rose: Interests and multiple meanings as elements of organizational culture. In P. Frost, L. Moore, M. R. Louis, C. Lundberg, & J. Martin (Eds.), *Reframing Organizational Culture*. Newbury Park, CA: Sage Publications: 90-103.

THE HOLLOWING OF AN INDUSTRIAL IDEOLOGY: JAPANESE CORPORATE FAMILISM IN AMERICA

Tomoko Hamada and Yujin Yaguchi

INTRODUCTION

Institutional anthropologists tend to regard organizational culture as an unfinished process of dialogical relationships where no sub-unit of an organization can create its own identity or world view without reconstructing its relationships with other units and the whole. While we look at diverse local experiences and local identities including those of workers and managers, we also look at how these diverse experiences are integrated into the identity of the whole organization. Industrial ethnography with an historical perspective simultaneously analyzes local autonomy and central control, or the intermeshing of decentralization and centralization. It also forces us to look at the culture in making, and the process of organizing, rather than organization.

However, by looking at the culture **in making**, organizational studies in the past tended to emphasize the "materialization" processes of culture, i.e. the development of culture from nothing to something. Organizational culture was often described as something that is "forming," "developing," "emerging," "transforming," "generating," or "expanding." In organizational studies in complex societies, our attention has been largely focused on the emergent process of culture, such as vibrant existence of informal culture, or the implementation of innovative ideas from the original muted stage to articulate materialization.

The attention to the creation or development process is perhaps based upon our professional "ethnologic" that tends to justify the use of kinetic and biological metaphors for evolutionary continuum, from nothing to something to something higher, bigger or whatsoever.

In contrast, the perspective presented here will give a different and hopefully refreshing angle for cultural change analyses. We look at a particular organizational process as the withering process, a process of emptying, or hollowing out. It is a chronological shift from "being" to "non-being."

According to this perspective, culture is considered not as the one that is "forming," "developing," "generating," and "perpetuating." Instead, culture is something that is being "refuted," "mutilated," "shrunk," "deformed," and "hollowed." It is the process of how the original meaning of a social phenomenon is being lost. We would like to use the term "hollowing-out" to describe this process because it clarifies two major characteristics of this process, i.e. (1) the process of growing dissonance between perceived social reality and underlying cultural assumptions, and (2) the process of growing dissonance between manifested symbols and their original meanings. It is a process of losing substance.

Our language includes hundreds of "lost" metaphors--words and phrases we still use figuratively, but whose original literal senses have been obscured or erased by time and change. While we may continue to use these words in our discourse, the original logic is gone with our loss of etymological knowledge.

Organization is full of "mislaid" ideas, half-spoken stories, and misplaced concepts that no longer mean anything. In this study we emphasize the existence of schism between manifested symbols and basic cultural assumptions underlying such symbols, by revealing the process in one particular business firm where a manifested ideological symbol is losing linkage with its original meaning and cultural logic.

We would like to make it clear that our study is not bound by a biological analogy that there is a uniform law requiring that every culture should pass through the stages of life from birth to death. We are not discussing a metaphor of the "rise and fall of civilization." Just as the substitution of one mode of living for another by an individual does not mean his death, so are the substitution of one fundamental form of culture for another is not equivalent to the death of the society and culture that undergo such a transformation. In fact, this process of hollowing out itself is required to maintain the vitality of culture in everyday life. We emphasize the fact that certain aspects of culture are forming and expanding at the same time other aspects are withering away.

Many of us are aware of this phenomenon, but very often, partly because of our search for the "existence of social facts," we may overlook this vital part of culture's creative process. If some aspect of culture is dying, we tend to equate it as the limitation of cultural creativity. Ethnographic cases of the hollowing-out process have often been limited to the politically and economically oppressed, who had no option but being stressed out and in many cases eliminated by more powerful outside forces. The tragedy and chaos, the horrors and sorrow of such transition periods are well known to anthropologists who study cases of cultural disintegration, deprivation, anomie, alienation, and ethnocide. However, one finds few examples of applying this classically anthropological "de-culturalization" concept to industrial organizational phenomena and to the so-called "powerful."

According to Mercus (1988), one critical intervention and contribution that an ethnographer can make in organizational studies is to clarify the traces of the roads not taken, or the possibilities not explored, because these traces do have life of their own, and would voice if given the chance. It also confirms that these voices are integral to the processes that form dominant and overt identities of the organization.

We argue that the defining and dominant ideology also has many possibilities not explored partly because the dominant ideology must be developed in its relationship to the ideology of the dominated. The dominant ideology cannot live without the ideology of the dominated because power control cannot be effective without taking into consideration the nature and target of domination. Mercus is wrong in assuming that anthropological analyses of the "traces" of possible paths should be limited to those of the forcefully silenced voices. We argue that domination occurs through inter-penetrating symbolic interactions between the two parties.

Most organizational processes contain both creating and withering of ideas, behaviors, symbols and power. The two are the Yin and Yang of any cultural process: the alleged death agony of a cultural ideology can be the birth pangs of a new form of culture, the travail attending the release of new creative forces. All the cultures, to remain creative, must undergo just such shifts.

The present study concentrates on the Yin side of the life of a particular dominant industrial ideology named "corporate familism." Corporate familism is a management ideology that equates the firm with a Gemeinschaft-like organization. The corporation is viewed as an amalgam of organic social relationships that is characterized by strong reciprocal bonds of sentiment and pseudo-kinship of individuals who are to share a common tradition and destiny. From this ideological stand, the company is considered as a community of people bound by their long-term membership. The company is not just a place for work that allows frequent changes of personnel. According to this ideology, individual responsibilities within the firm are defined not only by task functions but also by ever-shifting social relationships over many years. Corporate familism is a specific managerial ideology, with an emotion-charged metaphor of the Japanese family and with a strong insider-outsider distinction. It is supported by Confucian-style ethnologic on human relationships. The present study is based on the recording of symbolic interactions among key individuals in this firm. It will discuss the process in which symbols and original logic become incongruent with each other and the Japanese "family" metaphor begins to lose its power in Mid-West America. One of the authors has actually worked for this Japanese transplant, and has recorded a very detailed chronological history of the withering of corporate familism held by Japanese top managers. A total of nine individuals are involved in this case: Three Japanese men, and six locally hired men and women. The data presented here is a result of vivid human encounters across two cultures between 1989 and 1991.

CASE STUDY: METRIC TOOLS INTERNATIONAL

Metric Tools, International (MTI) is a joint venture between two Japanese firms, Boeki and Kogu, located in a small mid-western town. The management consists of only Japanese males. Since the president resides in Japan and only visits the company a few times a year, Takeo "Tom" Yamano, the Executive Vice President, is largely in charge of the company. Now in his early forties and a graduate of a prestigious university in Japan, Yamano has been working for Boeki for almost twenty years. Because he has had extensive overseas experience not only in the United States but also in Europe, the Middle East, and Northern Africa, he speaks English comfortably. However, the assignment in the United States is his first long-term international mission. He has been in the United States for five years, including three years at MTI. Yamano is affable and energetic in his private life. He is simultaneously cautious and aggressive in business. At MTI, the American staff members favor him for his friendliness: they call him "Tom," and under his influence, the Americans refer to all the Japanese by their English names.

The two other Japanese are Vice President (and also the Sales Manager), Yoshihiro "Josh" Takenaka, and supervisor in sales, Joji "George" Sonoda. Takenaka and Sonoda, both in their early thirties, graduated from regional colleges in western Japan and have been working for Kogu since their graduation. In Japan, Takenaka has been on the fastest promotion track to become a branch manager at the age of thirty-two. He is aggressive and at times emotional. He also takes good care of his Japanese subordinates by inviting them to his home when Kogu sends them to MTI. On the other hand, Sonoda, originally a salesperson at Kogu, is more subdued than the other two. However, he has such extensive knowledge about tools and machinery that not only the American staff but also Yamano and Takenaka rely upon him. Neither Takenaka nor Sonoda had previous business experience abroad, nor did they have a sufficient command of English to conduct business in the United States. However, their English has improved considerably in the past three years--enough to make the American staff insist that "there is no language problem anymore" at MTI.

The local American staff consists of three males and three females. Two of the men, Scott Smith and Carl Fischer, are salespeople, while the other man, Randy Brown and three women, Marge Bird, Emily Baker, and Jen Heart, are engaged in general administrative and secretarial work in the office. Scott and Marge, now in their forties, have widely diverse job experience. Marge, who has been engaged in secretarial jobs most of her career, is a meticulous planner. Scott, who lived in Japan for two years after completing an undergraduate degree in business, is the only person at MTI with previous exposure to Japanese culture and with the ability to speak Japanese. Emily, the only non-native of the state, is in her late twenties. She quit college one year short of completing her B.A. degree in business and was working as a secretary before MTI hired her. The other three are in their early twenties. Jen is trying to complete her accounting degree at a local vocational school. Carl and Randy, both graduates of local high schools, have little or no pervious job experience. In addition to the nine members mentioned above, at least one Japanese from one of the parent companies is always helping to ease the heavy workload at MTI. Thus, in total, about ten people work in the office.

At MTI, none of the local staff has been fired. The American staff members generally favor the management. Most of them have no intention of quitting in the future. Rather, a few have expressed their wishes to work at MTI "until retirement." Consequently, the turn-over has been low: in the past three years, only one man has quit for a personal reason.

PHASE ONE

The 500-square-foot temporary MTI office was crowded with four Japanese and two Americans, piles of tool catalogs, fax and telex machines, a copier, and six desks upon which the people stacked purchase orders, invoices, quotations, and telephone memos. All but two desks faced the same direction towards a large window at the front. Yamano, E.V.P., sat at the corner of the office facing the back of Takenaka, V.P., who faced the back of Scott, a salesperson. Marge sat across from Scott, also facing the window. The two Japanese, Sonoda and one of the authors ("I"), however, sat at the back of the office facing each other (Figure 1).

MTI's office style was unusual because it fit neither of the characteristic American or Japanese styles. It differed from the usual American layout where managers often enjoyed the privilege of retreating to their own offices while the staff members enjoyed privacy by having partitions surrounding their desks. It also differed from the usual open office style of Japanese companies, where people faced each other, and the manager sat at the top end of the line of desks (Yoshino 1986:176, Nevins 1988: 128). The Japanese at MTI had come from an environment in which they faced their colleagues across their desks while they could bump those sitting next to them with their elbows.

At MTI, the four people looking towards the window had no one facing or sitting beside them. Unless they attempted to peer at others' desks, they could not tell what their colleagues were doing. No partitions existed, but the order of the desks created an invisible partition that provided people with privacy. At the same time, however, absence of partitions allowed people to easily see and hear even the small incidents that took place in the office. Not only was this lack of visible boundaries important for the Japanese managers to supervise the American staff, but it was also necessary to enhance a sense of camaraderie between the two groups by facilitating better communication: one only needed to turn around to get some assistance or share information. Meanwhile, Sonoda and I sat in the back facing each other, in a purely Japanese style. Neither of us disliked this arrangement, nor regarded it strange, although Marge once commented she would not like her desk facing someone else's.

The office layout at MTI presented a hybrid of commonly observed Japanese and American systems with an emphasis on the Japanese style: it retained the open office style without partitions as well as some desks facing each other, thus suggesting the influence of the all-Japanese management. Significantly, even from the beginning, the Japanese management had altered the basic physical structure of the Japanese open office style to allow for a wider physical distance between the individuals in the office.

However, this initial alteration of the typical Japanese style appeared not so much as a result of the management's conscious effort to distance itself from the American employees as a simple copy of the style practiced at the headquarter of Boeki America. Far from creating an emotional and social gap between the Japanese and Americans, the management at MTI took the utmost care to create a harmonious relationship by establishing a sense of community or "family," as the management and staff called it, within the office. The Japanese firmly believed that MTI could not succeed without cooperation. Yamano, who used to be involved in plant exports, said from his personal experience, "No one person could win a contract for building a $100 million factory. We [at Boeki] needed a collective effort." For him, the tool and machinery business did not differ in that sense. Takenaka, originally a salesman at Kogu, convinced Scott of the impracticality of commission as a part of the wage system by showing how many people took part in one sale at MTI: Scott sold, Sonoda provided him with supplier information, and I issued an invoice to collect the money. In short, the management emphasized and valued collaboration, rather than competition.

Encouraged by this kind of atmosphere, Marge occasionally bought doughnuts at the company's expense which all the members enjoyed with free drinks. The Japanese and Americans teased each other about "getting fat" from eating the sweets. Sonoda and Scott made road trips for sales calls, and Scott, a native of the state, often took Sonoda through the back roads to show him the rural country scenes of the American midwest. Moreover, the management attentively listened to the opinions of the American staff members. Many times they praised the management for its "accessibility" and "not yelling" even when the staff made mistakes. The Japanese suppressed their occasional resentments when the Americans did not match their expectations in order to nurture a close "family" relationship in the office.

The Japanese at MTI kept the tie among themselves even stronger than their tie with the Americans. Takenaka and I often played catch behind the office building. Several times, the Japanese left the office at five o'clock to play a half round of golf together (though they usually returned to work after sunset). After a long day of work, just like they used to do in Japan, the Japanese at MTI often ate and drank together to relieve the stress from the work and engage in a relaxed conversation at one of the managers' homes.

The decision-making process of the Japanese revealed the harmony even more strikingly. Although the Japanese managers heeded and incorporated the American staff members' opinions, the management held occasional managerial meetings after the staff left at 5:00 p.m. The Japanese at MTI reached decisions consensually and cooperatively with a strong team spirit. They had active discussions but they rarely, if ever, disagreed with each other strongly. Not only did the Japanese seek consensus among themselves, but also they considered a consensus with the parent companies crucial. The parent companies cast a strong influence upon MTI; never a weekday passed without the Japanese at MTI calling or faxing to Kogu or Boeki in order to exchange information with their colleagues and superiors.

The Japanese management's main concern is to maintain the group's harmony (Pascal & Athos 1981:126). Thus the management gives meticulous attention to individuals to ensure their well-being; each individual is the basis of the company as a community model. The creation of the "family" atmosphere at MTI was a case in which the Japanese consciously attempted to implant their cultural assumption in American soil.

While the transplantation of the Japanese assumption about valuing "family" was quite successful at MTI, another assumption the management attempted to apply was less so. In Japan, the relationship between the customer and supplier is closely intertwined in such a way that makes them dependent upon each other. It creates a solid production chain in which a customer and supplier both work closely to creat a Just-In-Time delivery system. Through close and long relationships that often include the holding of one another's stock, companies "develop a sense of shared destiny" (Dertouzos 19889:181).

MTI completely failed to develop a sense of "shared destiny" with its American suppliers, despite its attempt to establish such relationships with them. Contacts with American suppliers to request quotations turned out to be difficult, not so much because of the language problem (Scott called often), but because of the prevalence of what the Japanese called "double-tongued" suppliers. Often the Japanese managers found a discrepancy between the actual price and the quoted price. Worse, the routine discrepancy between the actual delivery date and quoted date turned out to be disastrous and embarrassing for MTI, as the gap in turn delayed the company's delivery to customers and betrayed the "just-in-time" motto. Long delivery time often unexpectedly forced MTI to resort to an expensive way of importing goods from its parent company in Japan.

This lesson resulted in a feeling among the Japanese to "Never trust American suppliers." Scott shared this feeling because he made a number of contacts on behalf of the Japanese for quotations or order status. A phrase, "because they are Americans they lie," became common in the office to describe the failures of American suppliers. The Japanese pointed out every mistake among themselves in the office with the remark, "Are you an American?" which was an insult for them. When the American suppliers did perform well, they shared surprised feelings such as, "They do well for Americans!" The failure of American suppliers to satisfy the Japanese contributed to the formation of a sense of superiority to American business, a sense they had only heard and read about while they lived in Japan.

While the Japanese scoffed at American suppliers for their inefficiency, they prided themselves in sharing a sense of "destiny" with their customers that enabled them to provide the best service. Such services included quick delivery--a delivery even before the issuance of a formal purchase order. Requests for tools and machinery at customer plants were usually given to MTI salespeople by the Japanese supervising engineers who would then turn in their acquisition requests to the purchasing department. However, because of the extensive time required to process paperwork, the customers provided MTI with a written purchase order and its number only after a considerable lapse of time. Since the Japanese engineers wanted the goods as soon as possible, the Japanese at MTI opted to supply the requested goods, even without a purchase order number, to abide by their motto, "just-in-time," and to satisfy their Japanese customers. After all, Kogu's customers accepted such a practice in Japan.

However, this service boasted by the Japanese triggered a major controversy that ultimately forced them to drop their "flexibility." The purchasing and receiving departments, which consisted of American managers and staff, would not accept any goods without a purchase order number. MTI's ignoring of their policy created such considerable confusion among the American-managed accounts payable office at the customer plants that they threatened to refuse all payments and to sever their relationship with MTI.

At this moment, MTI could do nothing but to observe the instruction given by the Americans. No matter how customer-oriented MTI might have been, no money meant no business. Its policy not to deliver without a proper purchase order number outraged the Japanese engineers (who had nothing to do with the American-managed accounting office) at the transplants. MTI's Japanese managers and the engineers held a number of meetings in which the latter accused the former of "Americanizing," just like the Japanese management at MTI accused its American suppliers' lack of service spirit. Even though the "American" way could mean a delay in the delivery, the very betrayal of their proud motto of "just-in-time," MTI had to stand firm on adhering to the "American" way because its implementation could affect the survival of the company.

Thus, in the first year of its operation the Japanese management at MTI adhered to cultural assumptions they had brought from Japan. Some assumptions seemed to apply as well in the United States as in Japan. The most notable was the value of "family" atmosphere that made, as Yamano said, "people want to come to the office every morning." Even though the management arranged a wider physical distance than its Japanese counterparts, emotional and social distance among not only the Japanese but also the American staff remained close. On the other hand, the Japanese found out that not all Japanese assumptions fit well in the United States. Business based on the tight-knit, "destiny sharing" production chain was impossible in the United States because the suppliers could not cooperate with the concept of "just-in-time" service and customers required an indication of contractual agreement for every business transaction. The Japanese management felt frustrated with the difference. The Japanese managers depressurized their frustration with suppliers by routinely degrading them verbally in their conversation and confirming their own superiority. However, the problem with the customers provided them with no option but to adapt to the system in the United States in order for their business to survive.

PHASE TWO

On a freezing day in December of 1989, while the American staff members were enjoying their holiday break, eight Japanese men sent by Kogu transferred everything from the crowded temporary office to a brand new 14,000-square-foot building that was just completed in an industrial park, about six miles away. The new building had an office space of 4,000-square-feet with the remainder of the space serving as a warehouse. In anticipation of a future increase in personnel, the management at MTI decided to purchase six additional desks to bring the total number of desks in the new office to twelve.

The Japanese at MTI laid out the office arrangement in advance using a cardboard model. They decided that the open-style office would be continued; only the president's office was kept separate. The president's room was a luxurious space with a plush carpet, a $1,600 oak desk, a fancy clock, and two large windows, but it remained unoccupied. This room stood as a constant reminder that the president of MTI lived in Japan: he was, first, the president of Kogu, then he was the president of MTI. In other words, he who lived in Japan had the final control of the company.

Neither Yamanaka or Takenaka had any intention of retreating into their personal offices. They insisted on remaining in the open-style office because they were used to such an environment in Japan, after having worked over 19 and 10 years respectively for the parent companies. For them, a personal office did not symbolized prestige, but isolation, loneliness, and lack of supervision of others in the office. A personal office prevented developing a camaraderie which they believed was essential to the "family" atmosphere. In a sense, the Japanese at MTI preferred to have a relationship that was not "'dry', cool, and calculated, but 'wet' with human emotion" (Vogel 1979:152).

Yamano instructed me to make a model of the office according to some criteria he had defined. First, everyone would be in the same room except for the receptionist. Second, additional file cabinets would be given to everyone, thus providing each with a spacious work area of a 2'7" x 5' desk and a 4' 2" x 1' L-shape attachment. Yamano wanted to make the best use of the large office space; therefore, people were not to sit facing each other. The office layout provided everyone with her/his corner encompassed by a vertical attachment, a desk, an aisle, and a desk behind. Carefully, I created an office plan.

The arrangement of the non-facing desk order was a continuation of the previous office style. This time, however, the style became consistent: no one faced each other at all. The Japanese management completed the revision of its assumption on the physical structure of the office by providing a small alcove that gave everyone a greater space to work. Unlike the Japanese style, in which the managers have bigger desks, the area at MTI was large enough to allow the same amount of space for everyone. Consequently, the Japanese and Americans had more privacy than in a typical office style in which people could catch a glimpse of what others had in their drawers.

At the same time, however, a strong Japanese influence prevailed. The supervision remained strong. Since Yamano wanted to sit at a desk from which he could oversee the entire operation, he sat at the lower-left hand corner. Takenaka wanted to sandwich Scott in between himself and Sonoda in order to "watch" what Scott did in sales. In addition, Takenaka implemented a policy practiced in the parent company which required people to clean off their desks completely every day before they left; they had to go through everything on their desks in order to remind themselves how much work remained. Above all, management at MTI not only refused personal office space but also partitions. The absence of partitions continued to facilitate occasional casual conversations and jokes which brought laughter and, importantly, a sense of friendship, or "family," in a tangible way.

Even with greater physical distance among employees, the sense of family remained strong, thanks to conscious efforts not only by the Japanese but also by the American staff. By helping the Japanese managers in a strange land, Marge and Scott developed a feeling that they "helped to set up MTI." "MTI is part of me," said Marge.

Curiously, MTI's new location in an industrial park helped nurture a further sense of a cozy "family" atmosphere. After the move, the Japanese did not have enough time to drive into town to have lunch like they often did in the temporary office. Consequently, people at MTI started eating together in the kitchen. One person, either a young Japanese helper from Kogu or I, would take an order and go purchase lunch for everyone. Then people sat around a small dining table and had Wendy's hamburgers, chili, and fries. On other occasions, the Japanese brought in and cooked rice and noodles ("udon") in the kitchen. When Japanese noodles were made, Marge and Scott willingly tried them, much to the amazement and excitement of the Japanese.

Eating is a curious habit; it binds people. In Japan, the Japanese go out to eat and drink together after work to share their feelings, opinions, and reinforce their ties as members of the same corporate organization as well as to heal the "on-the-job psychic injuries" (Pascal & Athos 1981:127). This relaxed socialization functions as a "safety-valve in the Japanese management" to depressurize the need for competition and individualism (Chang 1982:87). True, lunch at MTI differed from after-work eating and drinking; no one drank alcohol, and language always caused a problem when it came to topics unrelated to tools and machinery. Nevertheless, the simple act of eating lunch together enhanced the sense of MTI as one "family" entity where "everyone liked each other."

Between the kitchen and office at MTI, there was a space called "computer corner." The move to the new office initiated full implementation of a computer system at MTI. The introduction of a computer system resulted from a careful decision by the management, despite an unusual opposition expressed by some members of Boeki in Japan. Those who expressed strong hesitation to computerization reasoned that the time was "premature" to make such a major investment. However, the management at MTI finally convinced them by indicating that "the majority of respectable companies in America" were computerized. As a result, MTI purchased a networked computer system with three stations.

Unexpectedly for the management, this introduction of new technology posed a challenging operational problem to the Japanese. For the first time it became necessary to make clear distinctions between individual job responsibilities in order to assure the input of accurate information to the computer. Information had to be keyed in collectively and systematically in order to avoid duplicate or loss of information. For example, someone had to become exclusively responsible for keying in information about the receipts of goods while another had to be responsible for the receipts of invoices. In addition, it was necessary to have someone oversee the entire operation to ensure the accuracy of information before it was posted each day.

At this moment, MTI had only seven people; it was impossible to have a purchasing department, a receiving department, an accounting department, etc. Yamano had stressed that in a small operation like MTI, "things had to be worked at collectively and responsibly." True, there had been some distinct divisions of labor. For example, Marge oversaw expenses, and I took care of all the translation and interpretation of jobs. Overall, the distinctions among the individuals' jobs had been blurred. With the beginning of full operation of the computer system, however, the Japanese managers made distinctions, for the first time, that I would be in charge of the receiving, Marge would issue the checks, and the helper from Japan, Matsuda, would take care of purchase orders.

The emergence of these distinctions in jobs challenged cultural assumptions held by the Japanese at MTI. Clear "job description" does not exist in Japan. Although companies in Japan have a formal structure based on the specialty of each section (in the case of Boeki, based on the geography and products), each individual's job under the section chief is hardly defined (Yoshino 1986:106). If Japanese companies provide written job descriptions at all, they give them to the section, and only in an extremely broad way (Yoshino 1986:113). Within the section, therefore, people are generalists who are capable of managing a variety of tasks. The Japanese companies prefer such generalists to specialists (Morita 1986: 184). Naturally, as seen in phase one, the Japanese at MTI had long resisted the idea of job descriptions by pointing out that no one job could be completed by one specialist; hence, a clear-cut job definition was not feasible and was unnecessary.

Nevertheless, in response to the introduction of a computer system, the task of creating job descriptions appeared unavoidable. Although at this stage the Japanese managers at MTI made informal, verbal distinctions ("Can you do this?"; "I think so."), they felt that more comprehensive job descriptions might be necessary in the future as the volume in business expanded.

During the second year, the effort by the Japanese at MTI to retain their cultural value of "family" continued. As a result, they maintained a close social and emotional relationship with each other. However, the introduction of a computer system and the subsequent emergence of job descriptions portended the widening of such distances by the creation of boundaries of responsibility around each individual. Despite a strong faith in the maintenance of a "family" atmosphere, the proximity of emotional and social distance would soon start coming apart in proportion to the wider physical distance of the new office. At that time, the Japanese at MTI were left with a deep sense of frustration because they were at a loss how to efficiently and effectively delegate the responsibilities to the staff. That is, coming from a culture where "job descriptions" did not exist, they could not provide proper job descriptions for their American staff members.

The sense of frustration over the difficulty in providing job descriptions continued to accumulate until it brought an outburst of emotion. The specific incident signaling the extent of the frustration occurred during the physical inventory count at the end of the second year, on December 22, 1990, almost a year after MTI had moved into the new building.

On that cold winter day, the lights at MTI were turned on at 6:45 a.m. By 7:00 a.m., two hours before regular office hours, all the Japanese and Americans were present. Normal operation had been shut down the day before, and the 22nd, the last business day of the year for MTI, was reserved for the warehouse inventory count.

MTI had an inventory of $800,000 with over 1,000 different items ranging from drill bits to rulers to industrial brushes. Despite the early start, the Japanese managers had predicted that the counting would not be finished until after sunset. Yamano and Takenaka "ordered" the staff to abide by Muto's instructions for that day's work. (Muto was a temporary helper from Japan who was about to return after a three-month mission.) He assigned everyone a section to count and the work began in the chilly warehouse.

Sometime between 9:00 and 10:00 a.m., Marge decided to go to the kitchen to have a cup of coffee. Almost at the same time, Scott left the warehouse to get a can of soda. Meanwhile, telephones rang frequently in the office with calls from several Japanese plants that were still in operation on that day. Sonoda, Muto, and Yamano left the warehouse to take the calls. Since some people had called for Scott, Emily, who was taking the phone calls that day, left the office to hand him the messages and found both Marge and him in the kitchen. They started chat, just as they often did on other days.

Jen had just started working for MTI to alleviate the heavy workload of Marge and Emily. Not familiar with the procedure of counting, she asked Takenaka a question. Not knowing the other had left the warehouse and wondering why she came all the way to ask him a question, Takenaka asked, "Why don't you ask your partner [Marge]?" Jen replied, innocently, "Oh, I think she's taking a break."

Takenaka looked around him, only to realize that he and Jen were the only people in the chilly warehouse struggling with counting the tools. He immediately went to the main building where he spotted the three American staff members in the kitchen. But first, he approached Muto, who had just been on the phone, and asked, "Did you tell them to take a break?" "No," said Muto. Then Takenaka turned around and strode into the kitchen. He was infuriated. For the first time in the two years since he had come to MTI, he yelled: "WHO SAID YOU CAN TAKE BREAK! GO BACK TO WAREHOUSE!"

A moment of silence prevailed. Scott, Marge, and Emily stood stunned. They had never been yelled at, even when they had committed disastrous mistakes (such as Scott having $1,500 in tools stolen from the unlocked delivery vehicle). Yamano came running from the office to find out what had happened. Finally, Scott mumbled in Japanese, "I'm sorry." Then he returned to the warehouse. In his mind, however, he angrily thought, "He didn't have to yell! If this is that important of a job, he should have told us!" Marge felt furious. Although she refrained from talking back, in her mind she repeated, "This wasn't really a break! Don't we always come in to the kitchen for coffee? He had no right to yell!" She later refused to take a break when Muto formally declared one. Emily was more astonished than angry. She had thought that Japanese people never yell since they disliked conflict.

The interesting aspect of this incident is how the Japanese and Americans perceived the reason for Takenaka's sudden and uncommon outburst of anger. The American staff members seemed oblivious to the instruction given by the management to follow Muto's orders. In the later interviews, they never mentioned their responsibility to abide by Muto's orders on that day. Rather, they attributed the incident to an aberration, based on a particular mood of Takenaka on that day. "He must have gotten up on the wrong side of the bed," they said. The staff members felt the anger was not their fault, and instead blamed Takenaka's caprice.

On the other hand, in Japan any strong expression of one's emotion in an office is a rarity. Rohlen, in his study of a Japanese bank, found that "an outburst of anger...receives immediate notice and often leads to interpersonal problems that take a long time to resolve" (1974:97). Such problems are nothing but detrimental for the Japanese, whose primary interest is to keep a sense of harmony ("family") within any organization. Thus, Takenaka's anger cannot be attributed to a simple mood. Rather, Takenaka and the other Japanese at MTI justified his outrage by claiming that the Americans failed to follow the instruction given by the management to follow Muto's orders on that day. Takenaka became infuriated not so much because Americans took a respite from work, but because the Americans neglected the order to follow Muto's instructions. The anger over the staff members' negligence to perform the assignment was combined with the pressure to complete the long and tedious physical inventory count within one day until the frustration could not have been repressed anymore.

This incident represents a crisis of appropriate leadership by the Japanese management. The management lacked an effective strategy for communicating with the American staff about even a simple assignment for a day's activity, let alone any job descriptions that covered the staff's everyday activity.

PHASE THREE

The Japanese at MTI never discussed the unpleasant December incident. Nevertheless, they sensed the necessity of "job descriptions." Since they had no experience in writing job descriptions, Yamano came up with the novel idea of asking the staff members to define their own descriptions.

The result was a two-page "Position Description Questionnaire," that Yamano made during the long holiday vacation after the December incident. On the first page, he defined the purpose of this questionnaire as "to assign a proper [i.e. particular] person to a proper job and responsibility." Then he asked three questions. In the first question, "Position Responsibilities Summary," he asked the staff members to "describe the basic function(s) or purpose" of their positions. Next he requested them to describe their "Principal Duties" in the order of importance. The last question asked them to "identify" their "knowledge and skills" that may be useful for their jobs at MTI.

The questionnaire was a strange, if not bizarre, approach to provide the staff with clear job descriptions: Why should the management ask the staff to define their responsibilities?, Why should the management, after hiring the staff, feel the need to assign them to "proper" jobs? This approach taken by Yamano inverted the normal hiring procedure in the United States in which the employers hire people to fill in the open "slots." It reflected a confusion of the Japanese management in their attempt to create job descriptions, something "American" they had never seen or made, which had not been given to the staff members upon their employment.

The Japanese assumption that ambiguous job descriptions for each individual would maintain a generalist attitude was deeply ingrained in the managers' minds. Therefore, they failed to provide any concrete job descriptions by utilizing the questionnaire, much to the disappointment of the American staff members who responded to the questionnaire hoping to have their jobs defined clearly. "I don't know what happened, but it must have drifted away," shrugged Emily, while Yamano quietly confessed, "It is so difficult to accommodate what they want to do."

Soon after giving out the questionnaire, the Japanese decided to hire two more men, Randy and Carl. Because the Japanese and Scott sold aggressively, this addition came concomitant with a continued increase in MTI's business volume. The management hired Randy and Carl because they were both young and inexperienced. Like its parent companies in Japan, MTI preferred someone whom it could mold over someone who had had considerable experience in other American companies. In the same month, Kogu sent another Japanese man, Hayashi, to replace Muto. Unlike Muto, Hayashi's mission was potentially long-term because he was to become a manager of sales administration (if he could obtain a working visa). The work volume of sales administration had been increasing dramatically at MTI without direction from an experienced Japanese manager.

Ironically, the increase in the number of personnel did not lighten the burden of others. Rather, their presence created further confusion among the American staff members because of the lack of individual job description and training. The management "experimentally" assigned Carl to sales and Randy to sales administrative work, after hiring them without "job descriptions." However, their assignments did not go beyond these generic categories. Consequently, to the eyes of the other Americans, Randy and Carl "were thrown in without explanation or overseeing" of their jobs. The older staff members believed that because of Randy and Carl's age and lack of experience, the management should give the two more detailed instructions about their jobs. Scott, who had lived in Japan long enough to familiarize himself with the Japanese culture and custom, was for a long time carefree about the necessity for specific job descriptions and was a believer in on-the-job-training (OJT). However, he came to feel the necessity of more specific assignments and training because the new employees were "not aggressive enough to look for their own jobs" like the more experienced staff had been left to do. Unlike the Japanese, the older staff members considered Randy and Carl's lack of experience a disadvantage that created the absolute necessity of providing them with concrete assignments and training.

The arrival of Hayashi brought further chaos to the understanding of job descriptions. His future title, the manager of sales administration, demanded that he learn every job performed by the sales administrative staff. For a long time, however, the management did not make it clear that Hayashi would become the "boss" of the sales administrative staff in the future. Consequently, the staff members were perplexed with this man "who tried to do everything." Marge, who had worked the longest at MTI among the administrative staff, felt "a power problem" when Hayashi, a temporary helper in her mind, gave her an order to report all the problems to him, rather than to Yamano. (Yamano, who wished to keep his accessibility, later overruled Hayashi's order.) Rather than considering Hayashi as a future "boss," all the American staff regarded him as an accountant from the accounting department of Kogu. In actuality, however, he had never belonged to the accounting department at Kogu. Rather, he "disliked" accounting and wanted to "stay away from it as much as possible." His responsibility, according to Takenaka, covered overseeing the entire sales administrative work and "accounting was [only] a part of it." Once again, this misunderstanding over the role of Hayashi was a case of ineffective communication regarding the responsibility of each individual.

The management sensed the confusion in the lowered morale of the staff. On behalf of other members, Marge talked with Yamano to express her concern over the problems: the management was not giving Randy and Carl proper assignments and training and Hayashi was acting like a boss. Marge thought Yamano had to be informed because he had "no idea how disastrous" the situation was. The crisis of leadership, the management's inability to communicate the basic messages that once manifested in Takenaka's yelling incident, had not improved. The situation continued to deteriorate. As a result, in the face of this chaos, the Japanese began expressing a need for a comprehensive "manual" that would not only include clear job descriptions but also how the jobs should be performed.

This need for the creation of a "manual" was the first open acknowledgement by the Japanese of the need to streamline the structure of MTI and to create formal job definitions and methods of training. They felt it necessary to start carefully supervising and controlling the activities of the Americans by defining their positions clearly and assigning them to particular slots. However, like "job description," "manual" remained a foreign concept to the Japanese. They continued to use the English term "manual" (pronounced ma-nu-a-ru) in their conversation; they had no equivalent word in Japanese. Through OJT, rotation of jobs, and a strong commitment to the company (rather than to one's own work), the Japanese had been working without any "manual." Sonoda, who holds an undergraduate degree in law, remembered how he was "thrown into" sales calls without much knowledge of tools or "how-to" in sales. The customers became frustrated and yelled at him, which in turn forced him to learn more about tools. Through trial-and-error on the job, he had gained a comprehensive knowledge of tools and machinery including the ability to discern the needs of the customers from rough sketches completed by the engineers. Likewise, Yamano, who represents Boeki--one of the largest companies in the world, had never worked with a "manual." Yamano, who majored in Spanish, had been involved in plant exports to various countries. He learned the extensive knowledge of "how-to" in plant export, an incredibly complex job differing from country to country and from one kind of plant to another, through on-the-job-experience and training. Considering these experiences of the Japanese, it may be said that a practical reason prevented the Japanese from making a "manual": they did not know how to make it because they did not have a concrete understanding of what a "manual" really was. In other words, they did not have a manual for making a "manual."

Another reason seems to have prevented the management from making a "manual." Inherent in the minds of the Japanese at MTI was a skepticism that if they delineated each staff member's realm of responsibility, she or he would not go beyond that prescription. Coming from a culture that valued generalists, the Japanese managers could not satisfy themselves with specialists. They were already seeing the disturbing result of specialization of work among the suppliers. Aside from the fact that the suppliers were not trustworthy (one of the first things the Japanese learned early in their first year of business), the Japanese always felt frustrated because the suppliers usually assigned only one sales representative to MTI and no one else could follow-up the person's job. "'I don't know' is a typical American stuff," griped Sonoda, "In Japan, 'I don't know' is not acceptable. If you belong to the same company, you should be able to take care of others' jobs."

Although the Japanese regarded the staff at MTI as "better than normal Americans," they feared that a "manual" could cause the same phenomenon among the staff: they would cease to work when they had fulfilled their stated job. This was far from acceptable for the management. Moreover, if the management described every aspect of the job, the staff would not be able to cope with exceptions, which the Japanese considered a "specialty" at MTI. As indicated in phase one, a close cooperation ("destiny sharing") between the Japanese supplier and customer is considered a unique strength that brings success to Japanese companies. Not surprisingly, at MTI, the Japanese emphasized such an unusual cooperation, even though the requirement by the customers to follow formal paperwork often trapped the Japanese. They took pride in their "flexibility" which was synonymous with satisfying exceptional requests by the customers. When Sonoda received phone calls at home on Saturday or Sunday from a customer asking for tools, he would try to deliver them. The Japanese wondered whether, after making a "manual," the American staff would become less flexible and more specialized, an idea that disturbed them, to say the least.

In this way, while feeling the need to create a "manual" in the face of confusion among the American staff, the Japanese remained helplessly frustrated in their inability and hesitation to create a "manual." Grudgingly, the Japanese who felt triumphant over American business admitted that they were "way behind" in their "technology of making a manual." They resented the fact that they had to create a "manual." After all, it was something "unnecessary" by Japanese standards. And if anything of the sort was made in Japan at all, the managers would only have needed to affix their seals as an affirmation, after the diligent and capable subordinates created everything (Nakane 1970:69). On the contrary, the Japanese at MTI had to try to create a "manual" for their subordinate American staff members. In a sense, then, by Japanese standards, the management at MTI did not have "subordinates."

The Japanese frustration that triggered an outburst of anger began to reveal itself, once again, but this time gradually in the management's loss of enthusiasm to retain the "family" atmosphere. The Japanese who had carefully and consciously created the "family" at MTI began to doubt its value and meaning. The management attributed its inability to communicate with and control the staff effectively to the freedom the staff was enjoying. The Japanese began suspecting they had been too tolerant. They feared that they had "indulged" the Americans so much that the staff members regarded the management as "soft." "We must tighten up the control where it's necessary," said Yamano.

Disintegration of the faith in "family" began to show itself in the kitchen. The place of conversation, laughter, and friendship at the lunch table started to change. Takenaka suggested that everyone take lunch at his or her own discretion, not altogether. This was overruled by Yamano, who was most responsible for creating the sense of "family." However, Yamano himself began going home at lunch hour, Sonoda was often out on business calls, and Takenaka often brought his own lunch. The kitchen lost its joviality. People ate quietly and returned quickly to their desks--to their alcoves. No one cooked in the kitchen anymore. There were no more doughnuts. Drinks, which were always free, became 25 cents.

The generally amicable relationship between the Japanese and Americans remained the same of the surface. There was occasional laughter and excitement in the office. Once, Marge brought a cake for Hayashi's birthday. But the ambience was quiet and less empathic than Yamano's birthday party two years before when everyone eagerly joined in hilarity to celebrate the day with crackers, presents, and a cake.

A series of crises that challenged the basic cultural assumptions of the Japanese characterized the third phase of MTI. The management came to realize that a "manual," a comprehensive document encompassing job descriptions and training methods, needed to be created. But this realization did not make the process of creating a "manual" a smooth one. While the Japanese felt the necessity of controlling the American staff members to avoid confusion by creating a "manual," which they did not know how to create, they feared the control would deprive the staff members of any potential to become generalists. In other words, while the Japanese at MTI keenly wished to create a "manual" because they felt the staff members were left too "free" and needed to be controlled, the managers possessed strong qualms about specifying the jobs too much because that might deprive their subordinates of the freedom to venture into unspecified job responsibilities. This vertiginous way of thinking was never resolved in phase three. Though the Japanese had determined to "do something" about the situation, they had not yet learned what to do.

CONCLUSION

In less than three years, the priority of the Japanese managers at MTI has shifted from establishing a "family" atmosphere in the office to creating a "manual," although they are still ambivalent about its value because they believe in the idea of a company "family" comprised of generalists. For the Japanese management, "family" and "manual" are not compatible concepts. Therefore, the effort of the Japanese to create a harmonious office under a people-oriented management has been superseded by an effort to establish a more mechanical and hierarchical relationship between the Japanese and Americans by assigning each individual staff member to a particular slot.

Although the Japanese have not been able to create a "manual" because of their ambivalence toward and their lack of knowledge about how to make one, the emphasis on "manual" and the simultaneous decline in "family" is likely to intensify at MTI in the future. A continual expansion of business will require the company to hire more American personnel, whereas the number of Japanese will remain the same because visa acquisition to work at MTI is becoming increasingly difficult. The growth in business will also allow MTI to open a branch office in another state. In that case, the Japanese management envisions promoting an American staff member (most likely Scott) for the first time to a managerial position as a branch manager. However, in order to assure a smooth operation of the branch office, the management considers effective supervision essential. For example, Takenaka thinks that in order to effectively supervise, every sale must be reported daily to the main office. In any case, the supervision and control of Americans will be an important concern for the Japanese management.

The establishment of a "manual" that defines each individual's realm of responsibility reverses the Japanese assumption of a group-oriented approach to jobs. Therefore, for the Japanese at MTI, the attempt to implement a "manual" came concomitant with the loss of faith in creating a "family" that incorporated their American subordinates.

This study has illustrated different phases of the life of a dominant cultural ideology. The growing incongruity between Japanese ethnologic and the local environment led to temporary interplay between denial and recognition of this particular corporate ideology vis-a-vis contending ideologies. While discord between their perceived reality and their ideology continued to grow, Japanese managers began to narrow the application criteria of corporate familism. First they kept the American staff and themselves at MTI as the members of the family against the "condemned" outsiders represented by American suppliers. In spite of this adjustment, the "family" membership continued to decrease while the Japanese kept on redefining the ideology in capricious, and constantly shifting social relationships with other organizational members. A further classification became necessary, and the Japanese began to doubt the effectiveness of this ideology itself. In a very short period of time, the application category for corporate familism shifted from the whole human community to the group of the Japanese managers, creating an insider-outsider boundary along the distinction between MTI managers and workers and between Japanese and Americans.

The "manual" symbolized an alternative but unacceptable ideology. At present there is no specific replacement for corporate familism, while the ideology itself is no longer perceived as an effective means for management control. While the effort to create familial atmosphere subsides, duality of Japanese top management and American staff steadily begins to emerge as defining principle of the intra-organizational relationships. The hollowing-out process is almost complete.

Our case has the following possible contributions to the field of organizational culture studies:

1. It emphasizes the Ying and Yan multiplicity of any cultural process that involves both becoming and decaying;

2. It discusses the importance of polysemic ways of observing any canon--we see a case where a dominant ideology is not a monolithic entity. It is constantly shifting, being fragmented, refuted and contested. Often an overt, central, and dominant canon turns out to be an amalgam of incomplete value pieces put together only by a symbolic label such as "family." A canon can contain contradiction or contention within.

3. The degree of cohesion of a dominant ideology can also depend upon a particular phase of the hollowing-out process it occupies at the time of observation. The case brings our attention to the existence of possible dissonance between manifested "symbols" and underlying cultural "logic" in organizational phenomena.

4. It also shows possible patterns of human responses toward such symbol-logic dissonance. Two possible responses are: (a) shifting the focus of application, and (b) shifting the taxonomy boundary.

Any and every dominant ideology is going to be obscured and eventually erased by time and change. Symbols that once brilliantly manifested central values and organizational goals may disintegrate as the organizational elite searches alternative means of power and control. Some ideologies may be replaced by new visions, but others may be simply cast aside into oblivion, as collective organizational memory fades. Like our usage of hundreds of "lost" metaphors, we may continue to employ these ideas in our discourse, while their creative functions are being lost with changing circumstances.

It is important to analyze the dynamics of these lost metaphors if we are to understand the true meaning of cultural change in organization. A multivocal perspective of organizational reality allows the idea that there are always more possibilities, other identities than those that have come to be enacted in organization. This study has shown that dissonance between symbol and logic is created by changing social relationships and social positions, most especially social class relationships within the organization.

REFERENCES

Chang, C. S.
  1982 "Individualism in the Japanese Management System." in Sang M. Lee and Gary Scwendiman, eds., *Japanese Management*. New York: Praeger. Pp. 82-88.

Dertouzos, Michael, Richard K. Lester, Robert M. Solow.
  1989 *Made In America, Regaining the Productive Edge.* Cambridge: MIT Press.

Mercus, George
   1989a Past, Present, and Emergent Identities: Requirements for Ethnographies of Late Twentieth Century Modernity Worldwide. Paper presented at the University of Maryland.

   1989b The Program of the Unseen World of Wealth for the Rich: Toward an Ethnography of Complex Connections. *Ethos* 17:110-119.

Morita, Akio
   1986   *Made In Japan.* New York: E. P. Dutton.

Nakane, Chie
   1970   *Japanese Society.* Berkeley: University of California Press.

Nevins, Thomas
   1980   "People Management Is What It's All About." in Daniel Okimoto and Thomas Rohlen, eds., *Inside the Japanese System.* Stanford: Stanford University Press. Pp. 127-129.

Pascal, Richard Tanner, Anthony G. Athos.
   1981   *The Art of Japanese Management.* New York: Simon and Schuster.

Rohlen, Thomas.
   1974   *For Harmony and Strength.* Berkeley: University of California Press.

Vogel, Ezra
   1979   *Japan As Number One, Lessons for America.* Cambridge: Harvard University Press.

Yoshino, Michael Y.
   1986   *The Invisible Link, Japan's Sogo Shosha and the Organization of Trade.* Cambridge: MIT Press.

RECONSTRUCTING A CULTURE CLASH AT GENERAL MOTORS: AN HISTORICAL VIEW FROM THE OVERSEAS ASSIGNMENT

Elizabeth K. Briody and Marietta L. Baba

INTRODUCTION

Knowledge of organizational history can play a crucial role in understanding human behavior in modern corporations. Embedded in history are clues to the origins of organizational structures (Stinchcombe 1965), managerial philosophies (Schein 1985), and employee behavior patterns (Allaire and Firsirotu 1984) that characterize the modern corporation. The imperatives of the past appear to leave an indelible impression on an organization, that continues to exert a pervasive influence on current organizational affairs.

In this paper we discuss the ways in which knowledge of organizational history enabled us to solve a perplexing human problem at General Motors Corporation (GM). Initially, the problem presented itself as variation in the repatriation experiences of GM's expatriate employees (known as International Service Personnel, or ISPs). Some ISPs return to the U.S. to find rewarding positions that exercise the skills and talents the developed overseas. Others, however, experience long periods of time with no viable return position and when finally placed, report low satisfaction in jobs that have not taken advantage of their professional capabilities.

Ultimately, we traced the root cause of these differences in repatriation experiences to the existence of two conflicting cultural patterns within GM -- one pro-international and the other anti-international (Briody and Baba 1991). Each pattern manifested a distinctive organizational domain within GM -- the international domain and the domestic domain. In spite of top management's efforts to integrate the two, these patterns continued to co-exist side-by-side and even appeared to grow stronger over time.

We originally stumbled onto the existence of the two patterns through an historical study of GM's international operations. Historical data on GM's early international organization clearly revealed the pro-international pattern, including its key structural, ideological, and behavioral features. Once this pattern was discovered, we were readily able to recognize its modern cultural equivalents, despite the fact that none of them were associated strictly with international organizations. Recognition of the modern forms was possible because the modern forms exhibited many of the same features as the earlier prototype, even though the prototype had ceased to exist many years earlier.

Recognition of the original pro-international pattern also allowed us to recognize its antithesis -- the mainstream anti-international pattern. We refer to this anti-international pattern as mainstream because it seems to pervade GM's North American operations, which are, in many ways, the mainstream of the corporation. Indeed, this mainstream anti-international pattern might have been too obvious for us to notice had it not been for the discovery of the pro-international pattern which presented a striking contrast to that which was familiar. The pro-international pattern, discovered through historical research, served as a conceptual template that enabled recognition of its opposite. As soon as we grasped the key features of these two cultural patterns, we were able to explain the variation in ISP repatriation experiences.

Historical research also provided important insights into the process by which organizational conflict unfolds within a corporation. As we discovered, antithetical cultural patterns in organizations do not necessarily clash unless they come into direct contact with one another. Contact appears to be a stimulus which can bring to the surface and exacerbate latent differences which are a prerequisite to conflict. In the case reported here, contact between the pro- and anti-international patterns came about as a result of actions taken by a third group -- GM's top executives -- whose efforts to enhance the company's international competitiveness inadvertently threw employees associated with each cultural pattern into direct contact with one another, thereby creating a whole new set of organizational problems. Our understanding of this process would not have been possible without detailed historical reconstruction.

Here we retrace the steps of our historical study, taking the reader back through the evolution of GM's international operations so that we may document carefully each of the findings that emerged from the historical materials. The objective of this review is to demonstrate that the past holds insights that are key to an understanding of the cultural present. We suggest here that historical reconstruction should become an integral part of the methodological tool kit carried by organizational anthropologists. Historical reconstruction enables anthropologists to identify and characterize organizational forms in an earlier state, when they are perhaps simpler, fewer in number, less geographically and/or organizational dispersed, and farther removed from the investigators' current and familiar experience and thus, less likely to be taken for granted.

A second objective of our paper is to suggest that once organizational structures, philosophies, and behaviors are established within an organization, they tend to persist over very long periods of time. Indeed, they may persist long after their initial utility seems to have ended and modern substitutes have evolved to take their place. It was Stinchcombe (1965) who originally showed that organizational structures persist through time. Our study extends his work by demonstrating that persistent structures are only one component of any given organizational context. Our discussion of distinctive cultural patterns within GM encompasses behavior and philosophy as well as structure. It is likely that GM encompasses behavior and philosophy as well as structure. It is likely that GM's organizational structures would not have persisted if they had not been enmeshed within a tradition that perpetuated their utility and salience across many generations of managers.

We present our findings in three parts, each focusing on a distinct period in GM's history. For each period we provide background information on the environmental conditions that surrounded the corporation, and the relevant organizational structures, ideologies, and behaviors of the time. Our focus is directed towards the overseas assignment at GM. The international assignment opens a unique comparative window on both the pro-international and anti-international cultural patterns since ISPs typically travel between and across units associated with these cultural patterns in the course of overseas duty.

DATA AND METHODS

The data for this paper are based on two different sources. First, we conducted semi-structured interviews with former ISPs and their families, ISP program administrators, and domestic managers whose staff members had overseas experience. Much of this information includes oral histories, highlighting both individual and organizational experiences. These reported experiences interweave ideological or attitudinal data with actions and events related to the overseas assignment. Approximately 75 individuals participated in our study, spending on average 90 minutes responding to our interview questions.

Archival documents were a second data source. Selected company magazines, annual reports, and policy statements were critical to our understanding of the development and changes in the overseas assignment and in GM's overseas operations during the twentieth century. Such information included vehicle production and sales figures, population data on overseas employees, official policies and viewpoints, and changes in organizational charts and reporting relationships. Other scholarly and business publications provided us with background data on the automotive industry and its environmental context.

PHASE I: THE INTERNATIONAL CADRE PERIOD (PRE-1970)

Expansion and Growth into Overseas Markets

New organizational forms emerge and develop in response to, specific environmental conditions which present particular sets of opportunities and constraints (Aldrich 1979). The characteristics of the new forms are shaped in large measure by environmental variables that encourage or inhibit certain types of responses. Our historical investigation revealed a unique configuration of environmental variables that existed during GM's early decades and contributed to the emergence and growth of a pro-international cultural pattern. The most important environmental condition shaping the development of this pattern was the opening and prolonged expansion of a global market for automobiles, particularly in Western Europe. From 1911 to 1960, GM was one of only a few American firms interested in markets beyond U.S. borders. During this period, GM successfully activated a sequence of business strategies, first designed to gain access to overseas markets, and then to ensure growth in these markets. These strategies transformed GM from a national to a multinational corporation, and provided an environmental and organizational context for the growth of a pro-international cultural pattern within the company.

The first strategy in the establishment of the GM Export Company in 1911 as a mail-order service to independent wholesale distributors in Europe and elsewhere. "Completely knocked down" (CKD) vehicles were boxed and shipped to these distributors who sold them, but often refused costumer requests to stock spare parts or to perform service operations when the vehicles needed repair. The mail-order business grew steadily from 1911 to 19, 415 in 1920 (*General Motors World*, 1961, 40(3):14).

During this period, some GM executives began to argue that GM also should invest in assembly plants overseas which would assembly plants overseas which would assemble these CKD vehicles shipped from the U.S. and Canada. The purchase of assembly plants overseas would offer several advantages to GM: decrease in freight, insurance and duty costs, reduction in damage to CKD vehicles during shipping (versus pre-assembled vehicles), and the establishment of overseas bases from which to launch direct dealerships offering a greater variety of models to customers and the provision of maintenance and repair services. The purchase of assembly plants also was as a way of competing more effectively with Ford, which was already assembling vehicles in Copenhagen and selling many more cars than GM in that market.

Thus, GM activated a second strategy to expand business opportunities abroad. It opened its first assembly plant in Copenhagen in 1923, and saw overseas sales grow from 54,000 to 64,854 during the following year (*General Motors World*, 1951, 3(1):8). As a result of this success, additional assembly plants were opened in Belgium, Argentina, Brazil, South Africa, New Zealand, Germany, Australia, Japan, Java, Sweden, Poland, and India -- all by the end of 1928. More assembly plants were opened in Switzerland and Mexico in the 1930s, and in Peru, Venezuela, and Pakistan in the 1940s. GM's strategy was to open assembly plants to serve primary markets absorbing 10,000 or more units per year. Smaller secondary markets continues to be served by the Export Company.

By the mid 1920s, GM faced a number of difficulties in its attempt to conduct business activities outside the U.S. These difficulties became increasingly important over time: mounting exchange and tariff barriers, nationalistic sentiments, and cultural preferences for European styling. Indeed, during the Great Depression of the 1930s, stiff tariff barriers were erected by many nations in the belief that employment could be increased by excluding foreign goods. Such socio-political conditions were significant factors in the initiation of manufacturing abroad as GM's third business strategy. GM acquired two European companies, Vauxhall Motors Ltd. in England and Adam Opel A.G. in Germany -- companies which made vehicles that were different from those produced in North America. These vehicles were smaller, more fuel efficient, and designed to withstand the geographical and climatic conditions of Northern Europe. Additionally, because these companies had previously established operation, a native work force, and a tradition of local ownership and management, they were strategically and operationally advantageous for GM.

Over the course of the Depression, CKD sales abroad from U.S. and Canadian factories dropped from 91 percent in 1929 to 52 percent in 1932 (*General Motors World*, 1951, 3(4):2). Clearly, vehicles manufactured by GM in Europe came to assume greater importance during this period. In fact, by 1960, seven out of eight vehicles sold by GM overseas were manufactured abroad (*General Motors World*, 1961, 40(3):18). Excluding the Depression years and period of World War II when most GM plants overseas were converted to the production of military equipment, the overseas operations oversaw a continuous period of global expansion from the early decades of this century until the mid-1960s. Especially important were the years after World War II when American-made vehicles were able to dominate European markets easily, given the war-related destruction and slow recovery of Europe's industrial capacity. Figure 1 depicts the growth of GM's overseas sales during this period and reflects the expansion of a new industry into open, unsaturated markets in the relative absence of intensive international competition.

Thus, in the five decades between 1911 and 1960, GM's overseas operations experienced a prolonged period of global growth and expansion. As GM responded to new market opportunities and constraints, its international activities grew from simple export, to overseas assembly, to full-scale manufacturing abroad. GM's increasing investments overseas represented by these developments reflected a strong organizational commitment to market growth and successful penetration. The growth orientation of GM's international activities during this period established a context for the birth of a strong pro-international pattern which we believe developed into a distinctive organizational subculture.[1] As we discuss below, the pro-international subculture both includes a distinguishing set of characteristics, and is an important component of the larger GM corporate culture.

Elements of the Pro-International Subculture

The steady growth of environment opportunities overseas encourages the simultaneous growth of an international organization within GM. Our historical research uncovered substantial descriptive material pertaining to specific features of GM's first international organization. In this section, we discuss the structural, ideological, and behavioral feature of this international organization. Together, they form the profile of the pro-international subculture at GM, a discovery critical to our research objectives.

Structural Autonomy. A key feature of the pro-international subculture, and one which probably enabled the development of other distinctive features, was structural autonomy. GM's overseas operations were not integrated into the main fabric of the North American organization but instead were organized as separate units of the company. As autonomous organizations, the overseas operations had considerable authority to plan and execute their own assembly and marketing programs based largely on the sales of American-made cars. Further, it appears that they were free to create and implement personnel polices which served their own needs rather than those of the domestic organization.

Geographical Separation. A structural corollary of the separate and distinct character of the overseas operations was the location of the overseas headquarters. With the exception of the four years between 1913-1917, the central office of GM's overseas activities was located in New York City (*General Motors World*, 1961, 40(3):6). In 1938, this office became the headquarters of a new division known as the GM Overseas Operations (GMOO). On average, between 900-1,000 people

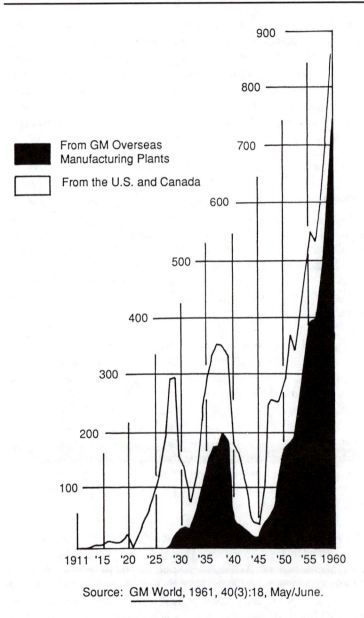

Source: GM World, 1961, 40(3):18, May/June.

Figure 1. GM Overseas Vehicle Sales by Manufacturing Location
(in thousands) 1911-1960

were employed in the New York office during Phase I (i.e., before 1970). The Foreign Distributors Division (FDD), which handled exports, also had its headquarters in New York. Like GMOO, FDD sent ISPs overseas.[2]

Domestic Headquarters in Support Role. Another indicator of the structural division between the overseas and domestic operations was the relationship between the New York and Detroit offices. Detroit, of course, was headquarters for GM's North American operations. However, a small staff averaging 136-150 employees associated with the overseas operations was located there as well. The New York office viewed its small Detroit office as a staff operation and received technical assistance from them. As reported in the *General Motors World* (1963, 42(3):13), "The location of the Detroit staff allows it to maintain a working relationship with the domestic plants, the manufacturing development and engineering activities of the domestic divisions...." Thus, the technically-based Detroit staff acted as a buffer between the overseas and domestic operations, reinforcing the structural separateness of the New York office.

International Focus of Personnel Selection. The new recruits flowing into GMOO and FDD intentionally applied for employment in GM's New York office because of their strong interest in overseas assignments. The majority of ISP candidates were hired directly in the New York office rather than through the Detroit office. According to one administrator, "Implicit in the hiring at the New York office was the fact that you'd be going overseas...(Potential hires would) know that, realize it ,and accept it, or (they would) go to work for another company." Most of the ISPs, particularly those hiring in through the New York office, had an "international outlook and were dying to go overseas," stated one individual.[3] Although some New York employees always worked and resided in New York, most of their new employees worked only for a limited period as a staff member in New York to gain knowledge of the overseas operations; then they engaged in a series of overseas assignments. As such, the GMOO and FDD Divisions were best characterized as an international cadre.

Career-Long Circulation within International Operations. Once they joined GMOO or FDD, overseas operations' employees spent most of their working lives abroad as "career internationalists." The assignment length was about three years, although according to program administrators, "You never expected anyone to come back in three years." ISPs were hired in New York or from one of the domestic car divisions or staffs through the Detroit office. Once they became affiliated with the overseas operations, they usually remained GMOO or FDD employees for their entire career. Figure 2 shows the model for the selection of personnel from both the New York and Detroit offices. Upon return from an overseas assignment, "You either stayed with the (GMOO) staff or took another overseas assignment (since) GMOO looked our for its own" stated one administrator. Another remarked,

> During the 1930s you really had career types. There were still many during the 1950s, fewer in the 1960s, and fewer yet in the 1970s and 1980s. When an ISP who had been a factory manager or a technical director would come back in the 1940s or 1950s, he[4] would probable sit around until another assignment came up. He would have some little projects to work on but we weren't trying to place these people back in the (domestic) divisions where they originated. They were career types.

Figure 3 depicts the repatriation pattern of an ISP during Phase I. The arrow shows the direction of the ISP return flow from their assignments overseas to the headquarter offices for reassignment -- usually to another overseas location. In this closed system, repatriation did not usually extend to the domestic staffs and divisions. Because personnel exchanges back to the domestic units of the company did not occur, the overseas operations developed their own unique, yet enclosed subculture.

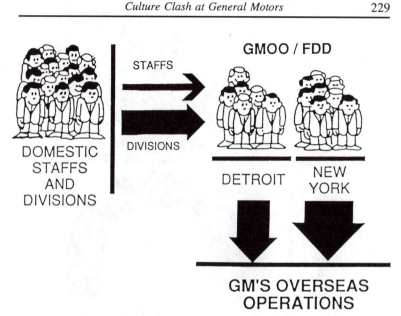

Figure 2. ISP Selection within GM's Overseas Operations (Pre-1970)

GMOO / FDD

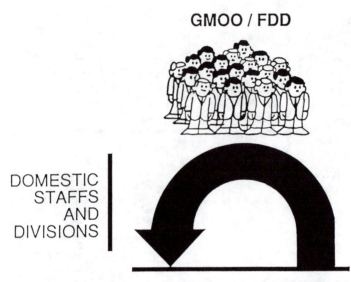

DOMESTIC
STAFFS
AND
DIVISIONS

GM'S OVERSEAS OPERATIONS

Figure 3. ISP Repatriation within GM's Overseas Operations
(Pre-1970)

International Skills Highly Valued. Members of the overseas operations shared a common ideology which centered upon the premise that overseas assignments were valued highly by the GMOO and FDD organizations. Indeed, ISPs filled critical positions overseas as GM expanded its operations between the 1920s and 1960s. Many of those sent abroad developed the general managerial and negotiating skills needed to interact with very diverse groups of host country national including employees of the particular GM overseas facility, government officials, and members of the local business community. Because such knowledge and experience represented one of the principal mechanisms by which GM was able to develop and maintain business contacts and relationships outside the U.S., the skills of these ISPs were critical to and highly valued within the international organization.

Upward Career Mobility. Perceived and actual upward career mobility was an important dimension of the overseas operations' homogeneous subculture. Although ISPs felt that they were expected to accept any overseas assignment offered to them, barring unusual personal circumstances, they usually viewed each assignment as an opportunity for upward mobility. An overseas job offer represented new career challenges and experiences because of the variation in job tasks and overseas locations. Indeed, ISPs commented that each assignment contributed to their career path because it was a "stepping stone to something better."

International Status Hierarchy. The overseas divisions were characterized by the importance attached to the relative status within and between the overseas locations. Most employees of the overseas division anticipated promotions within the managerial ranks as their careers within GMOO or FDD progressed. However, in any given overseas location, the managing director's position was the most prestigious. One ISP recounted, "The GMOO executives were gods. You stood at attention. You were a rookie. They commanded." The prestige that surrounded these executives seemed to stem in large part from their ability to communicate and negotiate effectively with host country nationals. Among the overseas locations, there was a ranking of the managing directors' positions such that the position held by managing director of Adam Opel A.G. conferred more status than the managing director's position in a smaller GM operation. Other high status positions to which some ISPs aspired included domestically-based managerial positions within the international organization, such as the position of general manager of GMOO. The overseas operations awarded high status and prestige to successful international personnel and protected the interests of such personnel by awarding them assignments of increasingly greater responsibilities in the overseas operations.

In summary, the expanding international market for automobiles encouraged the formation of a distinctive pro-international subculture at GM. This subculture attracted individuals with a strong, positive orientation to overseas work and retained such individuals for long-term careers abroad. Once a member of the pro-international subculture, the tendency was to stay there for life, circulating within a closed system - - a system which placed a high value on international experience and rewarded such experience with steady upward mobility.

PHASE II: THE TRANSITION PERIOD (1970-1977)

Beginning in the early 1970s, an environmental shift in the world market for automobiles triggered a series of events that created conflict between the pro-international subculture of GM's overseas operations, and the mainstream domestic environment. Prior to this time, these two domains had co-existed harmoniously in different market niches, separated structurally and geographically. However, an attempt by GM to integrate the domestic and international niches during the 1970s brought the pro-international subculture and domestic organization into direct contact for the first time, causing tensions and discord between them. In this section of the paper, we briefly reconstruct the historical events surrounding the environmental shift, and the adaptive responses at GM that led to the clash of the pro-international subculture and the anti-international dimension of the domestic environment. We then discuss the ways in which historical reconstruction enabled us to recognize the existence of the anti-international pattern.

Rising International Competition and Nationalism.

The economic growth associated with GM's expansion overseas began to slacken by the late 1960s, providing the first evidence of an environmental shift. GM's overseas operations entered into a transition phase during the early and mid 1970s characterized by two distinct phenomena. First, GM began to experience a rise in competition in the market place, particularly in Europe. As European industrial capacity recovered from the devastation of World War II and a number of European vehicle manufacturers began competing directly with GM and other American automobile manufactures, the strict domination of American-made vehicles in Europe ended. Despite an overall growth rate of 250 percent for vehicles sales in the 1950s, GM's overseas sales during the 1960s had grown by only 85 percent (Cray 1980:452). The relative loss of ground overseas was tied to the limited number of GM automobiles that satisfied European market demand for small, fuel efficient vehicles that could cope with varying topographical features.

Second, GM faced other difficult problems during the 1970s, many of which were related to a rise in nationalism around the globe (see for discussion Tepstra and David 1985:221-223). Host nations established "local content" legislation which required foreign firms to increase the proportion of raw materials and/or supplies produced within the host country (versus importing these materials/supplies from elsewhere). These nations also strongly encouraged or demanded that foreign companies hire larger numbers of local nationals to manage such enterprises, rather than selecting expatriates from the corporation's home base.

The Beginnings of Reorganization

To address the rise in competition and nationalistic sentiments overseas, GM identified and implemented several broad-based strategies. GM's intention was to redirect many of its efforts to enhance it international competitive position generally. One of these strategies was designed to "internationalize" the company so that it would be able to compete more effectively in a global market place. GM executives no longer considered the isolated overseas operations' office in New York to be adaptive in a changing world. One program administrator stated, "Detroit was more tuned into the pulse of the corporation. New York was isolated and was set in their ways. They had their own kingdom out there." The executive group believed that by integrating the functions performed in New York with those in Detroit, the company would benefit in at least two important ways: the overseas operations would receive greater managerial attention from company executives, and they would have access to larger numbers of skilled and talented personnel. AS a result of GM's new strategic direction, the dominance of the New York office began to decline. Gradually, many of the functions that were once performed in the New York office were transferred to Detroit and the New York employees relocated. Concurrently, the Detroit staff of GMOO increased to about 200 employees in preparation to take over more responsibility for international operations.

A second strategy, whose significance will become clear later, aimed at strengthening GM's overseas operations through a reorganization of the component operation (i.e., units devoted to the production of vehicle components such as electrical systems, batteries, and radiators). Throughout GM's history, the overseas component plants had been managed by GM's overseas organization. During the Transition Period, however, plans were underway to reassign the responsibility of these components plants from GMOO to the domestic component division (such as Delco Remy Division which manufactures electrical components). Each component division now would be charged with running its own domestic and international facilities. According to one program administrator, "tremendous overseas opportunities" were anticipated by those component mangers with a "global vision." Such managers were looking forward to their new international responsibilities because they afforded new business alternatives given the lower labor costs abroad and market expansion possibilities.

The third strategy established during Phase II (i.e., 1970-1977) consisted of changes in the size and composition of the ISP population. During the 1970s, the number of ISPs increased from about 300 in 1971 (*Annual Report* 1971:16)to 836 in 1982 (personal communication from a GM administrator 1986)[5]. This quantitative shift in hiring for the ISP program was a result of both GM"s diversification into joint venture contracts, largely with countries in the Far East, and GM"s expansion into South Africa, Brazil and Mexico. While GMOO was still charged with recruiting and selecting GM employees for assignments abroad, program administrators and other GM executives stressed that there were an insufficient number of ISP candidates within GMOO to meet the new and expanding overseas demands. One executive commented that, "We were beginning to lose our competitive edge...We needed to move (expand our pool) within the corporation because we needed its expertise."

Consequently, the composition of the candidate pool for overseas assignments was transformed. The overseas operations increasingly relied on the Detroit office and its ability to locate potential candidates from **within** the domestic staffs and divisions rather than hiring new personnel directly through New York[6] (see Figure 4). Increasing reliance on Detroit resulted both from an increase in the number of ISPs needed and in the type of skills required. Both because of new plant construction abroad, and because changes in the local content rules in various countries demanded that GM manufacture an increasingly higher percentage of its products overseas (rather than simply shipping in parts and whole units for assembly), the type of skills needed abroad were changing. One program administrator commented that, "More of the engineering, manufacturing, design, and service employees were needed to a greater extent than the financial, sales and supply people." In other words, the overseas operation had an increasing need for skills that would most likely be found within GM's domestic organization rather than in the general job market. By the end of the Transition Period, about one-half of the ISPs were selected by the Detroit office from within GM"s domestic operations.

Thus, the Transition Period witnessed the beginning of a series of changes for the pro-international subculture and the rise of a new domestic dominance over international affairs. Several features of the pro-international subculture were challenged and weakened during this period including the structural and geographic autonomy of the New York office, the international orientation of individual selected for overseas assignments, and the circulation of ISPs within a career-long international cadre system. Indeed, the existence of GMOO and FDD as a separate international enclave was seriously disrupted as increasing numbers of employees form GM's domestic operations were assigned to overseas duty through the Detroit office. For the first time in GM's history, the structural and geographic barriers separating the domestic and international organization were broken and the international arena was opened to direct contact with the domestic organization. As international administrators in Detroit worked to recruit employees form GM's domestic division, the first signs of a significant culture clash within the organization emerged. This clash, which first presented itself in our historical data as an ideological and behavioral conflict between domestic and international managers, was our initial clue to the existence of an anti-international pattern at GM.

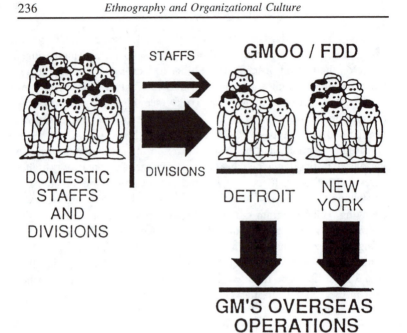

Figure 4. The Expansion of ISP Selection
(1970-1977)

The Manifestation of Ideological and Behavioral Conflict

During the Transition Period, international personnel managers, some of whom were now based in Detroit, needed to work closely with domestic managers to identify and select candidates for overseas duty. However, it did not appear that the domestic managers were particularly cooperative in this effort. Domestic managers seemed reluctant to recommend their most skilled and talented employees for overseas work. One individual stated,

> Why should they (the managers)? It is hard to separate the good engineers from an existing program that they are working on, particularly if it is a big important project. They (the managers) won't send their pride and joys...(When asked for candidates) they use it as an opportunity to clean out their organization.

According to ISP program administrators, the employees recommended by their managers for overseas duty were the ones that were expendable -- either they had reached a "plateau" or "dead end" in their domestic careers, or there were others with comparable skills at their work site. A New York program administrator remarked that when the domestic managers were approached for ISP candidates they would think, "Oh yeah, that little unit in New York ... Who do we want to get rid of?"

In addition to domestic managers' refusal to send forth their best personnel (contrasting with the GMOO/FDD effort to select the most highly qualified recruits for overseas duty), these domestic managers also did not want to accept returning ISPs on their staffs. Again, for the first time in GM's history, large numbers of technically-trained ISPs could not be accommodated within the overseas operations. There were now simply too many technically-trained ISPs to retain within the international enclave. Consequently, increasing numbers of ISPs had to return to the domestic car divisions and staff upon their repatriation to the U.S. (see Figure 5). Domestic managers, however, placed a low value on returning ISPs. One manager stated that the domestic managers looked upon the overseas assignment as a "touristic adventure." A program administrator commented that.

> For many years ... domestic managers have thought that taking an overseas assignment was like taking a vacation. Chevrolet was interested in making Chevrolet profitable. Someone would have taken

the ISP's job when he went overseas. we were provincial about it. This was one reason why repatriation was tough.

It became more clear that as more and more repatriated ISP's were assigned domestic positions, an increasingly negative image of the overseas assignment among domestic managers was evolving. These domestic managers had no history or value system which emphasized the importance of overseas work. The general perception was that high achieving, high quality GM employees from the domestic staff were not selected to go abroad. Instead, those who were expendable were sent overseas. These domestic managers appeared to be oriented towards the domestic operations exclusively and towards fairly traditional career lines such as engineering, computing, and finance. As such, they valued specialists, not generalists. ISPs, however, became "generalists" during their overseas duty in that they developed a general set of management skill. As one ISP stated.

> The type of people we need overseas -- the managing directors and GM reps over there -- were people good at dealing with governments, importation regulations, etc. They were personable people ... they had talents which were desirable ....

As generalists, ISPs were highly valued by the overseas operations. But, as far as the domestic managers were concerned, generalists were of little value. Indeed, some domestic managers indicated that the technical competence of returning ISPs was problematic because their specialist skills had not kept pace with the skills of their domestic counterparts in the domestic car division and staffs.

Thus, our reconstruction of the Transitional Period uncovered three key aspects of domestic managerial ideology and behavior which differed substantially from the ideology and behavior of the GMOO and the FDD managers. First, domestic managers selected ISPs on the basis of the employees' technical background and the degree to which they were "expendable" (verses selection on the basis of employees' interest in living and working abroad). Second, domestic managers did not value the skills of returning ISPs and, in fact, did not want expatriates in their organizations (versus the high value placed on experienced ISPs within GMOO and FDD). Third, underlying both of these patterns was the domestic managers' assumption that it was the *domestic* not the international operations, that were most significant to GM.

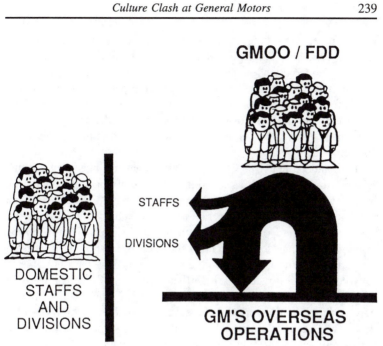

GMOO / FDD

DOMESTIC
STAFFS
AND
DIVISIONS

STAFFS

DIVISIONS

GM'S OVERSEAS
OPERATIONS

Figure 5. The Growth of Repatriation Options
(1970-1977)

Furthermore, the domestic managers seemed to believe that any upwardly mobile employee should concentrate on domestic, not international experiences. This last observation represents an inference that we drew on the basis of historical material pertinent to this period. This inference was supported not only by managers' recollections which suggested a pro-domestic bias within the company which provided much additional evidence that American managers focused almost exclusively on their home base.

It should be noted that the domestic managers' bias only became relevant to our research as a result of structural changes include the breakdown of organizational and geographic distance between international and domestic operations, and the new flow of domestic personnel into and out of the international enclave. The resulting reactions of domestic managers to these changes strongly suggested conflict within the managerial group. However, we were not able to fully confirm the possibility of conflict until we had reconstructed the third period of GM's international history (i.e., after 1977). It was only during this third period that the anti-international pattern revealed itself fully and international operation were brought even more completely within the sphere of domestics domination.

PHASE III: THE PERIOD OF UNEASY INTEGRATION (POST-1977)

Continuance of Competitive Pressure

In the late 1970s and early 1980s, GM continued to face intensive international competition in all of its markets -- particularly from th Japanese. Total world wide sales for GM dropped 34 percent, from 9,482,286 in 1978 to 6,244,458 in 1982. Sales in the U.S decline 41 percent from 6,878,119 to 4,042,464 during this same period, while overseas sales (excluding Canada) dropped 6.5 percent, from 1,751,260 to 1,637,401. (*GM Information Handbook* 1985-86:16-17). Gm continued to experience net losses in international sales and revenues from 1983 to 1985 (*Automotive News*, 1986:73). Such economic difficulties were critical motivators for carrying to completion these organizational changes begun during the 1970s and for instituting other policy changes during the 1980s.

Policy Changes and Domestic Responses

In Phase III, yet another group appeared in the foreground as a visible and active participant in GM's business pertaining to the overseas activities. Although the executive tier of the organization had activated a series of organizational changes during the 1970s to improve its performance overseas, their actions seemed to have occurred quietly behind the scenes. There was now a qualitatively different emphasis and response by the company's top executives to a perceived personnel problem. In this third phase, we see the decisions of the top corporate officers identified, implemented and discussed by those currently or formerly associated with GM's overseas operations. Their decision recognized and were intended to address not only the continuing competition the GM was experiencing worldwide, but also the role and status of the overseas assignment in the context of an individual's career and the company's operations.

On the one hand, the executives were interested in encouraging high quality candidates to apply for and accept tours of duty abroad. On the other hand, they recognized the existence of and wanted to address the repatriation difficulties ISPs faced as they returned to domestic assignments. The executive group now began to intervene actively in the Culture clash between the former overseas operations' employees and GM's domestically-based staffs and divisions. This intervention took the form of continuing structural and policy changes aimed at the internationalization process at GM and enhancement of the ISP candidate pool. The executives anticipated that such changes would positively affect ISPs, the overseas activities, and the company generally.

Probably the most dramatic change, and most striking symbol of this period, was the final dissolution of GMOO and FDD in 1978. To encourage further the internationalization of GM, the company moved its remaining New York office functions to Detroit where they were integrated within the domestic staffs. Organizationally, the formerly "isolated" New York employees were now located in the same city, same building, and on the same staffs as the mainstream domestic operations. In a similar way, the employees of the GMOO Detroit office were assigned to the other areas of the corporation. The principal organizational bastion of the pro-international subculture was now defunct.

In addition to this important structural change, a number of policy directives were issued which took aim at ISP recruitment and repatriation problems. First, GM executives identified the overseas assignment as an important step in the career progression of those interested in advancing to key positions within the career progression of those interested in advancing to key positions within the corporation . One 1979 GM document reported that the new ISP policies were intended to attract "high potential" employees,

> thus further improving the overall quality of our international management team as well as developing a group of executives who are better qualified to assume major corporate responsibilities based on their exposure to the world wide aspects of our business.

Such a statement was reinforced by a series of 1983 guidelines which encouraged the selection of high potential employees for managerial assignments overseas. The 1983 guidelines also were designed to facilitate the selection and repatriation of the ISP population. In particular, the guidelines suggested that ISPs either should receive a promotion prior to guidelines suggested that ISPs either should receive a promotion prior to departure or upon return to the U.S. when the assignment was completed (GM document 1983). Such changes in policy were indicative of an ideological shift at the corporate level.

As evidence of personal success and the movement of overseas assignments into the career mainstream, ISP candidates and some of their domestic managers singled out and affirmed high visibility role models among returning ISPs. Indeed, ISP candidates and some managers came to believe that the overseas assignment was an important means of progressing within the corporations. One ISP who left on an assignment in 1981 remarked,

> (One executive) was at Opel then. The corporation was pointing to the upper executives very carefully in emphasizing that overseas assignments would help your career. It seemed that there was some potential in taking an overseas assignment.

Another ISP stated, "A man ... who is now a VP ... was sent to Brazil and Mexico and perhaps some other places. These assignments seemed to have enhanced his career." Concurrently, the domestic managers held the same viewpoint. One manager commented, "Employees were told that they wouldn't get ahead unless they have overseas experience." One of the ISPs was told, "You won't get ahead if you don't go abroad." He subsequently told us, "They (management) felt that this was the coming trend."

A second intervention on the part of the executive tier involved changes in the responsibility for the career development of the American ISPs. While ISPs were associated with GMOO and FDD, guarantees of return employment (e.g., next overseas assignment) had not been a troubling issue. However, when the staffs and divisions were not necessarily open to placing returning ISPs, the executives established a policy which designated these domestic units as the ISPs' home units. ISPs returning stateside now were guaranteed return employment by their home units. Furthermore, the returning ISP had to be placed in a position equivalent to the one held prior to the overseas assignment (GM document 1979).

Third, top management instituted an improved ISP benefit package. The package consisted of a pre-departure cross-cultural training program, additional monies for language instruction, and a "look-see" trip to the new country of residence. These consideration, along with overseas premiums and allowances, tax protection, and annual home leave, relocation expenses, and provision of a company car were intended to attract higher quality candidates. In addition, the overseas assignment was shortened to about three years.

For those members of our sample who accepted assignments prior to Phase III, the assignment length averaged over 7 years. Many executives believed that such a long period abroad was contributing to the problem of placing expatriates upon their return home. Thus, unlike the career internationalists who took one international assignment after another for the course of their entire career, ISPs from domestic organizations were now forced to repatriate to the U.S. after a single three year assignment. While the three year policy was intended, in part, to help ISPs find return positions more easily, it ironically eliminated one potential avenue of escape from the problematic fate that awaited them upon return (i.e., it eliminated the possibility of them joining an international cadre on a permanent basis). Figure 6 shows the selection and repatriation process for ISPs during Phase III, in which

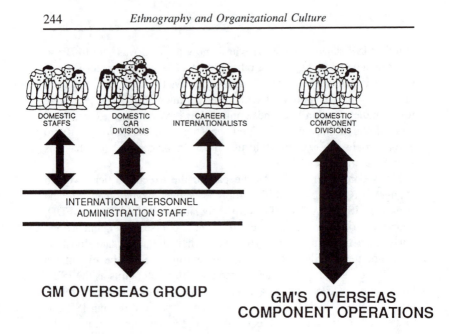

GM OVERSEAS GROUP   **GM'S OVERSEAS COMPONENT OPERATIONS**

Figure 6. ISP Selection and Repatriation (Post 1977)

most expatriates returned to domestic staffs and car division were processed through the International Personnel Administration Staff; while overseas, they usually were affiliated with the GM Overseas Group. Component division ISPs, described later, were selected from and repatriated to their division's domestic organization.

Through the combination of policy directives and role modeling strategies described above, GM executives hoped to improve and expand the ISP candidate pool and help contribute to GM"s internationalization process. What the executives did, in effect, was to force their own emerging pro-international value system onto the domestic organization. The executives assumed that domestic managers would follow their lead, based on an appreciation of the growing importance of GM's international markets.

While some domestic managers did begin to change their view of the international assignment, others were not so easily convinced. We were told that they continued to identify and recommend ISP candidates whom they considered to be expendable to the domestic operations. One individual remarked, "We are still sending has beens and never was (types of employees)." Many domestic managers had career paths that were tightly linked to success within GM's domestic, not international, organization. Because the domestic staffs and car divisions had not international affiliates and no international activities, the direct relevance of overseas experience to their administration was questionable. Instead, the domestic managers' interests continued to be vested in doing well at home.

The enactment of the pro-international policy changes by the executives coincided with the systematic devaluation of returning ISPs by the domestic managers. The more ISPs returned to domestic operations, the more difficulties they seemed to face. Despite all of the policy changes directed at enhancing the overseas assignment, many returning ISPs still found that domestic managers were not enthusiastic about their return placement. In many cases, ISPs reported that they had lost contact with their former peers and superiors, that younger colleagues had been promoted to positions over them in their absence, and that they had suffered from "falling off the career path" in a particular professional area. Some returning ISPs who had received a promotion just before their departure overseas actually were demoted to the status they held previously -- further evidence of ISP devaluation.

These same ISPs also began to question the credibility of the executive tier which was viewed as not having delivered on its career mobility promises.   Indeed, our historical data shows that the completion of an overseas assignment still was not linked to career success. One ISP who was sent overseas for a second time in 1980 stated, "For the last eight years GM has been saying, 'Go abroad. It will enhance your career' But your experience is not valued in practice. Once out of sight, out of mind." Another ISP who left the U.S. in 1980 reported, "It was believed that it was better for your career path if you stayed in the domestic divisions." An ISP who returned in 1987 pointed out,

> When I came back after eight years, no one knew me or knew what I could do. I almost went out of my mind for six months. I feel that I am at the same level as what I left eight years ago. Guys who were at my level then have gone ahead of me and I don't think they have done any more than I have ... I was taken out of the negotiating loop. This was my choice. A managing director's position was a step forward, I thought. But this was incorrect. The managing director's job is no longer the stepping stone to bigger things.

Furthermore, the views of these ISPs were corroborated by certain domestic managers, one of whom remarked,

> The overseas assignment may give you valuable experience but to date the philosophy that you need overseas experience to advance your career is not supported by top management. Both men you see over by the coffee machine were former ISPs. One has recently returned (to the U.S.). He keeps coming into my office and says, 'What am I going to do?' This man is competent. He is trying to elbow his way in.

Another discussed the 1979 policy change concerning guarantees of return employment. He said,

> What is happening is that the home units are abandoning their responsibility. {One division} talked to me about a potential ISP last week. They agreed to send the individual only if they didn't have to take him back upon his return to the U.S.

While comments such as these reflect the devaluation associated with ISPs, they are further confirmed by the apparent lack of enforcement of two of the 1983 guidelines instituted by the executive group. First, the guidelines stated that only high potential candidates "with ability to reach key executive positions" should be selected for international managerial assignments. However, according to one program administrator, only 61 (2 percent) of the 3,093 individuals designated as "high potential" employees in 1985 had been earmarked for an overseas assignment between 1986-1991. Clearly, GM was not achieving its goal of selecting high potential employees for overseas managerial assignments. Second, with respect to an ISP's promotion prior to or following an overseas assignment, we were told by a program administrator that, "The spirit of the procedure was clear but the issue was its enforcement. These guidelines give too many exits." This individual then commented on the experiences of those ISPs who left on an assignment after these guidelines were established.

> About 10-15 percent of the returning ISPs come back with a demotion even though they have received excellent ratings overseas. This would mean, for example, that they would be an eighth level before they left, get a promotion to unclassified right before going, and come back as an eighth level. They are told that there is no place for them in an unclassified position.

Thus, we can see that the executive group was not effective in protecting ISPs or in enhancing the value of the overseas assignment to the corporation.

Elements of the Anti-International Pattern

The historical reconstruction of Phase III provided the additional evidence we needed to confirm our suspicion that an anti-international cultural pattern was emerging within GM's domestic organization in response to the integrative pressures. In their reaction to policy changes instituted by GM's top executives, domestic managers increasingly displayed behavior and beliefs that were logically consistent with a strong domestic bias, clashing sharply with many features of the pro-international subculture identified earlier. While some of the features of the anti-international pattern were fully developed in the Transition Period, others were only initiated during the transition and emerged in full form during Phase III.

We purposely refer to this cultural pattern as "anti-international" rather than "domestic." The domestic managers' ideology and behavior was expressed primarily as a reaction to those aspects of the overseas operation and overseas assignment that directly affected them and their staffs. Thus, the conceptual core of this emergent anti-international cultural pattern exists in the relationship or linkage between the overseas and domestic operations, rather than the domestic environment in and of itself. While we may postulate the existence of a larger "domestic" subculture which might encompass the anti-international behaviors and beliefs of domestic managers, such a larger subculture was not the focus of our study. We list the distinctive elements of the anti-international pattern below.

Dominance to the Domestic Agenda. Domestic managers clearly were oriented to the needs and priorities of GM's North American operation, even when making decisions that affected GM's international organization. They put domestic needs ahead of international issues, basing ISP selection on their perception of what was best for the home organization rather than either the international organization of the entire corporation. As a symbolic reflection of domestic dominance, the center of ISP personnel administration was now in Detroit, which simultaneously continued to serve as headquarters for the domestic staffs and many domestic divisions.

Upward Mobility Based on Domestic Achievement. Along with their focus on domestic operations, domestic managers believed that their own career mobility and that of their employees, should be based on contributions to North American operations. Those going abroad were not viewed as serious contenders for higher corporate status and mobility, but as potential dilettantes who sought participation in a "touristic adventure." When asked to select personnel for international assignments, the domestic managers used that opportunity to "clean out" their organizations, leaving at home those individuals who would be most helpful to domestic advancement.

ISP Skills Not Recognized or Valued. The international and generalistic skills of returning ISP's had no perceived tangible value within the domestic organization. Domestic managers had no practical reason to seek advice and counsel on international matters, since they had virtually no involvement in any international activities.

Furthermore, they did not appreciate generalists skills but rather the skills of the technical specialists. Consequently, it was the specialists who continued to hone their skills on home turf, rather than the returning ISP generalists, who were rewarded.

Stigma on Expatriates. Because ISPs were selected, in part, on the grounds of "expendability," they carried a stigma when they returned home. Domestic managers assumed that these were the employees who were considered less competent than their peers prior to their overseas assignment, and even less competent upon their return to the U.S. as a result of having been abroad.

Career Stagnation for ISPs. The domestic managers' views of ISPs and their low evaluation of international experience meant that ISP careers often did not advance after their return stateside. Many ISPs were not placed in positions that allowed upward mobility; others were demoted following repatriation.

This distinctive set of features forms a logically consistent group of behaviors and beliefs. While this pattern is not the mirror image of that found in GMOO and FDD, and while it certainly does not represent a full domestic subculture, it has a set of distinguishing characteristics which define a fairly broad range of behavior and ideology. At the very least, this anti-international patter may be conceptualized as the international dimension of a domestic subculture which undoubtedly involves a fuller complement of characteristics than we have identified here.

Ironically, some of the policy changes instituted by GM's top executives may have stimulated resistance from the domestic managers and contributed to the growth and development of the anti-international pattern. It is possible that a deviation-amplifying feedback loop emerged between the behavior of the top executives and the domestic managers. As the domestic managers reacted negatively towards the integration of international and domestic operations, the executives responded by enacting policy changes aimed at solving a group of specific symptomatic problems facing ISPs. One effect of these policy changes was to force increasing numbers of ISPs to be recruited from and returned to the very organizations that had least to do with international operations. Managers of these domestic organizations, in turn, appear to have responded by stiffening their resistance to the returning ISPs. As a result, the devaluation of ISPs continued, serving only to heighten the problems of ISP recruitment and repatriation. Unfortunately, the executives did not seem to be aware of the underlying structural and ideological conditions associated with the ISP's problems. Even those policies that might have reversed the trend toward ISP devaluation (e.g., selection of high potential ISP candidates) were not consistently enforced and thereby failed to ameliorate the organizational conflict.

The Reemergence of the Pro-International Pattern

During Phase III, we noticed that not all ISPs reported negative repatriation experiences. Indeed, some indicated that they were able to use the knowledge and skills acquired abroad in their return assignments. As we attempted to understand what accounted for the variation in ISP repatriation experiences, we continued discussions and interviews with ISP program administrators and GM domestic managers who had participated in overseas assignments during their careers. We were told repeatedly that ISPs selected from and repatriated to the component division ISPs encountered positive reentry experienced and that the number of components division ISPs were rapidly increasing[7] (see Figure 6). Home units in the component divisions apparently planned for the return of their ISPs and typically placed them in positions which utilized their newly acquired managerial, entrepreneurial, negotiating, and cultural skills.

We knew from our historical reconstruction that one of the policy changes instituted during the Transition Period involved the component operations. The domestic component division had been placed in charge of the overseas component plants. Their headquarters were located in the U.S. but their personnel and operations were integrated with the overseas units which assembled or manufactured components. From our historical data, we were able to recognize that the component divisions exhibited an organizational structure similar to the structure of the former GMOO and FDD divisions (i.e., structural autonomy, linkage of domestic and overseas operations, and circulation of ISPs within a closed system). Furthermore, it appeared that component division managers shared some of the pro-international ideology of GMOO and FDD (i.e., high value placed on the international skills of returning ISPs).

Even though we did not have a full understanding of the component divisions since we had not focused on reconstructing their history specifically, we suspected that their organizational culture might be similar to that of GMOO and FDD because of similarities in structure, ideology, and behavior. If our suspicious were correct, it was possible that the current variation in repatriation experiences might be explained by differences in the return units. Perhaps the ISPs reporting positive repatriation experiences were the ones associated with the component divisions. Unfortunately, none of the ISPs in our sample had left from or repatriated to any of GM's component divisions. Consequently, we were unable to confirm our suspicion at that time. However, recognition of the pro-international pattern within the component divisions did alert us to the fact that modern day GM units might display the form of ISP selection and repatriation once associated with GMOO and FDD. Thus, we went forward from our historical reconstruction armed with the conceptual tools we needed to make an important future discovery.

SOLVING THE MYSTERY:
THE DISCOVERY OF COUPLED AND DECOUPLED SYSTEMS

As we thought about the parallels uniting GMOO, FDD, and the component divisions, we began to conceptualize a structural model which captured the substance of these organizations' similarities and could be generalized to other GM units beyond those whose histories we had reconstructed. This structural model can be described as a closed loop or a coupled system (see Figure 7). Coupled systems have both international and domestic operations. GMOO, FDD, and the component systems are organized in a way that allows ISPs to go abroad and repatriate without ever leaving their home organization. Administratively, these ISPs remain on their organization's headcount regardless of their geographic location. The coupling of international and domestic operations within a closed loop system helps to explain the shared ideology of such organizations which place a high value on the international dimension, the knowledge of returning ISPs is relevant to the management and operations of the system.

Conversely, the domestic car divisions and many domestic staffs we studied represent an opposite pattern which may be described as an open loop or decoupled system (see Figure 8). In this system, domestic

A   Domestic organization
A' International subunit of domestically-based organization

Figure 7. The Coupled System Model

organizations have no link to any international activities. To go overseas, an ISP must leave the home organization, work in an unrelated overseas division, and then cross back to some domestic organization upon repatriation. Clearly, the anti-international ideology of the domestic managers, which renders international experience irrelevant within the domestic framework, is consistent with a decoupled structure.

The conceptualization of the pro- and anti-international patterns as coupled and decoupled systems respectively, enabled us to create a more general hypothesis to explain repatriation variability. This new general hypothesis stated that ISPs who *return* to coupled systems will have positive repatriation experiences, while those repatriating to decoupled systems will share negative experiences. Significantly, this new hypothesis does not require ISPs to originate from a coupled system. The unit of repatriation is the one that determines the nature of the repatriation experience. Also, our general hypothesis suggests that *any* coupled organization, not just the component divisions, should foster positive experienced following repatriation.

The features of this general hypothesis allowed a preliminary test based on our ISP data set since every member of our initial sample of 15 ISPs could be categorized as having participated in either a coupled or decoupled system. As we discuss in Briody and Baba (1991), a preliminary test of the general hypothesis provided support for our idea that whether or not an ISP participates in a coupled or decoupled system explains a substantial amount of the variation in repatriation experiences (p. 10).

IMPLICATIONS OF THE STUDY

Our reconstruction of the history of GM's international organization provides several insights into the process by which cultural patterns and/or subcultures emerge and evolve within a complex organization. First, we see that cultural patterns represent organizational responses to specific historical and material conditions and that their fortune and lifespan are closely tied to changes within their material contexts. Both GMOO and FDD emerged during a period of domestic and overseas market expansion. They met their demise as a result of increasing international competition both at home and abroad. So long as both

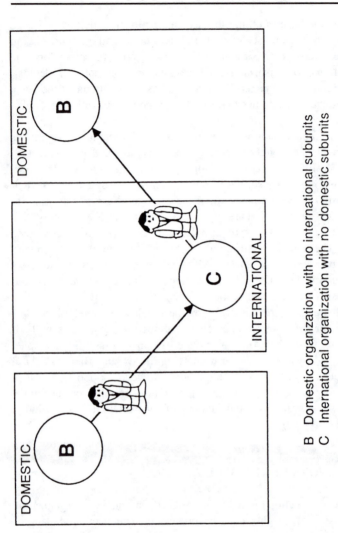

B   Domestic organization with no international subunits
C   International organization with no domestic subunits

Figure 8. The Decoupled Systems Model

domestic and overseas markets were growing, the pro-international subculture was able to maintain its own niche, co-existing peacefully with the domestic organization and developing a distinctive idealogy well suited to niche requirements. However, when markets contracted, the niche of GMOO and FDD was folded into the larger territory of a pre-existing organizational domain (i.e., the domestic staffs and car divisions), resulting in a clash over organizational priorities.

Second, we find that culture patterns operate as separate entities and are not easily integrated by policy change, particularly when such patterns continue to be grounded in distinctive material and structural contexts. In fact, forced contact between different organizational forms actually may stimulate the manifestation and sharpening of further differences between them that had been largely latent prior to contact. The anti-international ideology of the domestic managers remained unexpressed for the most part until environmental and subsequent policy and organizational change thrust pro-international functions and values upon them. These managers reacted to the invasion of their space by using their own agenda, refusing to expand their horizons beyond their structurally-grounded home base. It is clear that the efforts of top executives to ameliorate the culture clash were not effective, largely because they were not directed at the critical cultural problem facing GM: the differential focus and structure of GM's domestically-oriented and internationally-oriented units. Because this underlying problem was not addressed, policy changes aimed at enhancing the ISP candidate pool amounted to "tinkering" with the system without a clear understanding of the fundamental nature of that system (Deming 1982). As a result, the relationship between the two cultural patterns we described continued to fester, leading to a worsening rather than an improvement in the situation.

Third, we see that cultural patterns may vary in their degree of influence and status within an organization. While the tradition of the pro-international subculture at GM extends back to 1911, it has never been perceived as mainstream or pivotal to GM"s operations. Indeed, for decades, the domestically-based arm of the company has been the primary power and profit center. Material conditions, particularly the huge size and economic success once associated with domestic markets, played am important role in establishing a system of ranking. The pro-international domain appears to have been assigned a lower status relative to the anti-international sphere; in its formative decades, GM's international markets simply were not as important as the domestic market.   While status differentials between units associated with different cultural patterns have important implications for factors such as resource access, budget flexibility, and personnel expertise, they also play a role in career mobility.   As employees selected to be ISPs cross organizational boundaries, their passage from the high status cultural domain (anti-international) to the low status cultural domain (pro-international) is comparatively easy; the reverse pathway (i.e., low to high status) is much more difficult.   Indeed, with a few exceptions, it may be optimal for an employee's career progression to affiliate solely with one such domain during his/her tenure with an organization.

Fourth, our historical reconstruction elaborates and extends Stinchcombe's (1965) work on the persistence of organization forms. In this case, we document the persistence of cultural patterns within a corporation.   Both the pro- and anti-international patterns continued to exist within GM despite the efforts of top executive to reorganize, integrate, and otherwise influence corporate direction and operation. The pro-international pattern did not disappear with the dismantling of GMOO and FDD.   Instead, it reappeared in other units (e.g., the component divisions) that were organized around a coupled systems template.   Likewise, the anti-international pattern refused to die. Instead, it may have been strengthened by the very policy-related efforts that were intended to weaken it.   These two forms of persistence have different causes and may have very different consequences for GM's adaptation to environmental change.

In the case of coupled systems, executive-level policy change enabled persistence of an older cultural form through structural reorganization (e.g., the creation of component divisions which operated internationally).   Such persistence may be viewed as positive in an adaptive sense since it supports GM's objective to internationalize the company.   However, in the case of decoupled systems, we see a negative or maladaptive form of persistence, as domestic managers continue to further their own agenda at the peril of the larger corporation.   The persistence of the anti-international form may be viewed as a form of structural and ideological lag in which the status quo hangs onto its old response patterns long after such responses have outlived their usefulness.   The executives also play a role here in that they have permitted the continuing structural isolation of the domestic staffs and car divisions which underpins the domestic managers' anti-international ideology.   Thus, our study has begun to illuminate some of the forces underlying cultural persistence including environmental shifts (i.e., new market conditions made useful the old pro-international pattern), structural conditions (i.e., the administrative isolation of domestic managers precluded their interest in international affairs, and ideological traditions which cross generations of employees at all classification levels.

Finally, our study has highlighted the need for multiple sources of data in historical reconstruction. It would have been impossible to trace the path of GM's international evolution and the cultural consequences of this evolution without access to a range of different historical records. Of particular value was the triangulation of archival records and oral histories, a process which enabled the combination of complementary types of data, while simultaneously providing a built-in check on the historical accuracy of individual data items.

In conclusion, we reiterate our recommendation of the historical method as a tool of great power in the description and explanation of cultural phenomena in organizations. This method enable the conceptualization of structural and ideological forms and allows the tracing of their evolution over time. It is through the comparison of these evolving forms that our understanding of cultural process and cultural change in organizations is strengthened.

ACKNOWLEDGEMENTS

We appreciate the willingness of so many GM employees to speak with us about the wide variety of issues surrounding the overseas assignment. Special thanks go to members of the International Personnel Administration Staff for their help and guidance throughout the study. The comments from our many reviewers helped to make the paper stronger. They included Jacques Pasquire, Rich Rachner, Bob Szydlowski, Jan Benson, Ken Barb, Kathy Kay, Erine Smith, Plato Bageris, Dick Girling, John Meehan, Werner Volger, and the editors of this book Tomoko Hamada and Will Sibley. Judy Beeber Chrisman helped interview some of the GM managers and assisted with portions of the analysis. Library support was provided by Marilynn Alexander, Sara Bowker, and Suzanne Petre. The figures were designed by Ray Volger while the graphics were completed by Chuck Pycz.

NOTES

1. A subculture is a "pattern that is in significant respects distinctive but that has important continuities with a host or dominant culture" (Broom and Selznick 1973).

2. During Phase I, ISPs were known as HOSPs -- Home Office Status Personnel.

3. While many new hires were American born and had a strong interest in working and living abroad, others were foreign born, often schooled or trained in the U.S. The latter were particularly useful to the overseas operations because of their familiarity with other cultures and business practices.

4. By the late 1970s, some female employees accepted overseas assignments as ISPs. In 1987, for example, four of the 472 ISPs overseas were females.

5. Because we did not have aggregate data from the end of the Transition Period, we cited data from 1982, the first year in which this data was available.

6. GM began to recruit another source of ISP candidates from non-domestic operations to fill managerial and technical positions around the world. These ISPs were referred to as ISP-OS (overseas) in contrast to those who originated in the U.S., or ISP-US (*Annual Report* 1974:7). Reducing the proportion of American ISPs assigned to overseas duty, along with increasing the number of ISP-OS and local national employees, were viewed no only as responses to rising nationalism and as mechanisms to assist in GM's internationalization process, but also as means of cutting costs associated with overseas assignments.

7. During Phase II, the number of ISPs leaving from component divisions increased relative to those form car divisions. In 1982, 836 (29 percent) of the ISPs worldwide had home units in component divisions. By 1987, 472 (54 percent) of all ISPs overseas that year left from component divisions (personal communication with a GM administrator 1987).

REFERENCES

Aldrich, H. E.
1979   *Organizations and Environments.* Englewood   Cliffs, NJ:
            Prentice Hall.

Allaire, Y. and M. E. Firsirotu
1984   Theories of Organizational Culture, *Organizational Studies,*
            5(3):193-226.

Automotive News
1986   Pp. 73-74, April 30.

Briody, E. K. and M. L. Baba
1991   Explaining Differences in Repatriation Experiences: The
            Discovery of Coupled and Decoupled Systems, *American
            Anthropologist,* 93(2):322-344.

Cray, E.
1980   *Chrome Colossus: General Motors and Its Times.* New York:
            McGraw-Hill Book Co.

Deming, W. E.
1982   *Out of the Crisis.* Cambridge, MA: MIT Press.

General Motors Corporation
1971   *Annual Report.* Detroit, MI.

General Motors Corporation
1974   *Annual Report.* Detroit, MI.

General Motors Corporation
1951   *General Motors World,* 3(1).

General Motors Corporation
1951   *General Motors World,* 3(4).

General Motors Corporation
1961   *General Motors World,* 40(3).

General Motors Corporation
1963   *General Motors World,* 42(3).

General Motors Corporation
  1985-86   *GM Information Handbook.* Detroit, MI.

Schein, E. H.
  1985   *Organizational Culture and Leadership.*   San Francisco:
             Jossey-Bass, Inc.

Stinchcombe, A. L.
  1965   Social Structure and Organizations   In   *Handbook of
             Organizations.* J.G. March, ed., Chicago: Rand McNally, 142-
             193.

PART THREE

VOICES FROM THE FIELD:
WORKING ORGANIZATIONAL CULTURE

INTRODUCTION

Tomoko Hamada

The culture concept is now widely used by management consultants and practicing anthropologists in a variety of organizational situations. One major difference between theory-oriented academic anthropologists and applied behavioral scientists is that the latter needs to apply theories and concepts to solve problems in real situations. Here an important question becomes: How useful is the culture concept to solve administrative or managerial problems? Or is this the right kind of question to ask? Where is the meeting point between the praxis and theory of anthropology?

This part presents voices from the field of management consulting and applied anthropology. While each author's definitions of and ideas about the use of the culture concept differ significantly as discussed in the next five chapters, they all seem to agree that certain caution and care must be exercised in applying the concept to organizational phenomena. Like many powerful ideas that are recently employed in a fresh area of scientific investigation, without rigorous examination of the model, the application of the culture metaphor can become too loose or too wide a cognitive scheme for understanding organizational reality and/or for developing strategies and policies. Some authors emphasize the merits presented by this "new" view of looking at organization as a cultural system, while others point out the problem of employing traditional anthropological research methods in contemporary North American organizations. Some argue that differing expectations and goals between management scientists, managers, and anthropologists may create a particularly difficult problem of synthesizing theories in organizational culture studies.

Maccoby begins with a positive note that the holistic concept of culture developed by anthropologists can help managers to see more clearly the symbiotic relationship between corporate culture and its larger culture. His essay discusses the elements of corporate culture and its relationship to the societal culture of which it is a part. McLeod and Wilson, on the other hand, caution that anthropologists and students of corporate culture share a common problem because of their own cultural baggage which conditions and determines the kinds of research results. They note that the problems of such cultural blindness are particularly significant when the researcher is studying a culture similar to his or her own. Is there some risk that anthropologists studying their own culture might fail to see cultural patterns into which they are thoroughly acculturated? McLeod and Wilson's answer to this question is yes. They maintain that anthropologists must face this serious problem of cultural similarity as a fundamental theoretical problem of contemporary anthropology and analysts of corporate cultures.

Some authors are particularly concerned with the wholesale application of the organizational culture model as a management tool. After having experienced firsthand one company's attempt to "create" a corporate culture in Silicon Valley, it becomes abundantly clear to Reynolds that the idea of a single corporate culture that characterizes all levels of the organization is both naive and undesirable. It is inevitable that people in organization have differing conceptions of appropriate social action, but most significantly, cultural diversity is inevitable because their jobs require it.

Manning Nash stresses that the culture concept is useful as a powerful corrective to the current excess of individualist, utilitarian, and rationalistic modes of inquiry in the field of organizational studies. He maintains a view that the meanings of culture are chiefly carried in symbolic conveyances, and that they are directly related to social structure and individuals who make up ever-changing webs of social relationships. Nash emphasizes the interplay between levels of cultural meaning and spans of social organization. Like Maccoby, he believes that the "culture" of a particular organization can only be understood as a localization of certain meanings that are directly related to the wider set of cultural meanings in society. At the same time, he sees that these widest cultural meanings are also being defined, shaped, and changed in actual loci in the sphere of organizational activities.

Human knowledge and practice cannot be created in a vacuum; they are situated in historical, socio-political, and cultural contexts. Anthropologists and managers are both socialized and encultured into their own professional cultures. DiBella illuminates different meanings of culture developed in the anthropological discipline and that of management due to the two disciplines' different cultural orientations. DiBella argues that the difficulty in making culture a concept meaningful to the management profession stems from the latter's cultural orientation towards factors that can be manipulated, controlled, and managed. Generally speaking, the manager wants to understand organizational culture because he or she wants to make the organization more efficient or productive, while the anthropologist tries to understand cultures so that the dynamics of comparative human behavior, social, cultural, and economic change can be better understood. In spite of various difficulties in bridging the two different professional cultures, there are many areas of convergence, particularly in international management studies. Here the culture concepts can be applied successfully to solve managerial problems. Other areas that would benefit from the application of the culture concept include the fields of cross-cultural human resources; the impact assessment of joint ventures and mergers; and in the evaluation of implementing changes in organizations. These chapters clarify problems and challenges in applying anthropological perspectives to complex organizational phenomena.

THE CORPORATION AS A
PART-CULTURE

Michael Maccoby

The concept of corporate culture has rapidly become part of the common language of managers and business writers.[1] Before the 1980s, the concept was seldom, if ever, used. Now that corporations are being forced to adapt to a changing environment, they are learning that shared values and corporate practices will either facilitate or impede adaptation. As they attempt to change corporate culture, managers find this requires a holistic analysis. What they may fail to recognize is that corporate culture does not stand alone; it is a part culture. To change the corporate culture managers should understand its symbiotic connection to a larger culture. To influence this change in a way that benefits society, government officials who develop policy and regulate the corporations should also understand this connection. This essay describes the elements of corporate culture and its relationship to the societal culture of which it is a part.

WHAT IS CORPORATE CULTURE?

Most definitions of culture by anthropologists follow Taylor's description of "that complete whole which included knowledge, belief, art, law, morals, custom, and any other capabilities and habits acquired by man as a member of society."[2] Culture is not only the laws and customs which can be stated or written, it also includes the internalized values that drive behavior. A culture molds human nature, the inborn instincts, drives or dynamic tendencies into what might be called **value-drives**, motivated behavior patterns that have meaning for people. Family, school and workplace shape and give meaning to human needs for survival, relatedness, pleasure, knowledge, mastery, play and dignity.[3]

Following Kroeber, the modern business corporation can be considered a part-culture, since it cannot exist separate from larger national cultures. Kroeber described peasant society as a part culture because it depended on the larger culture of the city, its economic system, technology, political authority, religion, and educational practices. Kroeber writes: "Peasants are definitely rural -- yet live in relation to market towns; they form a class segment of a larger population which usually contains urban centers, sometimes metropolitan capitals. They constitute part societies with part cultures."[4] Often what appears uniquely part of peasant culture changes through contact with the city, and today peasant villages are changing rapidly, due in large part to the dynamism of the corporation which has become ever more efficient at delivering its products and services throughout the world.

The values and behavior of peasant culture have been rooted in the dominant mode of production of the small farmer who lives in a world of "limited good" where survival and striving for prosperity depend on family solidarity, hard work, and thrift. These values which have been adaptive for the peasant are formed within the family and reinforced by rituals and folklore.[5]

Unlike peasant culture which includes the institutions of family, school religion and work which form value-drives during childhood, the corporation selects some of the best-educated people formed by the larger culture and further molds them to fit its customs and strategic purposes. The corporation influences what is taught in university, school and home about the qualities required for success. While the peasant culture follows the innovation of the city like the caboose on the freight train, the corporation, particularly those employing the most advanced technology, is the engine that drives cultural change. The corporation creates new jobs and models productive relationships. It develops the technologies of communication and automation which wipe away jobs that are no longer needed. Its demand for resources, support, and protection influence domestic and foreign policy. The programs it sponsors and its advertising mould popular language and consciousness.

Because corporations use the institutions of society to create wealth for owners and employees, society has the right to regulate and tax corporations, to prevent them from spoiling the environment, to insist they support goal of fairness in hiring and promotion, to require that they share their wealth with the larger society that educates their employees, builds the infrastructure needed for corporations, and defends corporations with the police, judicial system, foreign trade agreement, and ultimately the armed forces. These national law and custom constrain corporate culture and keep it within bounds of accepted behavior. Correspondingly, because corporations generate wealth, society is willing to adjust education and political institutions to support corporate success.

Corporate culture is sometimes defined as the organizational values, customs, symbols and structures relationships which determine behavior and create a sense of shared meaning at work. As a consultant to managers forced to adapt to a changing environment, I find that they need operational definitions which focus attention on what needs to change and the resistances to change. Leaders of change processes need to see corporate culture holistically as connecting culture from both the historical point of view (diachronic) and in terms of how the culture is presently adapted to its environment (synchronic).

The diachronic approach describes what worked in the past. It is a method of contrasting present conditions with past practices and of challenging managers to plan for the future. It provides the reasons why some practices persist, even though they are no longer effective and may, in fact, impede adaptation.

The synchronic approach analyzes the formal and informal elements which adapt the corporate culture to its environment. The formal elements include strategy, structure, technology, rules, measurements, systems for recruiting, education and motivating employees and for dealing with the heavy flows of information required by a modern corporation. The informal elements include the quality of relationships, management style, symbols, and shared values.[6] These informal elements are determined in part by the behavior of leaders who model styles and use symbols. But they are also influenced by the larger culture of which the corporation is a part.

THE INTEREST IN CORPORATE CULTURE

The increased interest in corporate culture by managers is due to the demand on companies to change, to adapt to global competition that calls for innovation, quality, and increased productivity. This competition intensified during the 70's and 80,s as Germany and Japan recovered from World War II and developing low wage countries like Korea, Taiwan, Brazil and Mexico cost upgraded their manufacturing capability. At the same time, deregulation of telecommunications and airlines threatened the survival of companies unable to compete. However, as companies have attempted to implement new strategies to improve quality and productivity, they have discovered that the change they seek require profound transformation in the organization of work and the way people relate to each other. This is a transformation from, what might be called industrial bureaucracies to entrepreneurial "technoservice".[7]

The need to transform corporate culture results not only from competition, but from an increased complexity in products and processes. For the first 75 years of the 20th century, the strategy of industrial bureaucracies was to produce standardized products with the mass production, assembly line method pioneered by Henry Ford with the manufacture of the model T car.

This form of production used F. W. Taylor's theories of scientific management to design work. Lower level jobs were simplified and made so that relatively uneducated workers required little training and could easily be replaced. Given the standardized product, companies were organized into functional hierarchies. Given a view of human nature that each person would try to maximize his own gain, companies used internal competition and incentive systems as a way of motivating people and at the same time controlling them.

In theory, all the uniform corporate roles were controlled and coordinated up the functional hierarchies to the chief executive who was the single person responsible for the whole. In place, each individual, worker and manager alike, attempted to maximize autonomy and successful work relationships depended on negotiations at all levels.[8]

This corporate culture caused large class differences between workers and managers, reinforced by differences in dress, offices, dining rooms, etc., as well as wages. In large industries, workers joined unions which to some extent protected them from the dehumanization of the Tayloristic system and the arbitrary authority of foremen. Detailed contracts in the steel and auto industry, among others, institutionalized scientific management by prohibiting management from changing the job content once it had been determined by industrial engineers. As long as they held monopolistic positions in the market, American industries could accept the limitation on production and flexibility caused by these contracts and pass the added costs to customers who had no choice but to pay them.

Until they were hit by competition, American managers did not have to think about their corporate cultures. They were the world-class models of good management, and there was no reason for them to change.

JAPAN AND QUALITY MANAGEMENT

A major challenge to the Tayloristic industrial bureaucracy came from the Japanese companies which succeeded in producing higher quality products at a lower cost then American companies. In the 70's, Americans attributed this to lower Japanese labor costs. However, in the 80's, it became evident that labor costs did not explain the difference. The Japanese managed differently and more effectively, at least in the manufacturing industry. Unlike American managers, they worked at narrowing status differences. Rather than simplifying frontline jobs, they expanded them and gave workers more training and responsibility for quality and continuous improvement of products and processes. Rather than motivation through internal competition, they rewarded teamwork.

How much has the success of Japanese companies resulted from their embeddedness in Japanese national culture? The answer is not simple.

On the one hand, Japanese quality management was learned form American experts, such as W. Edwards Deming and Joseph Juran, who were brought to Japan after World War II to help the Japanese in rebuilding their industry.[9] The Japanese adopted quality methods that American companies did not consider necessary. Furthermore, in reducing status distinctions at work, the traditionally hierarchical Japanese followed General Douglas MacArthur's commands to become more democratic and to provide workers with lifetime employment.

On the other hand, the Japanese culture benefitted from a Confucian tradition which reinforced quality management by stressing reciprocal obligations, cooperation, and leadership as teaching. Furthermore, the Japanese educational system has supported industry. At Toyota in Nagoya, assembly workers with a high school education are capable of doing tests and calculations that are done by college educated engineers in the U.S.

Whatever the importance of national culture, Japanese managers have shown that their quality approach works as well with Americans and Europeans as it does with the Japanese. A dramatic example was a General Motors plant in Fremont, California which suffered from poor quality and adversarial labor relations. Under Toyota management, the same workers were superior to other GM plants in quality, and relations with the United Auto Workers became a model of cooperation.

ENTREPRENEURIAL COMPANIES

Another challenge to the industrial bureaucratic culture has come from small and middle sized companies. As large industrial bureaucracies have down-sized, these companies have expanded by a strategy of innovative and customized products and services and a culture that emphasizes self management and taking responsibility for solving customer problems.[10]

Technology has also forced change in the industrial bureaucratic culture. With computerized production systems, it is no longer possible to use Tayloristic principles. Workers close to the technology must understand the system and be empowered to take quick action. Otherwise management risks costly accidents and loss of capital investments.

In cases where companies like AT&T in the U.S. or L.M. Ericsson in Sweden sell and maintain large telecommunication and information systems for business customers, technical employees must work cooperatively with development engineers and customers. The boundary between supplier and customer practically disappears. Hierarchy, autonomy and narrow functional responsibility all get in the way of effectiveness. Innovation, customization, quality and productivity require teamwork and shared responsibility. The culture of the industrial bureaucracy is no longer adaptive. Corporate cultures must become entrepreneurial and service-minded, or they will disappear. Mass production must become technoservice.

NATIONAL AND SOCIAL CHARACTER

Although the strategy and structure of industrial bureaucracies throughout the world have been similar, important variations result from national institutions and values, as has been noted concerning Japan. Differences in the sense of equity influence reward systems. In egalitarian Sweden, a chief executive will make only 10 times the salary of a skilled worker, while in the U.S. the ratio in large companies can be 100:1. In Germany and Scandinavia, unions have cooperated with management to allow flexible work rules in exchange for political power and board membership.[11] In contrast American unions have defended individual rights at the shop floor, protecting worker owner-ship of job content at the expense of managerial flexibility and productivity. In Sweden, management develops consensus by strength-ening the informal organization through off site meetings, sometimes including spouses. In contrast, German managers maintain strictly formal relationships, and they even consider it unethical to develop special intimate relations outside work, since this might distort objectivity at work. European and Japanese managers view Americans as more individualistic and "political" in the sense that they tend to tailor their views according to what they believe the boss wants and what will most further their careers. Other researchers have also called attention to the influence of national differences on managerial behavior, even within the same corporation.[12]

In each country, corporations try to select employees with values that fit its culture. These values are then further shaped by corporate practices and incentives. Up until now, the majority of corporate employees have been brought up in a family structure that shaped attitudes and values which have fit industrial bureaucracy.

Typically, the employee of the industrial bureaucracy grew up in a family headed by a male who was the sole wage earner. The father represented the outside world of meritocratic work and the mother, the inside world of the supportive family. The father conveyed the demands of the industrial bureaucratic work world and became the model of a good authority. The goal of the future employee was to pass tests and on the basis of measured performance move up the hierarchies of school and work. The ideal boss, like a good father, respected autonomy and rewarded measured performance. The bad boss, like a bad father was over-controlling and punishing. Within the bureaucratic structure, employees at all levels sought to maximize personal autonomy and control, generally at the expense of those below them.

However, a new generation with different attitudes to authority and institutions is being raised in families with dual wage earners. In these families parents share authority, and there is less differentiation of sex roles. From an early age, this new generation has been sent to day care and pre-schools, where they have learned to be emotionally independent and at the same time get along with new groups, and strangers. They say their main goal at work is to further personal development. From childhood, they have been oriented to continual learning and sharpening skills at interpersonal relationships as a means toward successful adaption to changing conditions and new people. They distrust organizations and want to maintain their marketability and independence.

The new generation resents work that does not allow them to develop their skills. This not only includes work that separates hand from brain, but also specialized work separated from the whole purpose of the organization. They want to conduct business, be enterprisers, not perform in bureaucratic roles. They find teamwork natural and like work that demands learning from customers and co-workers.

Their values have been formed by a historical period of rapid technological innovation, relative prosperity, emphasis on individual rights, challenge to traditional authority, corporate downsizing at the expense of the loyal company men, and the growth of the dual wage earning family. This is the dominant orientation to work of 20 percent of over 3000 employees I studied in the early and mid 1980's, 25 percent under 40 years of age, and 30 percent under 30.[13]

CHANGING CORPORATE CULTURE

The corporation has no choice. It must change, adapt to its environment at the same time that it takes a leading role in changing the larger culture of which it is a part. Managers are starting to use the concept of corporate culture as an intellectual tool for facilitating this adaptation. Given that they must take account not only of strategy, structure, systems and technology, but also relationships and values, an anthropological approach is essential to holistic understanding. As a consultant, I have used interactive planning, based on Ackoff's approach, as a means of developing such understanding and facilitating a process of change.[14]

This process starts out by challenging top management to describe an ideal future of the corporation, to compare it with the present, and to agree on actions to close the gaps. This ideal vision is then interpreted by each division of the company and these interpretations are presented to the top for approval or modification. The process results not only in a shared holistic strategy, through the interactive process, it creates commitment to implementation.

How the corporation attempts to adapt depends not only on an analysis of the environment and its own capabilities, but also on values. A company can take either a long term or short term approach to profitability. It can seek not only to serve customers, but also to improve the working lives of its employees and to strengthen the larger culture from which it draws resources.

Rarely does corporate leadership see its role as one of improving the larger culture. In a highly competitive marketplace, leaders focus their energies on increasing their revenues and cutting their costs. However, the new demands for quality and innovation force companies to invest more in their human resources which benefits society as a whole, not only with better goods and services, but also with more competent people. For the larger culture to maintain its own adaptability, it must both nurture and control the corporation. At the same time that it supports the corporation with improved schooling and infrastructue it must restrain the unbridled power of the corporation. Regulation projects the environment from irreparable damage, customers from fraudulent claims and harmful products, and employees from damage to their health and limitation of their rights. The business corporation is modern society's most powerful tool for creating wealth. To remain a cutting edge, the corporate culture must be carefully controlled, but not so much that if loses its capability to adapt and innovate.

NOTES

1.   See, for example, Charles J. Fornburn, Corporate Culture, Environment and Strategy. *Human Resource Management*, Vol. 22, Number 7/2, pp.139-152.

2.   E. B. Tylor, *Primitive Culture.* Boston, 1971. Quoted in A. L. Kroeber and Clyde Kluckhohn, *Culture, A Critical Review of Concepts and Definitions,* New York, Vintage Books, 1952.

3.   The concept of value drives is described in Michael Maccoby, *Why Work, Leading and Motivating the New Generation.* New York, Simon & Schuster, 1988.

4.   A. A. Kroeber, *Anthropology.* New York, Harcourt, Brace & Co., 1948, p.284.

5.   George M. Foster, What is Folk Culture? In *American Anthropologist,* LV, No. 2 Part 1 (April-June 1953) pp.164-169.

      George M. Foster, *Tzintzuntzan.* Boston: Little, Brown & Co., 1976. p. 122.

      Erich Fromm & Michael Maccoby, *Social Character in a Mexican Village.* Englewood Cliffs, NJ: Prentice-Hall, 1970.

6.   Richard Tanner Pascale and Anthony G. Athos, *The Art of Japanese Management.* New York, Simon and Shuster, 1981.

7.   Michael Maccoby, *Why Work.* [*op. cit.*]

8.   Michel Crozier, *The Bureaucratic Phenomenon.* Chicago, University of Chicago Press, 1964.

9.   Lloyd Dobbins and Clare Crawford-Mason, *Quality or Else.* Boston, Little-Brown, 1991.

10.   John Case, *From the Ground Up.* New York, Simon and Schuster, 1992.

11.   Michael J. Poire, Notes on the Crisis of American Labor and the Crisis of Macro-economic Regulation. MIT, unpublished paper, September 1981.

12.   Andre Laurent, The Cultural Diversity of Western Conceptions of Management. In: Joynt, p. and Warner, M (Eds) *Managing in Different Cultures,* Oslo, Universitetsforlaget, 1985.

      G. Hofstede, *Culture's Consequence.* Beverly Hills, Sage, 1980.

13.   Michael Maccoby, *Why Work*, op. cit.

14.   Michael Maccoby, Move from Hierarchy to Heterarchy, *Research Technology Management*, Volume 34, No 5, September-October 1991.

CORPORATE CULTURE STUDIES AND ANTHROPOLOGY: AN UNEASY SYNTHESIS?

J. R. McLeod and J. A. Wilson

OBSERVING THE OBSERVERS

In his article, "The Medicine Man," David McCurdy notes:

> Anthropological fieldwork will always engender conflict between the ethnographer's personal relationships and his research goals. Informants will always make demands on time that are normal from their perspective and anthropologists will respond to these demands as best they can. In the end field work must involve a compromise, a willingness to recognize that informants are people, too, and that their needs are bound to impinge on research (McCurdy 1976:6)

Certifying the complete objectivity of the researcher within a specific cultural environment is not the issue here, but guaranteeing that the participant-observer is aware of the terminology of anthropology and the history and range of the lexicon of culture would certainly help to insure better analyses by experts in corporate culture. In return, anthropologists have much to learn from corporate culture specialists in terms of applying their lexicon to real world problems contemporary social contexts and gaining access to government and corporate elites. Through the interaction of the different perspectives on the "Culture paradigm", the goal of an anthropology of modern life (Boas 1986) might ultimately be achieved. However, the difficulties of such an enterprise were presaged by Franz Boas in his essay "Modern Life and Primitive Culture" (Boas 1986:204-5):

The scientific study of generalized social forms requires, therefore, that the investigator free himself from all valuations based on our culture. An objective, strictly scientific inquiry can only be made if we succeed in entering each culture on its own basis, if we elaborate the ideals of each people and include in our general objective study cultural values as found among different branches of mankind.

Anthropologists and students of corporate culture share a common problem, as the cultural baggage which they take to the field with them conditions and determines the types of research results which are achieved. Presumption, similarity, and familiarity are all connected in the framework process, and it is central to the research project to recognize them and analyze their effects on the investigative enterprise. These problems are especially acute in cultural situations in which the area under study resembles the analyst's own culture.

Presumption and similarity are connected in the fieldwork process in several ways. First of all, the idea that we can understand other cultures by doing fieldwork is presumptuous in the extreme. Science itself, in the last analysis, is a presumption about the ability of the human mind to comprehend the universe in which it finds itself, natural or social. But there are several presumptions built into anthropological training and fieldwork which can enable the fieldworker to overcome bias in ethnographic description and overcome presumption and similarity. Presumption and similarity work against the fieldworker on several levels, limiting valid description and preventing worthwhile analysis. The problem becomes especially acute as anthropologists and students of corporate culture study contexts which are profoundly similar to the cultures of the observer in many historical and cultural facets. As Stephenson and Greer note concerning the problems of Americans studying Appalachian culture:

> Ethnographers do not record observations and events randomly, but with regard for their meaning and pattern. Is there some risk that researchers studying their own culture might fail to see culture patterns into which they are thoroughly acculturated? Of course, it is quite possible that the reverse is true -- that familiarity aids perceptions. Our experience suggests that it does not. Certain patterns and practices may be so much a part of the "taken for granted" realm that extra caution and effort must be put forth not to overlook them (Stephenson and Greer 1981:124)

The use of the term 'ritual' in corporate settings (McLeod 1990a) is just one example of the lack of perspective in corporate culture research which could be overcome by a more complete knowledge of the anthropological literature and better training in the techniques of fieldwork.

This paradoxical difficulty of seeming to know a culture too well while actually taking important cultural features for granted is much more than a simple recognition of the importance of "cultural baggage" in the fieldwork process. Anthropology has historically been a business of cross-cultural comparison, and presuming similarity where there is difference is a fundamental problem of participant-observation. For the research anthropologists of the early 20th century, such difficulties seldom, if ever, came to light. Confronted as they were with cultures so vastly different from their own, perceptions of the "bizarre" were enough to guarantee descriptions which were, at the very least, interesting enough to read well. Malinowski's (1961:237-248) description of the famous *mulukwavsi* of the "flying witches" and of the *Kula* cycle of myth and magic (1961:392-427) in *Argonauts of the Western Pacific*, for example, were so profoundly divergent from western concepts of cause and effect that they clearly deserved academic attention. Similarly, his criticism of the Freudian Oedipus complex, based as it was on the matrilineal system of kinship and reciprocity, created an academic firestorm among psychoanalysts and anthropologists alike. Studies of witch craft and magic, such as those by Evans-Pritchard among the Azande (1937) and Wilson among the Nyakyusa (1963), highlighted magico-religious practices of a sort virtually unknown in contemporary Britain and America. As Ernest Gellner points out:

> The original concern of anthropology with culturally very distant, "primitive" societies naturally impelled anthropologists into a preoccupation with the problem of interpreting very alien ideas and mentalities. Handling this problem, like that of kinship, is one of their professional specialties (Gellner 1988:22).

That anthropology as a discipline (Mcleod 1990b) has a built-in bias concerning the study of similar cultural contexts, is derived from the history of anthropology as a science conducted in non-western cultures. As Messerschmidt notes:

In terms of differences in method, perhaps Yehudi Cohen is partly correct when he implies that the traditional anthropological enterprise is not adequately prepared to accomplish the objectives of research in societies other than those of tribal or peasant peoples (Cohen 1977:389). I am not altogether convinced, however, that we totally lack what he called the requisite "concepts, paradigms, and methods" to study all or part of modern industrial society. Rather the problem lies in the dearth of new and innovative strategies with which to employ our well-tested concepts, paradigms, and methods (Messerschmidt 1981:200).

This problem of concept, paradigms, and methods has been viewed rather differently by those in the study of organizational culture, who have adopted what they call the "culture paradigm" wholesale. The fundamental problem for anthropologists and others studying corporate cultures is to come to some decisions about whether or not they have any agreement concerning the culture paradigm.

If that simple goal of recognizing the importance of the culture paradigm could be realized by anthropologists somewhere outside of introductory cultural anthropology textbooks, the problems of **similarity**, **familiarity**, and **presumption** could be put in perspective and resolved to a large extent. The degree to which anthropologist and analysts of corporate culture are willing to come to some agreement about methods, concepts, and theories will determine their ability to do creative and useful work in the emerging new field of institutional anthropology. As Lewis point out:

> Historians, being professional obituary writers, prey necrophilically upon the dead; we cannibalize the living. The distance which separates historians from 'other cultures' of the past is of course temporal, not spatial as in our case. But in both disciplines it is surely the imaginative juxtapositioning of subject and object and the ability to achieve dramatic shifts of perspective which, as in painting, provide the ultimate source of our special significance and appeal. The nature of the historian's subject matter, however, excludes the possibilities of face-to-face field-work, and here we part company. For this is our enviable privilege, our distinctive way of confronting our subjects and sources, the cult we pay to our Muse through the hallowed ritual of participant observation (Lewis 1973:3-4).

As a result, the perspective of the *non-native observer* (Malinowski 1948, 1961) is not readily available to the practitioner of "institutional anthropology". *Similarity* in cultural form and process, not *difference* are the major impediments to analyses and description which are not culture bound and trivial. This may also be the major reason that so few anthropologists are involved in this study in a central way (McLeod 1990b). As E.T. Hall noted in February, 1991 *Anthropology Newsletter*:

> It has always been a mystery to me why more anthropologists do not work with business. Business needs them, and anthropologists can learn from working with business.

Unfortunately, the luxury of studying cultures with extremely divergent sets of cultural meaning and behaviors can no longer be afforded by the contemporary cultural anthropologist. While analysts of corporate culture have appropriated the essential insights from the disciplines, anthropologists have allowed the problems of presumption and similarity to stifle description and analysis of similar cultural contexts, especially business and corporate cultures.

Anthropological insights and techniques have invaded many other disciplines and have had significant influences on them. It is interesting to note that the use of the "Culture paradigm" in anthropology itself has seen a notable decline in the last two decades, while in other disciplines it has flowered as never before. While anthropologists spend an immense amount of time arguing about whether or not such a paradigm even exists, other disciplines have borrowed the "non-existent" paradigm wholesale. This trend is perhaps most notable in the field of organizational studies, where the term "culture" has become a watchword in management circles. Such studies borrowing from anthropology include Sanday's (1979) article, "The Ethnographic Paradigm(s), Barney's (1986) "Organizational Culture: Can it be a Source of Sustained Competitive Advantage?", Allaire and Firislow's (1984) "Theories of Organizational Culture," Trice and Beyer's (1984) "Studying Organizational Culture Through Rites and Ceremonial," Fine's (1984) "Negotiated Orders and Organizational Culture." The last study was perhaps the best review article of the literature to that date, and the authors were very specific about the importance of organizational culture studies to organizational research in general:

Few readers would disagree that the study of organizational culture
has become one of the major domains of organizational research,
and some might even argue that it is the single most active arena,
eclipsing studies of formal structure, of organizational environment
research, and of bureaucracy (Ouchi and Wilkins 1985:457-458).

However, as anthropology itself has moved into the study of
contemporary western societies, problems specific to the study of
similar cultural contexts have emerged. Wolf (1972) noted the
problems of American anthropologists trying to study their own society
analytically, and proposed a concentration by anthropologists on the
study of power within American society and culture. Nader (1972)
made a similar point when she called for "studying up" and observing
American power structures using anthropological techniques. Anthropologists have since then become involved in the study of very similar
cultural contexts, including Firth's study of Kinship in London, Moffat's
(1989) study of college and American culture, Plotnicov's (1987) study
of urban political economy, Susser's (1982) analysis of urban poverty
and politics, Stroup's (1984) study of utility regulations in Ohio,
McLeod's (1991) study of American political culture, Hinshaw's (1980)
study of anthropology and administration, Ginsberg's (1989) study of
the abortion debate in Fargo, North Dakota, Britan, Cohen's (1980)
analysis of administrative hierarchies, and Baba's (1986) analysis of the
cultures of business. These studies by anthropologists and many others
have all examined contemporary cultural contexts. As a result,
anthropologists are presently engaged in the study of fields which
overlap disciplines as divergent as public administration, sociology,
organizational studies, management, public policy, urban studies,
nursing, education, medicine, and political science.

While the problems of similarity, familiarity, and presumption have
bedeviled anthropologists engaged in the study of their own and similar
societies, the "culture paradigm" (Sanday 1979) has been wholly
appropriated by those engaged in the study of complex organizations.
Throughout the literature, names such as Malinowski, Geertz, and
Kluckhohn predominate in the newly energized field of organizational
culture studies. While it is true that anthropologists and anthropology
have no monopoly on the concept of culture, it is important to note that
few anthropologists have contributed to this literature and to this debate.
However, the importance of anthropology to the study of complex

organizations within similar culture contexts cannot be overstated. Ouchi and Wilkins assert:

> Many students of organizational culture would assert that their primary intellectual debt is to the anthropologist rather than to the sociologist... Most of the currently "popular" work on the organization culture...as well as other work written for management audiences and management scholars draws upon the spirit if not the details of the functionalist tradition in anthropology ... Malinowski and Radcliffe-Brown might be appalled by the explicitly proman-agement and change-oriented bias of many contemporary scholars, but the impact of their organic, whole view of the structure and functioning social systems on the contemporary or organizational culture is undeniable (Ouchi and Wilkins 1985:460).

The major reason for this failure among anthropologists to contribute substantially to this literature and this field is the problem of similarity and presumption in cultural anthropology. Cultural similarity prevents valid anthropological analysis, and is a fundamental problem facing contemporary anthropology and analysts of corporate cultures. If anthropologists are to contribute to the study of modern cultural forms, they will be forced to confront the problems of similarity directly and to come to terms with the difficulties inherent in an anthropology of meatier (and post-modern) institutional forms. It is also essential that anthropologists become conversant with the literature in organizational studies and corporate culture theory.

In the same vein, students of corporate and organizational culture need to be conversant in both the literature and field training of anthropologists; in short, *we need each other*. Anthropologists receive complex training the research methodologies of field ethnography and knowledge in cross-cultural studies; corporate analysts are well versed in the complexities of organizational process and access to organization-al cultures. As Schein has noted concisely:

> I do not see a unique role for the traditional industrial organiza-tional psychologist, but I see great potential for the psychologist to work as a team member with colleagues who are more ethno-graphically oriented. The particular skill that will be needed on the part of the psychologist will be knowledge of organizations and of how to work with them, especially in a consulting relationship. Organizational culture is a complex phenomenon, and we should

not rush to measure things until we understand better what we are measuring (Schein 1990:118).

CONCLUSION

Guaranteeing the absolute objectivity of the observer within a specific cultural context is not the goal, as it probably cannot be achieved with any certainty. All human beings are culture-bound, whether or not they have had the experience of living within another cultural context for an extended period of time. Participant observation in another culture is no guarantee of objectivity or scientific validity when one's own culture is the object of study. When anthropologists or students of corporate cultures are confronted by similar cultural contexts, their first requirement should be to recognize the categories which they bring into what Geertz (1983:151) calls the "significative world." The terminology of modern anthropology was derived and determined by the necessity to categorize modes of thought and social organization from those which exist in modern complex cultures (Gellner 1988). This is the major reason why fields of endeavor other than anthropology have brought the conceptions of culture to the study of modern institutional forms. However, whether one is operating out of an interpretivist paradigm, an organizational culture paradigm, a materialist paradigm, or a paradigm which proceeds from the assumption that culture is best understood as a text, the obligation of the anthropologist and the student of corporate culture alike must still be to distance their activities as analysts clearly from the objects of study. In the previous age of anthropology, this was accomplished by both the possession of a set of technical terms which made description of 'exotic' cultures possible, and by the automatic distance which was imposed by observing and analyzing cultures radically different from one's own. In the modern age of the 'culture paradigm', however, neither of these means of distancing the observer from the observed still holds sway. The continuing use of terminology derived from the study of non-western societies to analyze events in the modern world does indeed have significant academic worth; but anthropologists have a special role to play in determining that the terminology is used with comparative ethnographic significance. Geertz's 'significative worlds' must include the analysis of differences as well as similarity, and the only way to guarantee that is to insure that the observer has a real familiarity with the ethnographic reports written by anthropologists about other cultures. Simply citing Geertz, Kluckhohn, and Radcliffe-Brown, and then operating without an understanding of the ethnographic contexts from which their conceptualizations are derived is not enough. Such an understanding of the cultural and social anthropology of the twentieth century is bound to be culture bound, and guarantees that the problem of cultural similarity will obscure the observer's description and analysis. This problem does not apply to all modern organizational culture studies by any means, but it does occur often enough that the problem of similarity and science will be with us for a long time to come. The systematics of modern cultural forms challenge anthropologists and corporate culture analysts to overcome the limitations of method imposed by the history of their respective disciplines and to undertake a truly comparative ethnographic inquiry. This comparative ethnography could potentially yield a truly analytical ethnography, conscious of ethnoscience and hermeneutics, but apart from both.

Valid cross-cultural comparisons between cultural forms in the modern world and those from the traditional world are not, as some Foucaultians would have us believe, merely a profound kind of ethnocentrism. Rather, such comparisons follow in the best traditions of the anthropological muse; an analytical understanding of modern institutional forms derived from sociology, anthropology organizational culture studies, and so on. In fact, what anthropology must do in the modern context is to return to the holism which characterized its earliest roots as a social endeavor. What of students of corporate culture must do is to deepen their anthropological insights. In order to accomplish this goal, anthropologists have a special role to play in critically analyzing the use of their terminology and the 'culture paradigm' in the analysis of modern cultural forms. Corporate culture analysts have a special role to play through their knowledge of the real world of corporate cultures. By making other disciplines and themselves conscious of the problems of analyzing similar cultural contexts, contemporary anthropologists and corporate culture specialists alike can contribute to the goal set for them by Gellner (1988); that of developing an anthropology of modern institutions which is both analytical and comparative, and which reflects the best insights of a discipline conscious of its own place in the development of science. As Wilson (1990:15) has noted concisely:

Corporate culture researchers, along with those who attempt to deepen, correct, or largely change organizations via manipulations of factors within corporate culture, would do well to move toward a more significant understanding of the concept and process of culture itself and to attach their efforts to the findings and methods of cultural anthropology, ethnomethodology, and social-psychiatry -- both for the benefits to be directly derived and to "feed" the results back into these larger fields so that all can stimulate, cross-validate, and enrich each other.

REFERENCES

Allaire, Y. and M. E. Firisotou
    1984   Theories of Organizational Culture. *Organizational Studies.* 5(3):193-226.

Baba, M.
    1986   *Business and Industrial Anthropology.* Washington, D.C.: NAPA, American Anthropology Association.

Barney, J. B.
    196   Organizational Culture: Can it be a Source of Competitive Advantage? *Academy of Management Review,* 11(3).

Boas, F.
    1986   *Anthropology and Modern Life.* New York: Dover. First published 1928.

Britan, G. and R. Cohen
    1980   Toward an Anthropology of Formal Organizations. **In** *Hierarchy and Society,* Britain and Cohen, Eds. Philadelphia: Institute for the Study of Human Issues.

Deal, T and A. Kennedy
    1982   *Cultures.* Reading, MA.: Addison-Wesley.

Evans-Pritchard, E. E.
    1937   *Witchcraft, Oracles, and Magic Among the Azande* Oxford: Clarendon Press.

Gellner, E.
    1988   The Stakes in Anthropology. **In** *American Scholar* Winter,
               1988.

Ginsburg, F.
    1989   *Lives.* Berkeley: University of California Press.

Hellriegel, D., T. Slocum and R. Woodman
    1989   *Organizational Behavior.*   St. Paul, Minnesota: West
               Publishing.

Hinshaw, R.
    1980   Anthropology, Administration, and Public Policy. **In** *Annual
               Review of Anthropology* 9:497-522.

Johnsrud, C.
    1989   *Program or Profit? Traditional vs. Non-Traditional Linkages
               for the Commercial Development of Space.* PhD. Disserta-
               tion, Department of Anthropology, University of Florida.

Kroeber, A. K. and C. Kluckhohn
    1952   *Culture: A Critical Review of Concepts and Definitions.*
               New York: Vintage.

Lewis, I. M.
    1973   *The Anthropologist's Muse.* London School of Economics
               and Political Science. London: Broadwater Press.

McLeod, J.
    1985   The Labour Party and Administration in East London.
               Journal of Anthropology 4(2):17-39. Winter, 1985.

McLeod, J.
    1989   Ritual in Corporate Culture Studies: An Anthropological
               Approach. *Journal of Ritual Studies.* 4(1):85-97.

    1990b   The Anthropology of Modern Institutions. *Anthropology
               Newsletter.* 31(8). November, 1990.

    1991   The Cult of the Divine America: Ritual, Symbol, and
               Mystification in American Political Culture. *International
               Journal of Moral and Social Studies.* 6(2):1-24.

Malinowski, B.
1948   *Magic, Science, and Religion.* New York: Doubleday.

1981   *Argonauts of the Western Pacific.* New York: Dutton, First published in 1922.

Martin, J. and C. Siehl
1983   Organizational Culture and Counter Culture: An Uneasy Symbiosis. *Organizational Dynamics.* American Management Association (Fall):52-64.

McCurdy, D.
1976   The Medicine Man. In M.A. Rynkiewich and J.P. Spradley, eds. *Ethics and Anthropology.* New York: Wiley & Sons.

Messerschmidt
1981   Constraints in Government Research. In Donald A. Messerschmitd, ed., *Anthropologists at Home in North America: Methods and Issues in the Study of One's Own Society.* Cambridge: Cambridge University Press.

Merry, S.
1990   *Getting Justice and Getting Even: Legal Consciousness Among Working Class Americans.* Chicago: University of Chicago Press.

Moffat, M.
1989   *Coming of Age in New Jersey.* New Brunswick: Rutgers University Press.

Nader, L.
1972   Studying Up. In Dell Hymes, ed. *Reinventing Anthropology.* New York: Pantheon Books.

Ouichi, W. and A. Wilkins
1985   Organizational Culture in *Annual Reviews of Sociology*, 1985. II:457-483.

Pettigrew, A.
1979   On Studying Organizational Cultures. *Administrative Science Quarterly.* 24:570-81.

Plotnicov, L.
1987   The Political Economy of Skyscrapers: An Anthropological Introduction to Advanced Industrial Cities. *City and Society*, (1), June 1987.

Redfield, R.
1941   *The Folk Culture of Yucatan.* Chicago: University of Chicago Press.

Sanday, P.
1979   The Ethnographic Paradigm(s). *Administrative Science Quarterly.* 24:527-38.

Schein, E.
1990   Organizational Culture. *American Psychologist.* 45(2):109-120.

Stroup, K.
1984   *Administrative Politics in the Ohio Department of Energy*, Ph.D. Thesis, Department of anthropology, The Ohio State University.

Stephenson, J. B. and L. S. Greer
1981   Ethnographers in their Own Cultures: Two Appalachian Cases. *Human Organization*, 40(2).

Trice, M. and J. Beyer
1984   Studying Organizational Culture Through Rites and Ceremonials. *Academy of management Review* 9(4):653-669.

Wilson, J. A.
1990   Culture and Corporate Culture. *Working Paper (wp-700) Series, Joseph M. Katz Graduate School of Business.* University of Pittsburgh. Pittsburgh, PA.

Wilson, M.
1963   *Good Company.* London: Oxford University Press.

Wolf, E.
1972   American Anthropologists and American Society. **In** Dell Hymes, ed., *Reinventing Anthropology* . New York: Pantheon Books.

IS CULTURE "GOOD" IN THE
MICROCOSM OF THE FIRM?

Manning Nash

Culture is one of the more successful concepts developed in anthropology. Culture refers to the man made set of meanings exhibited in social life. As a concept culture focuses on publicly displayed behavior and the meanings of that behavior to people who share the symbolic leads to the displayed or implicit meanings. The meanings of culture are carried chiefly in symbolic conveyances, language being the most general and pervasive of symbolic system. But gestures, pictures, icons, artifacts, and even portents of nature may carry meaning. The important feature to keep in mind about culture as a meaning system, is that it is tripartate: something (symbol, act, artifact) means (conveys a content because it is part of a system of such conveyances) something to somebody. There is no meaning without public display of part of a system to a given audience. At least there is no meaning in the sense in which anthropologists use culture. If there are no intrinsic meanings, and no meanings apart from meaningful systems which actors fashion, construe and validate, then it follows that "culture" must be discovered in social life; it must be worked out by observing the displays of symbol act and artifact in society, and it must be played back against the understandings of the carriers, creators, and creatures of culture.

Working out, discovering, and describing a particular culture requires large amount of "field work" the actual act of immersion in empirical activity. But finding meaning embedded in symbol systems, as those system are interpreted by social actors is only part of the useful employment of the concept of culture. The meanings exist not as single items but in a syntax of items, and in fact much of the meaning can only be elucidated by reference to large parts of, or even the whole, syntactic relations.

So culture is a system of meanings, and the system is derived from observations and worked out and pieced together into some sort of architectonic arrangement. But that is not all there is to it. Meanings are often lodged in social and institutional arrangements, so that the syntactic system is given force by where it occurs in a social. Hence culture can be, and indeed must be, related to social structure if it is to be more than a body of somewhat spectral categories and disembodied meanings. And finally, the individual configurations of culture as they exist in real persons needs to be taken into account, if the motivational energy of social life is to be understood.

These are formidable tasks, and they are the agenda of social and cultural anthropologists when they study whole societies, parts of societies and special action structures. In a sense, the title of this paper -- Is Culture Good For The Firm -- is self-answering. In so far as culture is crucial, useful, good for understanding social life, it is to that extent crucial, useful and good for the understanding of the firm, a particular temporal, organizational, and cultural manifestation of social life. But caution must be exercised. Like all powerful ideas that are recently employed in a fresh area of inquiry, the use of culture for the explication of modern life, American life, or the institutions and structures that make up modern society, can be used loosely, too widely and to explain things and activities it can not encompass. This general tendency to reach for explanatory panaceas is not yet evident in the study of the firm or the world of economics and business. Rather the reverse is the case. The firm, the world of business, the realm of economics is still to narrowly conceived in the mold of individualistic, utilitarian, and rationalistic styles of explanations current in the policy sciences and their applied offspring. Culture is good in this realm as a corrective to the excess of habits of discourse and minds deeply ingrained in current thought.

The firm is a special action structure. It is instigated by conscious action to pursue particular ends. But firms exist only in certain kinds of social science, and in certain sets of cultural stipulations about them. First, private property must be one of the institutions in order for firms to come into being. Next mechanisms for engaging in and enforcing contracts must exist prior to the formation of a firm. And there must be markets for capital, for labor, and for other commodities in order for a firm to exist. Finally, there must be the notion, the legal fiction, that a firm is a person with defined rights, limited liabilities, and a life apart from its individual members. All of these structural and cultural aspects of the firm are antecedent to what we call the "market-exchange" economy of capitalism, but they came together under capitalism and matured into a single complex along with the development of the capitalist market economy.

Thus far we have chiefly been in the domain of economic history and sociology, touching but briefly on the realm of culture and anthropology. To get to the firm, or actual firms, we must move either up from cases of firms in action, or down from cultural syntax to expressions in concrete social instances. In practice, to see how culture is analytically central to an understanding of the firm, we shall slide both up and down this continuum.

The firm is patently a hierarchial structure. It has levels of power and levels of prestige, and it has unequal sets of rewards and privileges. Now, as Louis Dumont, anthropology's keenest analyst of the play of hierarchy and equality in social life, and others have argued, modern Western society is based on the premise of social equality. Hierarchial principles and structures are not easily tolerated in a culture whose denizens are *homo equalis*. It is not difficult to show that equality of persons and the formation of basic institutions to protect and foster that equality, is a idea and ideal at the heart of American culture and society and indeed at the center of European civilization since at least the end of the Middle Ages and the beginnings of the renaissance. Hierarchy and equality are, however, present in different mixes throughout the social structure. In the society at large and in the firm in particular, this incongruity is reconciled through a third cultural principal--merit. Merit allows for different social position and outcomes if they are achieved through means that are legitimate, and individual worth or merit is the mode of reconciling the structure of the firm with the dialectal tension between the value of equality and the structure of hierarchy. Merit, in the firm has two sub-categories, based again on principles in tension. The first idea of merit is that of property endowed rights. A stake in the ownership confers power in the firm, and the greater the property right the greater the power of command within the firm (the implicit notion is that the property was itself gotten properly and held in accordance with rules of ownership). The second notion of merit has to do with leadership. Power confers command, and the ability to command means leading or directing those below in the hierarchy. Leadership comes from skill, knowledge, and most importantly from success--the past track record of performance. This skill, knowledge and performance are located in an office, or position of nominal command, the actual exercise of which depends on the attributes of the occupant as much as it does on the office. This tension between merit and property is mediated in the firm by the idea of leadership, itself a compromise between structural office and individual talent. This compromise is seemingly harmonized by the cultural principle of efficiency. An organization is efficient if it uses the resources (human and otherwise) in a rational manner to meet its stated goals. The stated goals of the firm are clearly returns to stockholders. And firms are socially valuable insofar as they implement that goal, within, of course, the legal constraints of activity. These legal restraints are limits on the use of fraud, coercion, and market shares which restrict the free and competitive operations of price forming markets. This latter constraint is a judicial determination of extreme delicacy, and requires the cooperation of all sorts of experts--lawyers, economists, accountants, and advocates of the firms and speakers on behalf of the public and consumers, and finally politicians who can read the current winds of tolerance for various kinds of economic activity.

But in the larger culture the notion of efficiency is in opposition with the value of responsibility. This counterposing of values against value illustrates the general principle that value profiles invariably have counter value profiles. This general fact is necessarily so, for if the counter values were not socially latent, the dominant values would not need to be expressed. This observation is more than the mere assertion, long known in philosophical debate, that means and ends form chains and the nature of these chains determines the social meaning of "good" moral, and worthy.

The opposition and strife between the values of efficiency and the value of responsibility is at the heart of modern economies dominated by the special action structure of the firm. It is as central a dilemma to our epoch as the struggle between God and Satan was to the epoch that preceded ours, where the manor, not the firm, was the dominant economic organization. Responsibility means that effects of economic activities of the firm ought to be judged in a calculus other than, or wider than, efficiency, or profits, or returns to shareholders. Just what is involved in that wider calculus is evolving in American culture, and is a source of much debate in the society at large. Terms like "environment," "health," "equity" and even aesthetics are now part of the meanings in "responsibility." What the future holds for the resolution or reshaping of these tensions is unclear, but that the terms of judgement of the social worth of the firm will never shrink back to the narrow confines of efficiency or profits alone seems part of the new value profile of America.

The firm exists as a local manifestation of two of the chief values of contemporary society. Since the founding of the United States the idea of optimism and its twin, mastery, have been mainstays of the American ethos. Optimism means that problems can be solved and that the way of dealing with obstacles is to get to work and eliminate them. Optimism often appears in its more vulgar forms of boosterism and in the shallow forms of positive thinking, but it is clearly our central view of world, enshrined in the Declaration of Independence and in the preamble of the Constitution, and in the statements made and exhibited when we send message to ourselves in the recurrent national rituals of the Fourth of July, Memorial Day, Thanksgiving Day and other occasions reprising the nuclear experience of the birth, growth and maturation of America. These documents and rituals show men filled with hope, power, and moral vigor setting off in high spirits to build confidently a society suitable for life, liberty and the pursuit of happiness. No existential doubts that the task can be completed, and no begging forbearance from an implacable universe, nor wails about the intractability of human nature cloud or darken the optimistic vision of the founding fathers and their cultural descendants.

The handmaiden of optimism is the drive for mastery. To overcome a recalcitrant nature, to subdue a sprawling continent, to be the international power, and to pierce the heavens in the conquest of space are some of the manifestations of the drive to mastery. The attempts to eliminate poverty, to banish disease, end illness, and to make everybody young, sane, and beautiful are but the most exhuberant excesses of the mastery urge of a people dedicated to optimism and fueled by the energy such a view of a benign and tractable universe engenders. At the highest levels mastery is lodged in science, technology, and reason. These aspects of culture are the adaptive edge of problem solving. The institutional locus of problem solving has been the "enterprise" or what has here been called the firm. The problem solving firm has been in some institutional tension with the order maintaining government, the moral definitions of the organized religions, and the critical and innovative roles of the university and the expressive arts. The balance among these institutions for dominance and popular support varies with historical circumstance and with the performance of each in the business cycle, the shifting democracy of the representative organs, the probity and coherence of the churches, and the sharpness of vision of the arts and the universities.

It is of great importance to remember that the entrusting of the edge of change to one or another institutional locus is a function of current performance and past track record, in the same manner that leadership in the firm rests on merit and office. Hence the firm is a contingent form of combining men and resources for ends in the never ending chain of means and ends. Its role can not be deduced from doctrine, nor merely justified by the notions of efficiency and profit. Current institutional advertising by the larger corporations seems an implicit and partial recognition of the shifting cultural bases of legitimacy.

This alteration between the larger cultural premises and the firm as the special action structure in the economy, has not systematically shown the pattern of contemporary culture, nor the articulation of institutional order into a social structure. That has not been the intent of this essay. Rather the interplay between levels of cultural meaning and spans of social organization has been emphasized. That the "culture" of a firm can only be understood as a localization of certain meanings in the wider set of cultural meanings is the first part of the burden of this essay; the second message is that the widest cultural meanings are being defined, shaped, and changed in actual social loci of which the firm is, in the sphere of the economy, the most important.

Taking a firm as the actual locus of study results in a description of the style of that firm. That style is a function of the widest cultural meanings, the industry in which the firm is an entity, and the actual personnel in the organization of the firm, and finally the recent performance of the major organizations entrusted with combining men, material, and knowledge for the implementation of culturally stipulated ends.

A contrast merely in the advertising themes say between Coca-Cola and of the larger computer firms is instructive. Coca-cola stresses youth, movement, and vague satisfaction of imbibing something which is "it." These aspects of the product are a shorthand for the ideas of optimism and mastery, movement, youth, and this world satifaction so much so that non-Americans speak of "coca-cola" culture meaning the drive for pleasure in a world where all problems are solvable. Computer firms are in an industry which solves problems of information flow and must stress innovation, comprehensiveness, and efficiency. Computers offer technology that puts a firm in a better position in the dizzying flow of information. Innovation is at the heart of computers, differentiation at the heart of the soft drink industry. Other contrasts -- centralization versus decentralization; close supervision versus free form authority, and other meaningful contrasts could be spelled out, but the differences that the features enumerated above may make is fairly evident.

Culture is good for the firm in the very anthropological sense that to even think about firms, the cultural explorations of levels of meaning is the first requisite to understanding. It is also good for the firm in that it allows those in the workaday world to think in a productive context about what they and their firms are about. And culture is good for the firm in that it may help in an applied sense to make of them more reliable and humane instruments of the values (and counter values) of the larger society. Just as art, learning, and politics come more and more to be about culture in an ever more self-conscious sense, the economy and business world may come to be more and more about culture. The epigram that the business of America is business may slowly change to the business of America is culture (in the anthropological sense), and that what's good for firms is good for culture.

CORPORATE CULTURE
ON THE ROCKS*

Peter C. Reynolds

For a 15 month period during the early 1980s, I worked at a company I will call the Falcon Computer Company, a start-up manufacturer of microcomputers in the heart of Silicon Valley. When I joined the firm, a year after its founding, the future looked very bright, and during my time there the company quintupled in size to more than 250 employees. It was featured on the covers of important trade publications, and even *Time* magazine singled out Falcon Computer as one of the rising young stars of Silicon Valley that investors should be watching -- possibly another Apple.

The company did indeed bear scrutiny, but not in the way that *Time* had intended. Just two and a half years after its founding, it closed its doors for good, with a stunning loss of more than $32 million in investment capital and a debt of millions more. How 250 people can lose such a large amount of money in such a short period of time is an interesting story in itself, but a meteoric rise followed by a sudden descent into oblivion is not uncommon in the computer industry; the most unusual aspect of the Falcon debacle is that a professional anthropologist happened to be on the scene to record it.

*Reprinted with permission, from the publication *Across the Board*, October 1986.

I am an anthropologist by training, not a business man or a computer scientist, so I view the computer industry from a very different perspective. Before taking a job in Silicon Valley, I did field work among hunters and gatherers in the Malaysian rain forest, studied the stone tool making of Australian aborigines, did frame-by-frame analysis of films of social communication and videotaped folk technology in Papua New Guinea. I was an experienced observer of human interaction and technical processes long before I began my business career, and it was not too difficult to keep accurate notes of what went on at Falcon. At meetings, I would offer to take the minutes, and I made it a point to memorize interesting conversations, writing them down in my journal the same day. But I had been hired not as an anthropologist but as a software trainer through an executive-recruiting firm, so my observations were never confounded by people in the company playing a role for the benefit of the visiting scientist. Even those who knew that I had a doctorate in anthropology thought that anthropologists studied only savages, and that therefore my previous interests and experience had nothing to do with them.

Falcon Computer's infatuation with its own corporate culture, the subject of this article, is not a hot house creation conjured into existence by the bright lights of anthropological scrutiny. To the contrary, as a recently returned expatriate I was embarrassingly out of touch with the mega-trends of American life, and I first learned the term "corporate culture" from the natives themselves. In fact, shortly after joining the company, I was told by one of the managers that the president and vice presidents met periodically in closed session to develop a "Falcon culture," and that they had hired a management-consulting firm to help them define it. One goal, the manager said, was to preserve the atmosphere of a start-up even after Falcon became a big company. The manager referred to these sessions as "culture meetings," but later on they were officially designated "values meetings."

To an anthropologist, the conscious creation of a culture by management is amusing, because all human groups have culture by nature, and these systems of values and beliefs are shaped by experience, tradition, class position, and political circumstance -- all powerful forces that are extremely refractory to directed change, particularly by occasional committee. Nonetheless, behind closed doors, with middle management and nonmanagerial staff excluded, the president and his executive staff created a document called "Falcon Values" that expressed the culture of the company. This document was then distributed to all of the company's managers, who met, again in closed session, to further discuss and refine the premises of the corporate culture. By the time this document was ready for dissemination to middle management, I had been promoted to manager myself, reporting to the vice president of marketing, and this gave me a front-row seat at all subsequent cultural deliberations. At one of the meetings I attended, the president of the company and most members of the executive staff were present, so I was able to observe the deliberations of the upper echelons of the company, as well as those of middle management. In fact, since the tables at culture meetings were always arranged in a circle, unlike all other meetings in the company, where tables formed a rectangle, my vantage point was as good as the president's.

The Falcon Values document was two pages long, too long to examine in detail here, but it summarized such things as attitude toward customers and colleagues, the style of social communication, the desiderata of decision-making, and the working environment that the company wanted to create. Yet one of the most interesting things about it , from an anthropological fieldworker's point of view, was the disparity between the statements that were written down on paper and the social reality that produced the document in the first place. For example, in the values document under "customer orientation" one found: "Attention to detail is our trademark; our goal is to do it right the first time. We intend to deliver defect-free products and services to our customers on time."

Yet even as this policy was being adopted in executive session, it was generally known that defective computers were being shipped to customers -- and I was told by two company sources that the decision to send the new computers, despite evidence of defects, had been made at the highest level in order to squelch growing industry rumors that Falcon would miss its announced release date. As I did not witness the decision, I cannot ascertain the validity of that I was told, but there were reliability problems that were certainly known to the executive staff.

I was able to confirm the dismal state of the product for myself when I obtained permission to borrow some computers from the shipping room to use in a training class I was asked to organize. These were brand-new units, already packed in their printed cartons, and because so few machines were coming off the production line, only by great bureaucratic effort was I able to divert them from their intended destinations as customer machines. Yet only two of the four machines started up correctly when the start-up disk was inserted, and I only got them running because I happened to have a technician on my payroll.

In another example of the disparity between the official culture and the actual, consider this statement from the values document: "Managing by personal communication is part of the [Falcon] way. While we recognize the importance of group sessions, we encourage open, direct person-to-person communication as part of our daily routine."

"Open communication" was in fact a buzzword at Falcon, often used by software engineers to pry information out of management, but the culture creation process was nonetheless done in secret, strictly following the chain of command. The executive staff developed the initial document without consultation of middle management, middle managers were asked to affirm an existing document under the guise of "discussing" it, and the rank-and-file employees were told about open communication only after it had already been adopted by the company. Interestingly enough, democratic decision-making was also a written value: "We believe that rapid and sound decisions are the key to [Falcon's] success and that they should take place at the lowest common level. We encourage open discussion and honest feedback about the decisions that have been or will be made."

Even from these few examples it is clear that there was considerable disparity between the written culture and the behavioral culture observable in day-to-day social relations. From an anthropological perspective, this disparity was neither unusual nor unexpected. A century of fieldwork in non-Western societies has shown that cultures are not homogeneous like carrots but layered like onions, with context sensitive rules governing even widely held values. Who among us thinks that the injunction "Thou shalt not kill" applies to soldiers on the battlefield or to policemen confronting violent felons? Thus it is not surprising that the Falcon Values document encoded one system of values while the shipping room implemented another. Although we may deplore such moral hypocrisy, the decision to ship defective machines to large customers also fails by a worldlier standard best epitomized by Antoine Boulay de la Meurthe's judgment of the murder of the Duke of Enghien: "It is worse than a crime, it is a blunder."

Human beings, of course, are well aware of the disparity among systems of values, and the Falcon Values document did not fool very many employees into thinking they would get promoted by espousing open communication or blowing the whistle on defective products. In fact, skepticism about the Falcon values was itself an ethnographic fact, well documented in my field notes. For example, the vice president of software engineering seemed genuinely interested in the concept of open communication, and he circulated an initial draft of the an values document to all of the people on his staff, asking them to comment. Many programmers took the opportunity to compare Falcon with other companies where they had worked and many of these written replies, which were given to me after the company went bankrupt, reveal an undisguised skepticism about the possibility of legislating a culture. "You can't create values," wrote one engineer. "The way 'culture' is used at [Falcon] is pretty simple-minded, compared to say, anthropology," another responded.

The general impression one gains from reading these remarks is that most members of the software engineering staff were unimpressed by the Falcon Values document, and some went so far as to compare it to archetypal examples of corporate stupidity -- such as the executive charged with keeping desks neat at the Intel Corporation, known as Mr. Clean.

Cultures are shared models of social relations, and almost everyone knew that the operative values at Falcon were hierarchy, secrecy, and expediency, regardless of what the official culture said. My field notes, in fact, preserve a number of statements that can be interpreted as realistic models of the social relations, and these present a very different picture from that of the values document. "Make sure that training does not become a gating item for the software," the product marketing manager told me. Translation: Make sure that delays in software development cannot be attributed to delays in the training program. "I've seen this before," he continued. "Bill [a fictional name for the vice president of engineering] is going to kick the ball upstairs and try to say that Sam's group and marketing are not ready -- to get himself off the hook."

In computer companies, the sales department will normally tell the customer what he wants to hear, or even try to sell him products that do not exist, whereas engineering is expected to hold the line on truth. At Falcon, roles were reversed. As the manager of customer support reflected over lunch, "Sales is the conscience, while engineering is living on fantasies."

The Falcon Values document was both a model of the culture and a part of the culture, but it was so at variance with reality that few people took it seriously. Even some of the official communications seemed to contain ironic humor. For example, the vice president of finance and administration used Falcon culture to justify the institution of employee badges as a security measure. Although security badges are commonplace in the computer industry, probably few companies have ever presented this tactic to their personnel as an example of open communication. Yet at Falcon, the directive establishing the practice stated that employee badges would contain only first names, "in keeping with our casual culture."

The skepticism toward the official corporate culture was commonplace enough to be commented upon by members of the executive staff. For example, the vice president of marketing reported to the values meeting that he had conducted an informal survey among his own staff on the perception of Falcon Values. He said there were three main categories of responses:

1. It's all motherhood and apple pie.
2. So what?
3. Boy! Is this place becoming bureaucratic.

Clearly, a model of the culture must be close enough to the truth that it can be referred to without eliciting smirks, but this is not to say that ideal models of social relations are irrelevant to day-to-day life, or that cultural ideas are generally treated with skepticism by a society's participants. Human beings, in corporations as anywhere else, live in a moral universe, and the most interesting thing about the official Falcon culture is how little credence it gave to the moral standards already operative in the company. In reviewing my notes, I have come to the conclusion that people at Falcon did, to a large extent, hold the values of defect- free products and democratic decision-making; and, when among themselves, employees were not shy about evaluating the company by their own standard of right and wrong when corporate behavior was perceived as unjust. For example a software engineer told me: "Basically, if some people have to work the Labor Day weekend, then everyone should. Since the software had to be ready on the 6th, then everyone should work one weekend, or say the last three weekends in August -- everyone in the company."

Not only were there official ideals, encoded in values document, and unofficial ideals, expressed by employees in informal conversation, but there were also officially sanctioned ideals that never made it into writing at all -- except in the anthropologist's notebook. Each communicative channel in a complex social organization has a cultural system of norms that goes along with it, and the verbal ideal is different from the written ideal. Consider, for example, the dos and donts encoded in the following fragment of conversation: "At this morning's meeting, Winfield [fictional name for the company president] used the word 'mind set' and Zeke [pseudonym for the chief design engineer] said, 'We're not supposed to use that word; I've heard it twice in two days.' At the beginning of [Falcon], they decided never to use the words 'committee' or 'mind set' -- it was a reaction against buzz-words."

As the company's fortunes began to decline, about two and a half years after its founding, the disparity between the values meetings and the everyday culture became more and more grotesque. At a time when the public relations department was claiming "volume shipments of product to key accounts," the manufacturing division was essentially producing hand-crafted machines. The mother board on the Falcon computer, the circuit board containing the central processor and other important logic elements, had a design flaw that requires the hand soldering of jumper wires during manufacturing. These hand fixes were so expensive that they absorbed all the economies of scale that mass manufacturing is supposed to provide, and they were so time-consuming that production slowed to a trickle.

At this point in the company's history when state-of-the-art manufacturing lines were turning out handicrafts, when the mother board would take a minimum of six months to redesign, when a manager at Procter & Gamble reportedly shouted to a technical representative that he never wanted to see a Falcon computer again, and when financial reserves were hemorrhaging at the rate of $2 million a month, the disparity between the actual and the official cultures came to be expressed as sardonic humor.

In the irreverent asides of the now irrevocably cynical staff, the manufacturing division was dubbed "Research and Development." The more knowledgeable people, the more devastating their remarks. The service manager told me: "We do have a zero-defect program: Don't test the product and you'll find no defects." The manager of customer support gestured at the closed doors of the marketing conference room: "The sales meeting is taking so long because they're to get the regional sales managers to agree to the impossible -- sell the product as it exists."

The values meetings, however, gathered steam as the company itself was rapidly losing pressure, and personnel asked all departments to begin a series of regular meetings to discuss the values document and to devise plans for its implementation. The vice presidents, and sometimes the president himself, attended the values meeting organized for the departmental staff, and these kickoff meetings led to a series of round-table discussions that were just getting underway when the first big layoffs reduced the staff by a third. Several competing computers appeared in the marketplace, and the investment companies, which had floated three refinancings largely on the strength of the president's promises, finally lost patience and moved to slow the "burn rate" of their venture capital by cutting expenses as extensively as possible. The executive staff took the opportunity to find a scapegoat for all that had gone wrong, and they fired the vice president of marketing in the middle of the night, broke up his department, and allocated his staff among themselves by the time the sun came up. The next morning, the company was abuzz with stories, in spite of the official blackout imposed by the advocates of open communication. The marketing department secretary, now working for sales, asked me what I thought about the events of the night before. I told her I thought they were sleazy even by Falcon standards. She nodded, and then said, with ill-disguised anger, "It makes you realize what bullshit Falcon values are."

Fifteen months of participant observation at a microcomputer company confirms the importance of the concept of culture for understanding the structure of the modern corporation, but it also shows that "culture" is not an official system of values promulgated by management. It is a whole range of models of social action, containing both real and ideal elements, each layer cues by the social context and the channel of communication: the observed behavior, the official document, the things said at meetings, the things said to one's boss when the boss's boss is present, the situation that is said to be real, the verbal expression of what the situation should be, and the humorous renderings of all of the above. Will the real corporate culture please stand up?

When I began my research, I shared one of the assumptions of the Falcon executive staff -- that an effective company requires a homoge-neous corporate culture. But having had an opportunity to look more carefully at functional specialization, it is clear to me that the idea of a single corporate culture that characterizes all levels of the organization is both naïve and undesirable. A modern corporation, by its very nature, brings together disparate subcultures within a single organizational framework -- engineers and financial analysts, copywriters and cooks -- and not only is it inevitable that these people will have differing conceptions of appropriate social action, but, most importantly, their jobs require it.

Therefore, it makes sense to accept cultural diversity as a fact of life and ask instead how it facilitates or impedes the larger goals of the organization. Does the public-relations department's desire for good press facilitate the production of reliable products by manufacturing, or does it lead to premature shipment of defective machines? Does the model of social organization held by middle management match the model used by the executive staff, or do these levels of organization work at cross purposes because of differing conceptions of social realty?

If corporations are collections of subcultures, does this mean that departments and divisions have nothing in common that can be construed as the corporate culture -- the system of values and social traditions the characterizes the management style? No, for there are also company-wide values that cross-cut the subcultures, and this is true of Falcon as well. At Falcon, however, the overall corporate culture was most clearly revealed in the disparity between the official and the actual, in the mismatch between the real and ideal cultures. Although probably all societies have a disparity between idealistic and realistic models of social relations, because people are ethical animals and the world is imperfect, at Falcon the falsification of realistic models was sanctioned and encouraged by the social organization. Falcon culture was expressed not by the ethical ideals presented in the values meetings, but by the great intercultural disparity between the ideal and real: The implicit premise of Falcon culture was that there was no truth to the official documents. For example, a marketing manager, in charge of developing production schedules for the delivery of software, penned in some dates in the product plan that even I could tell were overly optimistic. She must have interpreted the expression on my face, for she smiled ironically, and said, "The *schedules* are the theology."

Was higher management itself aware of this disparity between the ideal and the real? Was the Falcon Values document an idealistic program that went wrong or a cynical use of rhetoric by people who communicated to their subordinates a far different model of acceptable behavior? Questions of motive are always the most difficult to answer, but the official development and production schedules relayed up the managerial hierarchy as attainable goals not only were meaningless but were known to be meaningless by all the participants in the review cycle -- except, perhaps, the venture capitalists on the board who dug into their pockets for three rounds of financing.

Culture is not a ideological gimmick, to be imposed from above by management-consulting firms, but a stubborn fact of human social organization that can scuttle the best of corporate plans if not first taken into account. If the venture capitalists had known that the key element in Falcon computer's culture was disparity between the official version and the actual situation, would they have continued to fund the company for as long as they did? In this case, the failure to apply even rudiments of the anthropological method can be measured in tens of millions of dollars.

APPLYING CONCEPTS OF CORPORATE CULTURE TO INTERNATIONAL BUSINESS MANAGEMENT[1]

Anthony J. Dibella

INTRODUCTION

Over the last ten years I have followed with interest, and initial envy, the introduction of the culture concept to the study of formal organization. I have always felt that anthropology, whose *raison d'etre* was its use of culture, had practical implications for contemporary concerns. Although several anthropologists working in the 1940s looked at life and behavior within administrative settings (Kluckhohn, 1943) and industrial organizations (Chapple, 1941; Whyte and Gardner, 1945; Richardson and Walker, 1948), neither management, nor other applied or contemporary issues, has ever been a legitimate pursuit within the profession of anthropology. When anthropologists had studied industrial work environments, their research focused more on the cultural rules of human behavior and interaction (Chapple and Arensberg, 1940) and less on the functioning of organizations as cultural wholes. It took a different scientific community seeking better theoretical explanations in its research domain to take ideas about culture and see how they fit or served the understanding of organization.

Beginning with the works of Ouchi (1981), Peters and Waterman (1982), and Deale and Kennedy (1984) culture became a popular, if not faddish, concept in management research. The intent of this essay is to show how concepts of culture can be applied to international business management. However, before going into actual areas of application, I discuss the different meanings within the disciplines about culture and how it can be used.

PERSPECTIVES ON CULTURE

Anthropologists have historically defined culture in holistic and relativistic terms. While anthropology is a comparative social science in which different cultural systems are examined, judgments about cultures are not customarily made. One culture as a whole is as acceptable as another.

This does not mean that anthropologists agree on what culture is or don't disagree on theories of culture. The scope of anthropological theory from cognitive to materialist explanations clearly reflects a diversity of opinion. However, among anthropologists there is a general consensus that culture is omnipresent, comprises patterned human behavior, develops historically, and is not optional to the human condition.

It is harder to generalize how culture is perceived and used within the field of business management since it incorporates a more eclectic group of researchers and practitioners, business managers, and organization theorists. When culture was introduced into business studies, it first became another factor in the search for increased productivity and efficiency. Typical of this orientation is the works of Akin and Hopelain (1986), Graves (1386), Kilmann (1985), and Sathe (1985). In general, this group treats culture as a discriminate factor in management performance and have no difficulty in characterizing or judging corporate culture. To many who use culture in business studies a corporate culture may be strong or weak, right or wrong, pervasive or narrow.

While anthropologists may describe or identify with "cultures of poverty", managers seek "cultures for productivity". A major problem in comparing these two approaches to culture is that there has been minimal interaction between the professions of anthropology and management. My sense is that culture became popular in management circles through the work of organization researchers rather than anthropologists because in the culture of the latter there is a general disdain for business. Corporate board rooms are not primitive enough for anthropologists. Perhaps more importantly the culture of anthropology (no wing-tip shoes) has never meshed well with the culture of the corporate manager (white buttoned-down oxford shirts and red ties).

Yet even if there was greater contact between anthropologists and corporate managers or business researchers that would not necessarily make an anthropological concept of culture and culture theory more

relevant in understanding organization. First, the missions of corporations and cultures differ. In formal organizations, either profit or
non-profit, the mission is some unit of service, productivity, or return
on equity. With organic culture, the mission is societal propagation and
evolution. Second, the manager and anthropologist play different roles
vis-a'vis the culture (or corporation) being studied. The manager tries
to understand corporations in order to make them more productive or
efficient; the anthropologist tries to understand cultures so that we can
better understand the dynamics of comparative human behavior, and
social, cultural, and economic change.

A third difficulty in relying on an anthropological concept of
culture to business pertains to the issue of whether organizations are
indeed cultural systems. Contemporary organizations function in one
or more complex societies whose predominating characteristics may
minimize cultural differences between organizations. From an
anthropological perspective, organizational boundaries may be too
permeable to establish or reinforce unique corporate cultures. In fact,
a traditional anthropological view (Steward, 1972) holds that autonomous bands are the only social systems that comprise integrated, unique
cultures.

Due to the values of their own discipline, anthropologists have
limited their entry and hence insight into complex organizations.
Meanwhile, the culture concept has evolved in more discriminating
ways within the business and management literatures to fit a range of
theoretical and methodological orientations. For example, Smircich
(1983, 1985) differentiates between theories that depict organizations as
cultures and those wherein organizations have culture that functions as
an independent or dependent variable. In the former schema cultures,
as systems, provide a conceptualizing device from which meaning
emerges. Ott (1989) starts with a similar distinction in defining an
organization culture perspective. However, he ends up with a typology
of organization culture theories using a modified version of Schein's
framework (1985) of culture as assumptions, values, and artifacts.

There have now been a large enough number of organization
culture studies to distinguish between three perspectives (Frost, 1991).
The integration perspective holds that culture within organizations is
monolithic and builds consensus. The differentiations perspective holds
that organizations are composed of sub-cultures that are often in
conflict. The fragmentation perspective views organizations as full of

ambiguity where there is no consensus either at the organizational or sub-cultural (group) level.

Methodological styles in the study of organizational culture have also emerged. Schein (1991) considers these styles to be competing approaches.[2] The survey research approach deconstructs culture and measures its dimensions through questionnaires (Hofstede, 1980; Kilmann, 1984). The analyical prescriptive approach empirically studies culture through its manifestations such as rituals and stories (Trice and Beyer, 1984). The ethnographic approach studies culture, as it is enacted, through observation and interviews with limited sets of informants (Van Maanen and Kunda, 1989). The ethnographic approach is the most closely aligned with anthropological techniques of discovery.

Another example of the different orientations taken by these two domains of work can be seen in the answer to the question: If culture is a problem in your corporation, who are you going to call? The anthropologist view is that we can only understand cultural systems over time, that to understand behavior we need to understand the contextual environment of that behavior. (Thus the need to walk in the shoes of the native.) However, many business managers feel that the ability of a participant-observer approach to solve corporate problems declines over time. In this view when a researcher spends more time in the corporation, his/her ability to understand and affect change will diminish. Over time the researcher becomes more and more like the native and can no longer see the trees for the forest.

This is an important distinction between anthropology and management research, especially when consulting and research time costs money. The management consultant/researcher's premise that he or she is most effective in a short time frame nicely fits the temporal and financial parameters of the corporate manager who has a problem and wants it solved tomorrow, if not today, at minimal cost. Long term anthropological studies might be interesting but are not tailored to put out fires and help organizations in crisis.

CULTURE AND CORPORATE STRATEGY

In the past, management specialists have focused on corporate strategy and corporate structure as key elements which determine corporate accomplishments and profitability. Chandler's thesis (1962) has for a long time been a popular one: that corporate strategy precedes corporate structure. Now that corporate culture has become an important concept, there are questions about where it fits in this sequence and what determines corporate culture.

In some circles it has been popular to view culture as a strategic tool (Schwartz and Davis, 1981; Fombrun, 1983; Scholtz, 1987; Sherwood, 1988) or a mechanism for control (Kunda, 1987; Barley, 1988). I regard corporate culture as tacit corporate strategy. Here I refer to all aspects of corporate strategy from mission to operational levels. Corporate strategy is the embodiment of corporate culture. In the past, the connection between corporate strategy and corporate culture may have been unintentional or covert at best. The growing recognition of how corporate values effect organizational performance has now made this link manifest and intentional.[3]

Schwartz and Davis (1981) argue that corporate culture develops through historical processes over time and is thus difficult to change. Consequently, it may significantly impact upon the realization of planned corporate strategies. They propose a methodology to assess how culture may jeopardize the implementation of corporate strategies. Behaviors that are reinforced by the corporate culture must be identified. Then how the behavior is linked to success factors must be determined. The result can indicate the feasibility of a new strategy given the culture.

What we need is more tools of analysis. We need techniques to understand the dynamics behind cultures of accomplishment, whether the ends be profit or cultural survival. Such tools need to analyze the cultural aspects of organizations in order to identify tactics which can help people more readily achieve personal and organizational goals.

I propose one simple method of cultural analysis here, in Chart A. It is a matrix to juxtapose cultural variables with the components of management in a particular organization. For example, compensation is a primary component of human systems. The role of compensation systems in organizational culture was considered by Kerr and Slocum (1987). They point out that who gets rewarded what is a reflection of an organization"s values and beliefs. However, compensation may also be examined in terms of how (language) it is discussed within the organization and how (behavior) it is implemented and what effect it has on employees. Likewise, the cultural traits of other management systems as shown in the sample matrix could be examined for multiple organizations.

CHART A

Management Component	Ideology (Values/Beliefs)	Behavior (Actions)	Language (Words)
Compensation			
Organization Design			
Performance Appraisal			
Performance Improvement			
Relations With Suppliers			
Relations With Customers			
Supervision			
"Time"			

Another tool could be a model in which some index of cultural characteristics is one of several independent variables that impacts upon an organizational dependent variable such as profitability, stability, survival, or evolution. Other elements in a model which could reflect the status of a corporate culture would be the number of organizational sub-cultures or occupational groups (Van Maanen and Barley, 1985). The problem in using any index of organization culture is that it deconstructs a culture thereby sacrificing its unique properties as a patterned whole.

What is presented above are primitive designs and need to be developed further. My intent is simply to present some ideas about tools of cultural analysis that could be helpful in a corporate setting. Consulting firms are already using numerous devices to measure and change elements of organizational culture and climate. However, whether they truly capture the essence and understanding of a cultural perspective towards organizations remains in doubt.

CULTURE AND INTERNATIONAL BUSINESS MANAGEMENT

How can concepts of culture help the international business manager? The following are several examples. They are based on a recognition that culture is hidden from view and that organizations are nested in societal cultures that affect the workplace from outside and cannot be controlled.

Culture and Human Resource Strategies and Policies

A first area where culture applies is in designing and implementing appropriate human resource (HR) policies. Multinational corporations must function in a variety of cultural environments where laws and individual attitudes toward personnel policies vary widely. Can or should HR strategies be consistent across national borders, or between subsidiaries or business units? For example, HR strategies are designed to attract, retain and motivate a workforce, and systems of compensation are one operational tactic of that strategy. However, for HR systems to meet these objectives they must take into account the value systems of employees. The cultural setting of a subsidiary, therefore, will be a determining force in the shaping of policy. Davis (1974) advocates flexibility in HR strategy implementation so that policies can be shaped to fit a particular work setting.

Still, to what extent should cultural factors be seen as barriers to or shapers of such policy? Cultures do change and do provide a legitimacy to forms of behavior. The feasibility of standardized HR strategies and practices is associated with the feasibility of standard forms of management which is a fundamental concern in the field of comparative management. Ronen (1986) identified three approaches to comparative management: universalist, economic cluster approach, and cultural cluster.

The universalist perspective holds that few major differences exist and that management theories and practices transfer easily from one culture to another. This would support consistent HR practices throughout a multinational. While there may be interaction between people from different cultures, their pattern of relationships can be discerned and will reflect a normative system of behavior.

The economic cluster approach holds that economic differences and similarities will determine management's tasks. Thus level of economic development will be the key determinant of behavior, and reward systems will be a critical component of HR strategy. The final perspective, culture cluster, maintains that behavioral and attitudinal differences will determine management's tasks. The implication of this view is that policy consistency across the business units of a multinational will be difficult to attain.

Hofstede's work (1980) falls into this latter framework. However, his establishment of four dimensions of national culture suggest that many cultural differences are not absolute but relative. While the cultural setting of a subsidiary is an important factor, it does not require totally new or different HR practices than are used in other parent held companies.

In considering factors that determine HR strategy, I have discussed the typology, purpose, and setting of the organization. While these characteristics are important, they are labels used to type organizations. An equally critical determinant of HR strategy is the essence of the organization itself. This encompasses its history, form of ownership, corporate culture, and the existing relationship between headquarters and subsidiaries or business units. HR practices in international organizations thus become a function of shared organizational values or traditions and localized practices. However, their realization requires top managers to tolerate cultural diversity.

The concept of the culturally diverse work environment is needed not only for multinational corporations but for organizational cultures in general. Diversity enables an organization to draw upon alternative solutions. Corporations with more harmonious cultures may be jeopardized by not having access to alternative strategies and courses of action that might free them from corporate traditions which have created the present problems.

THE ROLE OF CULTURE IN CORPORATE MERGERS AND JOINT VENTURES

A second area for the application of culture to international business management is in assessing the feasibility of international Joint ventures (IJV) and mergers. An IJV is an organizational offspring of different corporate (cultural) parents. Yet little is known about how the culture of an IJV emerges and what relationship it has to the cultures of the parent companies.

Corporate mergers are more than the rubbing together of two distinct cultures, known in anthropological circles as acculturation. Rather a merger is the combination of two corporate entities or organizational wholes. In some cases, one entity is subsumed or consumed by another. In other situations two corporations merge to form an entirely new corporation. Such mergers may be friendly or hostile but are customarily expected to generate efficiencies of scale due to decreased personnel and the rationalizing of production and product distribution. How can two corporate cultures be synthesized to generate a new and presumably more productive one?

Given the high level of mergers of domestic corporations during the last five years, management researchers have been looking for reasons why such mergers fail or succeed. Greater attention is now being paid to post-merger activities and how or whether the corporate cultures of the merged partnership fit or resist each other (Buono and Bowditch, 1987). However, the time has come to consider the role of culture in international mergers and joint ventures as well.

Salk (1992) used culture to explain the inter-group dynamics that occurred in three IJVs sponsored by pairs of American, French, German, and Italian companies. She found that differences in cultural assumptions and artifacts, especially ethnolinguistic ones, reinforced staff perceptions of stereotypes and social boundaries between groups. The result was often the emergence of a fragmented JV culture. Baba (1987) has described her efforts at a new analytical technique that considers the cultural perceptions of participants in IJVs. Her aim is to identify cognitive chronologies of the IJV process and determine the extent to which different actors/participants in an IJV share common objectives, values, and aspirations.

Related to these approaches is the link between corporate culture and decision-making. In multinational corporations, managers and workers often come from different cultural backgrounds and contexts that affect decision-making. From the field of ethnopsychology (Cole et alii: 1971; Price-Williams: 1975; White and Kirkpatrick: 1985) we know of multiple concepts of self, cognitive processes, and situations wherein such processes are applied. The greater the number of cultural contexts in which international businesses must function and the greater the disparity between organizational subunits, the larger the mix of cognitive processes that members will employ either in making decisions or in reacting to the implementation of decisions. How decisions about IJVs are reached can be one focus of analysis. How workers and managers at different organizational points react to decisions and either impede or facilitate their implementation is another.

ORGANIZATIONAL CHANGE IN INTERNATIONAL ORGANIZATIONS

A third arena in which a sensitivity to culture may aid the international business manager is implementing planned change. In his book on organizational culture, Schein (1985:271-272) lists eleven ways in which organizations change. Eight are forms of planned change; three are mechanisms in which organizations change in unplanned ways.

Planned change may also produce unexpected outcomes. Schein (1985:297-301) wrote about this process and how culture may account for unexpected outcomes. One explanation is that the parties who interact in a change effort may have different cultural assumptions or values. This leads to different frameworks in which the presence or direction of change is perceived in conflicting ways. The result is a set of changed behaviors valued and enacted by one group that were not anticipated by another group.

The distinction between intended and unintended deviation from change, first made by Alchian (1950), was subsequently developed further by Westney (1987) in her study of the cross-societal emulation of Western organizational forms in Meiji Japan. Unintended deviations in the change plan occurred when actors had incomplete information or alternate implicit models of what the change should be. Deliberate deviations occurred when features of the new form conflicted with local patterns or the institutional environment.

Schein and Westney consider how cultural differences across either group, organizational, or societal boundaries create problems and possibilities during the implementation of change. Understanding the impact of cultural differences across one level of analysis is a complex process. Unfortunately, the process of implementing change in international organizations is further complicated because change occurs across all three levels of analysis.

In my own research (DiBella, 1992) I used culture to explain how planned structural change in an international organization led to unintended outcomes. Differences between societal cultures in which the change took place affected the organization's internal processes of change thereby leading to unexpected outcomes.

Differences among group cultures within the organization led to conflict due to multiple perspectives about what the change was and why it was needed. Finally, a change in organizational leadership gave impetus to the values of a sub-culture which clashed with the values of the organization's dominant culture.

When an organization initiates planned change, the change becomes a phenomenon that over time acquires cultural meaning and value to the people engaged in its design and implementation. It thus becomes subject to an interpretive process. When change is implemented across boundaries of cultural difference, it is subject to a variety of interpretations. This process limits the extent to which there will be a shared vision of the planned change and increases the likelihood of outcomes that are unexpected to at least some of the affected parties. To understand these emergent processes requires close encounters with change events as they occur across boundaries of cultural difference and detailed knowledge of the contexts in which those events take place.[3]

MAKING THE CONNECTION BETWEEN THEORY AND PRACTICE

The above are several examples about how the culture concept has been used to understand and solve culturally related problems in corporations and organizations, particularly in the international business context. We must make the culture concept functional, practical, and useful in order for it to successfully persevere through the faddish domain of management concepts and practices.

The difficulty in making culture a concept meaningful to the management profession stems from the latter's orientation towards factors that can be manipulated. Yet culture is a lot like the weather. We know it is all around us. We can talk about it and learn how it works, but we can't do much to control it.

As the field of management research and organization studies develops techniques to better communicate to managers what culture is, the process of deconstruction makes culture's innate properties illusive if not ephemeral. Thus we are caught in a dilemma, whether to deconstruct and measure culture so that managers think they can control it, or to retain culture as a holistic concept but risk alienating those parties to whom a knowledge and understanding of culture may serve to benefit. Despite this apparent dilemma, the importance of culture in explaining organizational phenomena continues to grow whether in generating theories of organization freed of ethnocentrism (Boyacillger and Adler, 1991) or in developing companies that can transcend the ties of culture (Bartlett and Ghoshal, 1990). How best to achieve this remains an issue for further research, practice, and reflection.

NOTES

1. An earlier version of this paper was presented at the Annual Meeting of the Society for Applied Anthropology; Oaxaca, Mexico; April, 1987. Appreciative thanks are extended to John Van Maanen, Akbar Zaheer, and several anonymous reviewers for their comments on previous versions of this paper.

2. Schein (1991) advocates for a more encompassing methodology that focuses on three elements of culture (assumptions, values, and artifacts) and where research is based on a clinical perspective. According to Schein, this approach is most apt to capture the dynamism and shared pattern of culture. This orientation comes close to a traditional anthropological emphasis on the holism of culture.

3. A recent effort to make and tests this association is Kotter's *Culture and Corporate Performance* (in press).

4. Ethnographical fieldwork, a methodological tool once the sole of domain of anthropologists, is perfectly suited to this type of inquiry. This technique has become increasingly more popular among organizational researchers.

REFERENCES

Akin, G. and D. Hopelain
    1986 Finding the culture of productivity. *Organizational Dynamics*, 14(3):19-32.

Alchian, A. A.
    1950 Uncertainty, evolution, and economic theory. *Journal of Political Economy*, 58:211-221.

Baba, M. L.
    1987 Cognitive chronologies of international Joint ventures. Paper Presented at Annual Meeting of the Society for Applied Anthropology, Oaxaca, Mexico.

Barley, S. R., G. W. Meyer, and D. C Gash
    1988 Cultures of culture: Academics, practitioners and the pragmatics of normative control. *Administrative Science Quarterly*, 33:24-60.

Bartlett, C. A. and S. Ghoshal
    1989 *Managing Across Borders*. Boston: Harvard Business School Program.

Boyaciller, N. and N. J. Adler
    1991 The parochial dinosaur: Organizational science in a global context. *Academy of Management Review*, 16:262-290

Buono, A. F. and J. L. Bowditch
    1989 *The Human Side of Mergers and Acquisitions: Managing Collisions between People, Culture, and Organizations*. San Francisco: Jossey-Bass.

Caudill, W.
    1958 *The Mental Hospital as a Small Society*. Cambridge: Harvard University Press.

Chandler, A.
    1962 *Strategy and Structure*. Cambridge: MIT Press.

Chapple, E. D.
    1941 Organizational Problems in Industry. *Applied Anthropology* 1:2-9.

Chapple, E. D. and C. M. Arensberg
    1940 Measuring Human Relations. *Genetic Psychology Monographs*, 22:3-147.

Cole, M., J. Guy, J. A. Glick, and D. W. Sharp
    1971 *The Cultural Context of Learning and Thinking*. New York: Basic Books.

Davis, S. M.
    1974 *Comparative Management: Organizational and Cultural Perspectives*. Englewood Cliffs: Prentice-Hall.

    1984 *Managing Corporate Culture*. Cambridge: Bellinger.

Deal, T. F., and A. A. Kennedy
    1982 *Corporate Cultures: The Rites and Rituals of Corporate Life*. Reading, MA: Addison-Wesley.

DiBella, A. J.
    1992 *Culture and planned change in an international organization: Building a regional structure in South American and Asia*. Ph.D. dissertation. Cambridge, MA: MIT Sloan School of Management.

Dunham, H. W. and S. K. Weinberg
    1960 *The Culture of The State Mental Hospital*. Detroit: Wayne State U Press.

Fombrun, C. J.
    1983 Corporate culture, environment and strategy. *Human Resource Management*, 22: 139-152.

Frost, P. J., L. F. Moore, M. L. Louis, C. C. Lundberg, and J. Martin
    1991 *Reframing Organizational Culture*. Newbury Park: Sage.

Graves, D.
    1986 *Corporate Culture-Diagnosis and Change*. New York: St. Martins' Press.

Hofstede, G.
    1980 *Culture's Consequences*. Beverly Hills: Sage.

Kerr, J. and J. W. Slocum
  1987 Managing corporate culture through reward systems. *Academy of Management Executive*, 1:99-107.

Kilmann, R.H.
  1984 *Beyond the Quick Fix.* San Francisco: Jossey Bass.

Kilmann, R.H., M. J. Saxton, R. Serpa, and Associates
  1985 *Gaining Control of the Corporate Culture.* San Francisco: Jossey-Bass.

Kluckhohn, C.
  1943 Covert culture and administrative problems. *American Anthropologist*, 45:213-229.

Kotter, J.P. and J. L. Heskett
  Corporate Culture and Performance, in press.

Kunda, G.
  1992 *Engineering Culture: Control and Commitment in a High-Tech Corporation.* Philadelphia: Temple Univ. Pr.

Ott, J. S.
  1989 *The Organizational Culture Perspective.* Chicago: Dorsey Press.

Ouchi, W. G.
  1981 *Theory Z.* Reading, MA: Addison-Wesley.

Peters, T. J. and R. H. Waterman
  1982 *In Search of Excellence: Lessons from America's Best-Run Companies.* New York: Harper and Row.

Price-Williams, D.
  1978 Cognition: anthropological and psychological nexus, in G. D. Spindler (Ed.) *The Making of Psychological Anthropology* 586-611. Berkeley: Univ. of Calif. Press.

Richardson, F. L. W. and C. R. Walker
  1948 *Human Relations in an Expanding Company.* New Haven: Yale University Labor and Management Center.

Ronen, S.
   1986 *Comparative and Multinational Management*. New York: Wiley
        and Sons.

Salk, J.
   1992 *International shared management joint venture teams: Their
        development patterns, challenges, and possibilities.* Ph.D. disserta-
        tion. Cambridge, MA: MIT Sloan School of Management.

Sathe, V.
   1985 *Culture and Related Corporate Realities.* Homewood, IL: Irwin.

Schein, E. H.
   1991 What is culture?, in P. J. Frost, L. F. Moore, M. R. Louis, C. C.
        Lundberg, and J. Martin (Eds.), *Reframing Organizational Culture*
        243-253. Newbury Park: Sage.

   1985 *Organizational Culture and Leadership.* San Francisco: Jossey-Bass.

PART FOUR

ETHICS AND ORGANIZATIONAL CULTURE

INTRODUCTION

Tomoko Hamada

We have discussed how anthropological theories meet organization studies, and where anthropological theory and praxis take places. This part continues the theme of theory and application by examining the fundamental and central issue of doing ethnography, i.e. its ethical dimension. Some authors investigate crisis management by different business firms in America, and reveal that there are certain cultural patterns that can be considered as American institutional ways of thinking. Others probe the nature of the "institutional" ways of thinking that discourage organizational learning. Some authors also look at the relationship between the researcher and the client/employer. They ask such questions as: how does the researcher-client relationship affect anthropological research and action? How can one promote mutually beneficial interactive learning by shifting professional power relationships?

Weinburg advocates that industrial anthropology must go far beyond the "Hawthorne Effect" in ethical and methodological thinking to become an action science. The "action" scientist is interested in bringing change by teaching members of the system how to change themselves. Thus the focus of action-oriented research is more on problem definition than on problem solution--to help the client define what they mean by "success," who gets to define it, what problems exist, and what interpretations are possible. The role of the anthropologist-consultant, according to Weinburg, is to create an environment in which the clients can discover their own culture in order to make their own decisions. Weinburg believes that the anthropologist can begin more fruitful interactive learning by throwing away the myth that the consultant knows best, and by maintaining on-going, reciprocal, and collaborative relationships.

The view that business organization is a social entity within a given society, not just a part of its market economy, permits one to ask fundamental questions about the cultural orientation of business itself. One can look at business as an intersection between market-oriented economic values and broader human community-oriented values and ethics. Vetica considers the business corporation as a part culture, and he explores the junction and disjunction between community-oriented values and market-oriented economic values across different organizational lines. His examples of business firms provide a heuristic medium for his thesis that there are different sources of values in society with varying degrees of normative influence on corporate cultures, and that the intersection of different societal values across organizational levels constitute important variables for understanding organizational response to public demands. On the other hand, Nash and Kirsch's case study illustrates the normative orientation of an American company in relation to the public welfare of American people. They argue that, when General Electric executives disregard personal and moral responsibility in decision making that affects the life of workers and communities near the plants they control, they do so as actors within a larger capitalist system which promotes a cost accounting rationale. These executives are thus abiding by the economic values portrayed in the wider American culture. The PCB pollution case presented by Nash and Kirsch raises a question as to whether we can strike a balance between seemingly opposing values for organizational decision making.

Nash and Kirsch criticize the trend that "corporate culture" researchers ignore the underlying moral implication of the company's ideological primacy. Corporation stakeholders, including organization researchers, do not commonly perceive business decisions as containing moral components. According to Nash and Kirsch this lack of moral consideration is a significant short-coming in the conventional organizational theory building.

The fact that the anthropological perspective places "corporate culture" within the larger cultural context allows one to recognize that the corporation is still an actor, albeit an institutional one, of the larger culture with differing and contesting values and ethical concerns. The culture perspective lets one see the influence of culturally patterned thinking in organizational processing of information. Complex and often conflicting value relations within an organizational culture, such as one between market oriented ideology and corporate ethics, must be resolved ultimately by how we define corporate goals and corporate accountability.

Anthropologists are among the main stakeholders in international development assistance, and it is the profession's moral responsibility to confront the present failure of development agencies to create desired changes in host countries. In his study of the organizational cultures of international development aid agencies such as USAID and the World Bank, Nolan reveals that institutional forms that guide the decision-making of large agencies do not allow them to obtain grass-root level information and local knowledge and to apply diversity in any systematic way. Nolan shows that large international organizations' thinking is dominated by quantitative, econometric, approaches to analysis and planning. Consequently there is less and less opportunity for variation, experiment, or heterodoxy in international development projects.

The debates in this part which deal with the problem of normative orientations are addressed to those who strive to act both as problem solvers and change agents in organizational settings. It is the consensus among the authors of this volume that the field of organizational science must transform itself to multiparadigm, process-oriented, interdependent, globally oriented, organizational approaches. In search of new knowledge and action, practicing anthropologists will be involved inevitably in the messy reality of contrasting world views, inconsistent human values, differing ethical standards, dissenting interpretations, human alliances and power struggles in organizational settings. As Nolan states, the key to managing the world's diversity is an ability and willingness to learn, above all else. Thus the ultimate value of anthropological knowledge must be found in each individual research's contribution to organizational learning in diverse socio-political, symbolic, experiential worlds.

REAL WORLD ANTHROPOLOGY: THE ANTHROPOLOGIST-CLIENT RELATIONSHIP

Daniela Weinberg

The more I practice anthropology, the more I find myself reflecting on broad theoretical issues. Ethics is one of these. As a well socialized anthropologist, I have seldom had to think explicitly about ethics in the traditional sense of the disciple's "Principles of Professional Responsibility." I have completely internalized such principles as the obligation to respect and protect my informants. These principles constitute the moral code of the anthropological community. They serve me well, whether I am studying Swiss Alpine peasants or Swedish computer programmers. But when "informants" become "clients," I find the PPR to be necessary but insufficient. My relationship with clients is one of a different order than with informants. Not only must I treat the relationship differently, but I must also operate with a somewhat different ethical framework.

In this paper, I want to explore some of the relational implications of doing "real world" anthropology - in particular, the relationship between anthropologists and clients. Unless we understand this relationship, I believe we cannot fully realize the great potential of the anthropological perspective for the sociocultural system of any kind. We will then have to limit ourselves to what many of our detractors accuse us of doing: a kind of pale imitation, a caricature, of traditional anthropology. The people we work with will be quite justified in their contempt for anthropologists as mere "butterfly collectors" (Leach 1961).

In 1980 I began to divide my time between the "real world" of organizational consulting and the "academic world" of degree-oriented teaching and pure research. Both worlds, of course, are "real" to the natives, and each has pejorative connotations to the outsiders. The "real world," to the academics, is a mysterious place where people work themselves to death for crass monetary rewards. The "academic world," to citizens of the real world, is inhabited by people who do inane, uninteresting work and complain about being underpaid.

I have had one foot in both cultures, working as an organizational consultant in addition to doing "abstract anthropology" (Eddy and Partridge 1978) as a university professor. Most of my clients are organizations in the private sector, especially in the high technology areas. I function as a catalyst for change, helping organizations understand where they are, decide where they'd like to be, and find effective and humane ways to get there.

I do my work with the conceptual and methodological framework of anthropology. I treat an organization as a sociocultural system that exists within largely self-specified environment. I think about it in the standard anthropological framework - that is, in terms of its language, economy and ecology, social organization, and ideology. I take into account the dynamics of culture change and cultural evolution. My data-gathering approach is based on self-immersion and participant observation. In short, I see myself doing traditional anthropology in a non-tradition setting -- up to a point. That point is the crossover between research and action. It is the point at which the abstract and the real-world anthropologist part company. Doing real-world anthropology, I have found, creates some new challenges that may be usefully conceptualized as ethical.

The essential difference between real-world and academic, or abstract, anthropology lies in the relationship between anthropologists and-- what do we call it? In anthropological field research, we work with "natives," or "informant." Netting (1981) prefers to call them "consultants" in order to highlight the fact that they are not only active participants in the research process but, in fact, the true experts on their own culture. Unfortunately, the term "consultant" is used in the real world to identify someone who has not only expertise but the valuable perspective of an outsider. In applied or action anthropology, we may use the term "target group," or simply "community." Practicing anthropologists speak of "clients," or even "employers."

The fact is, we have no general term to designate the entity with which the real world anthropologist interacts. And, predictably, we have no general rules that describe and govern those interactions. I conclude, therefore, that, as the label changes, so too does the relationship. (This is good anthropology: we know, after all, that different kinship terms denote and prescribe different behaviors). And, as the relationship changes, so do the methodological and ethical principles that govern it.

Real world anthropology is client-centered. The very term "client" suggests a whole array of relationship changes. However we may have encountered one another, it is usually the client who initiates and terminates the relationship. It is the client who proposes the content and scope of the work to be done. It is the client whose needs must be served and satisfied. The client has confidence in my ability to help, partly because of research I have done in other organizations. Any research I do in their organization, however, must be directly related to their problem are rather than to my scientific interests, unless we have contracted explicitly otherwise.

In one company to whom I am consulting, I decided that it would be both interesting (to me) and valuable (to them) to collect and analyze professional life histories of a group of managers. When I proposed the idea to the managers, there was a mixed reaction. One manager in particular seemed to shrink from the idea of a personal disclosure. He hesitated and then said he would agree to a life-history interview -- "if it will help."

This incident reminded me of the great responsibility I have towards my clients. Although I work with them at their pleasure and for their needs, I become a very powerful person in their system. I am an "expert" with access to almost any information I want. I am a "friend" who can be relied on to serve and represent their best interests. The trust implicit in these status labels often verges on dependence. And indeed, the kind of consulting relationship I want requires a high degree of confidence in my competence and integrity. Yet somehow I must strike a happy balance between trust and dependence.

I am engaged by an organization as a problem solver and change agent, under the assumption that I will have all the necessary skills and knowledge to get the job done. But an important part of my conceptual and ethical tool kit is the idea that change will not be accepted or retained if it does not fit the cultural system. As an anthropological change agent, then, I must work with the culture. My clients must collaborate in the process -- both for reasons of efficacy and ethics. They may become dependent on me, but I too am dependent on them. This relationship of interdependency requires mutual trust and sharing of power.

In traditional anthropological research, the anthropologist assumes the role of "student," even "child" (Firth 1951), maintaining an open and humble posture that invites information.   The anthropologist is responsible to informants but accountable only to professional colleagues.

By contrast, the real-world anthropologist is both responsible and accountable to the client. At the same time, however, the client is at the mercy of the anthropologist.   By the very act of engaging a consultant the client has acknowledged an inability to handle the situation. To the extent that there is trust, the client has stepped into the role of "child" to the anthropologist's "parent,"   thus reversing the relationship that exists in traditional anthropological research. (I suspect that this is why we hear so many cynical jokes about consultants!) This delicate dynamic must be carefully managed to avoid the often stormy and destructive relationships in families where the parent-child gulf is exaggerated. The client may begin the relationship with a legitimate call for outside help and a willingness to trust the consultant. But later, like the child in disturbed families, the client may move through stages of unquestioning trust and total dependence, to feelings of "betrayal" (as perceived by the client), and finally to acts of "resistance" (as perceived by the anthropologist).

A way out of this dilemma is offered by the "action science" model proposed by Argyris and his colleagues (1985). They distinguish "basic" from "applied" researchers, and then contrast both with "action scientists." The basic researcher seeks only to understand the system under study. The applied researcher wishes to effect change in the system. The action scientist, too, is interested in bringing change but, in contrast with the applied researcher, works to teach members of the system how to change themselves.

For the applied researcher, the desired outcome of the research is established and accepted without further question. All that remains is to help children succeed in school. The action scientist, however, must focus the research on determining the desired ends as well as the means. For example, the action researcher might raise issues about what is meant by "success" and who gets to define it (teachers, students, or parent). Implicit in action research is the need to question (and help clients question) what exists and to confront value conflicts in the system. The action scientist must concentrate more heavily on problem definition than problem solution.

Argyris and his colleagues suggest that the most effective way to bring about long-term change is to teach the client how to do it, rather than doing it for them. They contrast the action scientist with the clinician (an "applied researcher") in this regard. Some family therapists, for example, discover and propose solutions but are not concerned with training the family to do its own problem-solving. For the Argyris group, then, the action scientist assumes the role of "teacher" -- a very non-directive and interactive kind of teacher whose primary mission is not to give answers but to teach people how to learn.

This model is very compatible with the anthropological model of culture change. The anthropologist/change-agent suggests rather than prescribes pathways to change and engages the client fully in the process. Client engagement offers the anthropologist feedback about, and the client ownership of the solutions as they emerge. Client and anthropologist thus alternate in the role of "teacher," together designing, building, testing and rebuilding the desired changes. This is what Maccoby aptly called "participatory research" (1986).

I offer the following example of this principle from one of my current consulting relationships. The client was well aware of the extremely hierarchical structure of organization when I reported discovering a high degree of "levels-consciousness." In fact, it was this very structure that the organization was trying to change in favor of a more participatory model. In Maccoby's terms, the organization was quite deliberately moving from an "industrial bureaucratic" to a "techno-service" model (1986).

My consulting colleague and I set about to design a culture change program which included a workshop for natural work groups. We proposed that each work group attending the workshop be a complete vertical slice -- third-level managers down through clerical support staff -- so that people could begin to experience the desired "new-culture" change.

The idea of a multi-level workshop hit the organization like a tornado warning siren. People at different levels expressed their anxieties in level-appropriate ways. Upper-level managers expressed concern for their subordinates who might feel "inhibited" in the same workshop with their bosses. The subordinates expressed concern for themselves and their careers if they should happen to "make fools of themselves" in the presence of those who had the power to promote them. Both kinds of concerns were rooted in the old culture of authoritarian hierarchy, and both would have been legitimate in that culture.

We listened quietly and added mental notes to our understanding of the organization. We realized that the organization was not yet ready to act fully on its new ideas. After much careful discussion with people at different levels in the organization, we redesigned the workshop to include only the three levels of management, excluding the technical and clerical workers below them. The client accepted the new design with relief and gratitude, reaffirming their confidence in our ability to understand and work with them. When all the commotion finally died down, some people realized that even three levels participating together in an intense learning experience might be two levels too many for comfort. It was at that point that we could help them make the decision, in full awareness, to trade off some immediate comfort for the possibility of achieving their long-term organizational goals.

We contracted to offer four of these workshops over a period of ten months, so that all work groups could participate. During the first hour of the first workshop, as participants became involved in the learning process, the dreaded specter of the Inhibiting Boss was forever dispelled. The opportunity to interact with colleagues as persons rather than as job-title-holders revealed that the old culture was fading into memory and the new actually taking hold. This was even more evident when, as the last workshop approached, one of the upper-level managers who was scheduled to come insisted that we admit his entire work group, down to the secretaries.

The point here is not that we, the omniscient and manipulative consultant, tricked the client but rather that we created an environment in which they could discover their own culture to make their own decisions. We started the process by acknowledging and respecting their concerns, and we stayed close to them as they tested and finally left behind their initial fears.

We further enabled their participation in the culture change process by insisting that the first group to attend the workshop constitute a feedback-gathering committee afterward. We asked them to report their findings to us so that we could make the necessary modifications to the succeeding workshops. The group sent us four pages of raw data, the notes from their meeting, and a concise summary of their conclusions. One statement in this material stands out as an emblem of the group's new empowerment: "we are ALL responsible for the success of future workshops."

In many respects, this reciprocal relationship is very similar to the one that exists in traditional anthropological field research. The reciprocity and collaboration in the real world, however, are even more crucial to the task at hand. Every good field worker in a traditional setting knows rapport can be built by giving as well as taking. A successful interview, then, leaves the informant a little better off than before, enriched by some new ideas or insights about the culture. The informant's satisfaction makes it more likely that future interactions with the anthropologist will be productive and reliable. In the end, however, the greatest gain will probably accrue to the anthropologist and the discipline at large, not to the informant.

In the real world, this spirit of reciprocity does much more than simply promote rapport and trust. It yields new information directly. It enables the anthropologist to test hypotheses. It promotes learning in the client. It empowers the client to construct their own solutions to problems.

To be effective in the real world, we must go far beyond the "Hawthorne Effect" in our ethical and methodological thinking. It is not just that working in a sociocultural system necessarily disturbs that system. It is not just that our data may be bias by this inevitable disruption. It is not even just that we are compelled to pay attention to ethical issues under these circumstances. This is a parental ethic, based on the notion that the anthropologist consultant know best - what to do, how to do it, and how to "protect" the client system from the iatrogenic effects of consultation. In other words, Hawthorne-Effect thinking raises the fundamental issue of power in the anthropologist-client relationship.

Working in the real world, the anthropologist is both more and less powerful than in the traditionally "anthropological" societies. The key to unlocking this paradox lies in understanding the special characteristics of the anthropologist-client relationship. We must treat this relationship as interactive and mutually enriching. We must begin to look at it -- and, for that matter, at any of our professional relationships -- in terms of power (Nader 1969, Wolf 1969). It may even be that, as we venture out into the "real world," we will be repaid by a deeper understanding of the "academic" mysteries of our discipline.

REFERENCES

Argyris, Chris, Robert Putnam and Diana McLain Smith
1985   *Action Science.* San Francisco: Jossey-Bass.

Eddy, Elizabeth M., and William L. Partridge, eds.
1978   *Applied Anthropology in America.* New York: Columbia
         University Press.

Firth, Raymond
1951   *Elements of Social Organization.* Boston: Beacon Press.

Leach, Edmund
1961   *Rethinking Anthropology.* London: Athlone Press.

Maccoby, Michael
1986   The Corporation as a Part of Culture. Paper presented at the
         AAAS symposium, "Studying Corporate Cultures," Philadel-
         phia.

Nader, Laura
1969   Up the Anthropologist -- Perspectives Gained from Studying
         Up. In Dell Hymes, ed., *Reinventing Anthropology.* New
         York: Random House.

Netting, Robert McC.,
1981   *Balancing on an Alp.* Cambridge: Cambridge University
         Press.

Wolf, Eric R.
1969   American Anthropologists and American Society. In Dell
         Hymes, ed., *Reinventing Anthropology.* New York: Random
         House.

CORPORATE SOCIAL RESPONSIBILITY: ECONOMIC RATIONALITY ENCOUNTERS SOCIETAL VALUES[1]

Thomas M. Vetica[2]

INTRODUCTION

One of the anthropology's traditional missions has been to study social institutions and the degree of integration of institutions in a given society. My research, of which this paper is a part, directly addresses the integration of institutions and values in our complex society. The modern business corporation is one of the most dominant organizations in society. Its place and role are being debated with an urgency that the traditional debate of the business-society relationship lacked.

My approach to this debate is to perceive the business corporation as part of society's culture, not merely part of the market economy. The corporation has a specific history and its development has been selected by social and cultural forces, as well as by market dynamics. It was made possible by the availability of resources and information as technology made the exploitation of resources possible and profitable. But social and cultural forces have also selected the corporation as it came into prominence in America. And social and cultural forces continue to influence change.

For example, until the mid 19th century, all corporations received a charter, or grant, from an act of the state legislature. They were considered an instrument for the advancement of public welfare, the public good, and sometimes an instrument of the state. The legal mechanism of chartering has since changed. So has the notion of advancing the public good. But society still claims a stake in the organizations that it legitimizes (Vetica 1991).

The purpose of this paper is to explore the problem of the integration of institutions in society and the junction, or disjunction of values across organizational lines. To do that, I am presenting a brief comparison of three companies that faced crisis. The response to crisis is a key heuristic medium for understanding the values that inform and motivate policy and performance.

JOHNSON AND JOHNSON: THE COMPANY BEFORE THE CRISIS

Johnson and Johnson was the world's most diversified health care company. Established in the 1880s by the Johnson brothers it has carefully cultivated an image of caring and responsibility. One of the first products offered by the company was a first-aid kit developed to service the needs of railroad workers laying tracks across the country. Since then the company has assiduously worked to service health care needs of American families.

By 1981 Johnson and Johnson ranked 74th in size among the top 500 industrial corporations. The company had sales of $5.4 billion (Annual Report 1981). The corporation was an organization of 150 semi-independent companies, or strategic business units, manufacturing a diverse line of products: dental floss, band aids, heart valves, contraceptives, and surgical sutures to name only a few. J&J led the market in painkillers. Its Tylenol line, produced by its McNeil subsidiary had the largest share of the analgesic market. Each of the 150 divisions had its own board of directors and chairman of the board. The companies were aggregated into eight groups according to geography and product similarity (Sturdivant 1985:436). An eleven member executive board met almost daily to manage the corporate affairs and hold the huge corporation together (Peters and Waterman 1982).

One further characteristic of the company is crucial to an understanding of the inner workings and value system of the organization. Johnson and Johnson had diligently and consciously nurtured an internal culture and value system of service, care, and responsibility to customers. Internal cohesion in the vast company is provided by the "Credo", the company's code of behavior (Table 1). The Credo was developed by Robert Wood Johnson, the son of one of the founders, who managed the company from 1938 to 1963. He wanted to sustain a 'strong company code of behavior and value system.

Executives continue to pride themselves on their rigid adherence to the code (*Fortune* Jan. 29, 1990:48-50). The company places service to its customers as its first priority, especially service to doctors, hospitals, nurses, and mothers. It serves employees second, communities third, and shareholders last of all. The commitment to servicing customers has caused the company to sacrifice earnings for the sake of consumer interests. For example, independently of the company's research apparatus, sunbathers discovered that Johnson's baby oil promoted sun tans very well. The company took advantage of that in a marketing campaign which targeted teenage sunbathers. However, as evidence grew concerning the deleterious effects of over-exposure to solar rays, J&J unilaterally withdrew the campaign at an estimated cost of about 15% of baby oil sales (Sturdivant 1985:437). Although the question of who profited and who gained in the removal of the add campaign and the nature of the values inherent in the decision is debatable, the issue will be discussed in a broader context in the conclusion to the paper.

TYLENOL: THE ANALGESIC MARKET

By the 1980s, the analgesic market was a $1 billion a year industry. There were two primary over the counter painkillers: acetylsalicylic acid (aspirin) and acetaminophen (nonaspirin). Tylenol was the leader in the market accounting for over 34% of market share in 1981. Although the competition was aggressive: Bristol Meyers offered Bufferin and Excedrin; American Home Products offered Anacin and Maximum Strength Anacin; and Sterling Drug marketed Bayer Aspirin. Nevertheless, Tylenol still accounted for $365 million in sales in 1981, and was J&J's best-selling nonprescription drug, accounting for 7% of the company's total worldwide sales and 15-20% of the company's profits (Annual Report 1981).

One of the main reasons for Tylenol's success is the way it entered the market. From 1955 until 1975 Tylenol was sold exclusively to medical professionals: doctors, hospitals, pharmacies. In 1975 Bristol Meyers introduced Datril, a nonaspirin pain reliever, to the market. This move by a competitor showed J&J that a consumer market existed for its product. Capitalizing on the success of Tylenol and the preference for it by medical professionals, Johnson and Johnson initiate a vigorous marketing campaign targeting the consumer market. Tylenol clearly remained the preferred non-prescriptions, nonaspirin, pain reliever (Sturdivant 1985:441).

THE INCIDENT: SEPTEMBER-OCTOBER 1982

The events surrounding the Tylenol-related deaths have been well document in the media. Time's account begins with the events on Wed., Sept. 30. "Adam Janus had a minor chest pain last Wednesday morning, so he went out and bought a bottle of ExtraStrength Tylenol capsules. About an hour later, in his home in the Chicago suburb of Arlington Heights, Janus suffered a cardiopulmonary collapse. He was rushed to the Northwest Community Hospital, where doctors worked frantically to revive him" (Tifft 1982:18). A few hours later his brother and sister-in-law, who had taken pills from the same bottle, were pronounced dead. By the end of the week four other Chicago citizens had died after ingesting cyanide-laced Tylenol. In all, seven people died that week. All had taken Tylenol.

Once the link to Tylenol had been established, stunned company executives took swift action (Waldholz 1982; More 1982). The two men responsible for the company's response were James Burke, Chairman and Chief Executive Officer of Johnson and Johnson, and David Collins, chairman of McNeil Consumer Products. The action taken was swift and determined.

Collins believed that the company was not at fault. He reasoned that if cyanide were introduced in the manufacturing process, the drug mixing machines would have diluted the contents such that no threat would have been posed. Yet, regardless of the sense of presumed innocence and a plausible logic to support his position, J&J ordered a recall of the entire lot of pills nationwide. Significantly, the FDA cautioned against such a move. Their position was also logical. In view of the strong arguments for company innocence they wished to contribute to the good name of the company and avoid widespread panic over the project. The recall entailed sending telegrams to 450,000 doctors, hospitals, and distributors at a cost of half a million dollars (Sturdivant 1985:450). All commercials for Tylenol were halted and production was ceased in one of the two manufacturing plants that produced the Tylenol implicated in the first deaths. The company then offered a $100,000 dollar reward for any information leading to the arrest of the person or persons responsible for the contamination.

The death of the sixth victim was attributed to Tylenol that was manufactured in the other of the two plants. This proved to the executives that tampering with the finished product was indeed the true cause of death and that the company was not at fault. The possibility that lethal doses of cyanide could have been introduced into the manufacturing process at both plants at the same time was so minimal that executives were convinced of company innocence. They quickly moved into the second, self-defensive, phase of managing the crisis.

First, Burke was concerned that the Johnson and Johnson name was associated with Tylenol. The company's image was at stake. According to company surveys before the Tylenol incident only one percent of the public knew that J&J manufactured Tylenol (Sturdivant 1985:450). After the deaths, 47% associated the company's name to the brand. Therefore Burke moved to rescue the company's image by pulling the Johnson name out of the press as much as possible. He assigned a crisis task force under the auspices of McNeil. The McNeil task force supervised the response, at least in the media and publicly, making a major connection between the drug and the subsidiary, rather than the parent corporation.

Next, the public relations department assembled a videotape of news reports and statements by company executives which was transmitted to all company employee television network. The task force established media relations and public relations offices which handled phone calls and media inquiries. Finally, Burke commissioned Young and Rubicam Consultants to begin polling the public on attitudes, the results of which would be used to assess the future of the brand (Sturdivant 1985:450-452).

By October 9, 1982 Johnson and Johnson stock fell more than six points for a paper loss of over $650 million. Distributors, in spite of all the media attention and demand by consumers to open packages to examine for tampering, trusted the company and remained loyal to J&J. The FDA initiated a policy requiring tamper-resistant packaging and a separate label calling attention to the presence and nature of the seal.

So for the first weeks the company took steps in favor of public safety and health, acted quickly to determine its own lack of culpability, tried to remove the Johnson and Johnson name form media attention, acted to reassure employees, and sought to assure the public of the good intentions of the company. Full disclosure to the media was key to the policy.

The competition was gentle to McNeil during the first phase of the crisis. But after the company's integrity was established, competitors moved in quickly. *The Wall Street Journal* of December 2, 1982 carried Dennis Kneale's report: "Rivals Go After Tylenol's Market, But Gains may Be Only Temporary." Competition moved in quickly and aggressively to go for Tylenol's market share. The third phase of the crisis encompassed all the moves undertaken to reestablish the brand in a highly competitive environment in which the name had lost value; that is, lost trustworthiness and credibility. The result is history. Ethical practice proved good for business. Today both J&J **and** Tylenol are alive and well. Market share of Tylenol is strong and J&J is prospering.

AUDI AND FIRESTONE: DEFENSIVE REACTION TO CRISIS

In 1986 nearly 1300 automobile accidents, among them several deaths, were attributed to quick acceleration in the Audi 5000. Audi's executive officers engaged in a prolonged battle with the public in which the company denied fault and attributed the accidents to drivers not knowing how to drive! The closest the company came to admitting fault was an offer to redesign the brake pedal which the company said was the real culprit in those cases where drivers could not adjust to the shape of the pedal. Rather than admit some fault or adopt an open posture with the media and provide design information to the public, audi fought it out in defiance of consumers and government agencies.

The Firestone Tire and Rubber Company has consistently maintained a position of leadership in the manufacture of tires for motor vehicles. In 1973 it ranked in the top two hundred industrial firms in the United States. Firestone was not a diversified company; throughout its history, which spans most of the 20th century, it has concentrated on the development and manufacture of tires for vehicles.

During the 1970s, the company came under attack. The 500 series of steel-belted radial tires was said to be defective, prone to blowouts, tread separation, and other deformities. Yet the company continued to market the product, refused to divulge information to the press and battled the Traffic Safety Administration for years. Hundreds of accidents and at least 34 deaths were associated with the tire.

The company refused to acknowledge fault in the design of the tire. It contended, rather, that tire failure could be blamed on consumer neglect and abuse. According to the company, consumers abused the tires by driving too fast, over-inflating the tires, banging them against curbs, etc. (Louis 1978).

When the Traffic Safety Administration (TSA) began an investigation, Firestone attempted to block it. The TSA undertook a survey of owners of the tire and Firestone went to court in order to suppress the publication of the results of the survey. When the TSA requested, under pain of prosecution, information on the tire design and manufacturing process, Firestone stalled in response, insisting that months of research would be needed to fully respond to the questions. Firestone not only objected to the types of information being requested but even questioned the authority of the Traffic Safety Administration to demand such data (Louis 1978).

Neither did Congressional hearings deter Firestone from resisting full disclosure of its records. As a result, the company lost millions of dollars to its competitors and for a few years experienced difficulty in selling any brand of radial tire.

Both Firestone and Audi were aware of technical defects in their products. Accidents and deaths were attributed to-the products! Yet both companies fought it out assuming a defensive and reactive posture. They denied fault, did not disclose information to the press not to the public, and lost money and customers in the process (Anderson 1989:232-233).

The brief summary of product failure by both Firestone and Audi is important because of the stark contrast to that of Tylenol. A corporation's concern viability, for product receptivity and value can be expressed in various ways in times of crisis. Firestone could have assumed the same, open posture as Johnson and Johnson but chose not to. As business, both organization seek to survive in the market by returning a profit on investment. Both opted for strategies in time of crisis which executives though would increase long-term profitability. Yet they opted for different and polar opposite strategies.

Research by management professionals has highlighted the positive aspects of Johnson and Johnson's response. According to Katz (1987) openness with the media and the public are crucial for a company's survival in the wake of a crisis. The company must demonstrate its concern for the public and make information available to the public as it becomes known by the managers. And crisis managers should have someone dealing with the media on a twenty-four hour basis, just as Johnson and Johnson did through their director of communications and their public relations department. And yet, as essential as Katz's comments seem to be, the reality is that both Audi and Firestone, companies that did not opt for the open and proactive stance, have continued to do business and survive. The posture of the executives was to fight any accusation, admit to no fault, blame the victims, and stall disclosure of information, even if it meant expensive and lengthy legal battles. There was short term loss, as with J&J's Tylenol, but overall both strategies worked well enough for those interested in economic rationality to support either position logically and theoretically. What then can one say of such apparent value contradictions in American corporate cultures?

ANALYSIS

It is fair to assume that the executives of the three companies believed that they opted for strategies that they thought would increase long-term profitability and survivability of their firms and products. Yet they opted for different and opposing strategies. Why?

One of the traditional avenues of response has been to discuss the difference in the realm of business ethics. However, an appeal to ethics alone to describe, explain, offer solutions, or to delineate the proper courses of action and response is not adequate.

For example, the benefit of seeking the greatest good for the greatest number might explain Johnson and Johnson's handling of the Tylenol crisis. The action taken by company executives responded to concerns of employees, customers, the public in general, distributors, shareholders and government. And within the last few months, J&J reached a monetary settlement for damages with the families involved.

What about Firestone and Audi? Their response was selfdefensive. Yet they got the same results.

My analysis invokes the notion of civil society and discusses it on two levels. The first is the level of the freedom of the parts. In each of these cases the following parties were present to the discussion and resolution of the particular problem. The companies, their employees, distributors, customers, and shareholders were all involved. Regulatory agencies of the federal government, state and local health administrators, and even committees of the United States Congress all had roles to play. The courts also entered the process. Consumer advocacy groups mounted pressure on both the government and the companies. The persons affected or relatives of the deceased pressed for just compensation. Individual parties brought law suits as did groups of affected parties in class-action. The health and welfare of the general public was a prime concern of most parties. The media played an aggressive role. And finally, the ominous cloud of public opinion loomed always overhead. Economics, politics and society are all intertwined here in an holistic interaction in which separation of social science domains diminishes, indeed obscures our understanding.[3]

What happened in these crises was an interplay of varied interest groups, each with its own agenda. And the drama was played out on a socio-political stage that allowed the acts to unfold. This, to me, is one of the most important aspects of the discussion. Because it was against the backdrop of our established cultural traditions which have asserted the right to freedom of the supposedly separate sectors of society that the interest of those sectors vied for recognition. One of the most significant underlying issues is not whether particular acts or decisions were unethical but rather whether the company should be free and able to continue to pursue its economic function in society. This cannot be overlooked.

I am not advocating that valid claims to ethical postures be subsumed into a political theory that might overlook those claims. The ethical debate is valid. Rather, I am saying that the ethical domain is part of a much broader picture. And it is that broad picture that is often overlooked or taken for granted in discussion of contemporary organizations.

The second level of analysis is just as essential as the first. It is concerned with the problem of how to account for the values that inform opposing corporate strategies. The notion of civil society has been most commonly used to defend economic freedom, as I mentioned a above. But that is only part of the concept. It sees society as composed of independent sectors, private and public, in which the intimate sector of family and community ties produced bond of solidarity in social relations and provides the moral background, the value system, for the functioning of the whole (Held 1987).

Corporations are important organizations within our society and culture. The relationship between the sectors of society and the intersection of values across artificially separated functions, from the intimate sectors to the public and vice versa, are a way to understand the opposing corporate strategies. Some of the business executives that I interviewed in a pilot study for this research spoke about the importance of community values and standards for business practice. In some cases I studied, the personal values of the executive influenced company policy toward the community.

For example, one of the executives in my pilot study has fostered a concern and even a sense of responsibility for children's health issues. The company contributes sizeable assets to the local children's hospital, assets in terms of money, time, and personnel. Employees are proud of their contributions and of the culture nourished by company leadership. The explanation for this is two-fold. First, the executive feels a sense of commitment to family and family values. Second, he feels a responsibility to share his personal success, as well as his company's, with the community. The values of the private and intimate sector, the bonds of family and community, have influenced the policy and practice of this company.

The same cannot be said of all companies. Corporate executives are persons whose values have been influenced by either the private and intimate sectors or by market principles or by both. My first attempt at explanation looks to variations of influence from all of these sources as they affect companies and executives and hence corporate cultures.

According to my perspective, the corporation is one form of social organization that is part of the social, economic, and political organization of our complex society. The market has its own rationality. There is no doubt that market dynamics are essential to understanding the functions of business corporations. And indeed, for some thinkers, it is the sole responsibility of business to pursue its economic function with little regard for issues of greater social import.

But corporations are, non the less, part of the culture. And significantly, the values of the market are not restricted to the marketplace. They are strongly represented outside the market. Economic rationality with its behavioral assumption that all individuals are rational decision makers that seek to maximize personal advantage has strongly rooted in our society. For some thinkers economic rationality is, or should be, the ethic for all social relations. For other thinkers, the private and intimate sectors would provide the values and the morality for social relations, even economic relations. The reality is that there are different sources of values in society with varying degrees of influence on companies, executives, and corporate cultures.

In order to examine this in greater detail, and to leave room for causal factors, I propose that there are at least three probable courses of evolutionary development in the business-society relationship. I discuss these as general propositions that address the integration of institutions in society and the junction, or disjunction, of values across organizational lines. They explain what is happening now and suggest courses of future development.

The first is that the dynamics of the market will diffuse across organizational lines and penetrate most aspects of society. The integration of values in our society will be dominated by market principles. Ours is either a society held together by nonbourgeois morality with a capitalistic economy or it is a society where market freedom is the moral code for all social relations. If the latter, then all social relations are organized according to the behavioral assumption of the market: rational decision makers seeking personal advantage. An organizational culture shaped by this principle would be least responsive to social demands.

The second proposition is that market forces will decline because a humanization of the marketplace is underway. Social pressures on business have been and will continue to be so strong as to effect change. Concern for the public good, in its myriad expressions, will mitigate against the unrelenting pursuit of self-interest, even in the non-economic transactions between business and society. Executives who have been influenced by community values and concern for "the other" would be most inclined to foster a responsive corporate culture.

The third proposition is that a steady-state in the business society relationship will be maintained and the value orientations remain constant. Our economy needs the self-interest of both corporations and individuals to energize it. At the same time our social system calls for the independence and the freedom of the parts for the sake of the whole. In debates and crises, such as the cases presented here, the independent sectors of society define themselves ever more precisely and delineate the interests at stake. The better those interests are defined and respected, the better the system works.

The influence of any one of these three possibilities could explain the differing postures of the firms discussed here. The intersection of values in society across organizations and the influence of market principles on organizational culture are extremely important variables in understanding varied responses to the public good.

CONCLUSION

I have learned two things from this research and from the greater body of work of which this paper is a small part. The first thing is that our commonly accepted way of thinking about business firms as a market instrument is too narrow and limiting. Business organization are part of culture. The firm is a form of social organization within a braoder social context. The traditional, holistic, and integrative epistemological stance of anthropology is extremely relevant for our study of contemporary institutions.

The second thing I have learned is the impact values can have on an organization. Indeed, the strength of the Credo at Johnson and Johnson is an example of values used as an organizing principle. And it is an attempt to tie into cultural values of responsibility.

To test these propositions and the hypotheses they generate, I have elaborated sets of independent and dependent variables that I am using in on-going research and field work. Executives are willing to talk about what their companies are doing. They are willing to talk about why they have decided to do what they do. My research will shed light on the values that influence corporate decision makers. And it will shed light on the direction the business-society relationship is moving.

TABLE ONE - OUR CREDO

We believe our first responsibility is to the doctors, nurses and patients, to mothers and all others who use our products and services.
In meeting their needs everything we do must be high quality.
We must constantly strive to reduce out costs in order to maintain reasonable prices.
Customers' orders must be serviced promptly and accurately.
Our suppliers and distributors must have an opportunity to make a fair profit.

We are responsible to out employees, the men and women who work with us throughout the world.
Everyone must be considered as an individual.
We must respect their dignity and recognize their merit.
They must have a sense of security in their jobs.
Compensation must be fair and adequate, and working conditions clean, orderly and safe.
Employees must feel free to make suggestions and complaint.
There must be equal opportunity for employment, development and advancement for those qualified.
We must provide competent management, and their actions must be just and ethical.

We are responsible to the communities in which we live and work and to the world community as well.
We must be good citizens -- support good works and charities and bear our fair share of taxes.
We must encourage civic improvements and better health and education.
We must maintain in good order the property we are privileged to use, protecting the environment and natural resources.

Our final responsibility is to our stockholders.
Business must make a sound profit.
We must experiment with new ideas.
Research must be carried on, innovative programs developed and mistakes paid for.
New equipment must be purchased, new facilities provided and new products launched.
Reserves must be created to provide for adverse times.
When we operate according to these principles, the stockholder should realize a fair return.

Source: Johnson and Johnson, 1982 Annual Report.

NOTES

1. Research for this paper is part of a larger project being conducted for the author's doctoral dissertation in anthropology at the university of Florida. A previous version was read at the annual meeting of the American Anthropological Association in Chicago, November 1991.

    I am grateful to Ronald Cohen for encouraging my interesting in these questions and for many helpful criticisms and suggestions. Fortunately or unfortunately the final product is, however, my own responsibility.

2. This article is not based on primary resource data. The issues raised in this paper inspired a larger research project which is currently underway. That project involves case studies and in-depth interviews with CEOs and corporate executives that deal with the theme of this paper; namely, the intersection of market values and broader, community values, within corporations. This article offers one perspective, one approach, to the study of business organizations within a social context. That approach is presented in the introduction and discussed in the analysis and conclusions to this article.

3. I wrote this before reading Robert N. Bellah's (1991) new book in which he makes the same point forcefully and eloquently.

REFERENCES

Anderson, Jerry W.
    1969   *Corporate Social Responsibility: Guidelines for Top Manage-
              ment.* New York: Quorum Books.

Bellah, Robert N., Richard Madsen, William M, Sullivan, Ann Swidler and
    Steven Tipton
    1991   *The Good Society.* New York: Alfred A. Knopf, Inc.

Fortune
    1990   Leaders of the Most Admired. Jan. 29, pp. 40-54.

Held, David
    1987   *Models of Democracy.* Stanford: University of Stanford
              Press.

Johnson and Johnson
    1981   *Annual Report*

Johnson and Johnson
    1982   *Annual Report*

Katz, A.
    1987   *Public Relations Journal.* November.

Kneale, Dennis
    1982   Rivals Go After Tylenols's Market But Gains may Be Only
                 Temporary. *The Wall Street Journal* December 2, p. 31.

Louis, Authur M.
    1978   Lessons From the Firestone Fracas. *Fortune* August 28.

Moore, Thomas
    1982   The Fight to Save Tylenol. *Fortune* November 29, pp. 44-
                 49.

Peters, Thomas J. and Robert H. Waterman, Jr.
    1982   *In Search of Excellence.* New York: Harper and Row.

Sturdivant, Frederick D.
    1985   *The Corporate Social Challenge: Cases and Commentaries.*
                 Homewood, Illinois: Irwin.

Tifft, Susan
    1982   Poison Madness in the Midwest. *Time*, October 11, p. 18.

Verica, Thomas M.
    1991   *The Evolution of the Business Corporation in America.*
                 Unpublished monograph. Gainesville: University of Florida.

Waldholz, Michael
    1982   Johnson and Johnson Officials Take Steps to End More
                 Killings Linked to Tylenol. *The Wall Street Journal*,
                 October 4, p. 16.

CORPORATE CULTURE AND SOCIAL RESPONSIBILITY: THE CASE OF TOXIC WASTES IN A NEW ENGLAND COMMUNITY

June Nash and Max Kirsch

In the spring of 1985, a group of Catholic laypeople posted themselves at the gates of the General Electric corporate headquarters in Fairfield, Connecticut, with signs protesting General Electric's extensive involvement in the production of nuclear weapons. Calling themselves "The Good Things Committee" (a play on the General Electric jingle about bring good things to life), the group of profession-al, business and working people presented their objection to the threat to deterrence posed by the MX and Trident missiles. Invited inside, the group questioned the executives as to what was the moral position of General Electric. The response was, "We're not responsible because it's the government that asks us to do this." When asked if they would reject a request by the government to build gas ovens, the executives said they would have to go back to the company for further guidance. Kelvin J. Cassidy, who reported the incident in *Commonweal*, (May 17, 1985), expressed dismay that "Not one assumed moral responsibility, either for himself or for the corporation."

Corporate responsibility is a growing issue as communities and the workforce are challenging existing practices affecting communities throughout the world. The production of destructive materials and by-products that can kill thousands in one accident heightens our awareness of the power over life and death wielded by these corporations. Although the issue of hazardous waste has been considered primarily a labor problem related to the work place, there is a growing awareness of the danger to entire communities and regions by toxic material produced in industry.

Businessmen and industrialists prefer to translate the moral aspect of pollution into cost accounting principles. This approach dictates that humanitarian concerns over employment, health hazards and even the survival of communities are subservient to the dictates of the market oriented ideology. Jack Welch, who became General Electric's Chairman in 1981, personally drafted a document of corporate values. Entitled, "*Where we want to be*," the core of the paper suggests that the corporation should operate on the principle of "diversity and unity", and earlier drafts suggested that workers who were uncomfortable with corporate policies, including an insistence that GE be first or second in any market it competed, should not feel pressured to stay employed. Indeed, GE's eighth Chairman has been nicknamed "Neutron-Jack", a reference to his elimination of 100,000 employees without the appearance of damage to the Company.

The ideology giving primacy to profits regardless of human costs has become the core of an amoral "modus operandi" often ignored by those who study "corporate culture." This literature tends to reify the company logos and public relations approaches to sell their image rather than to analyze the behavior and beliefs of corporate managers within the larger cultural context in which they are contained. In this analysis we look at the attempts made by community leaders to gain the cooperation of the corporation in reducing toxic waste disposal and compensating victims, counterpoised to the techniques of evasion pursued by the managers, and poses the issue of corporate responsibility in the context of the wider culture in which it acts. We argue here that while corporations influence the wider culture with this ideology and the power relations which accompany it, it is still only an actor, albeit an institutional one of the larger whole. Whatever these values are labeled, however, it is clear that they do not contain a moral component, and this fact has a direct effect on the problems posed by pollution.

The cost accounting approach resonates strongly with American cultural values and is gaining scientific credibility. In a recent issue of *Science*, Daniel A. Koshland Jr. published an article outlining what he termed the "undesirability principle." Given that some industries would like to dump toxic waste at lowest possible costs, that environmental groups would like to place severe restraints on that dumping, and that consumers desire to purchase the products of industry at the lowest possible prices, he maintains that society can obtain a goal that satisfies all contending groups simply by adjusting the relative costs. In order to put this principle into action, Congress could pass an Undesirability Impact Law requiring protagonists to state clearly to society the undesirable aspects of their proposal.

Koshland's suggestion does not acknowledge the profound differences in the degree to which different populations are subjected to the hazards of life and limb imposed by toxic substances in the work place and even in the home, or the relations of power which defines those differences. Production workers are those who are immediately exposed to the harmful substances that pass through their hands each day, not the executives sitting at their desks, and to a lesser degree supervisors in the work place. People of moderate and low income are those who buy the tract housing on place like Love Canal, not the movers and the shakers of industry, business and government. Navarro (1976) sums up his analysis of work hazards and industrial conflict with the statement that differences in power and privilege go along with differences in the hazards to life and limb. So long as this is the case, and in hierarchical society we assume that this will continue, a moral issue is involved in the determination of what should be done with toxic materials, before, during and after their use in production.

Our case study of the conflict regarding responsibility for hazardous materials is drawn from Pittsfield, Massachusetts, a city of approximately 50,000, which is the site of a large General Electric plant. Until relatively recently, a major product of this plant was large power transformers containing pyranol, a compound made with polychlorinated byphenyls (PCBs) and used as a fire resistant insulating agent. Once the mainstay and still the largest employer in the area, General Electric is reducing production of power transformers at the same time it is increasing the commitment to defense contracts. The local plant has worked on the Trident and Polaris missiles as well as automatic controlling mechanisms for army and navy vehicles. Some new engineering and technical personnel have been hired, but the hiring of blue collar production workers has experienced a steady decline. Overall employment has gone from ten thousand to seven thousand in a decade and a half. The population of the city has declined by almost the same number, from 59,000 in 1970 to 50,000 in 1985.

As a result of these changes, there is widespread apprehension concerning employment opportunities and community stability. Added to this is the fear about contamination of the environment and health hazards to the workers resulting from the accumulation of Poly-chlorinated Biphenyls (PCBs) used in the production of power trans-formers. Employees who have worked many years in the Power Transformer division appear to have higher than expected levels of cancer. An epidemiological study of illness and death rates of General Electric workers begun in 1979 has not yet been published, but one of the former managers of a testing division on Power Transformers told us that preliminary finding indicated high levels of cancer, approaching 62 percent in one building where workers and supervisors were constantly exposed to the substance. Added to this, the neighborhoods near the plant have been contaminated by PCB spillage that entered into the basements and gardens of the low-lying neighborhood to the south of the plant.

We shall argue that the differences in ideological perspectives, and specifically the differences in the commitment to an area over time, condition the morality of corporate decision making in such a way that the life-preserving interests of production workers and local residents in an industrial community are ignored. The corporate emphasis on short term profitability affects the way in which management perceives information on environmental hazards and how they respond to laws regarding the use of hazardous substances. The differential power and resources of corporate interests from those of workers and residents in a community influence the response of government agencies to scientific information regarding environmental hazards. Thus the immediate reaction to danger is forestalled and redirected by these power relations. Corporations control the basic information concerning the formulae, channels of distribution and disposal, and even the testing of the effects of the materials they use in production. Intervention by government agents may take a considerable length of time, as the effort needed to mobilize public support to move officials may be hampered by the reluctance on the part of the victims themselves to recognize and respond to danger. Too, the process of scientific testing and reassess-ment is a time consuming process that fortuitously plays into the hands of corporations. Even when the government establishes guidelines, the larger corporations have the legal wherewithal to circumvent the thrust of the regulations by securing exceptions to mandated use-laws.

THE THREAT TO A COMMUNITY

PCBs became a significant problem in Pittsfield when it was discovered that an Italian American community near the plant had been contaminated with the compound in 1977. Ray Del Gallo, a former mayor of Pittsfield and resident of the area referred to as Lakewood described his neighborhood:

> In the Lakewood area, most of the people work for General Electric. It's called Lakewood it was always under water off Lake Silver (the lake around which many of General Electric's buildings are located and into which oils containing PCBs were discharged up until 1977)...Many of the homes are old, but they are very well kept. Lakewood has always been a community, like the North End of Boston. We have some problems, but every one knows who they are. You don't even have to say anything: it's just 'watch that fellow!' and that takes care of it. Back ago, you didn't have police coming down here: they wouldn't come down here. We had our own police. Everyone knew what was going on.

Without advising people as to what they were doing, the company sent a crew to make test digs on a street in the neighborhood in 1980. Dolores, a resident of Lakewood, described her surprise:

> One day they started drilling on Lombard Street which is right over here. The man were around, and you know, if you see a gas company truck you think they must be putting in a gas line, or if you see a electric company truck, they're putting electric in, or whatever. It so happened that two or three people, not knowing what was going on, said 'What is this?' I was going out myself one day, and I said to one of the workers, "What are you doing?' No answer. That's crazy. I said "I hope it's not gas or it will blow up my house. He said, 'I don't know.' That's how it started. When anyone asked any question, they didn't answer. We went directly to Ray.

Ray questioned the workers who came to eat in his restaurant:

> I inquired as to what they were doing. They said they were just looking for the water level, but the truth is that they were looking for oil. They drilled 200 wells altogether at a cost of $1700-1800

a piece, I think -- they were shallow wells.   After that they
purchased some property in the area where PCBs were found.

Ray went to talk with community relations people at the General
Electric Company. He discovered that the tests revealed that PCBs
were found in 18 residential gardens and in 20 cellars, including
basements that housed a bakery and a grocery store. Later they started
to put dyes into the pipes that discharged wastes into Silver Lake. Ray
said:

> I went over and told them, 'I'm going to be cooperative and show
> you some places where you dumped the stuff. You're talking with
> a native!' They didn't appreciate that. All along the river bank are
> dump sites: Merrill road down New York Avenue -- when you ·
> have a heavy downpour, that stuff all just goes into the river. And
> they wonder where it comes from! I took them to a place on
> Newell Street where there were hundreds of barrels. I said, 'If you
> doubt me, I'll bring you the individuals who dumped it!'
>
> You see there above the railroad? General Electric used to have
> tanks with a capacity of 275,000 gallons. Those tanks leaked oil
> for years -- since the early thirties. When the trains used to go by,
> you could see the oil squishing up under the wheels. But they say
> we have no problem! In the old days, they used to bring in grapes
> in those oil tanks for the people to make wine.

The investigation continued throughout the summer of 1980.
Barrels containing traces of hazardous materials including arsenic and
PCBs were found in a landfill site adjacent to GE. When the environmental chief at GE was told of the dumped materials, he responded to
reporters with comments that jokingly belittled the seriousness of the
problem: "I looked at some 400 drums at the dump. It's an exotic
occupation. Some I took out because of some intellectual curiosity
about them." In examining samples from the Housatonic River, the
Lakewood area, and East Street, the Company found more PCB traces
than the State.   The State Department of Environmental Quality
Engineering (DEQE) agreed with corporation spokespersons that most
of the oil that leaked from underground storage tanks on GE property
was isolated in a "plume" on the GE side of East Street. An executive
committee was formed with representatives of city government,
including the mayor, the health commissioner, the Executive director of

the Berkshire County Regional Planning Association, and neighbors of Lakewood. We asked Ray Del Gallo about their actions:

> The consulting firm that handled Love Canal was called in. The Vice-President told us that it was fortunate for us that the oil flowed along that plume instead of following the water line. But we were afflicted no matter what he said about the miracle plume. We fought them all the way, since we are the natives. We have our own contacts in Boston. I have a cousin who is an engineer and knows the language. We went to a law firm in Boston with Representative Shelsy, a top law firm in the field of toxic wastes. And we fought with them in the council.

When the issue was discussed in city council, Ray showed up with a bucket of oil containing PCBs that he had taken from the basement of a bakery in Lakewood. The consultants asserted that there was little danger from the PCBs because the land in Lakewood was so closely knit that it wouldn't penetrate. But as Ray pointed out to them, "Lakewood was called Lakewood for a reason: when there are floods, that miracle plume floods also and the entire area is covered with it."

Undeniably, the environment was permeated with PCBs, but what was the real effect of this substance on humans? The earliest reported incident connecting PCBs with illness in human diseases comes from Japan. In 1968, a mass outbreak of Yusho, or oil disease, was reported in western Japan where rice consumed by the residents was contaminated with PCBs. One thousand residents were afflicted with oozing eye discharges, severe skin disruptions, neurological disorders and/or reproductive problems. In 1975, a follow-up report on these victims showed excess in the rate of cancer, particularly of the stomach and liver (*USA Today*, 1980). While later laboratory tests on animals which showed swelling, learning disabilities, severe susceptibility to disease and declines in fertility were discounted as irrelevant to human subjects, it has been harder to ignore the preliminary studies of workers exposed to PCBs. General Electric officials in plants north of Albany, New York, acknowledged that workers in contact with PCBs suffered from allergic dermatitis, asthma and bronchitis (*Berkshire Eagle*, December 6, 1975). A Study done at Mount Sinai hospital in New York on clinical findings among PCB-exposed capacitor manufacturing workers showed that workers who "swallowed, inhaled or absorbed the chemical" experienced skin disease, jaundice. and liver damage

(Fischbein, et. al. 1983). Warshaw and his research group reported in the New York Academy of Sciences (1979) that workers exposed to PCBs showed a decreased vital capacity similar to workers who has been exposed to asbestos, manifested in eye and upper respiratory irritations and tightness in the chest. They concluded that these significant findings warranted "further clinical, epidemiological, and experimental studies."

Pittsfield residents of Lakewood and workers exposed to PCBs were trying to get answers to these questions themselves. When we asked a Lakewood resident whether she thought people got sick from PCBs, she replied:

> They say yes. I think if I'm not mistaken, they have a suit going on because we've been talking an awful lot about cancer in this area. There was a case -- it's all died down now -- but we older, we people that have been here a long time could tell you that in almost every house, someone died of cancer. Now they don't want to ever hear about it. They say that in any other city, the percentage is just as much.

Her knowledge of the connection between PCBs and cancer is local and particular, but none-the-less the first step towards establishing a correlation:

> My mother was 61 years old. She had cancer. Across the street, the older ones, one of them had cancer. The next house were the Magis, he had cancer. He's fine now, but he was in his early thirties when he got it. The next house over there, there's a woman upstairs who has also had, well, Lil has had a lot of thing the matter with her, really a lot of things. Downstairs, the man has cancer at the moment. He's almost 57 or 58 years old..The colon seems to be the most affected. We all had a tremendous scare. We all had gardens here. The majority of everyone down here is Italian, and behind every house there is a garden. It's part of the house.

In 1981 a retired engineer initiated a study investigating PCB levels in the blood of area residents. The tests, conducted by a Professor of Public Health at the University of Massachusetts with the help of volunteer nurses, included 80 volunteer subjects, some who live in other areas. While work at General Electric seemed to be highly correlated with blood PCB levels, residence in Lakewood did not seem to result in higher levels than that of residents in other area. A later Massachusetts COSH study showed PCB levels often 15 times that of the general population: the general level is 20 or 30 parts per billion while their same of 43 GE workers showed 9 with more than 100 and 3 over 300. The highest was 378.

Workers and supervisors in General Electric Power Transformer Division were beginning to ask questions about what was causing an increasing number of deaths from cancer among their co-workers. In 1978, Ed Bates, who managed the Power Transformer Testing Department, tried to bring to the attention of other General Electric managers what he saw as a growing correlation between cancer-related deaths and those who had contact with pyranol. His motivation derived from his feeling that he had sent workers to their death:

> The guys who worked for me, and I remember this, they were saying, 'Jesus, I'm getting headaches and I don't feel good.' And I'd say, "Look, I sympathize with you, but there's nothing in the GE records that says this is bad. You have got to apply for another job.' And they go down maybe five steps and 60 cents an hour, the union couldn't help them. The union says, 'Hey, we're going strictly on seniority, you got to go down to the bottom if you want another job.' So the guys would stay out there (in testing). I was essentially sending guys to their death.

General Electric had already commissioned an epidemiological study of workers in 1979 and its results were scheduled to be made public in 1981. When it was still not published the following year, we called the principle investigator, who said that it would be another year before the results were tallied. Ed devoted himself to making the study public in order to gain corporate accountability for workers' compensation. His efforts resulted in his getting "the golden handshake:" he was, in other word, encouraged to retire early with attractive benefits.

Ed persisted in trying to get the results of the study published, and in a form that revealed the connection between pyranol and cancer. He took his complaint to the union in 1981, but the business agent of the Local dismissed it as a reaction to early retirement. Yet members of the Retired Workers Club associated with the union were impressed when he showed them records proving that his correspondence with

General Electric officials began well before his retirement, and that he had collected a great deal of data. They began to put together their knowledge of who was working on regulators and who was sick and had died. They remembered that Tony, John and Tom -- all of whom had worked in the testing department of the Power Transformer Division -- had died of head tumors. They were breathing pyranol fumes all the time at work. Others who had worked on repairs where the PCB laden oils spilled out on them as they reassembled the transformers seemed specially liable.

Ed Bates got together in 1985 with the head of the retirees club and others to present the material they had collected to state and national representatives. In the beginning, one of the political representatives remained cool to the issue, until Bates reminded him that his father had died of cancer after working in building 24, where they made small transformers. After this presentation, Senator Kennedy secured an allocation of $750,000 for further research on environmental problems in Pittsfield.

It was one thing to get money for further research, and another to make the results available to the concerned parties. The objectives that Ed Bates and some other retirees worked out were specific: first, they called for medical monitoring, paid for by General Electric, of workers who had worked directly with PCBs; second, continuation of medical insurance by the company past the age of 65, when it now stops; third, publication of the results of epidemiological studies, with specific data related to buildings were workers were most exposed to pyranol; and finally, financial reparation for the families of decreased workers. Preliminary results seemed to indicate a death rate from cancer among workers of 10.2 percent, just a fraction above State figures. But the cancer rate in building 12 was 64 percent and specific to lung and brain tumors. In our most recent conversation with the principle investigator of the epidemiological study in May, 1986, the results were still not ready and the researcher commented that there were many more toxic substances than just PCBs involved in the death rates.

Ed Bates did not blame General Electric for the use of PCBs when it was first introduced in 1934 as an insulating fluid that would, according to company spokespeople, save thousands of lives through its fire deterrent qualities. He limited his criticism to the years since the epidemiological study was initiated in 1979 and information withheld. In particular, the company's ability to thwart investigation, and to allay fears about the dangers by claiming that the data are inconclusive, served to mystify correlations that showed significant danger.

CORPORATE RESPONSE AND THE ROLE OF CORPORATE CULTURE

Corporate ideology in which the realities of potential danger are translated into cost accounting principles has gained momentum in the wider culture. Nonetheless there is significant resistance to the imposition of these priorities when communities are faced with the threat to life. The task of the ethnographer is to explore the interface between the corporation and the wider social setting so that the power relations are explored rather than masked.

Corporations are not closed systems. They developed as an integral part of industrial capitalism, and as powerful institutions, they play an integral part in the economic realities which shape every aspect of American life. Differences in value systems put forward by corporate leaders may provide general expectations of worker behavior, but say nothing about the way individuals incorporate attitudes and behavior into daily life. To posit a corporation as a unit of analysis negates not only the effect it has on wider sectors of the cultural whole, but the influences which instigate individuals inside the corporation to resist or accept the ideology presented.

In our case, the response of the corporation is to downplay not only its role in creating hazardous conditions, but the danger itself. In the three-year period of voluntary restrictions from 1972-1975, it was reported that there was no reduction in the amount of PCBs that escaped into the environment(*Wall Street Journal*, October 10, 1975-82). General Electric Corporation, as one of the principal users of the chemical, insisted that there was no comparable substitute for the chemical in transformers as currently designed, despite the fact that the Japanese had begun to use polydimethyl siloxane after the Yusho incident (Ibid.). It was not until 1977 that Monsanto stopped production of PCBs. This was almost a decade after the Japanese had discontinued production, during which time an estimated four to five million pounds were in the environment and 750 million pounds in economic use (Jacobs 1980:47), and two years after the U.S. Environmental Protection Agency called for a voluntary phase out.

The Environmental Protection Agency invited corporate leaders to hearings concerned with a phasing out of PCBs in January of 1976. In his statement, John F. Welsh of General Electric "welcomed the opportunity to undertake a cooperative effort between government and industry to reduce PCB discharges and find an acceptable substitute," emphasizing the "complexity of this issue and the potential consequences of precipitous action." He recommended a thorough and thoughtful consideration of the problem. E. J. Fitzgerald, Vice-President of Monsanto Chemical which was the major producer of PCBs, agreed "wholeheartedly" with the goal of eventually eliminating all uses of PCBs and stressed the record of the company in carrying out a voluntary program to implement this goal prior to the completion of a study done by the Federal Interagency Task Force in 1972. He emphasized the importance of replacing the compounds using PCBs in an "orderly manner without creating another hazard" and, at the same time, "avoiding serious power and transportation disruptions." Clifford Tuttle, speaking for the Capacitor Manufacturers Task Force of the Electronic Industries Association, gave a detailed technical and economic report on the difficulty at that time of switching to alternative methods (*Bureau of National Affairs*, 1976).

Following the hearings and investigations, Congress passed the Toxic Substances Control Act in October, 1976, specifying the production, distribution and disposal requirements for a wide variety of chemical products. The law set a thirty month timetable for eliminating the commercial production and use of PCBs, with some exceptions. They allowed, for example, the use of PCBs when "totally enclosed," ignoring the problem of leaks and fire damage. This code was revised after serious leaks were discovered in the transformers that had been installed in the Smithsonian Institution. It required a problem in the citadel of science itself to promote concern.

In the Pittsfield plant, there was a sharp change in the way that the "Community Relations" director dealt with the issue over time. As Ray put it:

> When the former heads of relations (those in office before 1982 when "headhunters" from other companies producing power transformers were invited to pick management personnel being laid off at the Power Transformer Division) were here, they sat down with us, discussed problems and offered to buy property if people were uneasy, although they kept telling us that there was no danger.

Now, with the new management over there, they are playing hardball. 'Your property is not a problem,' they say, 'We don't want to hear about it.'

A corporation spokesperson with whom it spoke in 1982 about the problem similarly downplayed the role of PCBs as an occupational or environmental health problem. He stated that:

Our experience in nearly forty years of use here in Pittsfield is similar to medical records over the country during the period. This record shows that the only adverse health effect experienced by workers exposed to PCBs have been limited to occasional skin irritations which clear up quickly.

This extremely selective reading of the situation could no longer satisfy those who were the victims of the chemicals in their work or community life.

CONCLUSIONS

Our conclusions regarding corporate responsibility are that, while the corporation responds to the letter of the environmental hazards laws, it delays actions to them and uses scientific studies to legitimize these delays.

The cooperative efforts of business and government personnel project an image of compliance to controls while at the same time delaying compliance through legal proceedings or the call for further studies to ascertain the "complexity" of the issue. Lenience in the interpretation of the environmental protection and OSHA laws gave further latitude for corporations to resist compensating the claimants during the Reagan presidency. Thus, from the time that the danger was first publicized to the time that definitive action was taken to eliminate further discharges into the lakes and rivers, a full fifteen years had elapsed. As yet, no action has been taken regarding the medical problems of workers, and there are no scientific guidelines that enable them to carry out individual suits against the industry.

When corporate executives disregard the personal and moral responsibility involved in making decisions that affect the life of individuals who work in or live near the plants they control, and indeed the general population, they do so as actors within a larger capitalist system which promotes an ideology that stresses a market orientation, and abiding by the economic laws governing the marketplace. The complexity of the way in which the ideology is played out in the context of the larger culture requires examination: As Cassidy complains in his *Commonweal* article (1985), the lack of any corporate response to environmental danger based on moral decision making comes uncomfortably comparable to the Eichman justification of the roles played in accepting the orders of Hilter's Third Reich. The problem of accountability becomes essential.

REFERENCES

Bureau of National Affairs, Inc.
 1976 *Toxic Substances Control Act*, United States Congress 2601. Washington, DC: Government Printing Office.

Fischbein, Alf, Mary S. Wolff, John Thornton, Ruth Lilis, Irving J. Selikoff, J. George Bekesi, John Roboz, and Julia Roboz
 1979 *Clinical Findings Among PCB-Exposed Capacitor Manufacturing Workers: Report to the National Institute of Enironmental Health Sciences 1977-1979.* New York: Center for the Study of Biological Effects of Environmental Agents, Mount Sinae School of Medicine.

Jacobs, Barry
 1980 The Poisoned Land; PCBs: Deeadly Footprints of the Chemical Industry. *The Progressive* 6(44):43-47.

Koshland, Daniel A., Jr.
 1985 The Undesireability Principle. *Science* 229-4707(July)(5):9.

Nash, June and Max Kirsch
 1988 The Discourse of Medical Science in the Construction of Consensus between Corporation and Community. *Medical Anthropology Quarterly* (June):158-171.

Navarro, Vicente
    1976   The Underdevelopment of Health of Working America: Causes, Consequences and Possible Solutions. *American Journal of Public Health* 66(June)(6)538-587.

ORGANIZATIONAL CULTURE AND THE DEVELOPMENT CRISIS

Riall W. Nolan

PART I: THE PROBLEM

A Crisis in Development Work

International development is in crisis: despite some notable successes, most development work has either failed to meet its stated goals, or has proved irrelevant or damaging to people's real needs.

The practice of development anthropology is also in crisis. Despite decades of research and writing on how to incorporate cultural factors into planned change, anthropologists have had little significant impact on development policy or practice.

For much of the world, what is termed 'development' is seen as ineffective, inappropriate, or damaging. And yet, despite the conspiracy theorists, large development agencies do not actively seek to undermine the aspirations of the world's poor, and anthropologists do not seek to destroy local cultures. Why, then, are outcomes so unsatisfactory?

The failure of development and of anthropology within development are connected, in my view; they arise, I believe, from one predominant problem: the inability of the development industry to learn. A capacity for **organizational** learning, and the ability to apply this learning, both essential in competencies in today's corporate world, seem largely lacking in development agencies.

In this paper, I want to talk about why I think this is the case, and what challenges this poses for development anthropologists.

Institutions and Development

The notion of development is a recent one. Like most cultural constructs, development is embodied in, and expressed through, our institutions. The "development industry" which has arisen since WW II is dominated by a few large agencies, among them USAID, the World Bank, and the various UN groups. Because they are the largest and most reliable source of funding, they now have a virtual monopoly on development work. Today, they constitute a multi-billion dollar network, dictating most of the world's development agenda, while remaining largely outside normal mechanisms of democratic scrutiny or control.

In one sense, it is perhaps normal that institutions should have a life of their own. Mary Douglas (1986) has pointed out to us how organizations and institutions shape our classifications and categories, influence our perceptions, and assign value to options. "The individual," Douglas says, "tends to leave the important decisions to his institutions while busying himself with tactics and details," (1986:111). In consequence, "the burden of thinking is transferred to institutions (1986:83)."

But large agencies do more than simply dominate development work--they also dominate our thinking about development: our ideas about what development is and how it should be done. In an important sense, Douglas claims, institutions determine "what can be counted as a reasonable question and a true or false answer," (1986:13).

It is therefore important to know how these agencies think, what they think about, and what values they use to guide them in their work. Looking at their organizational culture provides some useful answers here.

Institutional Cultures and Institutional Learning

As several observers point out, we tend to treat the organizational aspects of development as either given, or as peripheral (Honadle **et al** 1985:34; Moris 1981). I believe that by treating organization--and specifically, organizational culture--as central, we can begin to understand why we have the development outcomes we do--and more importantly, what we need to do to change these outcomes.

If pointing out that agencies have cultures were simply another way of saying that much of development work has a Western bias, the assertion would be true, but trite. The reality is more complex and ominous than this: today, the institutional cultures of these agencies are not so much Western-oriented as self-oriented. They have developed distinctive forms, into which newcomers--including nation-states--are quickly socialized.

None of this is necessarily bad in itself--most industries, after all, have distinctive cultures. But the institutional culture of the development industry has at least one characteristic which causes deep concern among specialists--it appears to find it very difficult to learn from experience. Although a great deal is known by individuals--anthropologists included--within these organizations about how to plan and manage change, little of this appears to seep into the agencies' institutional consciousness. The development industry itself seems incapable of processing and applying its own experiences in any systematic way.

The central question, then, is this: why do agencies seem to learn so slowly, if at all? The answer, I believe, lies in their organizational cultures.

PART II: ORGANIZATIONAL CULTURE AND DEVELOPMENT AGENCIES

Culture and Organization

Cultures, as anthropologists know, are shared systems of value and meaning, expressed through rules, symbols, categories and frameworks. Cultures stabilize and classify the surrounding environment, assigning "rightness" to some ideas and "wrongness" to others. Organizations, like societies, have--or more accurately, **are**--cultures.

And like societal cultures, institutional cultures create and shape reality. In the case of the development industry, their cultures shape both what is defined as a problem, and how it is subsequently dealt with. Mary Douglas says:

> Institutions systematically direct individual memory and channel our perceptions into forms compatible with the   relations they authorize. ... Any problems we try to think about are automati-

cally transformed into their own organizational problems. The solutions they proffer come from the limited range of their experience. (Douglas 1986:92)

Douglas cites examples from economics to demonstrate how analogies and classifications are implicit in our Western institutional arrangements, showing, for example, that there is an opposition between spiritual and physical, between luxuries and necessities, between basic needs and other needs (1986:64-65). Nowhere is the influence of culturally-patterned thinking more evident than in the use of information within institutions dominated by quantitative, econometric approaches to analysis and planning. I shall return to this point in a later section of this paper.

These modes of institutional thinking are useful in some situations, but limiting in others, because they reinforce the mistaken belief that the way in which the culture defines the world is the way the world really is. Krefting and Frost comment: "...members of an established culture do not for the most part perceive their culture as a social construction; rather, they see it as an objective reality" (Krefting & Frost 1985:155).

Let us look briefly, then, at the development industry: how it is structured and how it thinks.

The Development Industry

The development industry has a well-defined structure which links agencies together under a shared approach to planning which centers almost exclusively on projects, and is characterized by what one observer has termed an "ethnocentric tech-fix orientation" (Rhoades 1978).

Although complex and multi-layered, the industry responds to one overriding imperative: "move the money". This aspect of the development industry is too well-known to require much comment here (but see Bruneau **et al** 1978, Mickelwait **et al** 1979, and Tendler 1975 for further discussion). It is, however, crucial to an understanding of why agencies behave as they do.

To see how moving money influences things, we can use the US Agency for International Development (AID) as a model. AID's primary role is as a disburser of US government funds. It receives these funds in the form of yearly Congressional appropriations. The allocation and disbursement of this money are subject to many rules and regulations, some tied to Congressional agendas, and some designed to promote 'accountability' within the agency.

Getting, spending and accounting for funds are therefore the agency's top priorities. Because of the short life-span of Congressional appropriations, there is pressure to move money as quickly as possible down the AID 'pipeline'. And because AID, like most Federal bureaucracies, grows in accordance with its budget, the more money that can be moved in a given year, the better.

Rewards for AID staffers thus come primarily from moving funds rapidly and smoothly through the 'pipeline'. Officials spend much of their time and energy 'packaging' their proposed projects for funding, and 'walking them through' the agency's complex approvals process. A successful tour with AID is therefore one during which a maximum of money gets disbursed with a minimum of bother.

Burdened with paperwork, AID staffers can hardly do the leg-work necessary to make already-funded projects work, however. For this, they hire outsiders--contract technical assistants--who come in the main from US-based consulting firms. Several hundred of these firms--the notorious 'Beltway Bandits'--regularly do business with AID. Because there are many consulting firms, but few client agencies, the stage is set for some fast scrambling. Firms can only survive by getting contracts. Since these are temporary, they must continually market to the agencies, and maintain good relations with them.

Because of the plethora of requirements surrounding project funding, it is not unusual for several years to elapse between project design and implementation. By the time contractors arrive on site, everyone in the local AID office who originated the project may have been transferred. And by the time the contractors are finished, another group of AID staffers may have been rotated through. The experiential knowledge gained by both AID staffers and contractors, then, tends to dissipate.

Contractors' involvement on projects, furthermore, tends often to be piecemeal, and centered on phases in the project development cycle--the feasibility study, the training component, the implementation phase, or evaluation-- but on rarely all of these. This fact, coupled with the firms' need to seek continuing contracts, means that like AID itself, firms cannot afford much interest or involvement in long-term project outcomes.

What firms **do** pay attention to, however, is the development and maintenance of long-term relationships with their major agency clients. This tends to create an essentially a conservative approach: good performance is defined in agency terms (they are the ones who are paying, after all) and there is a general disinclination within firms to criticize either the funding agency or the host governments which receive development assistance. The development world is relatively small, after all, and news travels quickly: firms or individuals within firms who cannot or will not play the game are distanced, and ultimately denied contracts.

Outcomes and Consequences

Agencies and consulting firms are clearly partners in a collusive and symbiotic relationship, defined and maintained by transfers of money. This fact has consequences--some of them profound--for how development takes place.

Although the relationships as I have described them are long-term ones, the players, the minor rules, and funding priorities all change frequently. AID staffers are reassigned; technical assistants come to the end of their contracts; host country counterparts are shuffled off to other ministries; Congress forms a new foreign aid appropriations committee; a new development buzzword becomes a hot funding item. In such a situation of flux, only the overall relationships which keep the pipelines open are stable.

Agency reactions are predictable. Here again, conservatism is the general rule guiding action. Project designs tend to be safe, conventional, and familiar. They emphasize concrete things, such as money and equipment, which can be documented and controlled easily, and which can be displayed to constituents as proof of accomplishments. Less emphasis, naturally, is placed on 'soft' inputs such as training or institution-building. This tends to produce projects which are of the pre-planned 'blueprint' type rather than the more developmental 'process' type (Korten 1984). As a result, flexibility and local input are sacrificed to the agency's need for predictability and structure.

Since the movement of money is what the game is all about, there are many rules governing this movement, and many stakeholders to consult. The complexity of transfer procedures generates so much paperwork that everyone tends to become fixated on bureaucratic deadlines and procedures. The internal choreography of the project itself may be forgotten, or relegated to second place.

The rules, furthermore, are overtly political in nature and intent. Because AID's constituency is the US Congress, projects are designed to please Washington, and as Washington's mood shifts, so do fads in development. AID thus has little opportunity for true planning of a long-range type.

AID and the Congress are not the only players, of course: there is the host country bureaucracy to deal with as well, and sometimes local politicians. Most projects involve a seemingly endless series of decisions taken between major stakeholders over every conceivable aspect of planning and implementation. As Pressman and Wildavsky (1973) have shown, the chances for successful implementation diminish dramatically as the number of agreements required increases. The result is a lowest-common-denominator approach to planning, where the partners agree to projects which threaten no-one and carry virtually no risk.

Since this takes so much time and energy, there is a tendency to opt for larger and more expensive projects instead of smaller, cheaper ones. It is obviously better, the reasoning goes, to seek funding for a few giant projects totalling many millions of dollars rather than to pursue--and have to manage-- dozens of smaller projects totalling less money. In this way, more and more development eggs wind up in fewer and fewer (but larger) baskets. Put another way, as the portfolio becomes larger and more homogeneous, the risk increases, but the opportunity to program diverse learning experiences decreases.

And indeed, learning is not necessarily sought after, or even welcomed when it occurs. The conservative outlook encouraged by the risks of the development game have direct consequences for project development. Specification of project outcomes, for example, is often left purposely vague. To commit oneself in advance to a specified target is to risk not meeting that target. By keeping outcomes as vague as possible, almost any result obtained can be termed a success.

For this same reason, there is also little real concern with project evaluation. Completed projects are by definition successful ones, since they pave the way for more projects--and more funding. Evaluations tend to ask whether planned activities have been carried out, and not whether the activities had any real effect, or whether different activities and procedures might have produced better results.

Evaluations critical of players' efforts are often 'purified' before being officially transmitted to headquarters. In the same way, comparisons of different projects are not generally done, or if they are, they are not done in such a way as to enable planners to derive concrete lessons which would help them with future efforts.

Evaluations have another drawback: they are usually performed by outsiders. Since the players in the development game are in collusion, the main purpose of which is to maintain the closed system of money transfers, they will quickly close ranks against those who suggest that perhaps the game as it is presently played is flawed. Outside evaluators (IG, auditors, and rogue consultants) are seen as potential threats; they are outsiders and do not inhabit the same 'moral universe' as the other players, and are therefore unpredictable.

An Inability to Learn

In sum, there are few incentives for learning within the development industry (unless they relate to the funding pipeline) and few means for converting what is learned into better planning. Project planning, in this system, will be driven primarily by the rules for project approval and funding. Because of the need to move large amounts of money quickly, it is difficult to do true 'pilot' projects, since there is simply no time available to do them properly. Money for subsequent projects must be appropriated in many cases before the first--or 'pilot'--project has finished! And knowledge of local conditions is not merely irrelevant; it constitutes a potential stumbling block to the smooth working relationships between the major partners.

Those who learn the most from development projects, I would argue, are often the contract technical assistants themselves, because of the time they spend in the field. But here again, the temporary nature of much technical assistance work, combined with the high turnover in the consulting business means that much of this accumulated knowledge is lost, and little of it appears to have had a long-term impact on policies regarding planning.

The institutional arrangements which I have described lead to short time-horizons among players, and to a preference for large, relatively inflexible projects. Because attention focuses on maintaining relationships rather than on development outcomes themselves, little learning takes place about what actually produces these outcomes. Feedback from outsiders is not encouraged, since this injects 'noise' into the system.

Two short examples from the field will illustrate some of these points.

PART III: TWO SHORT EXAMPLES

Here, I want to illustrate how some of the points I have been making actually operate in field situations. My first example involves the World Bank, where efforts to promote agricultural policy in Senegal showed a consistent failure on the part of the Bank to learn. The second example is from Sri Lanka, where although a local ministry's innovative departure from AID planning models proved to be highly successful, it was ignored because of a lack of fit with the agency's established patterns of thinking.

The World Bank and Senegal

Today, virtually all government investment in Senegal is externally funded. To a large extent, therefore, the country's future is in the hands of the world's large lending organizations. For this reason, it is important to discover what large agencies understand about Senegal, and how they incorporate into their plans and strategies.

The Bank began working in Senegal in the early 1960s. As it engaged in lending, granting and advising, the Bank slowly began to confront Senegal's problems, as agriculture continued to stagnate and decline. Bank reports cited a variety of reasons for this decline, including population growth, the "influence of tradition" on rural farmers, and weak planning capacity. As drought patterns persisted and deepened, the weather began to loom ever larger in Bank reports, as did the long-term implications of dependence on groundnut cash-cropping.

By 1977, the Bank had also begun to worry about another obstacle to development: the parastatal agencies which planned and carried out most of Senegal's large agricultural projects. Many of these parastatals appeared to have serious management problems, particularly financial. But overall, the Bank remained optimistic about their role, despite increasing evidence of problems. Indeed, the Bank financed many of these operations, directly and indirectly.

The Bank had persistent difficulty, however, in understanding why Senegal worked the way it did. One of the reasons for this lack of understanding was that Bank policy was determined largely at the levels of Dakar and Washington, and took its cues largely from the prevailing orthodoxies of the day. But in the field, Bank projects faced other problems, some of which had received little or no attention in its sector work. The most serious gap in Bank knowledge concerned the Senegalese patronage system, and its implications for development funding.

Patronage, much of it linked to powerful Islamic brotherhoods, underlies almost every aspect of Senegalese life. The operation of the patronage system in Senegal has been described and discussed by numerous investigators (e.g., Waterbury 1978), and I will not attempt to summarize it here. The Bank understood very little of this system initially, learned little about it in the course of its work, and applied virtually nothing of what it did know to policy and planning.

As a society, Senegal uses patron-client relationships at virtually every level and in every aspect of life. But some relations of patronage are more important and widespread than others, and in Senegal, the main actors in the patronage system are the religious leaders, or **marabouts**, who are about as numerous in Senegal as civil servants.

Patronage in Senegal operates in many different ways, but one of the main outcomes is to spread resources and benefits among constituents. And one of the main benefits to be distributed is that of employment. Featherbedding through patronage turned out to be one of the main factors responsible for a problem plaguing many Bank projects--the institutional weakness shown by many of Senegal's implementing agencies.

Public bureaucracies which managed to acquire donor funding in the 70s often exhibited explosive growth in staff. ONCAD, the state marketing board, is a case in point: its temporary personnel grew from 1,500 in 1971/72 to 4,200 in 1975/76. During this period the wage bill grew by over 500%, from 184 to 945 million CFA (Waterbury 1978:23).

Although ONCAD was finally disbanded in 1980, the problem did not go away. Another Bank-funded project, the **Institut Senegalais de la Recherche Agricole** (ISRA), exhibited a similar pattern. Begun in the late 1970s as an exercise in institution-building, in part to address the weaknesses exhibited by ONCAD, ISRA fared little better.

Like ONCAD, ISRA's staff ballooned once outside funds were available. Between 1981 and 1985, ISRA's staff grew by over 260%, from 600 to 1,573. Most of the new staff were non-essential--and largely illiterate--"support" personnel, with scientists constituting a mere 14% of the total.

Bank reports reveal that some of these problems had in fact been recognized at the outset. In the case of staffing, financial support, and personnel management policies, for example, the Bank had received prior "assurances" from the Senegalese government that necessary reforms would be undertaken. When these failed to materialize, however, nothing was done. In the case of ISRA, the Bank watched the organization inflate its staff rolls for five years before it finally stepped in and forced a reduction in personnel.

In retrospect, it is clear that the Bank had bitten off a bit more than it could chew. Attempts to reform the way in which organizations in Senegal work are very difficult, for the simple reason that patronage in Senegal is not a failure of the system; it **is** the system.

Patronage acts on development efforts in two main ways: as input into the policymaking process, and as a way of reacting to policy once it is made. Waterbury and others have described how marabouts and patronage influence key policy areas in Senegal, including fertilizer and seed distribution, cooperative organization, rice marketing, and parastatal organization.

Although patronage obviously favors the already powerful, it does provide a passage within the walls, as it were, for people who have no other means of formal representation. Religious leaders, who today are the main conduit through which state-controlled resources reach the peasantry, are the only remaining members of the Senegalese ruling elite with strong roots in rural society.

The significance of this system and its implications for development assistance has largely escaped the official attention of the Bank, however. The Bank's 1975 report mentioned religious leaders only once, in these terms:

> The religious leaders, who receive remittances from their disciples, constitute an influential group... *however, they own or control no more than 4% of the cropped area in Senegal,* and their activities are considered to be beyond the scope of this report. (6:16) (Italics mine)

Here we see the operation of a highly restricted econometric world-view at work, where numbers--the larger the better--influence what you look at, and what you see. I had direct experience with this frequently during my time at the Bank, and one small anecdote may illustrate the form it often took.

In the course of my work on Senegalese agricultural policy, I found myself in conversation one afternoon with an Indian economist. He had never been to Senegal, but he was laboring to understand the correlation--or lack of correlation--between fertilizer inputs and groundnut production in Senegal. Using fertilizer imports, price levels, rainfall and government production figures, he was running regressions in an attempt to provide support for the Bank's position on subsidy reduction.

He wasn't getting what he wanted, and asked me if I had any insights to share. I described the patronage system to him, and sketched the internal distribution system through **marabouts** which might, I thought, have sent fertilizer sacks in a variety of directions. And I told him about the massive corruption and fraud which had plagued ONCAD, the government groundnut marketing agency, and suggested the possibility that this might tempt Senegalese farmers to sell their groundnuts across the border in Gambia, instead of to ONCAD. All of these factors and more, I said, were probably having a direct effect on his input-output model.

He listened to me politely, and then smiled. "Very interesting," he said at last. "But of course, all of these things you mention are what we in the Bank call 'non-price factors'." I looked at him for a moment, smiled back, and returned to my office.

Has the Bank learned anything from its projects? Bank reports over time show that there has been some development, at least, in the Bank's understanding of the Senegalese context. On one level, the fact that the Bank's discussion of development in Senegal now covers a wider range of variables--eg, institution-building--is cause for some optimism. On another level, however, the fact that the Bank has finally recognized something as being important does not necessarily imply that the Bank knows very much about it. Although the Bank appeared to recognize the importance of "institution-building" it did not, in the case of ISRA, demonstrate much understanding of how to actually go about doing it.

Although in print the Bank now pays somewhat more attention to the social and political factors underlying development, its understanding of these in Senegal, to the extent that this appears in official documents, is incomplete and superficial. A recent Bank report, for example, characterized the Senegalese as being "addicted to foreign aid" and having "national values and attitudes adverse to self-reliance, initiative, risk-taking and entrepreneurship" (6:31).

So there are problems on at least two levels with what the Bank knows--or believes--about Senegal. On the one hand, some of what the Bank thinks it knows is either wrong, or very partial, as the above quote shows. On the other hand, most of the rest of what the Bank knows--and which appears to be true--consists of things--such as the need for better management, or the need to build stronger institutions--which most anthropologists writing on development have known for decades.

USAID and Sri Lanka

As I have outlined in earlier articles (Nolan 1984, 1987), development donors usually carry quite specific general-purpose models around with them. Although due allowance is made for "local conditions" in theory, little attention is paid to this in practice. But all development projects are experiments, and they rarely unfold under controlled conditions. USAID's experience in the early 1980s with the Sri Lankan Million Houses Program (MHP) was an instance where although surprising--and positive--things happened, AID seemed hardly aware of this.

The USAID approach to low-income housing is derived from architecture, engineering and finance, and combines innovative design within a highly structured planning framework. Plans, typically, are made by specialists, and housing "solutions" are combined in "packages" and "delivered" to "recipients" by official agencies. "Messages" about how to implement these packages are sent by AID to host governments at policy conferences, whose participants sometimes complain that the dialogue is largely one-way.

Since AID's housing assistance is essentially a loan guaranty program, the agency tends to focus on the loan itself--its terms and conditions, the mechanisms for disbursement and recovery of payment from recipient households, and the determination of beneficiaries' income levels.

In these respects, the program is a fairly clear example of 'blueprint' development planning (Korten 1980, Moris 1981, Nolan 1984). The Sri Lankan blueprint, like all blueprints, was not value-neutral. It contained a number of crucial assumptions, including the following:

- That housing was best "delivered" to individuals representing families;

- That these individuals should pay the "full economic costs" of such housing;

- That the obligation to repay should not be transferred to a wider group through either cross-subsidy or collective organization; and

- That housing be made available **only** to those who could afford to pay for it.

These assumptions, innocuous enough perhaps in certain cultural contexts, created problems in Sri Lanka. As the costs of building rose (by 1982, it had become difficult to build a minimum house for much less than US$1,000), the numbers of people of below-median income able to actually afford repayments on a sum of this size began to decline. Ironically, although AID's mandate was to help "the poorest of the poor", it often wound up helping the richest of the poor.

Although AID was clearly well-intentioned, it also became clear as the program progressed that housing was simply not reaching large numbers of poor and needy people. Given the constraints imposed by the paradigm which underlay the AID program, it was inevitable that the needs of some would simply not be met. The limits of the model had been reached; if the program were to advance, a breakthrough was necessary.

The breakthrough came in response to orders from Sri Lanka's Prime Minister to expand the program; to create a 'Million Houses Program' (MHP). Working under intense pressure--and without input from USAID--a Sri Lankan design team hammered out the essential outlines of the new program. The principles which it embodied--although it took everyone some time to realize it--helped transform the paradigm which had up until now defined the housing program.

The most important of these principles could be summarized as follows:

- The improvement of existing housing stock was considered as important as the creation of new stock. Because of the relatively high cost of houses built with government-supplied materials, this approach was abandoned in favor of houses--or parts of houses--built with locally-obtained materials.

- It was recognized that housing needs varied too widely--across populations and across regions--to be satisfied by a single set of type-plans drawn by professional architects in Colombo. The MHP therefore called for plans to be drawn up by family members themselves. Instructional pamphlets were printed in Sinhala, illustrating procedures and techniques.

- It was also recognized that the program could not hope to provide enough loan money to everyone, if that loan must cover the entire costs of the house. And, as previous experience had shown, many needy families could simply not afford a large loan repayment. The MHP therefore made available fixed sums, from $150--$1000 dollars, on the assumption that families would somehow "find" any additional needed money themselves.

In this way, the MHP made a sharp break with previous housing programs, and, to a considerable extent, began to chart a new and relatively unexplored area. The government gave up a considerable amount of control--over what kinds of houses would be built, how, with what and by whom. The MHP also decided to rely on local mechanisms for house designs, construction work, and the mobilization of additional needed resources. And most importantly, it decided to learn by doing, through a "process" model fed by information from the field. Within the bureaucracy concern shifted from product to process, from instructing to learning (see, for example, Sirivardana 1986; Sirivardana & Lankatilleke 1987).

The people guiding the MHP knew that all projects are in some sense competing with existing local arrangements. It therefore became important to discover what these local arrangements were, and how they might affect the operation of the program. Since housing provision was now largely controlled by villagers at the local level, officials needed to understand the processes by which ordinary people built houses. This attitude of learning extended up as well as down: Ministry officials spoke of the need to understand the culture of their own bureaucracies, the better to transform them. Training programs for district officials had to begin by understanding what these officials did in reality rather than on paper (Lankatilleke 1985).

The MHP still faced the persistent problem of low rates of loan repayment, however.   The solution to this difficult problem involved still more decentralization of the program, and a further transfer of power to rural communities. Responsibility for both the granting and the recovery of housing loans became the responsibility of local rural credit unions, answerable to local constituencies, and responsible to local pressures.

In this way, a number of important issues were resolved. The sheer volume of loans could now be increased rapidly; instead of 25 district offices, there were thousands of rural village credit unions able and willing to process loan applications. Problems of determining creditworthiness were considerably resolved, too, since credit union members had intimate knowledge of the people in their own community. And since the unions would only receive extra housing funds as a function of loans already repaid, they had an incentive to not only loan money to reliable persons, but to ensure that such loans were repaid promptly. First tried on a small scale in 1985, and slowly expanded in 1986-1987, the rural credit union approach had the effect of dramatically increasing collection rates in areas where it was fully implemented.

In sum, the MHP transformed housing in Sri Lanka along several important dimensions. It changed both the rules and the procedures for obtaining **access** to housing finance, by decentralizing decision-making and accountability, moving both of these down to the community level. Beyond this, it redefined the **role** of government in housing, from that of a provider--and by implication a standard-setter--to that of an enabler, facilitator, and learner. It encouraged small-scale **private sector** activities and strengthened local community institutions. And--perhaps most importantly--it legitimated and enhanced the role of **local knowledge** in the design and construction of housing.

In a variety of ways, therefore, the MHP transferred power from government officials, planners and consultants to people in the community. Affordability levels were no longer determined by outsiders skilled in statistical analysis. House designs were no longer determined by architects working in their offices in the capital. Standards and materials were no longer dictated by engineers trained in Europe or America. And although financial managers still worried about loan repayments, local groups now had the power to choose loan recipients, and could exercise both judgement and pressure in encouraging repayment. So in some very clear ways, there was less for a planner to do under the MHP, as the kinds of knowledge necessary to plan and manage shifted from what the experts knew to what ordinary people knew.

And what of AID's role in this? To begin with, AID was almost completely absent during the crucial initial period following the Prime Minister's announcement that he would build one million houses. AID-funded technical assistance--and indeed, outside technical assistance of any kind--therefore played a very minor role in the design of the Million Houses Program, for several reasons. First, there was some concern on the part of Sri Lankan officials that outside consultants would "contaminate" the planning process with donor-derived agendas and requirements, at least in the early stages.

Second, donors--and AID in particular--proved unable to provide outside technical assistance in a timely manner. Like a large ship under way, AID could only change course slowly, a few degrees at a time. The Sri Lankan officials, under intense political pressure from their Minister, needed to move much more quickly than that.

Finally, AID was slow to understand the requirements of the new planning paradigm, with its emphasis on "soft" inputs such as social data, training programs, monitoring and evaluation systems, and local dialogue.

What did AID learn as a result of the program? When I last worked on the program in late 1988, the MHP was continuing, albeit under pressures of a new kind arising from political instability and civil war in the north. Despite these difficulties, the Ministry was continuing to learn and refine its approach, based on results from the field. But AID appeared to have absorbed little of the significance of the change of paradigm which the MHP had achieved.

As I drafted the document for the next funding authorization for the housing program, I became aware of how few people within the agency realized that a new model of housing provision had been designed and implemented, literally under their noses, and with their own money. Although some individual AID staffers had come to understand the implications of the MHP for housing, to a large extent the agency was continuing to ask itself the kinds of questions posed by the Logical Framework of the very first Project Paper of 8 years previously--how many houses have we built, how much did they cost, and are the occupants paying their loans?

Although these were legitimate questions, they were--and are-- probably among the least interesting and relevant aspects of the program.

PART III: LARGE AGENCIES AND LEARNING

So here are two examples of the failure of large development agencies to see what was happening right in front of them. Why and how does this happen?

The reasons for this state of affairs are complex, I think. There are a number of constraints which operate on the process by which agencies acquire and uses knowledge, many of them implicit in the descriptions offered here. Two are worth some discussion, I think: those which appear to arise from the international context in which the agencies work; and those stemming from methodological and disciplin- ary biases which control internal and external modes of analysis and action for these agencies.

On the international level, the quasi-diplomatic status and high prestige enjoyed by large agencies (and in particular the World Bank) works against the acquisition of ground-level knowledge. And because of the explicitly political nature of development work at this level, agencies must ensure that such policy "dialogue" as does occur accurately reflects agency doctrines, which, in the main, arise from predominantly political considerations originating outside the country in question, and which even when they are non-political, have more to do with theory than with experience.

This preoccupation with doctrine is one of the things responsible for the curiously flat, one-dimensional aspect to much agency analysis, where information is presented in sets of quite simple categories, and where the conclusions derived from this information are sometimes startlingly black-and-white. In the case of the Bank, for example, the fact that the analysis of quite different countries seems all too often to lead to quite similar policy recommendations (eg, cut subsidies, raise interest rates, privatize, etc.) leads some critics to speak of "cookie-cutter analysis".

This is not to say that shades of grey have not been identified and debated within the agencies. But agencies are highly sensitive to the need to "speak with one voice" to their clients, and the notion that alternative perspectives might emanate from the same division within an agency is a novel and somewhat unsettling idea to most staffers. In this sense, agencies resemble the African one-party states of the sixties, where disagreements were conducted privately, out of the public eye.

Finally, there is what might be termed a persistent over-optimism in much agency work, where yesterday's problems can almost certainly be overcome by tomorrow's loans, and where a doggedly positive attitude is maintained, whatever the evidence. This operated in Senegal with respect to the performance of the parastatal agencies, where--despite massive evidence to the contrary--the Bank persisted in believing that these agencies could somehow be effective planning and implementing bodies. This over-optimism is not unique to the Bank, and indeed, seems to be a feature of all large development agencies which are required to move money rapidly through a complex approvals process.

In terms of its modes of analysis, a preference within agencies for quantitative data and abstract modelling coupled with--in the Bank's case at least--a lack of in-country representation leads almost inevitably to an avoidance of field experience, of alternative data, and of complexity and ambiguity in the search for neat, quick, and categorical answers. Often--and many agency staff will openly admit this--data are "massaged" to justify a predetermined conclusion.

There is therefore a tendency toward "premature closure" in analysis, toward the over-extension of wide-ranging conclusions from narrow sets of data, and toward those data which are already judged "safe" by the agency. In practice, this means that agencies prefer to use mainly their own material in their work.

And part of this learning problem surely stems, in all the large agencies, from an over-reliance on numbers as the main--and sometimes sole--indicators of what is happening in the world. This distorts the description of the host-country situation, leads to a neglect of nonquantifiables in that situation, and promotes the development of unrealistic models.

Even models which are perfectly workable by some standard often become the only models used, whatever the context. AID's insistence on housing loans to individuals as the mechanism for recovering housing costs was one such model, which prevented alternative ways of recovering costs from being seriously examined.

Development agencies do not appear, in my experience, to search for alternative strategies to achieve their ends. Nor do they usually seek to innovate. Instead, they bring quite specific criteria to bear on the choice of pathways to a goal, value judgments which arise from aspects of their institutional culture. These include preferences for size, simplicity, quantifiability, predictability, and similarity to past experience. Local data, in this framework, tend to contaminate and destroy the simplicity of the models thus constructed, and so are avoided whenever possible.

This leads almost inevitably to a we-talk-they-listen format and the promotion of "institutionally correct" models of development.

PART IV: CONCLUSIONS

The invention of 'development' has created the first common global project for humanity; one which carries enormous risks as well as high promise. Almost without our noticing it, this global project has been captured by a few large bureaucratic agencies, which I have termed the development industry. These few agencies manage most of the world's development resources and control much of the thinking about development as well. They do both of these things in terms of quite specific organizational cultures.

As I have tried to show, these cultures favor simplicity and sameness. But as we are beginning to learn, the future of the world probably depends on those who can identify, understand and manage differences. The same challenge which faces us domestically--making differences work collectively--is that which faces the development industry on a global scale. For individuals and organizations alike, the key to managing the world's diversity is an ability and willingness to learn, above all else.

The enormous increase in donor power in the developing world does not appear, as far as I can see, to have been accompanied by any corresponding increase in donors' abilities to gather and use the information necessary to promote truly effective programs of change and economic reform. As the case of AID in Sri Lanka showed, development agencies may serve best as amplifying devices rather than as tape recorders. Having done an excellent job at getting "messages" about housing out to people, it was less good at receiving a "message" back.

In the process of broadcasting "messages", development increasingly becomes defined as "that which the agencies do". There is less and less opportunity for variation, experiment, or heterodoxy. This is hardly surprising, given the difficulty and complexity of development issues. Individuals with new approaches to offer find the going extremely rough in most cases. Douglas says:

> ...there is a tension between the incentives for individual minds to spend their time and energy on difficult problems and the temptation to sit back and let founding analogies of the surrounding society take over.   ...very little advantage lies with the privateer working under his own flag. (Douglas 1986:55)

Donor preferences for development are fairly cut and dried, favoring projects which are easy, familiar and appropriately cost-beneficial. Under intense financial pressure, host governments come to prefer these, too. Somerville notes:

> ...More and more, development in the Sahel is shifting from a North-South cooperative blueprint for action to one in which CILSS responds to donor ideas about development. (Somerville 1986:199-200)

What can be done about this sorry state of affairs? To begin with, we need to understand institutional cultures better if we are to have any chance of reshaping them for development purposes. Robertson, in his book on the anthropology of planning, makes the point this way:

> Until we have a better understanding of the state, we have no coherent basis for recommending its transformation. Such a quest must proceed from the presumption that the state apparatus is not beyond the analytical capacities of social science, and that its

structure and relations with society can indeed be laid bare. The state consists of people (often in surprisingly small numbers), institutions, symbolic systems, processes, networks of relationship--all phenomena with which anthropologists are familiar.

If anthropologists are among the best-equipped to analyze this problem, we are also one of the main stakeholder groups, since failure to confront the issues posed by the organizational cultures of development agencies will have profound consequences for how successfully anthropology will be used in future development efforts. Although as Mary Douglas reminds us, we have no other way to make our big decisions save through the institutions we build (1986:128), such institutions are human creations, products of our minds.

As we created them, so can we reshape them. And that, I suggest, should be one of the main goals of development anthropology for the rest of this century.

If we neglect this task. then we--and the rest of the world--will continue to have development defined and done for us by organizations which know much less than they should.

REFERENCES

Bruneau, Thomas C., Jan J. Jorgensen and J.O. Ramsay
>   1978   *CIDA: The Organization of Canadian Overseas Assistance.*
>   Working Paper #24, Centre for Developing Area Studies,
>   McGill University, Montreal.

Douglas, Mary
>   1986   *How Institutions Think.* Syracuse: Syracuse University
>   Press.

Frost, Peter J., Larry F. Moore, Meryl Reis Louis, Craig C. Lundberg and
Joanne Martin
>   1985   *Organizational Culture.* Beverly Hills: Sage.

Honadle, George H., S. Tjip Walker & Jerry M. Silverman
>   1983   Dealing with institutional and organizational realities. **In**
>   Morss & Gow 1985:33-63.

Horowitz, Michael M. and Thomas M. Painter (eds)
1985   *Anthropology and Rural Development in West Africa.* Westview Press: Boulder.

Korten, David
1980   Community Organization and Rural Development: A Learning Process Approach. *Public Administration Review* 40(5):480-511.

1984   Rural Development Programming: The Learning Process Approach. In *People-Centered Development: Contributions Toward Theory and Planning Frameworks*, David Korten and Rudi Klauss, (eds). Pp. 176-188, Kumarian Press: West Hartford.

Krefting, Linda A. & Peter J. Frost
1985   Untangling Webs, Surfing Waves, and Wildcatting: A Multiple-Metaphor Perspective on Managing Organizational Culture. In Frost *et al* 1985:155-168.

Lankatilleke, Lalith
1985   Training and Information for Institutional Development for the Implementation of the Million Houses Programme of Sri Lanka. University College, London (Development Planning Unit), International Symposium on the Implementation of a Support Policy for Housing Provision.

Mickelwait, Donald R., Charles F. Sweet and Elliott R. Morss
1979   *New Directions in Development: A Study of U.S. AID.* Westview Press: Boulder.

Moris, Jon
1981   *Managing Induced Rural Development.* Bloomington: Indiana University Press.

Morss, Elliot R. & David D. Gow (eds)
1985   *Implementing Rural Development Projects.* Boulder: Westview.

Nolan, Riall W.
1984   Development Anthropology and Housing: A Personal View. *Human Organization* 43(4):362-367.

Nolan, Riall W.
    1985   Anthropology and the Peace Corps: Notes From A Training
                  Program. **In** Horowitz & Painter (eds) *Anthropology and
                  Rural Development in West Africa.* Boulder: Westview,
                  93-116.

Pressman, Jeffrey L. and Aaron B. Wildavsky
    1973   *Implementation.* Oakland Project Series, Berkeley: Univer-
                  sity of California Press.

Rhoades, Robert
    1978   Peace Corps and the American Development Philosophy.
                  Human Organization 37(4):424-426.

Robertson, Anthony F.
                  *People and the State: The Anthropology of Planned Deve-
                  lopment.* Cambridge: Cambridge University Press.

Sirivardana, Susil
    1986   Reflections on the Implementation of the Million Houses
                  Programme. *Habitat International* 10(3):91-108.

Sirivardana, Susil & Lalith Lankatilleke
    1987   Some Key Issues in the Participatory Planning and Manage-
                  ment of the Urban Low Income Housing Process. Bangkok,
                  Second Congress of Local Authorities for Development of
                  Human Settlements in Asia and the Pacific.

Somerville, Carolyn M.
    1986   *Drought and Aid in the Sahel.* Boulder: Westview.

Tendler, Judith
    1975   *Inside Foreign Aid.* Baltimore: Johns Hopkins University
                  Press.

Waterbury, John
    1978   Policymaking in Senegal. World Bank Working Paper,
                  MADIA Project.

INDEX

NOTES ON CONTRIBUTORS

MARIETTA L. BABA is Professor of Anthropology in Wayne State University, with current research interests centering in Business and Industrial Anthropology. Her earlier interests involved extensive research in the areas of molecular evolution and primate ethology.

REBECCA L. HANSON BERMAN is a member of the Psychology Department in Northwestern Illinois University. Her research interest include organizational behavior, meetings, ethnography in public policy and bureaucracy.

ELIZABETH K. BRIODY is a Staff Research Scientist in the Operating Sciences Department, General Motors Research Laboratories, in Warren, Michigan, and is also Adjunct Associate Professor in the Department of Anthropology at Wayne State University in Detroit.

ANTHONY DIBELLA has augmented earlier training in applied anthropology with a recently-received Ph.D. from the Sloan School of Management at MIT. Formerly engaged in research and evaluation for Foster Parents Plan International, DiBella currently is an Assistant Professor of Organizational Studies at Boston College, and a Visiting Scholar at the MIT Organizational Learning Center.

404

SHIRLEY FISKE is a senior program officer working with the National Sea Grants College Program in the National Oceanic and Atmospheric Administration (NOAA), and has played significant roles in bringing anthropological approaches to resource management issues and problems at the Federal and community levels.

TOMOKO HAMADA is Associate Professor of Anthropology in The College of William and Mary and Department Chairperson. She has done extensive research concerned with both Japanese firms in America and American corporate activities in Japanese settings. Hamada is co-editor of this volume.

KATHLEEN GREGORY HUDDLESTON has studied the evolution of "start-up" corporations in Silicon Valley (in California), and taught in the Department of Information and Computer Science at the University of California at Irvine. At present, she consults about computers and their uses in Oregon.

MAX KIRSCH (Second author with June Nash) is Director of Research and Planning in the Office of Academic Computing of the City University of New York. He has responsibility for coordinating faculty and staff research and assessment efforts in the area of academic technology. He has done anthropological fieldwork in Japan, Latin America and the United States.

JILL KLEINBERG is Assistant Professor in the School of Business in the University of Kansas. She has spent many years in Japan, including dissertation research concerned with household-based pottery making enterprise in rural Japan. More recently, she has studied large Japanese firms in both American and Japanese settings.

MICHAEL MACCOBY is known widely for his books on management and the changing of work. He directed a pioneering union-management project designed to improve both productivity and the quality of working life. He heads The Maccoby Group offering consulting services for strategic development planning.

JAMES R. MCLEOD is Associate Professor of Anthropology in The Ohio State University-Mansfield. His research interests center in political and legal anthropology, organizational culture and the anthropology of administration. Geographical areas of concern include Great Britain, Europe and the United States.

JUNE NASH is Distinguished Professor of Anthropology in the City College of New York. Much of her extensive fieldwork both domestically and in Middle and South America has centered on the world of work from the village to the corporate level, from craft industries to large-scale mining.

MANNING NASH was earlier one of the first anthropologists to hold a position in a University-level School of Business; more recently Nash has held a professorship in the Department of Anthropology, in the University of Chicago. Much of Nash's extensive field research has taken him to Burma, Indonesia and other parts of Southeast Asia.

RIALL NOLAN has worked extensively with issues in international development and the cultures and organizational frames entailed. Currently with the University of Pittsburgh, Nolan guides programs of training for developers from many world areas, recently including many persons from Eastern Europe.

FRANK RACKERBY (second author with Donald D. White) is adjunct Research Associate in the Department of Anthropology, Denver Museum of Natural History. His work has spanned fieldwork in Japan, archeology in North America, University administration and the direction of social service programs.

PETER C. REYNOLDS received his doctoral degree from Yale University. Following fieldwork in the Pacific, he pursued a career in the computer industry. As a participant-observer in Silicon Valley, he studied corporate culture first-hand, and developed a radically new interpretation of high technology. In *Stealing Fire: The Atomic Bomb as Symbolic Body*, he argues that high-tech inventions are ritual re-enactments of scientific origin myths.

HELEN B. SCHWARTZMAN is a member of the Department of Anthropology at Northwestern University. Her research interests include the study of meetings as operating systems in organizations.

WILLIS E. SIBLEY, co-editor of this volume, is Professor Emeritus of Anthropology at Cleveland State University in Ohio. His recent interests include the study of modern urban technology as it influences and is influenced by urban culture and society through time. He has special interests in coastal and environmental management issues.

THOMAS VETICA is a Ph.D. recently received the Ph.S. in Anthropology from the University of Florida. His dissertation focussed on issues of corporate social responsibility, and was based in part on on scores of interviews with corporate CEOs and senior executives. Vetica now works with a management and marketing firm in Philadealphia.

DANIELA WEINBERG is an anthropologist who has moved from an academic setting to domestic and international consulting on organizational change. Recent work has included travel to Russia and Georgia to assist with massive organizational challenges resulting from political and economic changes in that world region.

DONALD D. WHITE is Professor of Business Administration in the University of Arkansas in Fayetteville, Arkansas. His research interests include the study of the transferability of Japanese management practices to American settings and work-related values as they pertain to regional subcultures in the United States.

JAMES A. WILSON (second author with James R. McLeod) is Professor Emeritus of Business Administration in the Katz Graduate School of Business, the University of Pittsburgh. A focus of his research and teaching has been the relationship of the person in the group and organization, with special emphasis on the field of mental health.

YUJIN YAGUCHI (second author with Tomoko Hamada) is a Ph.D. candidate in American Studies at the College of William and mary. He worked for a Japanese multinational firm, and is currently interested in the cultural borrowing of architectural designs between the United States and Japan.